BIBLICAL READINGS AND LITERARY WRITINGS IN EARLY MODERN ENGLAND, 1558–1625

Biblical Readings and Literary Writings in Early Modern England, 1558–1625

VICTORIA BROWNLEE

OXFORD
UNIVERSITY PRESS

OXFORD
UNIVERSITY PRESS

Great Clarendon Street, Oxford, OX2 6DP,
United Kingdom

Oxford University Press is a department of the University of Oxford. It furthers the University's objective of excellence in research, scholarship, and education by publishing worldwide. Oxford is a registered trade mark of Oxford University Press in the UK and in certain other countries

First Edition published in 2018
Impression: 1

Published in the United States of America by Oxford University Press
198 Madison Avenue, New York, NY 10016, United States of America

British Library Cataloguing in Publication Data
Data available

Library of Congress Control Number: 2017952325

ISBN 978–0–19–881248–7

Printed and bound by
CPI Group (UK) Ltd, Croydon, CR0 4YY

This publication received a subvention from the Publications Fund of National University of Ireland, Galway, for image and indexing costs.

For Andy, with love

Acknowledgements

The research for this book began during my doctoral work at Queen's University Belfast. This early research was generously funded by an AHRC Doctoral Award and enriched by discussions with staff and postgraduates in the School of English. I am deeply grateful to Adrian Streete who was an outstanding supervisor to my doctoral research. In 2007 I was privileged to be one of four students in an MA module convened by Adrian on literature and religion. I can trace the idea for this project to that class, and to my engagement with Adrian's important research. Since then, I have benefited enormously from Adrian's wisdom, advice, and readings, and I am grateful for his continuing support and interest in my work. Mark Burnett and Ramona Wray were my chief encouragers as an undergraduate at Queen's. Their classes were a joy, and I was fortunate to benefit from their insight throughout my graduate studies.

Without my year as an Irish Research Council post-doctoral fellow at University College Dublin this book might yet be unfinished. During that time Danielle Clarke was an enthusiastic and inspiring mentor, and an endless source of knowledge and encouragement. Danielle's rigorous engagement with the arguments in this book, and her professional advice, support, and friendship have been instrumental to the completion of this project.

I am grateful for the support of my colleagues in the Department of English at NUI Galway, especially Dan Carey, Marie-Louise Coolahan, Lindsay Reid, Sean Ryder, and Elizabeth Tilley, as well as for conversations with colleagues further afield, particularly Dermot Cavanagh, Laura Gallagher, Jane Grogan, Stephen O'Neill, Michele Osherow, Emma Rhatigan, and Shelley Troope. I would also like to thank warmly the two anonymous readers at Oxford University Press for the considerable time invested in reading and commenting on these pages. This book is better for their suggestions.

I am thankful for the assistance of the fantastic editors and staff at Oxford University Press, and to the University of Chicago Press for permission to reproduce material that appeared in 'Literal and Spiritual Births: Mary as Mother in Seventeenth-Century Women's Writing', *Renaissance Quarterly* 68.4 (2015): 1297–1326, in Chapter 5 of this book (© 2015 Renaissance Society of America. All rights reserved).

My deepest thanks are owed to my family. My mum, Roberta Brownlee, impressed upon me the importance of reading at a young age, and provided the resources for me learn. David Brownlee, Matthew Brownlee, Stephen Carroll, and Adeline and Roy Fleming have, in different ways, inquired about the progress of this project faithfully, and Naomi Reaney has listened and encouraged on more occasions than I can recall. My greatest debt is to Andy Carroll, who has cheered, consoled, discussed, and distracted since the beginning, and whose support for this book has been unwavering. To Reuben and Martha, you have provided joy and perspective in more ways than you know.

Victoria Brownlee

Contents

List of Illustrations

Note to the Reader

Original spelling and punctuation has been retained in quotations and in titles of early printed works. Unless otherwise noted, all biblical references are to the 1587 edition of the Geneva Bible: *The Bible that is, the Holy Scriptures contained in the Olde and Newe Testament* (London: Christopher Barker, 1587).

Introduction

OH that I knew how all thy lights combine,
  And the configurations of their glorie!
  Seeing not onely how each verse doth shine,
But all the constellations of the storie.

This verse marks that, and both do make a motion
  Unto a third, that ten leaves off doth lie:
  Then as dispersed herbs do watch a potion,
These three make up some Christians destinie:

Such are thy secrets, which my life makes good,
  And comments on thee: for in ev'ry thing
  Thy words do finde me out, & parallels bring,
And in another make me understood.

  Starres are poore books, & oftentimes do misse:
  This book of starres lights to eternall blisse.[1]

For a book examining the relationship between biblical reading and the literature of the early modern period, George Herbert's 'The Holy Scriptures (II)' is an evocative reminder of literary interest in matters of biblical interpretation. Herbert's sonnet ruminates on a core principle of reformed hermeneutics, namely, that the Bible is a collection of constellated writings that speak of one story, 'the storie'. The unifying metanarrative that the sonnet's opening quatrain celebrates is the life and death of Christ, who identified himself in the Gospels as the one written of in 'the Lawe of Moses, and in the Prophets and in the Psalmes' (Luke 24:44). Herbert's poetic meditation on scripture's Christological ligatures conveys much to us of early modern attitudes towards biblical reading. Of particular relevance to this book is the case made for typological reading. The comparison of scripture with itself and with history reveals a 'motion', as Herbert terms it, that stretches across biblical history and into the present.[2]

[1] George Herbert, *The Temple Sacred poems and private ejaculations* (Cambridge: Thom. Buck, and Roger Daniel, 1633), 50–1.

[2] For an explanation of typology as a reading practice in this period, see pp. 28–35.

Read in this way, the scriptures speak of 'Christians destinie' and 'me', as well as Christ.

The belief that the Bible's narratives were prefigurative of the present was a compelling one in the sixteenth and seventeenth centuries, and it is with this dominant supposition of early modern biblical reading that this book is concerned. *Biblical Readings and Literary Writings in Early Modern England, 1558–1625* considers how the Bible was read and applied to individual and national circumstances, and maps the connection between these readings and various forms of writing.[3] It argues that drama, poetry, and life writings, as well as sermons and biblical commentaries, bear the hallmarks of the period's dominant reading practices, and do interpretative work. In tracing the impact of biblical reading across a range of early modern writing, this book also demonstrates that literary reimaginings of, and allusions to, the Bible were common, varied, and ideologically evocative. As the chapters that follow illustrate the extent to which early modern literature participated in theological debate and articulated innovative programmes of exegesis, this book attests to the Bible's extraordinary impact on sixteenth- and seventeenth-century culture more generally.

The Bible was, as Hannibal Hamlin puts it, 'the age's most important book', and in recent decades the field of early modern studies has become much more attuned to the precise nature of scripture's profound influence.[4] Investigations into the circulation of the Geneva Bible, printed in England from 1576, and the 1611 Authorized Version Bible, have shown that the Bible was the book most likely to be owned in English households, and traced how the availability of the scriptures in the vernacular contributed to significant developments in domestic reading practices.[5] It is clear that Bible-reading and attendance at sermons shaped the education, religious

[3] The literary works considered by this book emerge during the reigns of Queen Elizabeth I and King James I & VI; yet, I have endeavoured throughout, where appropriate, to acknowledge how these writings engage with earlier and later traditions of biblical interpretation. Equally, although the literary writings that I address were published or performed in England, my discussion of the period's exegetical culture frequently addresses interpretative trends across Europe as a means of acknowledging the continuities, and fissures, in post-Reformation readings of scripture.

[4] Hannibal Hamlin, *The Bible in Shakespeare* (Oxford: Oxford University Press, 2013), 3.

[5] William Sherman, *Used Books: Marking Readers in Renaissance England* (Philadelphia: University of Pennsylvania Press, 2008), 72; Femke Molekamp, *Women and the Bible in Early Modern England: Religious Reading and Writing* (Oxford: Oxford University Press, 2013), 11, 19–50. See also Gordon Campbell, *Bible: The Story of the King James Version, 1611–2011* (Oxford: Oxford University Press, 2010); Hannibal Hamlin and Norman W. Jones, eds., *The King James Bible after 400 Years: Literary, Linguistic, and Cultural Influences* (Cambridge: Cambridge University Press, 2010); Euan Cameron, ed., *The New Cambridge History of the Bible: Volume 3, From 1450 to 1750* (Cambridge: Cambridge University Press, 2016).

beliefs, and day-to-day routines of individuals, and that the devotional habits of the laity could include various modes of reading.[6] The growing interest in early modern devotional practices has demonstrated the particular importance of writing to biblical reading habits in the sixteenth and seventeenth centuries.[7] Bible-reading frequently involved annotating scripture's margins, compiling commonplace books and note-making on sermons and spiritual conversations. These kinds of active reading habits were practised routinely by literate women, as well as men, as Femke Molekamp's study of female devotional habits has shown. 'Private Bible reading', Molekamp explains, 'was sometimes accompanied by rigorous acts of writing . . . the literate reader might annotate the scriptures and printed marginalia as she digested them.'[8] Certainly, biblical reading was generative in early modern England—those who could read the Bible frequently did so with pen in hand.

The kinds of writing induced by Bible-reading in early modern England were richly varied. Beyond markings and annotations, biblical reading shaped the information recorded in diaries, life writings, and advice manuals. Many such writings cite and encourage daily Bible-reading habits and contain religious reflection. Others, like Richard Stonley's diary, capture habitual reading through the transcription of a portion of biblical text before each entry.[9] Cultures of biblical reading are also traceable in the period's poetic writings. The Bible informs the structure and imagery of meditative poetry by writers including Anne Wheathill and Robert Aylett, as well as Passion poems, devotional lyrics, and epics. The Bible's impact on poets such as Mary Sidney, George Herbert, and John Milton has been established in several important studies, but there remains a sizeable chunk of biblical verse that has been little explored.[10]

[6] On daily habits of Bible-reading see Naomi Tadmor, *The Social Universe of the English Bible: Scripture, Society, and Culture in Early Modern England* (Cambridge: Cambridge University Press, 2010); Kate Narveson, *Bible Readers and Lay Writers in Early Modern England: Gender and Self-Definition in an Emergent Writing Culture* (Farnham: Ashgate, 2012); Molekamp, *Women and the Bible*, 84–118; Alec Ryrie, *Being Protestant in Reformation Britain* (Oxford: Oxford University Press, 2013), 259–92. For consideration of early modern sermon culture see Arnold Hunt, *The Art of Hearing: English Preachers and their Audiences, 1590–1640* (Cambridge: Cambridge University Press, 2010); Mary Morrissey, *Politics and the Paul's Cross Sermons, 1558–1642* (Oxford: Oxford University Press, 2011); Peter McCullough, Hugh Adlington, and Emma Rhatigan, eds., *The Oxford Handbook of the Early Modern Sermon* (Oxford: Oxford University Press, 2012).

[7] See Sherman, *Used Books*; Narveson, *Bible Readers*; Molekamp, *Women and the Bible*, 51–150.

[8] Molekamp, *Women and the Bible*, 34.

[9] Stonley's diary is in the Folger Shakespeare Library, MS V.a.459–61.

[10] Scholars who have considered the Bible's influence on these poets include: Danielle Clarke, *The Politics of Early Modern Women's Writings* (Harlow: Longman, 2001), 127–47; Hannibal Hamlin, *Psalm Culture in Early Modern English Literature* (Cambridge:

The Sidney Psalms aside, biblical verse paraphrase is particularly neglected by literary scholars, despite the popularity of this genre among sixteenth- and seventeenth-century poets and readers. One consequence of the critical marginalization of biblical verse is the side-lining of a great deal of writing by early modern women; another is a distorted impression of the output of some prolific and popular writers.[11] The paraphrases of women including Mary Roper and Anne Southwell deserve further study, as does the biblical poetry of William Baldwin and Frances Quarles. Although the biblical paraphrases penned by Quarles in the 1620s have been dismissed as pious, these poems, as Adrian Streete points out, make up a significant portion of Quarles' canon and warrant scrutiny alongside his better-known Caroline works.[12] Streete has shown that some of Quarles' biblical paraphrases offer sharp critique of the religious politics at the end of James' reign, while others, like *Sions Sonets* (1625), which I consider in Chapter 4, confront complex questions about the representative process and the limitations of language.[13]

While there remains much work to do on the period's explicitly biblical literature, biblical drama has fared somewhat better than poetry in recent critical history. Paul Whitfield White has demonstrated that biblical plays addressing Old Testament patriarchs and the Passion narratives, as well as parts of the Mystery Cycles, provided regular entertainment across rural

Cambridge University Press, 2004), 85–147; Michele Osherow, *Biblical Women's Voices in Early Modern England* (Farnham: Ashgate, 2009), 11–43; Margaret P. Hanney, 'Re-revealing the Psalms: Mary Sidney, Countess of Pembroke and her Early Modern Readers', in *Psalms in the Early Modern World*, ed. Linda P. Austern, Kari B. McBride, and David L. Orvis (Farnham: Ashgate, 2011), 219–34; Barbara K. Lewalski, *Protestant Poetics and the Seventeenth-Century Religious Lyric* (Princeton: Princeton University Press, 1979); Alison Knight, '"This verse marks that": George Herbert's *The Temple* and Scripture in Context', in *The Oxford Handbook of the Bible in Early Modern England, c.1530–1700*, ed. Kevin Killeen, Helen Smith, and Rachel Willie (Oxford: Oxford University Press, 2015), 518–32; James H. Sims, *The Bible in Milton's Epics* (Gainesville, FL: University of Florida Press, 1962); Mary Ann Radzinowicz, *Milton's Epics and the Book of Psalms* (Princeton: Princeton University Press, 1989); Philip J. Donnelly, *Milton's Scriptural Reasoning: Narrative and Protestant Toleration* (Cambridge: Cambridge University Press, 2009).

[11] Notable exceptions include Adrian Streete, 'Frances Quarles' Early Poetry and the Discourses of Jacobean Spenserianism', *Journal of the Northern Renaissance* 1.1 (Spring 2009): 88–108, and Sarah C. E. Ross, 'Epic, Meditation, or Sacred History? Women and Biblical Verse Paraphrase in Seventeenth-Century England', in *The Oxford Handbook of the Bible*, ed. Killeen, Smith, and Willie, 483–97.

[12] See, for example, the comments about Quarles' Jacobean poetry in Karl Josef Höltgen, 'Quarles, Francis (1592–1644)', *Oxford Dictionary of National Biography* (Oxford: Oxford University Press, 2004; online edition, Jan. 2008), <http://www.oxforddnb.com/view/article/22945>, accessed 30 Sept. 2016. For a useful overview of Quarles' critical history see Streete, 'Frances Quarles' Early Poetry', 88–95.

[13] See Streete, 'Frances Quarles' Early Poetry', and pp. 130–6 in this volume.

England until the mid-seventeenth century.[14] Inside London there was an audience for biblical drama too. A flurry of plays reimagining biblical narratives were performed on public stages at the turn of the sixteenth century, and some of these plays, like George Peele's *The Love of King David and Fair Bethsabe* (*c.*1581–94), were replayed countless times.[15] Michele Ephraim and Beatrice Groves' attention to stage dramas devoted to the narratives of Deborah, Esther, Rachel, and Jonah has illustrated the cultural significance and political bent of some biblical plays, and Peele's play, which I explore in Chapter 2, is no exception.[16] The representation of court politics and succession in *David and Bethsabe* reminds that although biblical dramas frequently appear, from their titles, to offer straightforward retellings of scripture, these plays must be understood to offer readings of scripture. The movement from biblical page to another medium necessarily involves elements of reconstruction or renovation. The act of rewriting the scriptures is, as this book explores, always an interpretative one.

Biblical Readings and Literary Writings is interested in the interpretative work undertaken in biblically inspired plays and poems, but also in biblical readings that occur on a more subtle, ideological level in the period's writings. Biblical imagery and allusions are embedded regularly within ostensibly secular narratives. This has been shown to be the case in much of Shakespeare's work, where the study of biblical allusion is an established and vibrant field of study. Biblical and religious references in Shakespeare's plays have been catalogued, direct and indirect allusions to scriptural imagery and language have been traced across individual plays, and the Bible has also been discussed in the context of wider considerations of Shakespeare's religious beliefs and engagement with Christian doctrine.[17]

[14] Paul Whitfield White, *Drama and Religion in English Provincial Society, 1485–1660* (Cambridge: Cambridge University Press, 2008).

[15] For a list of these plays see pp. 17–19, and for more on Peele's popular play, see pp. 73–8.

[16] Michelle Ephraim, *Reading the Jewish Woman on the Elizabethan Stage* (Aldershot: Ashgate, 2008); Beatrice Groves, '"They repented at the preachyng of Ionas: and beholde, a greater then Ionas is here": *A Looking Glass for London and England*, Hosea and the Destruction of Jerusalem', in *Early Modern Drama and the Bible: Contexts and Readings, 1570–1625*, ed. Adrian Streete (Basingstoke: Palgrave Macmillan, 2012), 139–59.

[17] Some notable book-length studies that have considered biblical usage in Shakespeare include Roland Mushat Frye, *Shakespeare and Christian Doctrine* (Princeton: Princeton University Press, 1963); James H. Sims, *Dramatic Uses of Biblical Allusions in Marlowe and Shakespeare* (Gainesville, FL: University of Florida Press, 1966); Naseeb Shaheen, *Biblical References in Shakespeare's Plays* (Newark: University of Delaware Press, 1999); R. Chris Hassel, *Shakespeare's Religious Language: A Dictionary* (New York: Continuum, 2005); Steven Marx, *Shakespeare and the Bible* (Oxford: Oxford University Press, 2000); Beatrice Groves, *Texts and Traditions: Religion in Shakespeare, 1592–1604* (Oxford: Clarendon Press, 2004); Hamlin, *The Bible in Shakespeare.*

Most recently, Hamlin has argued in his book-length investigation into biblical allusions in Shakespeare's plays that 'no book is alluded to more often, more thoroughly, or with more complexity and significance than the Bible'.[18] Although scholarship addressing scripture's literary impact in the sixteenth and seventeenth centuries has focused disproportionately on Shakespeare, the Bible's influence on a wider range of commercial theatre is becoming better established. We now know that playwrights including Christopher Marlowe, Thomas Heywood, Philip Massinger, Thomas Dekker, and John Webster invoked biblical imagery, narratives, and text in their works in a variety of ways for different purposes.[19] What scholarship on the Bible in drama has made clear is that the scriptures were ideologically evocative in early modern England—'even a brief allusion to a biblical story', as Groves explains, 'could open up a fund of associations, ambiguities and analogies' to audiences and readers.[20]

That there is a strong and discernible relationship between the Bible and literature in this period is in no doubt, and yet there is still work to be done on the particularities of this relationship. To this end, *Biblical Readings and Literary Writings* examines not simply those passages of scripture commonly read and used in literary writings, but *how* they were read, reworked, and applied. Biblical interpretation, that is, the effort to understand what the Bible means, was central to early modern understanding of the world and its effects are visible across a variety of contemporary thought. Since Deborah K. Shuger illuminated the shaping influence of biblical scholarship on politics, gender, and subjectivity in *The Renaissance Bible* (1994), others have shown how developments in Christian humanism and the English language were indebted to the vernacular scriptures, and traced the effect of biblical reading on science and understanding of the natural world.[21] Book-length studies by Christopher Hill, Achsah Guibbory, Elizabeth Clarke, and Kevin Killeen have illustrated the Bible's pervasive presence in early modern politics.[22] It is

[18] Hamlin, *The Bible in Shakespeare*, 3.

[19] See, for example, the essays gathered in *Early Modern Drama and the Bible*, ed. Streete, as well as Victoria Brownlee, 'Imagining the Enemy: Protestant Readings of the Whore of Babylon in Early Modern England, c.1580–1625', in *Biblical Women in Early Modern Literary Culture*, ed. Victoria Brownlee and Laura Gallagher (Manchester: Manchester University Press, 2014), 213–33.

[20] Groves, *Texts and Traditions*, 25.

[21] Deborah K. Shuger, *The Renaissance Bible: Scholarship, Sacrifice, and Subjectivity* (Berkeley: University of California Press, 1994). See also Brian Cummings, *The Literary Culture of the Reformation: Grammar and Grace* (Oxford: Oxford University Press, 2002); Kevin Killeen and Peter Forshaw, eds., *The Word and the World: Biblical Exegesis and Early Modern Science* (Basingstoke: Palgrave Macmillan, 2007).

[22] Christopher Hill, *The English Bible and the Seventeenth-Century Revolution* (London: Allen Lane; New York: Penguin Press, 1993); Achsah Guibbory, *Christian Identity: Jews &*

now clear that the scriptures invaded a large and diverse corpus of political writings—sermons, tracts, and treatises, as well as poetry and plays—and images too, as several chapters in this book attest, disseminated biblical-political ideas to significant effect. Killeen's neat summation that 'the scriptures provided both a sledgehammer and a scalpel for political analysis, amenable to subtle as well as crude deployment' is applicable across a variety of media.[23] The amalgam of uses to which the Bible could be put is clear in debates about female silence. Michele Osherow has argued that early modern women and men found that the Bible authorized a 'freedom to resist' and a means of celebrating the female voice through 'the rhetorically powerful women scattered throughout the Bible's pages'.[24] Certainly, Dorothy Leigh, whose maternal advice text, *The Mothers Blessing* (1616), is examined in Chapter 5, looks to a catalogue of biblical women to authorize her writing, but she also identifies with the apostle Paul, using his words in Galatians to fashion her voice.[25] Aside from studies that have illustrated the Bible's importance to women who wrote, several Marian scholars have weighed the impact of the Gospels on early modern ideas of suffering and grief, while Streete, Ephraim, and Guibbory have demonstrated the extent to which the scriptures were enmeshed with conceptualizations of identity and subjectivity in this period.[26]

My study builds on these approaches in recognizing that Bible-reading fed into writing on almost all fields of knowledge in this period, and that cultures of biblical reading were inflected by the concerns and circumstances

Israel in Seventeenth-Century England (Oxford: Oxford University Press, 2010); Elizabeth Clarke, *Politics, Religion and the Song of Songs in Seventeenth-Century England* (Basingstoke: Palgrave Macmillan, 2011); Kevin Killeen, *The Political Bible in Early Modern England* (Cambridge: Cambridge University Press, 2016).

[23] Kevin Killeen, 'Hanging up Kings: The Political Bible in Early Modern England', *Journal of the History of Ideas* 72.4 (2011): 549–70 (551). See also Killeen's 'Chastising with Scorpions: Reading the Old Testament in Early Modern England', *Huntington Library Quarterly* 75.3 (2010): 491–506.

[24] Osherow, *Biblical Women's Voices*, 9. For scripture's importance to women writers see also Molekamp, *Women and the Bible*; Clarke, *Politics, Religion and the Song of Songs*, 134–73.

[25] Dorothy Leigh, *The mothers blessing. Or the godly counsaile of a gentle-woman not long since deceased* (London: Iohn Budge, 1616), 9–12. For Leigh's reading of biblical women, see pp. 143–68.

[26] On Mary see, for example, Helen Hackett, *Virgin Mother, Maiden Queen: Elizabeth I and the Cult of the Virgin Mary* (New York: St. Martin's Press, 1995); Gary Waller, *The Virgin Mary in Late Medieval and Early Modern English Literature and Popular Culture* (Cambridge: Cambridge University Press, 2011); as well as the essays in Regina Buccola and Lisa Hopkins, eds., *Marian Moments in Early Modern British Drama* (Farnham: Ashgate, 2007). See too Ephraim, *Reading the Jewish Woman*; Adrian Streete, *Protestantism and Drama in Early Modern England* (Cambridge: Cambridge University Press, 2009); Guibbory, *Christian Identity*.

of individual readers. The chapters that follow elucidate the extent to which biblical interpretation was wedded to the realities of everyday life in early modern England. Herbert's sonnet speaks to this assumed relationship by stating that reading the Bible involves ascertaining how scripture's words find 'parallel' with the circumstances of individual readers. The challenges and blessings of the people of Israel, the sufferings of Job and the Psalmist, and curses lavished on the enemies of God were for many readers the normal means of understanding, and commenting upon, national, local, domestic, and personal circumstances.

Christopher Hill's now famous description of the Bible as a 'huge bran-tub from which anything might be drawn' pithily captures scripture's perceived relevance to all aspects of early modern life, and speaks to the seemingly arbitrary nature of this applicatory process from a modern standpoint.[27] Yet, for early modern readers, the process by which scripture's contemporary relevance was discerned was no haphazard lottery. Indeed, so seriously was biblical reading taken in this period that some individuals were willing to die for the right to read and interpret the scriptures.[28] Chapter 1 makes clear the seriousness with which Bible-reading was undertaken in the sixteenth and seventeenth centuries. Complex calendars of reading, cross-referencing systems, memory aids, and the tradition of scriptural commonplacing supported the painstaking effort of many readers to discern scripture's personal relevance. Of course, the fact that readers understood the interpretative process to be divinely guided by the Holy Spirit lent credibility to this interpretative pursuit, and meant that a variety of applications could be brought to bear on a single text without being considered contradictory. For early modern readers of scripture, a single biblical narrative could contain concurrent identifications without difficulty.

This book investigates the diverse uses to which biblical texts were put in this period and, to that end, is structured around five popularly interpreted biblical narratives. In this regard, this book differs from the majority of previous investigations of the relationship between literature and the Bible that have clustered around a particular author or genre.[29]

[27] Hill, *The English Bible*, 5.

[28] For the relationship between Bible-reading and martyrdom in this period see James Simpson, *Burning to Read: English Fundamentalism and its Reformation Opponents* (Cambridge, MA: Harvard University Press, 2007), esp. 10–33.

[29] See note 17 for a list of titles that have focused on drama, and particularly Shakespeare's work. Although research on the early modern Bible has disproportionately centred on drama, scholarly awareness of biblical usage in other genres is growing. A number of works have explored the relationship between poetry and the Bible, particularly the Book of Psalms, such as Rivak Zim, *English Metrical Psalms: Poetry as Praise and Prayer, 1535–1601* (Cambridge: Cambridge University Press, 1987); Hamlin, *Psalm Culture*; Beth Quitslund,

Taking a biblical text or figure as my starting point in each chapter, I explore scripture's shared and varied applications by a range of writers working across a variety of genres. My aim, however, is not to offer an encyclopaedic record of biblical use. Rather, as suggested earlier, I am interested in exploring the diverse ways that biblical texts were read and applied, and in the interpretative practices that facilitate mapping the biblical past on to the early modern present. The biblical texts and figures addressed in *Biblical Readings and Literary Writings* received widespread attention in the century of writing considered by this book, and this popularity accounts, in part, for their inclusion in this study. My selections have been influenced by the work of previous critics too. I have not, for example, considered the Book of Psalms, as recent scholarship has made clear that the Psalms were sung, paraphrased, and rewritten with staggering frequency across the sixteenth and seventeenth centuries, and traced the wider influence of this biblical book on early modern culture.[30] The biblical texts and figures selected for inclusion in this volume have also been shaped by my desire to showcase the diverse fields of knowledge that biblical reading informed. Biblical hermeneutics was a buoyant and varied field of discussion that influenced most other intellectual disciplines. The chapters that follow demonstrate how interpretation of the scriptures informed domestic politics and foreign policy, underpinned how history and language were conceptualized, and shaped attitudes towards bodily suffering and childbearing.

The Bible's centrality to such discussions reinforces that early modern readers did not approach scripture's sacred narratives as remote histories. Instead, the Bible was understood to record a history that was, as Killeen observes, 'omnipresent'.[31] The narratives of scripture, although historical in their own right, were understood to be prefigurative of the present. In subsequent chapters I examine the exegetical principles that underpin the shuffle between biblical past and early modern present, and facilitate the recapitulation of the Bible's narratives within myriad contemporary debates and literary contexts. In this regard, biblical typology emerges as an interpretative tool that was fundamental to the application of scripture

The Reformation in Rhyme: Sternhold, Hopkins and the English Metrical Psalter, 1547–1603 (Farnham: Ashgate, 2008). See also Thomas Luxon's consideration of John Bunyan's prose writings, *Literal Figures: Puritan Allegory and the Reformation Crisis in Representation* (Chicago: University of Chicago Press, 1995), and Clarke's *Religion, Politics and the Song of Songs.*

[30] See, for example, Zim, *English Metrical Psalms*; Hamlin, *Psalm Culture*; Quitslund, *The Reformation in Rhyme*; Austern, McBride, and Orvis, eds., *Psalms in the Early Modern World.*

[31] Killeen, 'Chastising with Scorpions', 493.

to the present. This manner of reading the scriptures prioritized the connectedness of the Old and New Testaments and sought to ascertain the bonds between this sacred history and the present. My interest in the use of typology to discern 'constellations' across Christian history has also led to the scrutiny of a key hermeneutic principle of the reformers, namely, that scripture has, as William Tyndale put it, but 'one sence which is ye literall sence'.[32] Several of the chapters that follow suggest that biblical typology was a more figural and contested reading practice than the literally minded reformers claimed it to be. Figurative and highly symbolic readings of the scriptures abound in Protestant commentary, and allegory—a reading practice much maligned by reformers—could, as Chapters 4 and 6 make clear, have its uses. With this in mind, *Biblical Readings and Literary Writings* argues for a brand of Protestant literalism that was much more flexible and capacious than the soundbites of reformed hermeneutics imply.

Although many of the writers included in this book can be termed 'Protestant', or be said to be in broad agreement with the central tenets of reformed theology, writers are addressed whose confessional stance is ambiguous.[33] Shakespeare is a case in point. He has been labelled Catholic and Protestant, and, as Hamlin notes, identified as an atheist and a Jew.[34] While the religious outlook of well-known writers is an avenue of study that continues to pique critical interest, ascertaining the confessional beliefs or doctrinal particularities of individual authors is not an objective of this book. Early modern writers, irrespective of their religious beliefs, can be familiar with, and influenced by, popular reformed interpretations of scripture, and by the broader Protestant imperative to read and apply the scriptures to the present. To this end, as this study considers how various writers read Solomon, Job, and Christ's mother, Mary, and the narratives of the Song of Songs and Book of Revelation, it elucidates how

32 William Tyndale, *The Obedie[n]ce of a Christian man and how Christe[n] rulers ought to governe* (Antwerp: J. Hoochstraten, 1528), R2v.

33 I use the terms 'reformed', 'Protestant', and 'Protestantism' in this book as a means of referring to a religious outlook that, however fragmented by the understanding of the Eucharist or the limits of free will, was theologically distinct from Catholicism. Reformed theology, or Protestantism, maintained a belief in the key doctrines of justification by faith, the power of grace to save the elect, *sola scriptura*, rejection of intermediaries between man and God, and a broadly defined anti-Catholicism. This list is not designed to be exhaustive but merely serves to demonstrate key points of general agreement in reformed thinking. For this list of the central tenets of reformed theology I rely on Streete's *Protestantism and Drama*, 9.

34 Hamlin, *The Bible in Shakespeare*, 2, and see 3, 9–16 for an overview of these arguments, and 43–76 for an overview of the various studies addressing Shakespeare's confessional beliefs.

Protestant interpretative practices shape literary constructions of a range of theological, political, and social debates.

With the exception of the first chapter, which takes a broad look at the reception and circulation of the Bible, the chapters have been ordered according to biblical sequence. This format is designed to reflect how the Bible was read typologically from Old Testament to New. That said, individual chapters regularly cross-reference a variety of biblical texts in line with trends in early modern exegetical practices. The conventions of early modern Bible-reading and the influence of the period's exegetical culture are the subject of Chapter 1. Lay engagement with the scriptures in this period could take place through traditional modes of Bible-reading, or via non-textual media such as public sermons, catechizing, household readings, as well as biblically inspired drama, ballads, and songs. The question of how the Bible was to be read in early modern England is central in the first chapter, which addresses the emphasis on sequential and typological reading, and the complexity of the reformers' literal claims.

The ideological scrutiny of reformed reading practices continues in Chapter 2 as part of an investigation into the importance of King Solomon to visual conceptions of monarchical authority after the break with Rome. Although popular, figurations of England's monarchs as antitypes of Solomon were complex and exegetically demanding, not least because Solomon ended his life as an idolater. Unsurprisingly, contemporary applications of Solomon's narrative use this biblical text selectively. Yet, when scrutinized more closely, many such readings struggle to occlude fully the unhappy death of scripture's famously wise king. Attention turns in Chapter 3 to the Old Testament figure of Job, and to a consideration of the resonance of his biblical narrative amid a climate of religious persecution in Europe. Job's narrative was typically understood to mark bodily suffering as test of faith and, for many readers, affirmed that their suffering, like Job's, was divinely authorized for a finite period of time. A wave of theological and literary writings affirm the remarkable impact of the Joban trajectory of suffering in early modern culture. Shakespeare's *King Lear* is no exception. Yet, instead of upholding the Joban paradigm of eventual restoration, this play is notable for its deliberate disruption of the typological process of promise and fulfilment, and for its shocking inversion of established exegetical traditions of suffering more generally.

Chapter 4 concludes consideration of the Old Testament with the Song of Songs. This biblical book, as a poetic dialogue between two lovers, presented literally minded biblical commentators with a thorny exegetical dilemma: either accept the presence of a purely erotic text in scripture, or make the case for a literal reading that was figurative. Like early modern exegesis of the Song, poetic recapitulations of this biblical book rely on complex figural reading practices to substantiate a spiritual meaning not directly implied by the biblical text. But this dependence on human words to secure the relationship between sign and spiritually signified exposes reformed anxieties about the inherently fallen nature of the human mind, and the broader inadequacy of language to articulate spiritual truth.

In Chapter 5 focus shifts to the New Testament, and to female readings of the fleshly connection between Christ and his mother, Mary. For Aemilia Lanyer and Dorothy Leigh, Mary's material labour had spiritual consequences because, in delivering Christ, she delivered God's plan for salvation and inaugurated the new covenant which atones for Eve's sin. Yet a typological reading of the scriptures also allows these writers to suggest that the new covenant initiates a form of maternity that has, within the Christological dispensation, profound spiritual resonance. For if, as *Salve Deus* and *The Mothers Blessing* advocate, the Bible is read typologically, Mary's maternity becomes a mechanism of deliverance for all women, and inaugurates a form of maternity rich in spiritual issue and consequence.

Fittingly, *Biblical Readings and Literary Writings* concludes with a consideration of the end-point of typological history, apocalypse. The discussion of the Book of Revelation in Chapter 6 focuses on the ways in which the ongoing struggle between Protestantism and Catholicism was filtered through an eschatological lens. Post-Reformation interpretation of this biblical book claimed a special revelation, one that understood the historic juncture of religious change as the final battle between good and evil. Within this schema, the narratives and figures of this biblical book became a mechanism to delineate Protestantism visually and ideologically from Catholicism, and not just within sermons, biblical commentaries, and woodcuts. The work of Spenser, Dekker, and Middleton illuminates the extent to which drama and poetry participated in the extrapolation of Revelation's meaning for the present. Yet these literary interpretations also point up the intrinsic difficulty of reading Revelation's apocalypse in relation to the early modern present, namely, the progression of time. In revelations that are fractured, obscured, and stalled, these reimaginings of apocalypse question if the final typological uncovering will be delayed indefinitely.

Together these chapters showcase the extent to which Bible-reading was rooted in the practical reality of early modern life. The words of scripture, made available through public sermons, plays, and ballads, as well as private study, were an instinctive means for many individuals of understanding the world around them. Bible-readers understood their rulers, their enemies, and themselves through a series of ideologically inscribed biblical narratives, and the prevalence of such associative readings reveals the extent to which Protestantism, for all its insistence on literalism, remained reliant on figures. The societal impact of the reformers' interpretative practices is detectable in the period's cultural output, in which the dominant reading strategies and principles of Protestantism contribute to, and problematize, literary constructions of contemporary debates and ideas. By re-examining the relationship between literature and biblical interpretation, *Biblical Readings and Literary Writings in Early Modern England, 1558–1625* reminds that scrutiny of how the Bible was read can transform our understanding of early modern culture.

1

'The engrafted word'

Reading and Receiving the Scriptures in Early Modern England

The education of James Ussher, Archbishop of Armagh (1623–35), begins, according to the seventeenth-century biographer Samuel Clarke, with two women. Clarke records in *A collection of the lives of ten eminent divines* (1662) that '*James* was taught first to read by two of his Aunts'. That the early instruction of this prominent figure took place at the hands of female relatives is certainly interesting, but what is extraordinary is that these women were blind. Amidst his account of Ussher's education, Clarke pauses to note that the aunts 'were blinde from their Cradles, and so never saw letters, yet were they admirably versed in the sacred Scriptures, being able suddenly to have given a good account of any part of the Bible'.[1] This momentary insight into the lives of these unnamed women is revealing, for it makes clear that the ability to discern letters was not a prerequisite for biblical literacy. Likely from listening to the Bible read aloud and attending sermons, Ussher's aunts apparently garnered sufficient biblical knowledge to recall swathes of biblical text and, remarkably, teach a child to read.

The acquisition of this level of biblical knowledge among these women is suggestive of the emphasis placed on individual engagement with the scriptures during the sixteenth and seventeenth centuries. But familiarity with the scriptures was not necessarily dependent on biblical ownership or personal study. As this chapter explores, individuals could become conversant with biblical narratives through a variety of non-textual means, as well as via more traditional modes of Bible-reading. Scripture's words could be heard in playhouses and taverns, as well as from pulpits and street corners, and the Bible's figures appeared in royally commissioned artwork as well as in cheap print. Because each relocation of the Bible's words and

[1] Samuel Clarke, *A Collection of the lives of ten eminent divines* (London: William Miller, 1662), 190–1.

topoi to other formats must involve a biblical reading, a study of the Bible's impact on early modern literary culture must take account of reading practices, and their relationship to the core principles of reformed hermeneutics. Simple though the reformed commitment to reading scripture literally sounds, the interpretative practices of Protestants are complex and inconsistent, their literalist principles more capacious and accommodating than they initially seem.

THE BIBLE IN SOCIETY AND CULTURE

Individual access to the scriptures evolved markedly during the sixteenth century. Although the Bible had long been important to those seeking to reform the Church, a number of studies have made clear that, from the 1520s onwards, the readership of vernacular Bibles mushroomed in England, as well as in many parts of Europe, in response to the reformed insistence on *sola scriptura* as the authority of the faith.[2] Because only the pages of scripture were understood to contain 'all thinges necessarie to saluation', the ordinary individual was now obliged to scrutinize scripture for personal meaning.[3] Tyndale explains this injunction to readers of his vernacular translation of the Bible: 'endeuour thy selfe to searche out the meanyng of all that is described therein, and the true sence of all maner of speakinges of the Scripture . . . and note euery thyng earnestly, as thynges pertainyng vnto thyne own hart and soule'.[4] The reformed emphasis on the Bible as the only authority for ascertaining matters of doctrine and church practice, as well as the stress on individual scripturalism, was of

[2] Prior to the sixteenth century steps had been taken to produce a vernacular Bible in English by John Wycliffe, and in Czech by Jan Hus. Tyndale's New Testament in English was published in Antwerp in 1526, and Luther published the New Testament in German in 1522. The Bible was also published in Dutch in 1522, and in French in 1566. For more on these developments see Matthew Spinka, *John Hus and the Czech Reform* (Hamden: Archon Books, 1966); Mary Dove, *The First English Bible: The Text and Context of the Wycliffite Versions* (Cambridge: Cambridge University Press, 2007); Molekamp, *Women and the Bible*, esp. 1–18; G. R. Evans, 'Scriptural Interpretation in Pre-Reformation Dissident Movements', in *Hebrew Bible/Old Testament: The History of Its Interpretation* (Vol. 2), ed. Magne Sæbø (Göttingen: Vandenhoeck & Ruprecht, 2008), 295–317; Henry Wansbrough, 'History and Impact of English Bible Translations', in *Hebrew Bible/Old Testament*, ed. Sæbø, 536–51; and the essays gathered in 'Part II: Producing and Disseminating the Bible in Translation', in *The New Cambridge History of The Bible*, ed. Cameron, 159–386.

[3] Church of England, *Articles, whereupon it was agreed by the archbishoppes and bishoppes of both prouinces, and the whole cleargie* (London: Richarde Jugge and John Cawood, 1571), 5.

[4] William Tyndale, *The vvhole workes of W. Tyndall, Iohn Frith, and Doct. Barnes, three worthy martyrs, and principall teachers of this Churche of England collected and compiled in one tome togither, beyng before scattered, [and] now in print here exhibited to the Church* (London: Iohn Daye, 1573), 7.

course aided by the development of commercial printing. Practically, increasing numbers of publishers and a rapidly expanding network of booksellers across Europe ensured that the Bible became widely available.[5] Indeed, before long, as Kevin Sharpe and Steven N. Zwicker have observed, 'an English Bible in every parish and nearly every household literally placed Scripture within everyone's reach'.[6]

It was the Geneva Bible, first published in English in 1560, that, as Molekamp points out, brought the vernacular scriptures to the English laity on an 'unprecedented scale'.[7] Cheaply produced and widely available, this translation also offered the reader access to biblical scholarship in the form of marginal notes, book prologues, and chapter summaries. It has been estimated that between 1575 and the 1640s more than 140 editions of the Geneva Bible were printed in England, which contributed to as many as one million copies of the vernacular scriptures in circulation by the mid-seventeenth century.[8] That the numbers of Bibles in England might have reached such staggering proportions in a matter of decades attests to Protestantism's status as, to use Alec Ryrie's phrase, 'a book-religion'.[9] While the impact of Protestantism in early modern England can be measured numerically in the Bibles, reading aids, commentaries, sermons, and scriptural indexes that flooded the English marketplace, less quantifiable is the fact that it remained, as Ryrie observes, entirely possible to be biblically informed and unlettered.[10] Those who could not read

[5] See Ian M. Green, *Print and Protestantism in Early Modern England* (Oxford: Oxford University Press, 2000), 45–51.

[6] Kevin Sharpe and Steven N. Zwicker, *Reading, Society and Politics in Early Modern England* (Cambridge: Cambridge University Press, 2003), 4.

[7] Molekamp, *Women and the Bible*, 5. It should be said that although the Geneva Bible was never authorized for use in English churches, this version remained popular with the laity into the seventeenth century, and continued to have large print runs after the publication of the 1611 Authorized Version: see Molekamp, *Women and the Bible*, 5–8, 19–50. For further discussion of Bibles in English see Green, *Print and Protestantism*, 45–51; David Daniell, *The Bible in English: Its History and Influence* (New Haven: Yale University Press, 2003); and the essays in 'Part I: Translations', in *The Oxford Handbook of the Bible*, ed. Killeen, Smith, and Willie, 19–112. It should be said that although there was a decisive shift towards lay reading of the Bible in English, Nicholas Hardy reminds that 'there was no movement away from Latin as the language of biblical scholarship, towards the vernacular': 'The Septuagint and the Transformation of Biblical Scholarship in England, from the King James Bible (1611) to the London Polyglot (1657)', in *The Oxford Handbook of the Bible*, ed. Killeen, Smith, and Willie, 117–30 (129).

[8] Molekamp, *Women and the* Bible, 14; L. B. Wright, *Religion and Empire* (Chapel Hill: University of North Carolina Press, 1943), 53. See also the figures noted in Sherman, *Used Books*, 71.

[9] Ryrie, *Being Protestant*, 259.

[10] See Ryrie, *Being Protestant*, 259–69, for an extensive overview of the acquisition of biblical knowledge among illiterate Protestants. For a list of the best-selling religious works in the period see Green, *Print and Protestantism*.

heard the scriptures at weekly church services during which the Bible was read and preached, and metrical Psalms were sung before and after the sermon.[11] Ian Green has shown that the new Protestant liturgy, used in church services in England from 1549, was an important oral means of disseminating and enhancing biblical knowledge. Services ran according to a yearly cycle of readings drawn from the Old and New Testaments, and short passages of biblical text were used to direct worshippers in thanksgiving, confession, and exhortation.[12] For the illiterate, 'the passages of the English Bible declaimed regularly in church continued to be the primary source of their scriptural knowledge', says Green.[13] In addition to the readings and biblically infused set prayers and responses in the liturgy, the laity could acquire knowledge of the scriptures and key points of doctrine by attending catechizing classes.[14] Outdoor sermons too, like those held at St Paul's Cross, provided regular opportunities to hear the Bible read and explained.[15]

The scriptures were also disseminated to the laity in less regimented and formal ways as the early reformers harnessed the century-old tradition of using drama to popularize the Bible's contents.[16] In the 1530s and 1540s Thomas Cromwell commissioned biblically inspired interludes and morality plays as part of a government effort to promote lay reading

[11] Church attendance was compulsory in Elizabethan England with heavy fines imposed for abstentions. Groves notes that by 1581 the increasing fear of Catholicism drove fines from twelve pence per abstention to twenty pounds: *Texts and Traditions*, 11–12.

[12] Ian Green, '"Hearing" and "Reading": Disseminating Bible Knowledge and Fostering Bible Understanding in Early Modern England', in *The Oxford Handbook of the Bible*, ed. Killeen, Smith, and Willie, 274. Green also notes that the new liturgy, devised under Cranmer in 1549 and revised in 1552–61, retained some of the emphasis and practices of medieval services of worship, if not the words (275–5). For consideration of the Prayer Book's cultural importance and popularity more broadly, see in particular Judith Maltby, *Prayer Book and People in Elizabethan and Early Stuart England* (Cambridge: Cambridge University Press, 2000).

[13] Green, '"Hearing" and "Reading"', 285.

[14] For the catechizing of children and servants in this period see Ian M. Green, *The Christian's ABC: Catechisms and Catechizing in England c.1530–1740* (Oxford: Clarendon Press, 1996).

[15] Several studies of public sermons have emerged in recent years: see especially Hunt, *The Art of Hearing*, 60–116; Morrissey, *Politics and the Paul's Cross Sermons*; McCullough, Adlington, and Rhatigan, eds., *The Oxford Handbook of the Early Modern Sermon*; as well as the essays in 'Part III: Spreading the Word', in *The Oxford Handbook of the Bible*, ed. Killeen, Smith, and Willie, 257–350.

[16] Drama had been a key means of teaching the laity about the Bible in the medieval period. Medieval mystery cycles, based on the scriptures, were used by the Church to mark the liturgical year and for devotional purposes. On the persistence and influence of this tradition in early modern England see Michael O'Connell, *The Idolatrous Eye: Iconoclasm and Theater in Early-Modern England* (Oxford: Oxford University Press, 2000), esp. 21–5, 87–91; White, *Drama and Religion*; Groves, *Texts and Traditions*, 10–59.

of the Bible. John Bale, for instance, who was in receipt of patronage from Cromwell, wrote a number of plays based on seminal biblical episodes, such as *John the Baptist's Preaching in the Wilderness* (1538) and *The Temptation of our Lord and Saviour Jesus Christ by Satan* (1538). Such plays not only familiarized audiences with the narratives of key biblical episodes, but were used to make political comment and even to teach the basic principles of biblical hermeneutics. Bale's *King Johan* (1538), for example, which invokes Moses and David as kingly types, stresses the reciprocal relationship between the Old and New Testaments, and suggests how these biblical leaders find their antitype in the figure of Henry VIII.[17]

Biblically inspired drama was, however, more than a didactic tool wielded by England's early reformers. The tide of biblical dramas that were staged in commercial theatres between 1590 and 1602 suggests that the Bible—its perceived contemporary relevance and the popularity of its stories—continued to stimulate public interest in, and demand for, plays based on biblical narratives.[18] George Peele's *The Love of King David and Fair Bethsabe* is a case in point. The frontispiece of the printed edition of the play, published in 1599, states that the drama 'hath ben diuers times plaied on the stage', testifying to sustained public interest in the work since its initial performance in 1593/4.[19] *Abraham and Lot* (1594) and *Nebuchadnezzar* (1596–7) also emerged in the same decade and, in 1602, several plays were staged bearing the names of central biblical figures, including *Judas*, *Job*, *Pontius Pilate*, *Jephthah*, *Samson*, and *Joshua*, all of which are now lost.[20] Importantly, biblically derived plays like these were more than straightforward regurgitations of the biblical texts they

[17] For more on the political resonance of this play see Robert Zaller, *The Discourse of Legitimacy in Early Modern England* (Stanford, CA: Stanford University Press, 2007), 357–64.

[18] See Groves for a fulsome discussion of the debt later Elizabethan drama owed to medieval mystery plays, and for the ways in which cycle plays persisted in England's cultural memory into the seventeenth century: *Texts and Traditions*, esp. 33–59.

[19] George Peele, *The Love of King David and Fair Bethsabe With the Tragedie of Absolom*, in *The Dramatic Works of George Peele*, ed. Elmer Blistein (New Haven: Yale University Press, 1952), title page.

[20] For a record of biblical drama performed in the period see Alfred Harbage, *Annals of English Drama 975–1700: An Analytical Record of all Plays, Extant or Lost* (London: Routledge, 1989), 4–45; Philip Henslowe, *Henslowe's Diary*, ed. R. A. Foakes (Cambridge: Cambridge University Press, 2006); and O'Connell, *Idolatrous Eye*, 91. It should be said that while biblical dramas continued to emerge until the early seventeenth century, the onset of censorship in the 1570s made overt stage representation of religious matter more difficult. The complete ban of such representations in 1606 sealed the decline of the overt biblical dramas noted above, yet it by no means marked the end of theatrical engagement with scripture. See Groves, *Texts and Traditions*, esp. 16–21; and Annabel Patterson, *Censorship and Interpretation: The Conditions of Writing and Reading in Early Modern England* (Madison: University of Wisconsin Press, 1984).

addressed. In *The History of Jacob and Esau* (1557/8), the Genesis account of Isaac's twin sons is used to consider election and reprobation and scrutinize the Calvinist doctrine of predestination.[21] In a different vein, Thomas Lodge and Robert Greene's *A Looking Glasse for London and England*, which was staged several times during the 1590s and published in 1594, dramatizes the reformed call to examine scripture for personal meaning through a retelling of the Book of Jonah. In this play, the sins of Nineveh are also the sins of London and England, and the audience is called repeatedly, like their biblical antecedents, to recognize their need to repent.[22]

In addition to drama, the laity could experience the Bible's narratives and topoi in the form of ballads and songs. Throughout the sixteenth and the seventeenth centuries numerous editions of the Psalms and the Book of Proverbs appeared in metre and, in 1569, William Samuel completed the task of translating the entire Old Testament into Sternhold's metre.[23] Many of Christ's teachings, particularly the parables, were set to familiar ballad tunes, including the mustard seed (Matt. 13), the rich man and Lazarus (Luke 16), and the beatitudes (Matt. 5).[24] The Old Testament too seems to have steadily attracted the attention of balladeers with works such as 'Sampson judge of Israell' and 'David and Berseba' circulated in broadside form for several decades.[25] Yet the reach of biblical ballads extended further than those who physically possessed a broadside copy. Itinerant sellers of ballads, like dramatic touring companies, orally disseminated the biblical works they sold as they advertised their wares through

[21] While scholars agree that the play uses this biblical narrative to tackle predestination there is some disagreement over how it represents the finer points of this doctrine. See Helen Thomas, 'Jacob and Esau—"Rigidly Calvinistic"?', *Studies in English Literature* 9.2 (1969): 199–213; and Paul Whitfield White, 'Predestination Theology in the Mid-Tudor Play *Jacob and Esau*', *Renaissance and Reformation* 24.4 (1988): 291–301.

[22] For further discussion of this play see Groves, '"They repented at the preachyng of Ionas".'

[23] William Samuel, *An abridgeme[n]t of all the canonical books of the old Testament written in Sternholds meter* (London: William Seres, 1569). Other popular editions of the Psalms include Robert Crowley's *The Psalter of Dauid newely translated into Englysh metre* (London: R. Grafton and S. Mierdman, 1549) and Thomas Sternhold's *The whole booke of Psalmes collected into Englysh metre* (London: John Day, 1562). For an example of the Book of Proverbs in metre see John Hall, *Certayn chapters take[n] out of the Prouerbes of Salomo[n]* (London: Thomas Raynalde, 1550). For a more fulsome discussion of these and other metrical versions of the scriptures, see Ryrie, *Being Protestant*, 302–5; Quitslund, *Reformation in Rhyme*.

[24] See the examples and discussion in Tessa Watt, *Cheap Print and Popular Piety, 1550–1640* (Cambridge: Cambridge University Press, 1991), 119.

[25] For a full list of ballads with their circulation and publication dates see Watt, *Cheap Print*, 336–41.

reading and song.[26] In doing so, these sellers facilitated the transmission of printed ballad content to those who could not read. Circulated orally, as well as in print, the ballad became, as Tessa Watt has shown, an important mechanism through which the reformers could 'give unlearned people direct access to the concepts of the Christian faith'.[27]

Just as one singer had the potential to make the contents of a ballad available to countless others, a single reader in a household or community could play an important role in orally disseminating scripture's words to those who could not read. There are accounts of servants reading to other servants and there is evidence to suggest that individuals became renowned in villages for their willingness to read the Bible to others.[28] John Foxe records in *Actes and Monuments* (1583) how one Edward Allen, 'a milner', prevented 'many poore people' from starving by selling corn at half the price of his competitors 'but also fedde them with the food of life, reading to them the scriptures'.[29] Certainly, as Andrew Cambers, Kate Narveson, and Ryrie have shown, Bible-reading could be a communal, even social, activity that brought together demographically diverse individuals.[30] Masters read to their households—children and servants—maids read aloud to their mistresses, and illiterate parents heard the scriptures from children who had been taught to read.[31] Presumably it was the result of Bible-reading aloud that enabled James Ussher's blind aunts to learn the scriptures.[32] Evidently, an inability to read, or see, was no excuse for the absence of biblical knowledge.

While Bible-reading aloud was one way the illiterate could access the scriptures, learning to read was a more satisfactory means of becoming personally familiar with the Word of God.[33] To this end, the pages of

[26] Madeleine Gray, *The Protestant Reformation: Belief, Practice, and Tradition* (Brighton: Sussex Academic Press, 2003), 127; Jonathan P. Willis, *Church Music and Protestantism in Post-Reformation England: Discourses, Sites and Identities* (Farnham: Ashgate, 2010), 190.

[27] Watt, *Cheap Print*, 119.

[28] See Andrew Cambers for an overview of the variety of contexts in which the Bible was read: *Godly Reading: Print, Manuscript and Puritanism in England, 1580–1720* (Cambridge: Cambridge University Press, 2011). For examples of individuals who became renowned for reading aloud see Ryrie, *Being Protestant*, 259–62.

[29] John Foxe, *Actes and Monuments of matters most special and memorable, happenying in the Church with an vniuersall history of the same.* Vol. 2 (second half) (London: Iohn Daye, 1583), 1979.

[30] Cambers, *Godly Reading*; Narveson, *Bible Readers*; Ryrie, *Being Protestant*, 259–97.

[31] See the examples of servants and children reading aloud in Ryrie, *Being Protestant*, 260–1, 272, and the instructions given to masters in Thomas Tuke, *The practise of the faithfull containing many godly praiers both of morning and euening and other necessarie occasions* (London: Io. Beale, 1613), 238.

[32] See Clarke, *A Collection of the lives*, 190–1.

[33] For a discussion of Protestant attitudes towards illiteracy see Ryrie, *Being Protestant*, 259–70, and for an assessment of literacy levels in this period see David Cressy, *Literacy and*

scripture frequently provided the means, as well as motivation, for literacy, as Ryrie explains: 'once the Reformation was properly under way, almost everyone who learned to read, learned, at least in part, by reading the Bible. Therefore, to be literate was to be, in some measure, Biblically literate'.[34] Guides for biblical reading reveal that an individual's access to scripture was, at least in theory, not to be restricted by age, gender, or rank. Dorothy Leigh explains to her sons that one of her reasons for writing *The Mothers Blessing* (1616) is 'to command . . . that all your children, be they Males or Females, may in their youth learne to read the Bible in their owne mother tongue'.[35] Such is the importance of this task that Leigh permits little excuse for failure asserting 'let none of you plead pouerty against this' command for, if idleness is avoided, she charges, might 'all brought vp to read the Bible'.[36] Thomas Cranmer similarly seems to discount financial means and social rank as a bar to biblical reading when, in the prologue to the 1540 edition of the Great Bible, he claims that 'publicanes, fyshers, and shepherders maye fynd their edifycacion' in the scriptures.[37]

ROUTINES AND MODES OF READING

Although it is difficult to assess the practical impact of the reformers' literacy ideals on those who worked in the professions Cranmer mentions, among those who did learn to read, Bible-reading, according to Molekamp, 'was practiced more frequently than any other kind of reading in early modern England'.[38] The popularity of Bible-reading in this period was in large part due to the Protestant emphasis on the individual's need to adhere to a regular, and preferably daily, routine of reading. Tyndale argued that the Bible itself authorized 'lay men' to 'read dayly scriptures', and, writing later in 1622, John Downame advised individuals to set aside a particular time each day for Bible-reading, and to 'keepe themselues constantly (as neere they can) to a settled course'.[39] Guides for biblical

the Social Order: Reading and Writing in Tudor and Stuart England (Cambridge: Cambridge University Press, 1980); John S. Pendergast, *Religion, Allegory, and Literacy in Early Modern England, 1560–1640: The Control of the Word* (Aldershot: Ashgate, 2006).

34 Ryrie, *Being Protestant*, 272–3.

35 Leigh, *The mothers blessing*, 24.

36 Leigh, *The mothers blessing*, 24–5.

37 Thomas Cranmer, 'The Prologue', *The Byble in Englyshe that is to saye the conte[n]t of al the holy scrypture, both of ye olde, and newe testame[n]t* (London: Rychard Grafton, 1540), ii, v.

38 Molekamp, *Women and the Bible*, 10.

39 Tyndale, *The vvhole workes of W. Tyndall*, 287; John Downame, *A guide to godlynesse or a Treatise of a Christian life* (London: Felix Kingstone, 1622), 649. See also the

reading frequently offered assistance to the reader in this pursuit. Tables and calendars prescribing chapters to be read daily abounded. Many of these rotas took readers through the whole of scripture in a year, while others aimed at coverage in a matter of months.[40] Individuals who were zealously committed to programmes of daily reading were used in sermons and devotional writings as exemplars to spur others to similar diligence. In Francis Rogers' funeral sermon for William Proud, the scriptural commitment of the deceased marks him as 'a true Christian Noble' for, in addition to attending weekly sermons and lectures, 'he did dayly vse to reade in the Bible'.[41]

Among women too, observance of regular biblical reading was considered exemplary. In *The Christall Glasse* (1592) Philip Stubbes commends to readers the example of his dead wife, Katherine, whose 'whole delight', he claims, 'was to be conuersant in the scriptures, & to meditate vpon them day and night: in so much that you could seldome or neuer haue come into her house, and haue found her without a bible'. This image of Katherine Stubbes with a Bible ever in hand is central to Stubbes' effort to position his wife not only as a 'Myrrour of womanhood' but also as the 'perfect patterne of true Christianitie'.[42] It reminds that in this period Bible-reading was more than an act of Christian duty. Reading the scriptures was widely understood to be an outward manifestation of inner godliness and spiritual health. Leigh elucidates the perceived connection between regular biblical reading and spiritual health in *The Mothers Blessing*. She explains that:

> spirituall food of the soule . . . must be gathered euery day out of the word, as the children of Israel gathered Manna in the wildernesse . . . For as the children of Israel must needs starue, except they gath'red euery day in the wildernesse and fed of it, so must your soules, except you gather the spiritual

encouragements towards daily reading in Andreas Hyperius, *The course of Christianitie: or, As touching the dayly reading and meditation of the holy Scriptures* (London: Henry Bynneman, 1579), 168; Edward Vaughan, *Ten introductions how to read, and in reading, how to vnderstand* (London: A. Islip, 1594), Bir.

[40] For an example of a reading calendar that allowed the Bible to be read in one year see Nicholas Byfield, *Directions for the priuate reading of the Scriptures* (London: Printed by E. Griffin, 1618), A4v. For a more ambitious reading calendar see Hyperius, *The course of Christianitie*, 168–204. The parallel reading streams in the Book of Common Prayer, if followed, offered readers impressive coverage of the scriptures in one year and of the Psalms in one month. See Green's discussion of these liturgical rotas in '"Hearing" and "Reading"', 276.

[41] Francis Rogers, *A sermon preached on September the 20. 1632 . . . at the funerall of William Proud* (London: Iohn Norton, 1633), D3v. See Ryrie for more cases of exemplary 'biblical over-eating': *Being Protestant*, 271–2.

[42] Philip Stubbes, *A christal glasse for christian vvomen containing, a most excellent discourse, of the godly life and Christian death of Mistresse Katherine Stubs* (London: [T. Orwin], 1592), A3v.

> Manna out of the word euery day, and feed of it continually: for as they by this Manua co[m]forted their harts, strengthened their bodies, and preserued their liues; so by this heauenly Word of God, you shall comfort your soules, make them strong in Faith, and grow in true godlinesse.[43]

Just as God provided manna to sustain the Israelites physically, Leigh considers the Bible to be the means through which God offers spiritual succour to subsequent generations of his people. Because this 'spiritual Manna' is a source of comfort and a means to grow in faith and godliness, it must, like the Israelite's manna, be treated with appropriate seriousness and regularity.[44] From God's instructions to the people of Israel in Exodus 16 Leigh extrapolates the central tenets of biblical reading: reading must be daily, continual, and effectual. What underpins Leigh's advice is an expectation that the words of scripture are transformative, and it is an expectation that she shares with others who sought to promote individual reading. Stubbes, for example, suggested that the outcome of his wife's fervent biblical study was that 'her whole heart was bent to . . . the Lord', and Downame extols the Bible's power to alter the condition of the heart when he encourages individuals to 'read with affection and deuotion . . . framing and fashioning our hearts vnto it'.[45] In a similar vein, Grace Mildmay explains in her *Autobiography* (*c.*1617–20) that those who read the Bible 'every day in some measure' will find that their 'heart, soul, and spirits, and whole inner man' will 'receive the true stamp and lively impression thereof'.[46]

The idea that the heart could be stamped or fashioned by the Word of God has its basis in scripture itself. The Book of James calls readers to ensure that 'the worde . . . is graffed in you' because such implantation will make 'ye doers of the worde, and not hearers onely' (James 1:21–2) and, in Deuteronomy, the people of Israel, having received the Ten Commandments, are instructed to 'lay vp these . . . words in your heart & and in your soule' (Deut. 11:18). But the process by which such internalization of the scriptures could be achieved was not straightforward, and demanded more than passive, daily reading. Margaret Hoby's diary is revealing in this regard in that it demonstrates how biblical reading was to be complemented by a range of practical activities, each designed to aid

[43] Leigh, *The mothers blessing*, 5–6.

[44] God instructed the Israelites to collect and prepare manna daily, with the exception of the sixth day, on which they were to collect and prepare enough for the Sabbath too. See Exodus 16:4–5.

[45] Stubbes, *A christal glasse for christian vvomen*, A3v; Downame, *A guide to godlynesse*, 647.

[46] Grace Mildmay, *Autobiography* in *Women Writers in Renaissance England: An Annotated Anthology*, ed. Randall Martin (London and New York: Routledge, 2014), 211.

personal familiarity with the scriptures. In her entry for Friday 7 September 1599 Hoby recounts a day demarcated by various tasks connected to personal scripturalism:

> After private prayers I writ my notes in my testament, which I gathered of the lecture the night before: then I did eat my breakfast, then I walked abroad and talked of good things, so that I found much comfort: after I came home I writ my sermon that was preached the Sabbath day before, then I went to private prayer, and so to dinner . . . then I prayed with Mr Rhodes, and after walked abroad: and when I came home I prayed privately, and soon after went to supper: after which I went to the lecture and then to bed.[47]

One of the most striking things about Hoby's diary is the way in which it records the effort to internalize what is read and heard from the scriptures through the process of writing. The Bible text is annotated, in this instance with pertinent observations from a lecture, sermons are recalled and logged, likely in the commonplace book mentioned elsewhere, and interactions, both prayerful and on matters of theology, with the household chaplain, Mr Rhodes, are memorialized in the diary itself.[48] Hoby's diary reminds that, when it comes to the Bible, reading and writing are not discrete activities. Biblical reading was frequently a generative process, and the act of writing had the potential to enrich and consolidate what had been read.[49]

It is because the act of writing was thought to aid the process of internalization that biblical reading guides frequently advocated the practice of annotation. Recent work on readers' material engagement with their Bibles, such as that by William Sherman, has illuminated how many 'found some method of annotating an indispensable practice for digesting and mobilising the text'.[50] The margins of Bibles offered a physical space to record an individual's response to the Word, either in the form of brief reflection or scriptural cross-reference.[51] Readers were also encouraged to develop their own system of markings to memorialize sections of scripture

[47] Margaret Hoby, *The Diary of Margaret, Lady Hoby* in *Women Writers*, ed. Martin, 194.

[48] In the entry for 14 September 1600 Hoby mentions writing notes on a sermon in her commonplace book. It should be noted, as Martin observes, that Hoby's daily devotional activities are not prioritized to the same degree after Rhodes moves out of her house in 1601, or at least less time is spent recording them: *Women Writers*, 194. See also Dorothy Mead's observations on this issue in *Diary of Lady Margaret Hoby* (London: George Routledge and Sons, 1930), 280.

[49] For an in-depth consideration of the relationship between lay biblical reading and writing see Narveson, *Bible Readers*, and Molekamp, *Women and the Bible*.

[50] Sherman, *Used Books*, 76. Narveson, *Bible Readers*, 19–100; Molekamp, *Women and the Bible*, 34–65; Ryrie, *Being Protestant*, 270–314.

[51] See the marked Bibles discussed in Sherman, *Used Books*, 71–86.

that had personal relevance.[52] Such markings functioned as discernible evidence of affective biblical reading, as in the case of Ignatius Jurdaine, who, according to Clarke, 'did not onley read the Bible above twenty times over, but read it with special observation (as appeareth by the *Asterisks*, and marks in the Bible which he used) making particular application to himself'.[53] The acts of writing that accompanied biblical reading resulted in material changes to the text. Clearly the Bible, as Sharpe and Zwicker put it, was 'not only an authority but a text to be edited, emended, retranslated, glossed, interrogated and, *in fine*, deconstructed'.[54]

This kind of active Bible-reading not only encouraged alterations to be made to the Bible's pages, but led to the creation of truncated and reformatted biblical texts as readers relocated portions of scripture to commonplace books. As Molekamp has made clear, biblical reading and commonplacing often happened concurrently in this period.[55] Before the reader begins using Nicholas Byfield's year-long track for reading the Bible they are advised to 'first make thee a little paper booke of a sheete or two of paper, as may be most portable' to record verses that will later be committed to memory.[56] William Gouge's impressive recall of the scriptures is credited to his practice of writing in 'a little book which he always carried about him'. By this means he is said to have 'made himself so expert in the Text, that if he heard any phrase of Scripture, he could presently tell where it was to be found'.[57] To commit something to memory was, then, to undertake the most literal act of internalization, and it is for this reason, Ryrie explains, that memory aids became an important component of the printing industry that grew up in support of biblical reading.[58] Among such works is John Lloyd's rather unwieldy memory retrieval system, *A good help for weak memories, or, The contents of every chapter in the Bible in alphabetical dysticks* (1671). By memorizing a related dystick after daily reading, the individual, Lloyd promised, would have embedded a means of remembering the key points and scriptural reference of that biblical

[52] Downame, for example, calls readers to observe those 'Chapters of lesse ordinarie vse, and others . . . most profitable for our edification, and as we goe, to prefix before them, with our pen, a seuerall marke: as for example; before the former sort, this *; before the other, this +, or some such like': *A guide to godlynesse*, 648–9.

[53] Clarke, *A Collection of the lives*, 453.

[54] Sharpe and Zwicker, *Reading, Society and Politics*, 4.

[55] On this relationship, see Molekamp, *Women and the Bible*, 13, 55–9.

[56] Byfield, *Directions for the priuate reading*, A8r–9v. For further discussion and examples of commonplacing in this period see Narveson, *Bible Readers*, 35–7.

[57] Clarke, *A Collection of the lives*, 98. Clarke also attributes the 'vast and tenacious' memory of Robert Harris to his regular commonplacing (312).

[58] For an overview of the practice of memorizing the scriptures, as well a list of texts written to aid memorization, see Ryrie, *Being Protestant*, 277–9.

narrative. For example, if the user wanted to remember in which chapter of the Bible Noah builds the Ark the relevant dystick can be called to mind: 'Flouds of sin cause the Lord the Floud to send; *Noah* finds Grace; th' Arks measure, form, & end'. Once recalled, the individual may discern that 'F' is the first letter of the dystick, which is the sixth letter in the Christ-cross-row. According to Lloyd's model it may then be concluded that this narrative is recounted in Genesis 6.[59]

While the methodologies for memorizing the scriptures may have varied from writer to writer, the motivation remained the same. If the words of scripture are laid up 'orderly in our memories', Downame encourages, then 'when we haue most neede, wee may know where to finde them'.[60] A case in point was the persecution of the Protestant faithful across Europe. Foxe's *Actes and Monuments* popularized stories of scores of martyrs who regurgitated scripture during their trials and went to their deaths with the words of the Bible on their lips.[61] While the threat of persecution may have passed for Protestants living in Elizabethan and Jacobean England, the ability to recall the scriptures functioned as a useful guard against heresy. It is presumably because Katherine Stubbes had implanted the words of scripture in her memory that she is able to discourse successfully on matters of faith. Her husband notes that 'if she chanced at any time to be in place where either Papists, or Atheists were, and heard them talke of Religion, of what countenaunce or credit soeuer they seemed to be, she would not yeeld a iote, . . . and conuince them, yea, & confound them by the testimonies of the word of God'.[62] The reformed emphasis on lay reading of the vernacular scriptures was, then, not simply a call to read. It was an injunction to memorialize the scriptures in the heart. In copying, glossing, and memorizing biblical text, individuals engaged in a form of active reading designed to inscribe hearts as well as pages.

INTERPRETATIVE PRINCIPLES AND APPROACHES

Although the spiritual benefits of purposeful biblical reading could be established relatively easily by writers, the subject of *how* the Bible was to be read, that is, how its words should be understood, was much less

[59] John Lloyd, *A good help for weak memories, or, The contents of every chapter in the Bible in alphabetical dysticks* (London: Thomas Helder, 1671), 2.

[60] Downame, *A guide to godlynesse*, 644.

[61] See, for example, the recorded trial of Richard Woodham in Foxe, *Actes and Monuments*. Vol. 2 (second half), 1994, as well as the examples discussed on pp. 90–3.

[62] Stubbes, *A christal glasse for christian vvomen*, A2r–A3v.

straightforward. The question of how to read the scriptures was invariably bound up with acceptance of the core principles of reformed exegesis, which, in spite of claims that the sense of scripture is both 'literall' and 'easie', were complex and fluid.[63] While the intricacies of reformed hermeneutic principles were largely reserved for discussion by theological writers, the relationship between biblical reading and understanding was of interest to writers of reading guides aimed at the laity. Such writers frequently broached the topic of how to read the scriptures via the question of order. Indeed, the order in which the books of the Old and New Testaments were read emerges as a central concern in biblical reading guides from this period. Clergyman Elnathan Parr cautioned against 'disorderly and confused reading', urging instead that 'Order; and Methode which is a great furtherance of knowledge, and a singular helpe of memorie' govern biblical reading.[64] Readers were similarly dissuaded from haphazard selection of scripture in Downame's *Guide*. Rather than read 'as the book hapneth to open', daily devotions were to be undertaken with 'constancie, not by fits and snathces, here a Chapter and there another'.[65]

Orderly reading could be as straightforward as reading through the Old or New Testaments, or involve more complicated formulas for reading through particular books or genres.[66] Readers were sometimes encouraged to begin 'with the easiest and playnest Bookes' and conclude with the more complex Pauline Epistles.[67] Less commonly writers, like Perkins, advised readers to tackle difficult books such as Romans first.[68] The Psalms were commended in many guides as a mainstay of lay daily reading, and individuals often followed a rota for reading through this book, such as the monthly cycle in the Book of Common Prayer.[69] The rota of morning and evening readings in the Prayer Book also took

[63] Tyndale, *The Obedie[n]ce*, R2v; Byfield, *Directions for the priuate reading*, A5v.

[64] Elnathan Parr, *The grounds of diuinitie plainely discouering the mysteries of Christian religion, propounded familiarly in diuers questions and answeres* (London: N. O[kes]), 1614), 30. See also the comments on sequential and orderly reading in Edward Vaughan, *A method, or briefe instructio*, Bir.

[65] Downame, *A guide to godlynesse*, 647–8. For an in-depth discussion of the advice Downame offers Bible readers see Narveson, *Bible Readers*, 24–8.

[66] See Ryrie, *Being Protestant*, 273–5, for a comprehensive overview of common strategies for reading through the whole Bible.

[67] Parr, *The grounds of diuinitie*, 32.

[68] William Perkins, *The arte of prophecying, or, A treatise concerning the sacred and onely true manner and methode of preaching* (London: Felix Kyngston, 1607), C3v–r.

[69] Writers who encouraged regular meditation on the Psalms include: Lewis Bayly, *The practice of pietie directing a Christian how to walke that he may please God* ([London]: Robert Allott, 1616), 244, 247; Perkins, *The arte of prophecying*, C3v–r; Richard Bernard, *Dauids musick: or Psalmes of that royall prophet, once the sweete singer of that Israel vnfolded logically* (London: Felix Kyngston, 1616). See Ryrie for more on the particular popularity of the monthly track for reading the Psalms in the Book of Common Prayer: *Being Protestant*, 275.

readers systematically through large chunks of the Old and New Testaments, and was just one of many parallel daily reading tracks that individuals could follow to bring order to their Bible-reading.[70] Individual Bible-readers devised unique rotas for reading too, with some reading sections of the Pentateuch, the Prophets, the Gospels, and the Epistles daily.[71] Although systems for daily reading differed, they typically prioritized sequence—the incremental movement through Testaments, genres, or books.

The reformed emphasis on reading the Bible progressively led a number of writers to advise their readers to use the Bible's configuration to direct selection. By 'reading of the Bible in order', counselled Lewis Bayly, readers will 'better vnderstand both the *Historie* and the *Scope* of the holy *Scripture*'.[72] What Bayly contends here is that sequential reading will enable the individual to discern more easily the unity of scripture's narratives, an idea that is more fully explained by Downame: 'the best way is, in our ordinarie course to begin at the beginning, and so to proceed till we come to the end. The which will be a notable helpe both for the vnderstanding of the matter, and the History of the Bible, when as we obserue the coherence, and how one thing dependeth vpon another: which if it be interrupted, causeth much obscuritie.'[73] Underpinning this advice to read progressively through the Bible is, then, a belief in the coherence of biblical history. Those who read the scriptures in this way are expected to be in a better position to discern how the Bible is a continuous narrative overseen by a sovereign God.[74]

In advocating a methodology designed to drive home the hermeneutic unity of the scriptures, Downame articulates a specifically typological understanding of biblical history. A typological reading of the Bible was used to establish and produce connections between the Old and New Testaments. Within this interpretative framework, the Old Testament was understood to have resonance beyond its literal, historic meaning and

70 Richard Finch, for example, commends the daily cycle of readings in the Prayer Book in *The epiphanie of the church gathered out of the Holy Scriptures* (London: Roger Ward, 1590), A4v. See also Green who notes that many likely relied on the English Prayer Book to order their private reading: '"Hearing" and "Reading"', 285.

71 See the discussion of the reading tracks of Grace Mildmay and others in Ryrie, *Being Protestant*, 274.

72 Bayly, *The practice of pietie*, 247.

73 Downame, *A guide to godlynesse*, 648.

74 The reformers' understanding of biblical history was intimately connected to the doctrine of providence. Among Protestants broadly, God was understood, as Alexandra Walsham has shown, to be 'an assiduous, energetic deity who constantly intervened in human affairs. His finger could be discerned behind every inexplicable occurrence': *Providence in Early Modern England* (Oxford: Oxford University Press, 1999), 2.

was found to speak of Christ. Biblical typology had been practised from the early church and, as alluded to earlier, was among the most commonly practised, and influential, exegetical methodologies of the early modern period.[75] The apostle Paul laid the foundations for this manner of biblical reading when he rebuked the Christians in Galatia and Colossi for believing that observance of the law was necessary for salvation. The law, he insisted, is 'but a shadowe of thinges to come' the 'body is in Christ' (Col. 2:17).[76] It is, then, this biblically authorized hermeneutic relationship between Old Testament shadow and Christological fulfilment that motivates an orderly approach to biblical reading. The reader who traces the precise ways in which the Old Testament anticipates the New Testament will understand the Christological metanarrative of the scriptures.

Of course, for the ordinary reader, observing how Christ was promised across the pages of the Old Testament was easier in some books than others. That there was concern that lay readers might fail to perceive the Christological ligatures running through biblical history is suggested by the emergence of interpretative aids specifically designed to assist readers in discerning the coherence of scripture's two Testaments.[77] One such work is William Guild's *Moses vnuailed: or Those figures which serued vnto the patterne and shaddow of heauenly things, pointing out the Messiah Christ Iesus, briefly explained* (1620). While Guild's title, which includes a paraphrase of Hebrews 10:1, suggests that he reads the Bible typologically,

[75] For an overview of typology's influence on Christian thinking see Lisa Freinkel, *Reading Shakespeare's Will: The Theology of Figure from Augustine to the Sonnets* (New York: Columbia University Press, 2002), 1–46; Earl Miner, ed., *Literary Uses of Typology from the Middle Ages to the Present* (Princeton: Princeton University Press, 1977); Hugh T. Keenan, *Typology and English Medieval Literature* (New York: AMS Press, 1992). As many of the chapters that follow attest, typological interpretations of scripture increased in popularity after the Reformation acquiring fresh relevance in the context of personal scripturalism. For an assessment of typology's importance to early modern exegesis see Lewalski, *Protestant Poetics*, 111–46; Luxon, *Literal Figures*, 34–76; Kevin Killeen, '"Veiled Speech": Preaching, Politics and Scriptural Typology', in *The Oxford Handbook of the Early Modern Sermon*, ed. McCullough, Adlington, and Rhatigan, 389.

[76] See also Paul's teaching on the relationship between the old and new covenant in II Corinthians 3:13–18, and Galatians 3–4.

[77] See, for example, William Guild, *Moses vnuailed: or Those figures which serued vnto the patterne and shaddow of heauenly things, pointing out the Messiah Christ Iesus* (London: John Budge, 1620); Thomas Taylor, *Christ revealed: or The Old Testament explained* (London: Miles Flesher, 1635). See also the work of Richard Bernard, which encourages readers towards a typological reading of the Psalms and the Book of Revelation: *Dauids musick*, 47 and *passim*, and *A key of knowledge for the opening of the secret mysteries of St Iohns mysticall Reuelation* (London: Felix Kyngston, 1617), 'To the Christian Reader'. For a more extensive list of typological works devoted to the Old Testament, and an assessment of Luther and Calvin's influence on this tradition, see Johann Anselm Steiger, 'The Development of the Reformation Legacy: Hermeneutics and Interpretation of the Sacred Scripture in the Age of Orthodoxy', in *Hebrew Bible/Old Testament*, ed. Sæbø, 732–40.

it is the work's opening lines that definitively reveal a reliance on this particular reading practice: 'darke shaddowes were the fore-runners of that bright substance, obscure types were harbingers to that glorious Anti-type the Messiah'.[78] Like comparable interpretative aids in this period that were designed to be a source of reference during biblical reading, *Moses vnuailed* uses charts and tables to excavate, book by book, and verse by verse, the relationship between type and antitype. For example, in a detailed table on Abraham, a number of connections, including one between Genesis 21 and Mathew 22, are posited:

Abraham put *Hagar* and *Ismael* out of his house, *Gen*. 21. 14.	*So shall Christ expell out of the number of his Church all bastard hypocrites, despisers and mockers of the godly,* Matt. 22.[79]

As this example suggests, Guild's painstaking endeavour to illuminate how Christ is foretold across the pages of the Old Testament is not limited to broad comparisons of sacrificial or redemptive themes. Rather, *Moses vnuailed* demonstrates how typological readings could stretch from more plausible identifications of the kingly relationship between David and Christ to associations that required much greater imagination.

Biblical typology as understood in this period governed more than a reciprocal reading of scripture's two Testaments. This reading practice was to guide understanding of the relationship between biblical history and the early modern present, and facilitate scripture's personal application. This usage was possible because, during the sixteenth century, the Christological focus of typology evolved to include all of history in a continuing process of typological fulfilment.[80] Within this enlarged application, a biblical type could find its antitype, or fulfilment, in the present as well as

[78] Guild, *Moses vnuailed*, A4v. Hebrews 10:1: 'For the Lawe hauing the shadowe of good things to come, and noe the very Image of the things.'

[79] Guild, *Moses vnuailed*, 18. Thomas Middleton's treatise *The Two Gates of Salvation; or, The Marriage of the Old and New Testament* (1609) is similarly devoted to demonstrating the interrelated nature of the two Testaments of scripture, and proves, unambiguously, that early modern dramatists were steeped in typological exegesis. See *The Two Gates of Salvation* in *Thomas Middleton: The Collected Works*, ed. Gary Taylor and John Lavagnino (Oxford: Oxford University Press, 2007).

[80] Lewalski attributes the expansion of typology in the sixteenth and seventeenth centuries to the reformed directive for individuals to scrutinize scripture's personal relevance: 'Typological Symbolism and the "Progress of the Soul" in Seventeenth Century Literature', in *Literary Uses of Typology*, ed. Miner, 81. For further discussion of the development of typological applications in this period see Joseph A. Galdon, *Typology and Seventeenth-Century Literature* (The Hague: Mouton, 1975), and Keenan, *Typology and English Medieval Literature*, 262.

in scripture. For early modern exegetes, ascertaining the precise relationship of the Old Testament and the New, and both Testaments and the present age, was a significant task because the typological connections discovered proved the Bible's contents to be part of, what Killeen terms, an 'omnipresent history'.[81] Understood typologically, the narratives of the Old Testament did not only recount the history of Israel but spoke of the people, circumstances, and practices of the English Church. In a baptismal prayer prescribed in the Book of Common Prayer the salvation of Noah from the flood, and the flight of the Israelites from Egypt, foreshadow both the baptism of Christ and the individual presented for the sacrament:

> ALMIGHTY and everlasting God, who of thy great mercy didst save Noah and his family in the ark from perishing by water, and also didst safely lead the children of Israel thy people through the Red Sea, figuring thereby thy holy baptism; and by the baptism of thy wel-beloved Son Jesus Christ in the river Jordan, didst sanctifie water to the mystical washing away of sin; We beseech thee for thine infinite mercies, that thou wilt mercifully look upon *this Child;* wash *him* and sanctifie *him* with the holy Ghost, that *he* being delivered from thy wrath, may be received into the ark of Christs Church.[82]

Scuttling from Genesis 6, to Exodus 14 and into Matthew 3, the prayer traces an unbroken line of divine deliverance from the Pentateuch to the present. God's promise of rescue, although made in biblical times, could be read and applied in this way because, ultimately, as Joseph A. Galdon explains, typology is 'a theology of history which postulates the presence and relevance of an eternal God at every individual moment of time'.[83]

It is because the reformers understood the Bible to be, in the words of John Bale, 'the eternall Testament' of an 'eternal & everlastyng God', that scripture's figures, narrative, and text could be mapped on to the present. The history of the Israelites was the history of God's chosen people who, in reformed exegesis, were invariably Protestant.[84] The proximity of biblical history to the history of English Protestants is clearly suggested

[81] Killeen, 'Chastising with Scorpions', 492.

[82] 'The ministration of Publick Baptism' (1662), *The Book of Common Prayer: The Texts of 1549, 1559, and 1662*, ed. Brian Cummings (Oxford: Oxford University Press, 2011), 409. For further discussion of the typological references in the Book of Common Prayer see Galdon, *Typology and Seventeenth-Century Literature*, 14.

[83] Galdon, *Typology and Seventeenth-Century Literature*, 5.

[84] For consideration of the relationship between England and Israel see Patrick Collinson, 'Biblical Rhetoric: The English Nation and National Sentiment in the Prophetic Mode', in *Religion and Culture in Renaissance England*, ed. Claire McEachern and Debora K. Shuger (Cambridge: Cambridge University Press, 1997), 15–45; Guibbory, *Christian Identity*.

by the structure and biblical allusions used in Perkins' prayer of thanksgiving in *The arte of prophecying* (1607):

> Hee hath dispelled the duskie clowdes of Popish darknesse as palpable as that of Egypt, and hath caused the Sunlight of the Gospell to shine cleerely in all our coasts. Hee sheweth his word vnto vs, as he did vnto *Iaacob*, his statutes and his iudgements, as he did sometimes to *Israel.* He hath giuen vs his Prophets and Embassadours, which doe serue like that cloude and pillar of fire to direct vs in our pilgrimage through the wildernesse of this wicked world into celestiall Canaan.[85]

In these lines, a typological understanding of the Old Testament facilitates the composition of England's own providentially determined history, as the English nation and its enemies become participants in the events of sacred history. Following covenant theology, the English fulfil the role of God's chosen people, and, as an elect nation, become the recipients of divine favour.[86] It is typology too that allows Perkins to anticipate a point in history when, like the Israelites, the English will reach 'celestiall Canaan'. This brief expression of expectation is revealing because it illuminates how typology could work forwards as well as backwards. Typology enabled current circumstances to be filtered through the promises and outcomes of the biblical past, but it also allowed the present to be read in light of what was to come, as prophesied in books such as Revelation. As a reading practice, typology is, at its heart, what Northrop Frye describes as a theory of 'historical process'. It posits that the entirety of sacred and secular history builds towards a single point that gives meaning to past, present, and future.[87] The Second Coming of Christ, understood by the reformers to be, in the words of Bale, the 'complet summe' and 'whole knitting vp' of history, is the final antitype in a chain of meaning that stretches from Genesis to the present age.[88] It is the

[85] Perkins, *The arte of prophecying*, A2r–A3v.

[86] Ideas of covenant and providence in this period were, as Zur Shalev has shown, frequently tied to visions of 'the Promised Land as an emblem of divine promise', a notion promoted by the period's fierce debates about sacred geography. See Zur Shalev, 'Early Modern *geographia sacra* in the Context of Early Modern Scholarship', in *The Oxford Handbook of the Bible*, ed. Killeen, Smith, and Willie, 207.

[87] Northrop Frye, *The Great Code: The Bible and Literature* (New York: Harcourt Brace Jovanovich, 1982), 80–1.

[88] John Bale, *The image of bothe churches after the moste wonderfull and heauenly Reuelacion of Sainct Iohn* (London: Richard Iugge), A3v; 194. Importantly, Scott Mandelbrote has shown that the reformers' compulsion to tie 'the past more firmly to the contemporary world and even to its future' was bound up with the compilation of sacred chronologies, a hugely popular genre in which writers drew on mathematical and scientific skills, as well as theology, to understand the relationship between scripture and history. See Scott Mandelbrote, '"The doors shall fly open": Chronology and Biblical Interpretation in England, c.1630–c.1730', in *The Oxford Handbook of the Bible*, ed. Killeen, Smith, and Willie, 176–95 (194).

moment that gives meaning to everything that has gone before because it promises eternal victory to the true church of believers.[89]

As subsequent chapters attest, a typological understanding of the relationship between the Bible and history was not only the preserve of churchmen and theologians. Rather, because the applicatory principles of typology frequently formed the backbone of weekly sermons, as well as more complex commentaries and reading aids, this method of reading the scriptures was imparted to regular churchgoers. In every sermon preachers were to demonstrate how the words of the Bible applied to those in attendance, as the Oxford minister Richard Harris reportedly advised: 'a Preacher had three Books to study, 1. The Bible. 2. Himself. 3. The People'. For Harris, 'room for Application' differentiated sermons from 'Divinity-Lectures'.[90] There is also evidence that some preachers not only modelled the applicatory principles of biblical reading, but used their sermons to teach their congregations how to discern scripture's contemporary relevance for themselves. The Lincolnshire clergyman Thomas Granger seems to have been particularly concerned with teaching his parishioners how to read and apply the Word to their personal circumstances. In a sermon entitled *Pauls crovvne of reioycing. Or The maner how to heare the word with profit* (1616), he encourages his listeners to 'welcome, entertaine, embrace the word . . . and to apply the same particularly to [your] owne hearts and consciences' as well as to 'your towne in particular'.[91] Granger's sermon reminds his listeners that the scriptures can be applied in a variety of ways, and reiterates that the Bible's words have both personal and collective application. John Donne in a sermon on the Psalms similarly alerts his congregation to concurrent applications of his biblical text. The words of Psalm 38:3 are, he explains, 'historically, and literally to be understood of *David*; And secondly, in their *retrospect*, as they look upon the first *Adam*, so they concern *Mankind collectively*, and *so you*, and *I*, all have our portion in these calamities.'[92] Donne's exposition of Psalm 38 is revealing because it calls the reader to a

[89] The concept of the true church receives its fullest explanation in the Book of Revelation. For example, a contrast between the true and false churches is drawn figuratively through the woman of Revelation 12 and the harlot in Revelation 17. For more on how these women were read in the period, see Chapter 6, pp. 169–210, as well as Brownlee, 'Imagining the Enemy'.

[90] Harris in Clarke, *A Collection of the lives*, 313–14. For a broader discussion of the relationship between preachers and their congregations see Hunt, *The Art of Hearing*, 228–91.

[91] Thomas Granger, *Pauls crovvne of reioycing. Or The maner how to heare the word with profit* (London: T. S[nodham], 1616), 8, 36.

[92] John Donne, *The Sermons of John Donne*, ed. George K. Potter and Evelyn Simpson, 10 vols. (Berkeley: University of California Press, 1953–63), 2:75. For further discussion of Donne's reading of Psalm 38, and additional examples of the influence of typology on his exegesis, see Lewalski, *Protestant Poetics*, 137–8, and 'Typological Symbolism', 82–5.

recognition of the foundational principles of typological exegesis. Read retrospectively, that is, from a Christological vantage, the words of this penitential Psalm have resonance beyond their literal, historic meaning and speak of the ongoing sins of mankind. The sinful David finds his antitype in '*you*, and *I*'.

This practice of reading the scriptures backwards and forwards demonstrates that, although typology was premised on an understanding of the Bible and history as a continuous, progressive narrative, typological methods helped to foster non-sequential modes of reading as exegetes worked to illuminate the meaning of a passage through biblical cross-referencing. The comparison of scriptural texts with one another was a central component of reformed hermeneutics as it was believed to affirm the unity of the Bible's narratives and attest to scripture's capacity to interpret itself. The meaning of a tricky passage or verse could be ascertained by comparative reading, as Tyndale explains: 'the scripture geueth record to himselfe and euer expoundeth it selfe by an other open text'.[93] It is for this reason that even those sermons devoted to the exposition of a particular biblical passage abound with cross-references to other portions of scripture, either in the form of passing allusion or direct citation. George Gifford, for example, in a sermon focusing on James Chapter 2 invokes quotations from the Gospel of Luke, the writings of Paul, and the Book of Acts to elucidate and support his interpretation of the text.[94] Topical sermons roam even more freely and hastily over the pages of scripture and commonly cite dozens of biblical passages. In the course of a few short paragraphs, Thomas Adams' sermon on hypocrisy, *The White Deuil* (1613), addresses the Genesis serpent, the betrayal by Judas, the Ten Commandments, Samson's encounter with the Philistines, the Baal worshippers of the Pentateuch, and Daniel in the lion's den, among other narratives.[95] While cross-references could be declared plainly by preachers, they could also be presented more subtly, at the level of linguistic allusion. Henry Ainsworth's comparison of the Roman Catholic Church to the Old Testament queen, Jezebel, clearly is intended to suggest this Church's affiliation with another biblical woman, Revelation's Whore of Babylon.

[93] Tyndale, *The vvhole workes of W. Tyndall*, 173.

[94] George Gifford, *A godlie, zealous, and profitable sermon vpon the second chapter of Saint Iames* (London: Thomas East, 1582).

[95] Thomas Adams, *The white deuil, or The hypocrite vncased in a sermon preached at Pauls Crosse* (London: Melchisedech Bradvvood, 1613), 10–15. Peter Stallybrass makes clear that the division of the Bible into chapters and verses made it 'an entirely navigable book and facilitated the custom in Protestant sermons of persistently cross-referencing'. See 'Books and Scrolls: Navigating the Bible', in *Books and Readers in Early Modern England: Material Studies*, ed. Jennifer L. Andersen and Elizabeth Sauer (Philadelphia: University of Pennsylvania Press, 2002), 44.

His description of 'this *Iezebel*' draws on the words of Revelation 17:2: she is one who has 'enamoured the Nations with her beauty... and made them drunken with the wine of her fornications'.[96] The subtlety, variety, and rapidity of biblical allusions in early modern sermons made the pew a site where ears became attuned to scriptural gestures. In fact, so influential was this weekly hearing of the Word that Hamlin contends that 'the experience of hearing the Bible in worship conditioned early modern audiences to recognize biblical allusion in plays'.[97]

Whatever the medium of communication, it is clear that typological reading and cross-referencing was an integral part of early modern Bible-reading. Such non-sequential methodologies were central to the reformed effort to make sense of scripture, as the typography of many Geneva editions of the Bible attest. Here, margins crammed with cross-references and commentary invite the reader to turn to multiple scriptural locations during their reading. In many cases, such discontinuous reading is designed to impress upon the reader the Bible's linear Christological narrative. The marginal notes of the Song of Songs, for example, suggest that this book should be read through the lens of passages such as Matthew 25, Ephesians 5:25, and Revelation 19:7, cross-references which recast the lovers' dialogue as a communication between Christ and the 'Church... his Spouse'.[98] Similarly, the suffering servant of Isaiah 53 speaks, according to the chapter headnote, 'of Christ and his kingdome', and the reader is encouraged to ascertain this connection for themselves by turning to passages including Matthew 8:17, I Peter 2:24, I Corinthians 15:3, and Romans 6:9. Lay familiarity with this method of reading is suggested by the way in which many readers supplemented the references printed in the margins of Bibles with their own cross-references. Sherman's study of the early modern Bibles and prayer books in the Huntington Library has shown that as many as one in five Bibles contain significant inscriptions by readers, many of which are handwritten cross-references.[99] There is also

96 Henry Ainsworth, *An arrovv against idolatrie Taken out of the quiver of the Lord of hosts* (Amsterdam: G. Thorp, 1624), 90.

97 Hamlin, *The Bible in Shakespeare*, 41. For further discussion of the circumstances and effect of hearing sermons see Hunt, *The Art of Hearing*, 60–116, 229–91.

98 The Song of Songs, The Argument. In Matthew 25 the bridegroom who is awaited by the ten virgins of the parable is Christ, and in Ephesians 5:25 husbands are instructed to 'loue your wiues, euen as Christ loued the Church'. The Church's position as the Bride of Christ was also supported by Revelation 19:7 where, as the Geneva marginal note explains, Christ's bride the lamb was commonly understood as the Church: 'God made Christ [the] bridgrome of his Church' (*The Geneva Bible*, 1560). For more on the relationship between these verses and the Song of Songs, see Chapter 4.

99 Sherman, *Used Books*, 73. See also Molekamp's discussion of cross-references and notes in Geneva Bibles in *Women and the Bible*, 23–43.

evidence that readers jotted biblical cross-references in the margins of printed sermons and commentaries, and replicated systems of cross-referencing common in Bibles in their own devotional works, as is the case in Grace Mildmay's diary and Anne Wheathill's *A handful of holesome (though homelie) hearbs gathered out of... Gods most holie word* (1584).[100]

Such works affirm that many lay readers had become exceedingly familiar not only with the Bible's words, but also with the central principles of reformed exegesis. Wheathill is a case in point. Her prayers contain copious biblical allusions and citations, but they also suggest that she was proficient in reading biblical history typologically in relation to her own circumstances. In one instance, she responds to Jacob's encounter with the angel (Genesis 32:22–31) by praying that, like 'Iacob, who wrestled with thine angel, and prevailed... Even so make me a strong wrestler against mine enimies in this world.'[101] Wheathill's identification with Jacob and her prayer for empowerment further affirm the generative nature of biblical reading. Her Bible-reading necessitates personal application, prayer, and the production of her devotional text. Mildmay's diary entries similarly indicate an awareness of typological reading strategies. The medical care she offers to her community is, as Narveson notes, indebted to readings of Luke 10:37 and Acts 3:1–7, and is presented as a fulfilment of these biblical directives: 'I minister thy mercyes but as the servant and disciple of my Lorde, as I have learned of him, and as he hath commanded me.'[102] It seems that, among certain strands of the laity, there was familiarity with, and reproduction of, the period's dominant interpretative processes.

The chapters that follow make clear, though, that individuals without formal theological training could not only explore the implications of typological reading strategies within the more personal genres of life writing. A typologizing imperative underpins the published poetry of writers such as Robert Aylett and Aemilia Lanyer, and is discernible in Peele's biblical drama, *David and Bathsabe*, and in the apocalyptic play, *The Whore of Babylon*, written by Thomas Dekker to critique King James I's foreign policy.[103] The impact of typology on writers of more traditional

[100] For an overview of Mildmay's engagement with scripture see Narveson, *Bible Readers*, 177–98.

[101] Anne Wheathill, *A handful of holesome (though homelie) hearbs gathered out of... Gods most holie word* (London: By H[enrie] Denham, 1584), E4v.

[102] Grace Mildmay in Kate Narveson, 'Authority, Scripture, and Typography in Lady Grace Mildmay's Manuscript Meditations', in *English Women, Religion, and Textual Production, 1500–1625*, ed. Micheline White (Burlington, VT: Ashgate, 2011), 175.

[103] For typology's influence on the work of Robert Aylett see pp. 137–42; on Aemilia Lanyer see pp. 143–68; on Peele see pp. 73–8, and in Dekker see pp. 181–204.

literary genres is also detectable in works that declare their scriptural debts in more subtle, and strained, ways than these biblical poems and plays. It is possible to read Shakespeare's *King Lear* as an inversion of the typological pattern of promise and fulfilment and the Christological promise of hope, as Chapter 3 explores. A work such as this demonstrates how literary writings can be a means of exploring and disrupting dominant biblical readings and interpretative practices. Indeed, like sermons and commentaries, drama and poetry can do interpretative work, and disseminate innovative and complex ideas about biblical reading and meaning.

Lanyer's poetic retelling of the Passion of Christ, as recorded in the Gospels, is an evocative example of the sophisticated exegesis achievable within literary genres. *Salve Deus Rex Judaeorum* (1611) reimagines Gethsemane as a second Eden—a 'blessed' space pointedly beset by 'Vipers'—in an effort to expose the sins of biblical men, as well as women.[104] But the poem's attempt to challenge dominant, male-authored readings of the life of Christ, which is bolstered by the inset reassessment of responsibility for the Genesis Fall in 'Eues Apologie', is not simply evidence of the complex biblical interpretation undertaken by some members of the laity in literary writings. *Salve Deus* raises an important question about where exactly interpretative authority lies in this period. Because, although Protestantism may have emphasized the need for personal reading of the scriptures, and writers like Lanyer attest that independent exegetical work was undertaken by ordinary readers, individuals were not understood to function as authoritative interpreters in post-Reformation thought. 'Everybody should study the scripture' but, as Green reminds, 'the soundest interpreters were those with knowledge of the original languages in which the Bible was written'.[105]

INTERPRETATIVE COMMUNITIES

That interpretation was not straightforwardly devolved into the hands of the laity is suggested by the production of the wealth of interpretative aids detailed earlier, and of course the textual apparatus found in printed Bibles themselves. The marginal notes, chapter headings, and book prologues of the Tyndale (1526), Matthew (1537), and Geneva (1560) Bibles operated as a means of guiding the reader towards an appropriate understanding of

[104] Aemilia Lanyer, *The Poems of Aemilia Lanyer: Salve Deus Rex Judaeorum*, ed. Susanne Woods (Oxford: Oxford University Press, 1993), 67, lines 363, 365.

[105] Green, *Print and Protestantism*, 106. On this point see also Narveson, *Bible Readers*, 20–2; Hardy, 'The Septuagint and the Transformation of Biblical Scholarship in England'.

what they read.[106] The way in which these marginal notes sought to clarify and explain scripture's meaning demonstrates that there were clearly exceptions to the early reformers' claims that the Bible had been written in such a manner that the 'speciall intent and purpose might be vnderstanded and perceiued of *euery* reader'.[107] Guides for individual biblical reading had, then, to reconcile the reformed insistence that all of scripture was useful for reading, with the knowledge that some passages and books likely would prove difficult for ordinary readers to understand. It is for this reason that Downame advises that once the Bible had been read through, some books and chapters

> may be read much more seldome then others, especially by common Christians of meane knowledge and capacity, who are able to make little vse of them, as the Chapters which containe nothing but Genealogies, those in the New Testament excepted, the Leuticiall law abrogated by Christ, contaying the ceremonies of Gods seruice, wherof we can make vse only as they were types and shadowes of Christ, which cannot easily be done by ordinarie wits.[108]

To those of 'mean knowledge' and 'ordinarie wits', some portions of scripture may not simply be unintelligible, but unhelpful. The Song of Songs is the most obvious and commonly cited example. As an erotic account of human intimacy, biblical expositors deemed the spiritual meaning of this book to be 'darkely hyd', and, as Chapter 4 considers, frequently insisted it be read alongside a paraphrase or commentary, or indeed not at all by those who were spiritually immature.[109]

The expectation that lay reading of the Song, and scripture more generally, would be informed by a variety of external, and expert, sources reoccurs in clerical instructions for individual reading. Authors of biblical reading guides often reminded prospective readers of the need first to 'lay a sure foundation, by reading diligently some profitable Catechisme, containing the maine points of Christian Religion... till we so thorowly

[106] The Great Bible (1539) made use of Prologues. Some versions of the Bishops' Bible (1568) and Authorized Version Bible (1611) carried notes but these were much less extensive than those found in the Geneva Bible. For a discussion of these differences see Vivienne Westbrook, *Long Travail and Great Paynes: A Politics of Reformation Revision* (London: Kluwer Academic, 2001). For a discussion of medieval and Catholic Bibles see Beryl Smalley, *The Study of the Bible in the Middle Ages* (Notre Dame, IN: Notre Dame University Press, 1964); Eamon Duffy, *The Stripping of the Altars: Traditional Religion in England, 1400–1580* (New Haven: Yale University Press, 1992).

[107] Cranmer, 'The Prologue', *The Byble in Englyshe*, iir (my emphasis).

[108] Downame, *A guide to godlynesse*, 648.

[109] William Baldwin, *The canticles or balades of Salomon, phraselyke declared in Englysh metres* (London: William Baldwin, 1549), 1.

vnderstand & remember it, that we are able to giue an account'.[110] Of course, this foundation had likely been laid decades earlier. Catechizing typically took place in childhood, ensuring that individual reading of the scriptures was, to some degree, always filtered through an awareness of the central tenets of the Christian faith.[111] Moreover, the repeated calls for readers to familiarize themselves with 'the maine points of Christian Religion' reaffirm that ordinary individuals were, as Narveson reminds, not called 'to *interpret*' the Bible's words freely, but to weigh them in a manner that verified, and reinforced, the doctrines which they already knew.[112] The extent to which the ordinary reader operated within a larger interpretative community is suggested by Hoby's diary. Many of her entries demonstrate that her biblical reading was informed by a number of external sources, including her interactions with the household chaplain, Mr Rhodes, attendance at church sermons and religious lectures, and reading of devotional and theological works, including writings by William Perkins and John Foxe's *Actes and Monuments*.[113] There are, it seems, many midwives who bring Hoby's private readings to being.

Hoby's diary is suggestive of the way in which hermeneutic authority could slip between reader and professional preacher or textual expositor. The lay religious writings mentioned in this section affirm that individuals did interpretative work, but many also reveal how these readings were, to varying degrees, inflected by the ideas and models circulating in catechisms, sermons, biblical paratexts, and printed interpretative aids. The reformed call for *sola scriptura* must, as Narveson cautions, 'be qualified by an awareness that no reading happens "sola"—without framing contexts'.[114] Importantly, the existence of these framing contexts speaks to a tension inherent in the reformers' other mantra regarding scripture; that is, that 'scripture hath but one sence which is ye literall sence. And y^t^ literall sence is ye rote and grou[n]de of all.'[115] For if scripture does indeed speak literally, this seems to negate the need for interpretation or, at the very least, exegetical clarification by external sources. Yet, in spite of the reformers' literalist claims for the Bible, Protestantism remained reliant on a wealth of interpretative methodologies, which, to the modern observer,

[110] Downame, *A guide to godlynesse*, 642.

[111] See Green, *The Christian's ABC*, for a comprehensive discussion of catechizing in the period.

[112] Narveson, *Bible Readers*, 22.

[113] See, for example, the entry for Monday 7 January 1600 in *The Diary of Margaret, Lady Hoby* in *Women Writers*, ed. Martin, 195. See also Downame's advice that those with 'leysyre, learning and liberty' seek 'the helpe of some good commentary to cleare their doubt [in places of difficulty]': *A guide to godlynesse*, 644.

[114] Narveson, *Bible Readers*, 30.

[115] Tyndale, *The Obedie[n]ce*, R2v.

cannot easily be reconciled with literalism. Even if we accept, as James Douglas Fleming explains, that there are, or can be, exceptions that are 'consistent with literalism, in some overarching, non-arbitrary way, then the target of literal interpretation would appear, bewilderingly, to be something other than the merely literal'.[116] The reformers' continuing use of figurative reading practices, such as biblical typology, and reliance on commentaries and marginal glosses to elucidate scripture's meaning, demonstrates that the Protestant commitment to literalism is rather more conditional, and its literalist credo more complex, and contradictory, than otherwise might be supposed.

LITERALISM, REFORM, AND EXEGESIS

The reformed insistence on the Bible's literal sense arose from a frustration with the medieval practice of interpreting the scriptures according to a hermeneutic programme commonly known as the *Quadriga*. The *Quadriga* was a four-fold methodology used to ascertain a number of higher (that is non-literal) senses of scripture. According to this schema, exegetes, after establishing the literal sense of a biblical passage, could discern three spiritual senses: namely, the allegorical, moral, and anagogical.[117] From the outset of the Reformation, religious reformers criticized this four-fold methodology on the basis that it warped scripture's meaning and confused lay readers. The presence of 'so many' senses, Luther chided, meant that 'silly poor consciences could receive no certain doctrine of anything'.[118] Rather than multiple senses, Luther advocated that the Bible has only 'one, literal, legitimate, proper' sense.[119] Writing at the beginning of the next century, Perkins affirms that, despite the lapse in time, Protestants continued to hold tightly to this early Reformation principle: 'there is but one full and intire sense of euery place of scripture, and that is also the

[116] James Douglas Fleming, 'Making Science and the Literal: Modern Semantics and Early Modern Hermeneutics', in *The Word and the World*, ed. Killeen and Forshaw, 46.

[117] See Alistair McGrath, *Reformation Thought: An Introduction* (Oxford: Blackwell, 1988), 157. It should be said that while the term '*Quadriga*' typically refers to the four senses listed this was not a fixed interpretative system and '*Quadriga*' could be used to refer to some or all of the approaches cited. See G. R. Evans, *The Language of the Bible: The Earlier Middle Ages* (Cambridge: Cambridge University Press, 1984), 114–22.

[118] Martin Luther, *A Commentary on Saint Paul's Epistle to the Galatians* (London: J. Duncan, 1830), 402. For more on Luther's hermeneutic, and for a more extensive overview of the reformers' understanding of scripture's literal sense, see Luxon, *Literal Figures*, 83–101.

[119] Martin Luther in Siegfried Raeder, 'The Exegetical and Hermeneutical Work of Martin Luther', in *Hebrew Bible/Old Testament*, ed. Sæbø, 375.

literall sense'.[120] The reformers' commitment to a single, literal sense of scripture was bound up with the accusation that medieval and later Roman Catholic writers had, at best, marginalized this manner of reading the scriptures. Calvin explains that because the literal sense was thought to be 'too mean and poor', generations since Origen have tortur[ed] Scripture... by beating out allegories'—an interpretative approach that Luther similarly denigrates when he describes allegory as a 'beautiful harlot who fondles men'.[121]

While the reformers may have made vocal claims for the literal and staunchly disavowed the usefulness of allegory, this oppositional rhetoric shrouds a much more complex hermeneutic picture. The *Quadriga* itself, requiring as it did exegetes to establish the literal sense of a passage first, demonstrates that the medieval Church did not straightforwardly abandon the literal.[122] Neither did the reformers, as Richard Muller notes, 'simply trade allegory for literal interpretation'.[123] Protestantism's commitment to scripture's literal sense actually marks a continuity, rather than a contrast, between sixteenth-century biblical interpretation and medieval exegesis. What changes is better understood as a shift in the emphasis of biblical hermeneutics in the sixteenth century, for what the reformers advocated was a single sense that, although termed literal, accommodated figurative readings; as David Steinmetz explains, theirs was 'a letter pregnant with spiritual significance, a letter big-bellied with meanings formerly relegated by the *quadriga* to allegory or tropology'.[124] The reformers' continuing

[120] William Perkins, *A Commentarie or Exposition upon the First Five Chapters of the Epistle to Galatians* (Cambridge: John Legat, 1604), 346.

[121] John Calvin, *Calvin on the Epistle of Paul to the Galatians and Ephesians*, trans. William Pringle (Edinburgh: Thomas Clark, 1841), 115; Martin Luther, *Luther's Works: Volume 5 (Lectures on Genesis, Chapter 26–30)*, ed. J. J. Pelikan, W. A. Hansen, G. V. Schick, and P. D. Pahl (St Louis: Concordia Publishing House, 1968), 347. Luther's description of allegory as a 'harlot' chimes with the reading practice's association in reformed thought with Catholicism. Frances Dolan reminds that the reformers' persistent association of 'the Roman church with fallen women' allowed them to 'acknowledge its seductive appeal while simultaneously repudiating it': *Whores of Babylon: Catholicism, Gender, and Seventeenth-Century Print Culture* (Ithaca: Cornell University Press, 1999), 52. The accusation of harlotry made against the Roman Catholic Church was bound up with the association of Roman Catholicism with the Whore of Babylon who appears in Revelation 17. See Brownlee, 'Imagining the Enemy'.

[122] For more on the importance of the literal within the *Quadriga* see Alistair McGrath, *The Intellectual Origins of the European Reformation* (Oxford: Blackwell, 1987), 148–53; Richard A. Muller, 'Biblical Interpretation in the Era of the Reformation: The View from the Middle Ages', in *Biblical Interpretation in the Era of the Reformation: Essays Presented to David C. Steinmetz in Honor of his Sixtieth Birthday*, ed. R. A Muller and J. L. Thompson (Grand Rapids, MI: Eerdmans, 1996), 3–22.

[123] Muller, 'Biblical Interpretation', 12.

[124] David Steinmetz, 'Divided by a Common Past: The Reshaping of the Christian Exegetical Tradition in the Sixteenth Century', *Journal of Medieval and Early Modern*

reliance on figural readings of scripture resulted, then, in a broadening of what is typically implied by the term literal. Sixteenth-century theologian William Whitaker works to define what is meant by the reformers' enhanced understanding of a literal reading of scripture in *A Disputation on Holy Scripture against the Papists* (1588). He insists that the sense of 'Scripture is one only, namely, the literal or grammatical' but explains that this 'is not that which the words immediately suggest, as the Jesuit defines it; but rather that which arises from the words themselves, whether they be taken strictly or figuratively'.[125] Suggesting that the literal can, paradoxically, encompass both a strict (or literal) reading of the words as well as a figurative reading, Whitaker's text posits an understanding of the literal that is much richer than it initially seems.

What Whitaker attempts to reconcile in this portion of the *Disputation* is the reformed commitment to scripture's single, literal sense with a defence of using other non-literal interpretative practices. This prevarication was practically necessary as not all of scripture claimed to speak literally. Jesus had used parables to teach the crowds that followed him, and invoked metaphors and figures of speech to explain his divinity to his disciples. Beyond the Gospels, entire books, such as Revelation, termed a 'prophecie' (Rev. 22:10) by its writer, John, declared themselves to be written figuratively. In addition to accommodating the figural interpretation of those portions of scripture that were written symbolically, a literal interpretation, in the reformed tradition, might include the use of biblical typology as a means of demonstrating a relationship between the Old and New Testaments. Yet as the earlier discussion of typology suggested, this reading practice could yield highly figurative results. The extent to which typology encouraged figural reading of the Old Testament is suggested in Thomas Taylor's *Christ Revealed* (1635). Much like Guild's work, Taylor's text is dedicated to mapping 'the Types and Shadowes of our SAVIOVR contained throughout the whole SCRIPTVRE: All opened and made usefull for the benefit of Gods Church'.[126] Taylor's painstaking progression through the scriptures locates traces of Christ in the minutiae of Old Testament narratives. For example, the pillar of cloud that

Studies 27.2 (1997), 249. See also Debora Shuger's overview of reformed understandings of the literal: 'Isaiah 63 and the Literal Senses of Scripture', in *The Oxford Handbook of the Bible*, ed. Killeen, Smith, and Willie, 149–63.

125 William Whitaker, *A Disputation on Holy Scripture against the Papists*, trans. William Fitzgerald, Parker Society, No. 45 (Cambridge: Cambridge University Press, 1849), 406, 405.

126 Taylor, *Christ revealed*, title page.

appeared to guide the Israelites in Exodus 13 is dissected and found to reveal Christ in a variety of imaginative ways:

> As a Pillar it signified Christ; who as a Pillar is firme, stable, straight, strong, and as a Pillar able to support his Church, and to beare up all the living stones layd on this foundation... 1. as the cloud naturally engendreth fruitfull raines and showers: so Christ properly, by the influence and raine of grace, makes the field of the Church fresh, fruitfull, flourishing; 2. as the cloud mitigates the heat of the Sunne: so Jesus Christ quencheth and allayeth the parching heat of his Fathers wrath... 3. as the cloud covered Israel from the Aegyptians fury: so Jesus Christ defends his Church, from the fiery darts and assaults of Satans temptations; 2. from the furious rage of our owne lusts, and inflammation of sinne: 3. shelters it from the heat of the Sun of persecution, and from all bodily woes that they cannot doe what they will, but what he permits.[127]

In these lines, the brief biblical description of the pillar of cloud ('the LORD went before them by day in a pillar of a cloude, to leade them the way' (Exodus 13:21)) is found to testify to the character and work of Christ, and his ongoing provision for the Church's protection—an interpretation that chimes with much older spiritual readings of this episode in Exodus.[128]

The fact that reformers like Taylor used typology to facilitate, and legitimize, elaborate and textually obscure readings of the Bible is telling, particularly because of Protestant concerns regarding allegory. What the reformers detested most about allegory was, as B. A. Gerrish summarizes, that 'a sufficiently astute theologian could, without much difficulty, find any of the church's beliefs hidden or symbolized in the most unlikely corners of both the Old and the New Testaments'.[129] Taylor's reading reminds, though, that deeply symbolic and figural readings of the scriptures persist in the reformed tradition, as well as in medieval and Roman Catholic exegesis. Albeit under the banner of typological rather than allegorical exegesis, reformed readers enriched obscure biblical passages with figurative meaning, producing readings that sometimes cohere with patristic and medieval approaches to, and interpretations of, the Bible.[130]

While biblical readings like Taylor's attest to the continuing importance of figural and symbolic readings in the reformed tradition, many

[127] Taylor, *Christ revealed*, 246.

[128] See, for example, Origen's interpretation of Exodus: *Homilies on Genesis and Exodus*, ed. Ronald E. Heine (Washington, DC: Catholic University of America Press, 1982), 275–84.

[129] B. A. Gerrish, *The Old Protestantism and the New: Essays on the Reformation Heritage* (Chicago: University of Chicago Press, 1982), 52.

[130] For a more fulsome discussion of how the reformers' figural readings of the scriptures built on centuries of reading see Chapter 4.

Protestant expositors insisted that there was a resolute distinction between typological and allegorical approaches to the scriptures.[131] Whitaker insists in his *Disputation* that 'A type is a different thing from an allegory. The sense, therefore, of that scripture is one only, namely, the literal or grammatical.'[132] Whitaker's polemical work elucidates how, for the reformers, typology was not only distinct from allegory, but entirely compatible with scripture's literal sense. Perkins' influential guide on preaching, *The arte of prophecying* (1607), likewise contended that there was no similarity between typological readings of the scriptures and the interpretative practices of the medieval Church. 'The fourefold meaning of the scripture must be exploded and reiected', he asserts, '*There is one onelie sense, and the same is the literall*.'[133]

The accommodation of typology within the reformers' understanding of scripture's literal sense rested on a belief in the historicity of both type and antitype. Both reference points were, as Galdon explains, understood to be 'literal and historically perceptible scriptural events', and, as such, typology was considered to be a more stable and objective reading practice than allegory by reformers.[134] Lewalski outlines how the historical origins of typology informed the reformers' effort to distinguish this reading practice from allegory: 'Allegory was understood to involve the invention of fictions . . . to represent underlying spiritual truth or reality. Typology by contrast was recognized as a mode of signification in which both type and antitype are historically real entities with independent meaning and validity, forming patterns of prefiguration . . . by reason of God's providential control of history.'[135] Lewalski's comments elucidate how the distinction drawn between these reading practices turns on the fictiveness of allegory, that is, on the reader's ability to discern the literary from the historical. Yet such a distinction is, as Lisa Freinkel's work on the theology of figure has shown, 'strictly speaking . . . impossible', for 'one cannot rigorously distinguish between typology and allegory any more than one can rigorously demonstrate the legitimacy of a given meaning'.[136]

[131] Galdon suggests that prior to the Reformation there seems to have been little inclination to distinguish typology from allegory: *Typology and Seventeenth-Century Literature*, 25.

[132] Whitaker, *A Disputation*, 406.

[133] Perkins, *The arte of prophecying*, 31.

[134] Galdon, *Typology and Seventeenth-Century Literature*, 31–2. Other scholars who have scrutinized the relationship between history and typological and allegorical reading practices include Luxon, *Literal Figures*, 34–76; Freinkel, *Reading Shakespeare's Will*, 1–46; and Pendergast, *Religion, Allegory, and Literacy*, 8–12.

[135] Lewalski, *Protestant Poetics*, 111.

[136] Freinkel, *Reading Shakespeare's Will*, 4. See also Luxon's critique of this distinction in *Literal Figures*, 41–3.

Another difficulty with the reformers' understanding of typology's literal and historical surety emerges when the processes of this reading practice are scrutinized.[137] Unlike medieval readings that viewed the Old Testament as containing a people who were, as James S. Preus puts it, 'unaware that their whole history was an allegory', the reformers championed typological readings on the basis that they preserved the historical independence of both type and antitype.[138] In other words, typology read the Old Testament both *within* its historical context and resonating *beyond* it.[139] The historicity of the Old Testament is, however, destabilized when, as Thomas Luxon points out, one considers that the reality that gives significance to these biblical narratives always lies within a future revelation, chiefly, in the Second Coming of Christ, the final fulfilment in typology's chain of meaning.[140] Luxon elucidates the difficulties inherent in typology's focus on such future revelations when he states that 'the real, the true and the literal have all been evacuated from this world and projected into the next, with the result that the Protestant Christian's grasp on reality is by way of faith (*sola fides*) and word (*sola verbo*) alone'.[141] Although typology was accommodated within reformed literalism on the basis that it prioritizes that which is 'real' and 'historic', these definitive categories are unsettled by the cycle of figurations that typological readings precipitate.

THE DEFICIENCY OF THE INTERPRETER

Typology's continual deferral of meaning has problematic consequences not simply for the historicity of typology as a reading practice, but for reading as a way into biblical truth, as Freinkel explains: 'from its Pauline

[137] In this point I build on Luxon's arguments in *Literal Figures*, 40–76.

[138] James S. Preus, *From Shadow to Promise: Old Testament Interpretation from Augustine to the Young Luther* (Cambridge, MA: Harvard University Press, 1969), 33; Luxon, *Literal Figures*, 25.

[139] For example, a type, such as the High Priest in the Book of Exodus who is understood as a figure of Christ because he undertakes the annual sacrifice of atonement for the people of Israel, attains additional significance beyond its Old Testament historic context. See Perkins' reading of the High Priest in *Christian oeconomie: or, A short survey of the right manner of erecting and ordering a familie according to the scriptures* (London: Felix Kyngston, 1609), 67. For further discussion of the historicity of type and antitype see Erich Auerbach's comments in *Mimesis: The Representation of Reality in Western Literature* (Princeton: Princeton University Press, 1968), 195, as well as his essay 'Figura', in *Scenes from the Drama of European Literature: Six Essays*, trans. Ralph Mannheim (New York: Meridan, 1959), 11–76. See also Galdon, *Typology and Seventeenth-Century Literature*, 31–2; Luxon, *Literal Figures*, 34–101; Freinkel, *Reading Shakespeare's Will*, 1–46.

[140] Luxon, *Literal Figures*, esp. 42–4, 51–6.

[141] Luxon, *Literal Figures*, 66.

inception Christian figurality grounds itself not in history per se but in the readerly, promissory construction *of* that history'.[142] What Freinkel's comment makes clear is that typology is not an objective reading practice but one that, like any other, relies on human perception. It is precisely because, at some level, this reality must be confronted that attempts to define typology's place within the reformers' understanding of the literal sense are so fraught. Whitaker's attempt to reconcile the reformers' enriched understanding of literalism with scripture's single sense reveals the extent to which the interpretative process relies on perception:

> When we proceed from the sign to the thing signified, we bring no new sense, but only bring out into light what was before concealed in the sign. When we speak of the sign itself, we express only part of the meaning; and so also when we mention only the thing signified: but when the mutual relation between the sign and thing signified is brought out, then the whole complete sense, which is founded upon this similitude and agreement, is set forth.[143]

As Whitaker clarifies that scripture's single, that is its literal, sense is that which mutually considers the grammatical-historical meaning and broader spiritual meaning, he inadvertently confronts the weak spot in reformed exegetical theory. The relationship between sign and signified ultimately relies on 'similitude'. In this admission Whitaker discloses how, in spite of a commitment to the words of the text and emphasis on its historicity, ascertaining biblical meaning rests, in the end, on the perceptive abilities of the human interpreter. In this admission, reformed hermeneutics finds itself in tricky territory. Because, as Calvin asserts in the *Institutes of Christian Religion*, after the Fall humanity 'lack[ed] the natural ability to mount up unto the pure and clear knowledge of God'.[144] So entirely depraved, the human mind was considered to be 'a perpetual factory of idols', an outlook which inherently problematizes both perception and representation of things divine or invisible.[145]

The reformers' understanding of the human mind was influenced by, and part of, the broader philosophical debate concerning the precise relationship between *res* ('things') and *verba* ('words').[146] A number of medieval thinkers, often referred to as Nominalists, posited a separation of

142 Freinkel, *Reading Shakespeare's Will*, 4. 143 Whitaker, *A Disputation*, 407.

144 John Calvin, *Institutes of the Christian Religion*, 2 vols., ed. John T. McNeill, trans. Ford Lewis Battles (Louisville: Westminster John Knox Press, 2006), 68, 1.5.15.

145 Calvin, *Institutes*, 108, 1.11.8.

146 For an overview of this debate see Diana B. Altegoer, *Reckoning Words: Baconian Science and the Construction of Truth in English Renaissance Culture* (London: Associated University Presses, 2000), 29–50; Hugo Keiper, Christopher Bode, and Richard J. Utz, eds., *Nominalism and Literary Discourse: New Perspectives*, Critical Studies 10 (Amsterdam: Rodopi, 1997).

things and words.[147] Among these was William of Ockham who argued that 'words are signs subordinated to mental concepts or contents' and, as such, are only able to signify 'secondarily what the impressions of the mind import primarily'.[148] This problematic relationship between mental thought and language logically destabilizes the representative process—both spoken as well as written—for, as Marion Trousdale observes, it places a gap between the thought, or *res*, and the words on the page.[149] Martin Elsky elucidates this difficulty when he explains how the disparity between speech and mental language ensured that every 'utterance can potentially render meaningless the meaning of which it is the necessary vehicle'.[150] This understanding of language leaves reformed exegesis in a problematic position.[151] Metaphysically separated from the biblical text, the reader's attempt to ascertain the relationship between biblical sign and signified is inherently hampered by their only resource, the fallen human mind.

The consequences of relying on the human mind to discern scripture's meaning become further apparent in Donne's 1624 sermon on the Book of Revelation. In this work, Donne defines the literal sense as that which is 'the principall intention of the Holy Ghost, in that place'.[152] This description not only illuminates the reformers' difficulty with defining scripture's literal sense, but identifies the truly precarious nature of their exegetical programme. For a faith that considered humanity to be 'dull' to the 'manifest testimonies' of God in the universe, ascertaining the mind, or 'intention', of the divine must ultimately be doomed to fail.[153] Having placed scripture's meaning at the mercy of the frail human mind, Donne's advice to his listeners on Bible-reading contains further contradictions. He explains that, in different places in scripture, the literal sense is both that which is immediately implied and that which is not:

> In the first book of the Scriptures, that of Genesis, there is danger in departing from the letter; in this later book, this of Revelation, there is as much danger in adhering too close to the letter. The literall sense is alwayes

[147] For the complexities of defining Nominalism see McGrath, *Intellectual Origins*, 70–85, and Martin Elsky's discussion in *Authorizing Words: Speech, Writing, and Print in the English Renaissance* (Ithaca and London: Cornell University Press, 1989), 29–35.

[148] William of Ockham, *Summa totius logicae*, in *Philosophical Writings*, ed. Philotheus Boehner, rev. edn. Stephen Brown (Indianapolis, IN: Hackett Publishing Company, 1990), 48. See also Adrian Streete, 'Reforming Signs: Semiotics, Calvinism and Clothing in Sixteenth-Century England', *Literature and History* 12.1 (Spring 2003): 1–18 (3).

[149] Marion Trousdale, *Shakespeare and the Rhetoricians* (Chapel Hill: University of North Carolina Press, 1982), 31.

[150] Elsky, *Authorizing Words*, 33.

[151] For a more fulsome discussion of these difficulties see Chapter 4, pp. 114–15, 135, 142.

[152] Donne, *The Sermons*, 6:62.

[153] Calvin, *Institutes*, 1.5.11.

> to be preserved; but the literall sense is not alwayes to be discerned . . . the literall sense of every place, is the principall intention of the Holy Ghost . . . And his principall intention in many places, is to express things by allegories, by figures; so that in many places of Scripture, a figurative sense is the literall sense.[154]

The principles for reading Genesis and Revelation that Donne sets down leave the reader in a rather ambivalent position. Beyond these named biblical books, how were readers to be sure which portions of scripture required them to remain close to the implied meaning, or letter, and in which places they should search out a higher, spiritual meaning? And, if the literal sense is, as Donne says, 'not always' discernible, surely the entire interpretative process is itself destabilized as the possibility of certainty is eliminated? Donne's final attempt to bring clarity to the reformers' understanding of the literal sense by claiming that the 'figurative sense *is* the literal sense' renders the literal a hermeneutic category that lacks definitive meaning.[155] Donne's 'literal' is interpretative and, by implication, figural.[156]

Regardless of the reformers' desire for the 'literal' to simply be literal, attempts to define, explain, and attain the 'literal' are inevitably hampered by language itself, which as figurative, defies literalism. While the reformers may have sought to define themselves by their anti-allegorical principles, and through an insistence on a single, literal approach to the scriptures, explanations of Protestant interpretative methodologies reveal that a purely literal hermeneutic was impossible. The contemporary relevance of the scriptures depended on a figurative, and flexible, approach to the Bible's words, one that understood the Bible's sacred history as ever-present. In this regard, the hermeneutic principles of biblical typology did not only shape early modern Bible-reading but could inform most other spheres of knowledge and daily life. As a reading practice, typology enabled the translation of the biblical past to the present, and brought the realm of the sacred to the world of the individual. The history, literature, and art of this period reveal that mothers, monarchs, martyrs, and milners could be biblically literate, and possess the interpretative skills necessary to read and apply the Bible's pages to their own lives.

[154] Donne, *The Sermons*, 6:62. [155] Donne, *The Sermons*, 6:62 (my emphasis).
[156] As Fleming reminds, 'figurative meaning is the very idea of interpretative meaning': 'Making Science and the Literal: Modern Semantics and Early Modern Hermeneutics', in *The Word and the World*, ed. Killeen and Forshaw, 47.

2

'Our King Salomon'

Biblical Typology and the Kingship of Solomon in Tudor and Stuart England

On 19 June 1621 William Laud preached a sermon on King David's prayer in Psalm 122 before King James I and IV. David's prayerful petition for peace in Jerusalem was a fitting choice for the royal occasion, particularly as England's king was facing opposition to his policy of peace from Parliament. Aptly, Psalm 122 is not simply read by Laud as an account of a biblical king's commitment to private prayer for his kingdom. Rather, this Psalm is understood as a command to pray for the peaceful prosperity of London, the New Jerusalem, which is paralleled with Israel's sacred city throughout the address. Indeed so powerful are the analogies Laud draws between the circumstances of England and those of David's Jerusalem that the sermon ends with the following confident summation: 'Thus hauing made my *Text* my *Circle*, I am gone round it, and come backe to it; and must therefore end in the poynt where I began: *Pray for the peace of Jerusalem; Let them prosper that loue it: Peace be within the walles of it, and prosperity within the Palaces.*'[1] By the end of Laud's address London is not simply analogous with Jerusalem. Instead, a typological understanding of the connectedness of biblical past and early modern present has fused England's metropolis with its biblical counterpart. The separate identity of these cities is indecipherable: 'Jerusalem' is London.

The elision of Israelite and English history was by the reign of 'Great Britains Solomon', James, commonplace.[2] The Bible's narratives were regularly mapped on to the events of Tudor history, and Old Testament leaders in particular became a popular means of celebrating, and consolidating, the

[1] William Laud, *A sermon preached before his Maiesty* (London: F. K[ingston], 1621), 44.

[2] John Williams, *Great Britains Salomon A sermon preached at the magnificent funerall, of the most high and mighty king, Iames* (London: Eliot's Court Press, 1625), title page. On the paralleling of English history with Israel in this period see in particular: Guibbory, *Christian Identity*; Beatrice Groves, *The Destruction of Jerusalem in Early Modern English Literature* (Cambridge: Cambridge University Press, 2015).

authority of many early modern English monarchs. The centrality of biblical leaders to conceptions of monarchical authority in this period has, in recent years, become more familiar terrain for scholars. Studies have shown the importance of David, Josiah, Deborah, and Solomon to the respective reigns of Henry VIII, Edward VI, Elizabeth I, and James I.[3] While the commemorative use of biblical leaders under the Tudors and Stuarts has become better established, the reading practices that facilitate these comparisons have received limited scrutiny.[4] As early modern readers pondered the contemporary relevance of the Bible's sacred histories, and engaged in the process of applying these narratives to the political circumstances of their cultural moment, common exegetical strategies emerge. Biblical typology, prioritizing as it did the relationship between scripture's two Testaments as well as biblical history and the present, is central to the Bible's application in this period, and the political and social functions of this reading practice warrant further exploration. Typological reading strategies enabled Israelite and English history to be elided and thus became integral to the formulation of a new, Protestant history. But more than this, the figuration of England's monarchs as antitypes of biblical kings like Solomon became an important, yet problematic, means

[3] For royal comparisons to David see: John N. King, 'James I and King David: Jacobean Iconography and its Legacy', in *Royal Subjects: Essays on the Writings of James VI and I*, ed. Daniel Fischlin and Mark Fortier (Detroit: Wayne State University Press, 2002), 421–53; P. Tudor-Craig, 'Henry VIII and King David', in *Early Tudor England: Proceedings of the 1987 Harlaxton Symposium*, ed. Daniel Williams (Woodbridge: Boydell Press, 1989), 183–206; for Josiah see Diarmaid MacCulloch, *The Boy King Edward VI and the Protestant Reformation* (Berkeley: University of California Press, 2002), 57–104; for Deborah see: Anne McLaren, 'Elizabeth I as Deborah: Biblical Typology, Prophecy and Political Power', in *Gender, Power and Privilege in Early Modern Europe*, ed. Jessica Munns and Penny Richards (Harlow: Pearson, 2003), 90–107; Alexandra Walsham, '"A Very Deborah?" The Myth of Elizabeth I as a Providential Monarch', in *The Myth of Elizabeth*, ed. Susan Doran and Thomas S. Freeman (Basingstoke: Palgrave Macmillan, 2003), 143–68; and for Solomon: Michael Hattaway, 'Paradoxes of Solomon: Learning in the English Renaissance', *Journal of the History of Ideas* 29.4 (October–December 1968): 449–530; John N. King, *Tudor Royal Iconography: Literature and Art in an Age of Religious Crisis* (Princeton: Princeton University Press, 1989), 86–9; Guibbory, *Christian Identity*, 33–55.

[4] Killeen's 'Chastising with Scorpions', which considers the reading strategies that underpin the application of the biblical kings Rehoboam and Jeroboam in the present, is a notable exception. See too Killeen's *The Political Bible*. It should also be said at this point that reading strategies surrounding biblical kings have received some attention in discussions of kingship in Shakespeare's works. See in particular David Evett, 'Types of King David in Shakespeare's Lancastrian Tetralogy', *Shakespeare Studies*18 (1981): 139–61; Marx, *Shakespeare and the Bible*, 40–58; Adrian Streete, '"What bloody man is that?": Questioning Biblical Typology in *Macbeth*', *Shakespeare* 5.1 (April 2009): 18–35. See also the literary uses of biblical kings discussed in Lily B. Campbell, *Divine Poetry and Drama in Sixteenth-Century England* (Cambridge: Cambridge University Press, 1959), 93–107; Inga Stina Ewbank, 'The House of David in Renaissance Drama: A Comparative Study', *Renaissance Drama* 8 (1965): 3–40; Groves, *Texts and Traditions*, esp. 89–120.

of responding to the relocation of sacred authority to the monarchical body after the break with Rome. For a faith that claimed to reject symbols in favour of the literal word the difficulty lay not only in the use of Solomon's image to promote a brand of sacred kingship that, at times, borders on political idolatry, but in the very biblical text itself. The life of Solomon, recounted in I Kings and I & II Chronicles, demanded careful negotiation. For although celebrated for unmatched wisdom and wealth, and the erection of Israel's long-awaited Temple, Solomon ended his life in idolatry and disobedience.[5] The process of mapping Solomon's life on to the reigns of England's monarchs was, then, complex and exegetically demanding. Such typologies depended upon a selective reading of the biblical narrative that consistently occluded the shadows of the biblical whole.[6]

BIBLICAL HISTORIES, POLITICAL TYPOLOGIES, AND REFORM

The Bible's importance to conceptions of political authority in early modern England was bound up with the need to establish a distinctively Protestant history after the break with Rome. In renouncing the Roman Catholic Church, the reformers also relinquished an ecclesial history that claimed to trace its origins to St Peter. Having lost this authorizing lineage, there was in England, as Guibbory has shown, 'a turn to things Jewish', and as the institutions of monarchy and the Church 'were given a foundation in the Hebrew Bible, so was the nation'.[7] This legitimizing endeavour intensified Old Testament reading, and the history of Israel was found to connect with that of English Protestants on a number of levels. The Old Testament became, as Bruce Gordon notes, 'a mirror in which the evangelicals saw themselves and their enemies reflected; their religious leaders were the prophets, those suffering persecution were the Israelites in Egypt, their godly rulers were Josiah and Hezekiah, and their enemies were Pharaoh's servants'.[8] But the sacred history that scripture recorded

[5] Unlike I Kings, the account of Solomon's reign in II Chronicles is silent on his idolatry.

[6] The tendency to read biblical narratives selectively was, perhaps, an inevitable consequence of the typological practice of reading the type in relation to the self in the period. Certainly, given the monarchical associations Solomon accrued, a refit of the Solomonic story was essential.

[7] Guibbory, *Christian Identity*, 20–1.

[8] Bruce Gordon, ed., *Protestant History and Identity in Sixteenth-Century Europe, Volume 2: The Later Reformation* (Aldershot: Scholar Press, 1996), 'Introduction', 4.

was, as Chapter 1 suggested, more than a straightforward reflection of the circumstances of English Protestants. The Old Testament was understood to be an omnipresent account of the trials and deliverance of God's chosen people who, in the early modern present, were English.[9] Read typologically, these pages of scripture were not simply an historical account of Judaic history and record of Jewish law. 'The actors of the Old Testament', as Killeen explains, 'engag[e] in prefigurative deeds they do not understand—of either the New Testament or the seventeenth-century divine drama of England.'[10] The anointed kings and wicked tyrants, and the enslavement, exile, and victories of the Israelites were part of the continuing history of England. In this regard, a typological understanding of the relationship between the scriptures and contemporary history enabled English Protestants to be participants in the Bible's covenantal promises.

The way in which reformed readers turned to the Bible to excavate their own providentially determined, covenantal narrative is suggested in an ornate woodcut in the opening pages of Thomas Morton's *Salomon or A treatise declaring the state of the kingdome of Israel as it was in the daies of Salomon* (1596) (Figure 2.1). The woodcut figures Queen Elizabeth I and the Old Testament king, Solomon, standing either side of the royal crown and Tudor coat of arms. The connection between the two monarchs is further suggested by the scrolls placed over their heads; Elizabeth is 'Flos de Iesse' and 'Reg. Pacis', and Solomon, 'Leo de Iuda' and 'Rex Pacis'.[11] In these related biblical titles the woodcut implies, as John N. King states, 'that the new Israel of Elizabethan England is a throwback to the Solomonic kingdom'.[12] Certainly, the placement of the monarchs and the titles which they are awarded work to elide biblical past with political present, typologically positioning England as a new, Israelite nation, and Elizabeth as a new Solomon. The accompanying biblical citation, taken from Jacob's prophecy for Israel in Genesis 29:8, is further suggestive of the applicability of Israel's covenantal promises for England:

[9] The perceived connection between the Bible and the present depended on the reformers' understanding of the unchanging nature of God, the relationship between scripture's two Testaments, and the doctrine of providence. See Chapters 1, pp. 31–3, and 3, pp. 85–7. For the Old Testament's omnipresence, see Killeen, 'Chastising with Scorpions', 492.

[10] Killeen, 'Chastising with Scorpions', 494. See also Killeen, *The Political Bible*, esp. 22–51.

[11] Thomas Morton, *Salomon or A treatise declaring the state of the kingdome of Israel, as it was in the daies of Salomon* (London: Robert Robinson, 1596), A2v.

[12] King, *Tudor Royal Iconography*, 257. I am indebted to King's study for first introducing me to Morton's woodcut, and to the Holbein watercolour and King's College window series discussed later.

Figure 2.1. 'Regni Angloisraelitici Typus', from Thomas Morton, *Salomon or A treatise declaring the state of the kingdome of Israel* (1596 M88). The Burke Library at Union Theological Seminary, Columbia University, New York.

> *Jvdah* thy brethren shall praise the[e]:
> Thy hand in the necke of thy enemies:
> The Sonnes of thy father shall bowe themselves vnto thee:
> *Jvdah* my Sonne, a Lions whelp, thou shalt come vp from thy spoiles.
> Thou hast crouched like a Lion, yea as great as a Lion: and who shal raise him vp?
> The sceptre shall not depart from *Jvdah*, nor a lawgiuer from betweene his feete till the Messias come:
> And to him shall be the obedience of the people.[13]

Placed under a woodcut that clearly figures Elizabeth, 'Flos de Jesse', as part of the Judaic line, '*Jvdah*' is positioned as a type of England, and Jacob's words are understood to have living relevance. His prophecy continues to promise the prosperity and deliverance of God's elect at the turn of the seventeenth century. The typological connections that dominate this page of Morton's text, not least in the woodcut's title, 'Regni Angloisraelitici typus', reinforce that the identification of the English as God's chosen people is not only scripturally rooted, but specifically traceable through the leaders of biblical and contemporary history. Indeed, the symbolism used elucidates how the process of aligning scripture's rulers with an early modern monarch could position leaders on opposing sides of the cosmic struggle between Christ and Antichrist, and anticipate the eventual triumph of the Protestant faithful over their enemies. This strategy is clearly exemplified in clergyman John Prime's typological reading of Elizabeth I as Solomon. The Queen's enemies, broadly conceived as 'papistes', are 'traitors to Ierusalem and enemies to Sion'.[14] As in Morton's text, a Solomonic Elizabeth is deployed by Prime to make a comment on England's national, and religious, election. In visualizing the transferral of Solomon's divine appointment and kingly attributes on to Queen Elizabeth, Morton's text presents an Anglo-Israelite monarchical line, or 'Regni Angloisraelitici typus', in a way that reinforces Elizabeth's providential appointment as head of the English Church and state, but also of God's people at this junction in history.

While the use of King Solomon to bolster the authority of early modern English monarchs is the central concern of this chapter, this Old Testament leader was by no means the only biblical figure symbolically used to confer political and ecclesial authority on to Tudor and Stuart monarchs. Queen Elizabeth, for example, had multiple biblical personages attached

[13] Morton, *Salomon*, A2v.

[14] John Prime, *A sermon briefly comparing the estate of King Salomon and his subiectes togither [sic] with the condition of Queene Elizabeth and her people* (Oxford: Ioseph Barnes, 1585), B5r.

to her image over the course of her reign. She was commemorated in her coronation pageant on Fleet Street as an English Deborah, praised because of her role in effecting religious reform by John Norden in *A progresse of pietie* (1596) as 'a Hester in this land', and paralleled at length with the godly biblical kings David, Josiah, and Hezekiah in William Leigh's 1612 sermon *Queene Elizabeth paralleled.*[15] Reformed readers evidently found no difficulty with concurrently overlaying several typologies on a single monarch, or criss-crossing gender lines that were typically bifurcated in traditional patterns of exemplarity. In a recorded prayer in Thomas Bentley's *Monument of matrones* (1582), the queen herself demonstrates the flexible amalgam of identifications that were possible through typological readings of the scriptures. She thanks God for allowing her to be: 'Thy peoples Ioseph, their Moses, their Iosua, their Dauid, their Iosias, their Samuel, and their Salomon: finallie, to be their Deborah, their Iael, their Hester, their Iudith, and their *Elizabeth*; that is . . . their shepheard and ring-leader in the waie of vertue, holinesse, zeale, and sincere religion.'[16] The range of typological readings that could be imposed on a monarch was further complicated by the conflicting polemical purposes that the Bible's figures could be turned to promote. In the 1550s, political theorists such as John Knox and John Ponet used, as Adrian Streete has shown, the wicked Old Testament queens Jezebel and Athalia to condemn the female rule of Queen Mary I; yet, these writers also embraced the fearless female warriors Jael and Judith as exemplars of acceptable resistance to tyranny.[17] King David too functioned as a mutable figure through whom opposing voices could call individuals to obedience and rebellion, and Deborah, the Israelite judge, was invoked both to authorize and restrict female authority and speech.[18] When it comes to political typologies derived from the scriptures, biblical leaders, in the hands of various readers, operated differently at different moments.

Interpretative variation aside, lay familiarity with the details of Israel's political history enabled the kings, queens, and judges of the Old Testament

[15] William Leigh, *Queene Elizabeth paralleled in her Princely vertues with Dauid, Josua, and Hezekia* (London: T[homas] C[reede], 1612), 56; John Norden, *A progresse of pietie* (London: I. Windet, 1596), 8.

[16] Thomas Bentley, *The monument of matrones conteining seuen seuerall lamps of virginitie* (London: H. Denham, 1582), 262. For a discussion of Elizabeth's association with various monarchs see King, *Tudor Royal Iconography*, esp. 255–66.

[17] Adrian Streete, 'Christian Liberty and Female Rule: Exegesis and Political Controversy in the 1550s', in *Biblical Women*, ed. Brownlee and Gallagher, 59–74.

[18] See the 'Homily Against Disobedience', in *Certain Sermons or Homilies 1547–1571*, ed. Mary Ellen Rickey and Thomas B. Stroupe (Gainesville, FL: Scholars' Facsimiles and Reprints, 1968), and John Goodwin, *Anti-Cavalierisme, or, Truth Pleading* (London: G.B and R.W, 1642).

to function as, what Killeen neatly terms, 'a ready shorthand' for lengthy political commentary.[19] Because when Solomon is invoked in praise of Queen Elizabeth in Morton's woodcut, there is an expectation that the viewer will be aware of his peaceful reign and prominent position in the Israelite line, and therefore will be able to decipher the contemporary implications of the comparison. The assumption that readers of Morton's treatise will be familiar with the biblical account of Solomon's reign is not surprising given the various opportunities for lay engagement with the Old Testament by the turn of the century.[20] Indeed, out of the more than forty kings and queens whose reigns are mentioned in the Old Testament, after David, it was Solomon who garnered the most political and theological comment during the reign of the Tudors and early Stuarts.[21] Biblical commentaries addressing his sacred writings, thought to be gathered in the biblical books of Proverbs, Song of Songs, and Ecclesiastes, abounded, and these works were frequently selected as the subject of sermon series, such as those by George Gifford, John Dod, and John Dove.[22] Biblical paraphrases of Solomon's writings were also common, and the character and deeds of this biblical king seemed to have loomed large in the imagination of literary writers including Robert Greene and Michael Drayton.[23] Indeed, the poetry of John Hall and Gervase Markham attests to a trend in setting Solomon's life and works to verse.[24] Records also show that Solomon's narrative influenced the content of early modern drama. Sections of his reign form the plot of the Latin play *Sapientia Solomonis* (1565/6) and Pageant 16 of the Stonyhurst Pageants (1605–25), and the titles of the lost Jacobean masque *Solomon and the Queen of Sheba*, and lost play by Robert Cox, *King Solomon's*

[19] Killeen, 'Chastising with Scorpions', 498.

[20] See pp. 14–37 for an overview of lay knowledge and awareness of the Bible.

[21] King more specifically notes that Solomon was 'second only to David as the most enduring biblical type for Tudor kingship'. King, *Tudor Royal Iconography*, 81.

[22] George Gifford, *Fifteene sermons, vpon the Song of Salomon* (London: Felix Kingston, 1598); John Dod, *A plaine and familiar [on] chapters of the Prouerbs of Salomon* (London: Humfrey Lownes, 1607); John Dove, *The conuersion of Salomon A direction to holinesse of life* (London: W. Stansby, 1613).

[23] For an example of a paraphrase, see Thomas Rogers, *A golden chaine, taken out of the rich treasurehouse the Pslames of King Dauid: also, the pretious pearles of King Salomon* (London: Henrie Denham, 1579). See also Robert Greene, *Greenes vision written at the instant of his death* (London: E. Allde, 1592), and Michael Drayton, *The harmonie of the church* (London: T. Orwin, 1591).

[24] See Hall, *Certayne chapters of… prouerbes*; Gervase Markham, *The poem of poems. Or, Sions muse contayning the diuine song of King Salomon* (London: Iames Roberts. 1596). It should be said that Solomon was not a marginal figure in literary imagination prior to the sixteenth century. His narrative inspired poems during the Anglo-Saxon period, several philosophical and theological paraphrases in the medieval period, and was invoked in Jacobus de Voragine's 1483 collection of hagiographies, *Legenda aurea* (1483).

Wisdom (1650), suggest that their authors also drew on the biblical account of Solomon's life.[25]

Works addressing Solomon during this period, as Morton's woodcut suggests, frequently had an overt political bent. Early modern preachers advanced political applications of Solomon's narrative to the present, as is the case in Prime's *A sermon briefly comparing the estate of King Salomon and his subiectes togither [sic] with the condition of Queene Elizabeth and her people* (1585), Richard Crakanthorpe's *A sermon at the solemnizing of the happie inauguration of our most gracious and religious soueraigne King Iames* (1609), and John Williams' famous *Great Britains Salomon A sermon preached at the magnificent funerall, of the most high and mighty king* (1625). In these works, as Prime's title in particular suggests, the circumstances of Solomon's reign, recounted in I Kings 1–11 and II Chronicles 1–9, are found to resonate strongly with those of early modern England.[26] Prime, after a lengthy disquisition on Solomon's rule, is moved to urge his listeners to 'looke . . . homeward a little' and 'out of the looking-glasse of this scripture . . . consider what blessing also on us GOD hath bestowed'. The subsequent paralleling of Elizabeth and Solomon is, importantly, not considered to be an arbitrary means of paying homage to the queen. Listeners are pointedly reminded that 'flatterie becommeth no place, but least of all the pulpit'. Rather, the typological connectedness of biblical and Tudor monarch is perceived as a relationship that is textually rooted and historically verifiable: 'it is a trueth', Prime insists, that 'God hath blessed her maiestie with a wise, a wealthy, a peaceable and a godlie raigne', an assortment of blessings which, as the preceding section of the sermon has reinforced, are clearly identifiable as Solomonic.[27]

Richard Crakanthorpe also credits historical circumstances with his choice of Solomon's narrative for a sermon marking the inauguration of King James I. He explains at the outset that the time has 'mooued me to make' a study of II Chronicles 9:5–9, the Queen of Sheba's praise of Solomon, and demonstrate what 'a fit correspondence to our *Salomon*', King James, it presents.[28] In Crakanthorpe's reading, the homage paid by Sheba operates as 'a worthy example of the loue wee owe to [our

[25] Groves also notes a reference to Henry VIII as Solomon in Shakespeare's *Troublesome Raigne of King John*: *Texts and Traditions*, 95–6.

[26] The practice of mapping Solomon's life on to the current political landscape was not a distinctively post-Reformation practice. Solomon's importance to constructions of political authority is suggested, as Hattaway and King observe, in the use of his image on the crown of the Holy Roman Empire, and in the pageantry commemorating the ascension of Henry VII: see Hattaway, 'Paradoxes of Solomon', 524; King, *Tudor Royal Iconography*, 28, 35–6.

[27] Prime, *A sermon briefly comparing the estate of King Salomon and his subiectes*, B3v.

[28] Richard Crakanthorpe, *A sermon at the solemnizing of the happie inauguration of our most gracious and religious soueraigne King Iames* (London: VV. Iaggard, 1609), B2v.

Salomon]'; yet the consideration of the graces and virtues of this biblical king also vocalizes contemporary expectations of the newly crowned monarch.[29] A warning is implicit when Crakanthorpe laments: 'what an heauy iudgement and curse an vnwise King is vnto the Land and people: but that Kingdome is happy, that people, and those Subjects are happy ouer whom *Salomon* a wise and prudent King is placed by the Lord'.[30] King Solomon could, then, be deployed in a contemporary, political context to commemorate the virtues of a reigning monarch, but also as an exemplar of the ideal relationship between ruler and nation. This twin function of Solomon's regal example is certainly at work in Williams' funeral sermon for King James, where the biblical narrative functions as a means of commemorating the graces of England's recently deceased king, and a reminder to the new king, Charles, of his responsibilities. Amid protracted praise of Solomon's virtues, Williams pinpoints the worth of this Old Testament king as a royal exemplar; Solomon's selection of wisdom from the '*pandora* of royall *graces*' is a choice that 'hath taught all *Kings*'.[31] But Williams' lengthy comparison of the biblical Solomon with 'our King Salomon', which is used to honour the practical successes of James' reign, issues a more specific, and subtle, challenge to Charles with the rather taunting remark: 'There was no King before or after to be compar'd for happinesse with our King Salomon. His *Sayings*, his *Doings*, his *Wisedome*, his *Fame* in Histories, his *Citie*, his *Empire*, and his *long Raigne*, far surmounting all Kings in *Scripture*.'[32] Importantly, in this reading, James is not simply *like* Solomon. The successes of his reign outstrip those of Solomon's, indeed of all biblical kings, and provokingly, those kings who come 'after'.

As these sermons commemorating royal occasions suggest, political readings of Solomon's narrative work to elucidate and conceptualize monarchical authority. The question of why English Protestants came to rely on this biblical king, among others, to visualize monarchical authority, foster ideas of national election, and establish a Protestant account of Christian history is an important one. Certainly, the practice of mapping the lives of biblical monarchs on to the early modern present can in part be explained by the Protestant emphasis on personal scripturalism. Yet, the boom in biblically derived political typologies under the Tudors and

[29] Crakanthorpe, *A sermon at the solemnizing*, A4v.

[30] Crakanthorpe, *A sermon at the solemnizing*, B4v.

[31] Williams, *Great Britains Salomon*, 14. In Prime, Solomon's narrative is even more overtly deployed as an instrument to effect change: *A sermon briefly comparing the estate of King Salomon and his subiectes*, B8r.

[32] Williams, *Great Britains Salomon*, 28.

Stuarts seems also to be bound up with the broader reformulation of spiritual authority in the wake of the break with Rome.

VISUALIZING SACRED AUTHORITY AFTER THE REFORMATION

Debora K. Shuger has argued that, after the loss of a unified Christian church, and a single, visible figurehead of all Christendom, as well as the removal of church artefacts and erosion of the perceptible rituals of the medieval Church, there remained among Protestants a need for 'a visible locus of the sacred'.[33] Indeed, the reformers' general aim to prioritize the word over the image 'somewhat paradoxically... led to (or at least coexisted with)' what Shuger terms 'a massive endeavour to instantiate the holy in some sort of institutional form'.[34] In 1534, the Act of Supremacy made the 'King our Sovereign Lord... the only Supreme Head in earth of the Church of England, called Anglicans Ecclesia'.[35] The English monarch was now the locus of sacred as well as political authority, a shift that, according to J. J. Scarisbrick, precipitated 'a powerful new national epic, indeed, theology of history'.[36] The monarch's position as head of the realm's spiritual, as well as temporal, well-being was understood to encapsulate true Christian kingship and re-establish a biblical model of monarchy after centuries of misdirected papal authority.[37] Certainly, from the earliest days of the English Church biblical images of sacerdotal kingship were an important means of explaining and authorizing the expanded authority of the monarch.

It is no coincidence that one of the first images of Henry VIII produced after the break with Rome represents him as the Old Testament king famed for establishing a permanent home for the Ark of the Covenant.[38] In *c.*1534, Hans Holbein the younger produced a small watercolour that

[33] Debora K. Shuger, *Habits of Thought in the English Renaissance: Religion, Politics and the Dominant Culture* (Berkeley: University of California Press, 1990), 122–3. See also Richard C. McCoy, *Alterations of State: Sacred Kingship in the English Reformation* (New York: Columbia University Press, 2002), 2–22, 88–97.

[34] Shuger, *Habits of Thought*, 123.

[35] 'Act of Supremacy' (1534), *Selected Documents of European History: Volume Two, 1492–1715*, ed. W. F. Reddaway (New York: Henry Holt & Co., 1930), 73.

[36] J. J. Scarisbrick, *Henry VIII* (Berkeley: University of California Press, 1968), 386. On this point, see also McCoy, *Alterations of State*, 16.

[37] It should be said that some reformers found the association of the sacred with the monarchical body blasphemous. See John Calvin and Richard Hooker's comments in Hooker, 'The Laws of Ecclesiastical Polity', *The works of Mr. Richard Hooker... in eight books of ecclesiastical polity* (London: Thomas Newcomb, 1666), 460.

[38] See I Kings 6:1–37, and II Chronicles 3:1–17 for Solomon's erection of the Temple.

uses Solomon's narrative to celebrate King Henry's position as Supreme Head of the Church. Henry VIII is figured as Solomon receiving the Queen of Sheba who kneels in submission (Figure 2.2). The homage Sheba pays to the enthroned Solomon/Henry is important because, as King observes, she was recognizable as 'a traditional type for the church'; as such, her deference to the king symbolically affirms that the painting

Figure 2.2. 'Solomon and the Queen of Sheba', *c.*1535, by Hans Holbein the Younger. Reproduced by kind permission of the Royal Collection Trust / © Her Majesty Queen Elizabeth II 2017.

'commemorates the recent submission of the Church of England to Henry as the head of the church'.[39] The miniature's resonance with the religious-political changes afoot in England is made explicit in the Latin inscription placed above Solomon/Henry's head:

> SIT DOMINVS DEVS TVVS BENDICTVS
> CVI COMPLACIT IN TE VT PONERETTE
> SVPER THRONVM SVVM VT ESSES REX
> (CONSTITVUS) DOMINO DEO TVO.[40]

This text is based on the words of praise given to Solomon by Sheba in II Chronicles 9:8: 'Blessed be the Lord thy God, which loued thee, to set thee on his throne as King, in the steade of the Lorde thy God.' The extraordinary power that this verse vests in the monarch—so appropriate after the break from Rome—goes some way to explaining the popularity of Solomon as monarchical figure in early modern England. Certainly, in Holbein's watercolour the words of Sheba's blessing have omnipresent relevance, functioning as an endorsement of Henry VIII, as well as his biblical antecedent, Solomon. In 1534/5, II Chronicles 9:8 celebrates Henry's position as the anointed king of God's covenantal nation, and confers divine approval on his position as head of Church and state.[41] It affirms that there can be no intermediaries. Henry, placed 'in the steade' of God, is God's sole representative on earth.

The fact that Solomon's narrative authorized a sacerdotal model of kingship further reinforced his applicability to an English monarch newly charged with the spiritual care of the faithful. Solomon, who had been divinely appointed to oversee the construction of the Temple in Jerusalem, is seen functioning as a priestly intercessor during its dedication. I Kings 8 records that he prays and petitions God for Israel and presents multiple sacrifices on the nation's behalf. While royal supremacy may not have officially afforded Henry an intercessory role, his oversight of the realm's spiritual health did amplify older ideas of sacred kingship, as Richard C. McCoy explains: monarchical ideology under the Tudors drew 'on ancient traditions of sacred kingship' in a way that 'redefined them and

[39] King, *Tudor Royal Iconography*, 81.

[40] Hans Holbein the Younger, 'Solomon and the Queen of Sheba', *c.*1535. Holbein also was responsible for a similar image, that of Henry as King David, which appeared on the cover of the Coverdale Bible (1535). For more detailed discussion of the Solomon watercolour, including how it relates to the portrayal of Henry as David in the border of the Coverdale Bible, see King, *Tudor Royal Iconography*, pp. 81–4.

[41] It should be noted that Solomon was also deployed in a Roman Catholic context as suggested in the pageantry commemorating Charles V and Philip II in Europe. See King, *Tudor Royal Iconography*, 85; Vaughan Hart, *Art and Magic in the Court of the Stuarts* (London: Routledge, 1994), 109.

gave them new ideological force'.[42] The monarch's responsibility for the nation's spiritual well-being can be traced back to the medieval belief in the healing powers of the royal touch, and the idea of the king's two bodies, theorized at length by the Tudor jurist Edmund Plowden, affirmed the monarch's sacred nature by imbuing the ruler's mystical body with divine qualities.[43] The monarch possesses, what Plowden terms, a body that 'cannot be seen or handled' and is 'not subject to . . . Death'.[44]

Analogies between the monarch and God were also used to reinforce the reverence subjects owed to their rulers.[45] In Thomas Smith's *De Republica Anglorum* (1565), for example, the advice offered is reminiscent of the conventions that were to be observed by the Levite priest entering the Holy of Holies as recorded in Exodus: 'The prince is the life, the head, the authoritie of all thinges . . . in the chamber of presence . . . no man may dare walke, yea though the prince be not there, no man dare tarrie there but bareheaded.'[46] Under James I, the sacred nature of the monarch was propagated by the king himself when, in a speech before Parliament in 1610, he famously declared 'Kings are not only GODS Lieutenants vpon earth, and sit vpon Gods throne, but euen by GOD himselfe they are called Gods'.[47] James' comments allude to the Bible's role in the expansion of theories of sacred kingship under the Tudor and Stuarts.[48] The power that the Bible conferred on monarchs, and the models of sacerdotal kingship that it contained, were central to the inscription of sacred authority in the English monarchy after the split from

[42] McCoy, *Alterations of State*, 15.

[43] McCoy, *Alterations of State*, 16. For more on medieval and renaissance notions of sacred kingship see Ernst H. Kantorowicz, *The King's Two Bodies: A Study in Medieval Political Theology* (Princeton: Princeton University Press, 1957, rpt. 1997); Marc Bloch, *The Royal Touch: Sacred Monarchy and Scrofula in England and France*, trans. J. E. Anderson (London: Routledge, 1973).

[44] Edmund Plowden, *Commentaries or Reports* (London: S. Brooke, 1816), 212–13, 233.

[45] For consideration of early modern analogies between the king and God see Stephen Greenblatt's discussion of Thomas Wyatt's understanding of the monarchy: *Renaissance Self-Fashioning: From More to Shakespeare* (Chicago: University of Chicago Press, 2005), 116; Kantorowicz's *The King's Two Bodies*, 47; and Stuart Clark, *Thinking with Demons: The Idea of Witchcraft in Early Modern Europe* (Oxford: Oxford University Press, 1997), 621.

[46] Thomas Smith, *De Republica Anglorum*, in McCoy, *Alterations of State*, 18. See Exodus 25:31 and 35:40 for the instructions given to those entering the Holy of Holies.

[47] James I, *The Works of the Most High and Mightie Prince, James* (London: Robert Barker, 1616), 529.

[48] For a discussion of how James used the Bible to support his view of monarchy see King, 'James I and King David', 421–47; Guibbory, *Christian Identity*, 33–4; Jane Rickard, 'Mover and Author: King James VI and I and the Political Use of the Bible', in *The Oxford Handbook of the Bible*, ed. Killeen, Smith, and Willie, 371–83.

Rome.[49] Yet, Solomon's image, commonly mobilized to visualize this shift, could be used to encourage the kind of 'excessive royal adulation' that Stuart Clark understands aligns 'political conformity' with 'something like an act of religious worship'.[50] Nowhere is the proximity of these acts clearer than on the walls and windows of late Tudor church buildings that became home to various forms of biblically inflected royal iconography.

ROYAL ICONOGRAPHY AND KING SOLOMON

In testament to the relocation of sacred authority to the royal body after the Reformation, the monarch became visually present in many English churches, appearing on the cover pages of popular religious texts, such as the Coverdale Bible and Foxe's *Actes and Monuments*, and in stained-glass windows.[51] One of the most symbolically sophisticated forms of royal iconography to appear in churches during this period is the elision of a monarch's image with that of a biblical figure, as is the case in a series of stained-glass windows completed by Henry VIII's royal glaziers in King's College Chapel, Cambridge. Amid a series of twenty-six windows, which were commissioned to represent the relationship between the Old Testament and the New, stands a pane in window four depicting Solomon receiving the kneeling Queen of Sheba who is bearing gifts.[52] This Solomon bears a striking resemblance to England's reigning monarch, and, according to King, the original placing of Henry's monogram, 'H.R.', would have 'indisputably identifie[d]' Henry as Solomon and made the pair's typological connection explicit to viewers.[53] In figuring Henry as an antitype of Solomon, the window affirms the prefigurative nature of the

[49] In addition to II Chronicles 9:8, see, for example, I Samuel 18, Isaiah 9 & 11, I Peter 2:17, and Hebrews 13:17. See the Gospels too for Christ's kingship, especially John 12 & 18, as well as Revelation 17:4; 19:16. For early modern readings of some of these verses see Kim Ian Parker, '"A king like other nations": Political Theory and the Hebrew Republic in the Early Modern Age', and Anne Lake Prescott, 'A Year in the Life of King Saul', both in *The Oxford Handbook of the Bible*, ed. Killeen, Smith, and Willie, 384–96, 412–26.

[50] Clark, *Thinking with Demons*, 621. On the relationship between royal obedience and religious duty see also McCoy, *Alterations of State*, 14–18.

[51] For more on royal iconography in churches see King, *Tudor Royal Iconography*, 17; Duffy, *The Stripping of the Altars*, 566, 58.

[52] For a comprehensive discussion of the iconography of the windows in King's College Chapel, see King, *Tudor Royal Iconography*, 86–9; Hilary Wayment and Kenneth Harrison, *The Windows of King's College Chapel, Cambridge: A Description and Commentary* (London: Oxford University Press, 1972).

[53] King, *Tudor Royal Iconography*, 86.

Old Testament, and the traceability of an Anglo-Israelite royal lineage that stretches across Israelite and English history.

Although this Solomonic Henry reiterates the sacred roots of the Tudor line, the wider visual context of these panes advances a yet more powerful typology of political authority. The Solomon panes are paired with Christological images from the New Testament—Solomon's receipt of Sheba's gifts sits above a pane representing the adoration of the magi who similarly bear gifts in homage to the infant Christ, and the representation of the Old Testament king's coronation is, as King notes, connected visually to a neighbouring image of Christ being crowned with thorns.[54] Seen together, the windows propose a series of concurrent typologies; Solomon is a type of Christ, but Henry too, as an antitype of Solomon, is, by logical extension, also an antitype of Christ. The windows' symbolism figures Henry as the recipient of a Solomonic model of sacerdotal kingship, as well as a Christological one, bolstering the notion of the sacred status of the monarch. Indeed, the excessive majesty these windows grant to the king chimes with Henry's views of his own kingship. Before Parliament in 1545 Henry declared himself to be one 'whom God hath appoyntcd his Vicare, and high mynyster here', a comment which affirms that he conceived of his kingship in priestly terms that resonate strongly with the vision of royal supremacy advanced in the chapel windows.[55] Although Protestantism claimed to have abandoned visual signifiers of holiness, the elaborate commemoration of Henry's reign in the chapel windows of King's College attests to a need for the sacred to remain, in some way, tangible. But there are inherent problems with this effort for reformers, particularly given the location of the images. Erected in a church, this visual affirmation that Solomon-Henry, rather than the pope, rules 'in the steade of... God' (II Chron. 9:8) intertwines veneration of the monarch with divine worship. The images of Henry as Solomon compete with the panes depicting Christ in a manner that unsettles the windows' revelation of messianic kingship. For, rather than a type of Christ, a Solomon who is Henry becomes the typological endpoint, as the windows herald the bonds between the Old Testament and New, and the New Testament and the present. Amid these concurrent typologies, Henry has the potential to be worshipped, as well as to rule, 'in the steade of... God'.

[54] King, *Tudor Royal Iconography*, 86. See also 85–9 for a detailed assessment of how the windows dedicated to Solomon invoke New Testament models of kingship and authority, and correspond to medieval iconography.

[55] King Henry VIII, *King Henry VIII: Volume Two*, ed. Edward Hall (London: T. C. & E. C. Jack, 1904), 357. See McCoy for a more fulsome discussion of Henry's theory of kingship in *Alterations of State*, 15–16.

The use of biblical models of sacerdotal kingship, such as Solomon's, to encourage adulation of the monarch also occurs in the royal iconography fostered by King James I and VI. The Bible was, as Guibbory has shown, central to James' divine right theory of kingship: 'He used the Hebrew Bible, exaggerating the power of Judah's kings to place England's king beyond the reach of the Pope and above the power of Parliament and the law. . . . He imagined himself a Solomonic monarch even in Scotland, and he brought that preoccupation to England.'[56] James had been associated with Solomon as early as 1579, when, as a boy of fourteen, his state entry to Edinburgh was marked by a pageant depicting Solomon's judgement over two mothers in I Kings 3:16–28. By the end of his reign, James' identification with this particular biblical king was, as Williams' funeral sermon attests, firmly entrenched.[57] This association had, in part, been nurtured over the course of James' reign through his support of architectural projects, such as the restoration of St Paul's Cathedral.

James' commitment to repairing St Paul's—religious hub of London and iconic pulpit of many a reformed preacher—symbolically marked him as a second Solomon, who had similarly overseen the erection of House of the Lord. The parity between these holy projects was announced in specially commissioned paintings and sermons, as well as in the lions, cherubim, and palm trees—features of the Temple described in I Kings 6, II Chronicles 3, and Ezekiel 41—which were planned, as Vaughan Hart has noted, for the Cathedral's west front, nave and frieze.[58] In this regard, the restoration of St Paul's visualized the popular Protestant view that, typologically, the erection of the Temple foreshadowed the regeneration of the true church at the Reformation, and announced that the monarch who oversaw its preservation was Solomon's antitype, James.[59] Certainly, King James' involvement in these building projects was used to confirm his status as a second Solomon: 'Salomon beautified very much his *Capitall citie* with *Buildings*, and *Water-workes*, 1 Kings 9. 15', Williams declared, 'So did King *Iames*'.[60] The strength of James' identification with

[56] Guibbory, *Christian Identity*, 34–5.

[57] For James' entry into Edinburgh, see Roy Strong, *The Tudor and Stuart Monarchy: Pageantry, Painting, Iconography* (Woodbridge: Boydell Press, 1998), 134.

[58] Hart, *Art and Magic*, 117. Hart explains that these plans, compiled by Inigo Jones, were unexecuted: *Art and Magic*, 105–6. Guibbory notes that paintings commissioned by Henry Farley were used to encourage the St Paul's renovation: *Christian Identity*, 53–4.

[59] For readings of Solomon's Temple in relation to the Reformation in England see the Epilogue of *Sapientia Solomonis*, ed. Elizabeth Rogers Payne (New Haven: Yale University Press, 1938), 129, and Williams, *Great Britains Salomon*, 38.

[60] Williams, *Great Britains Salomon*, 39.

Solomon, and the continuing importance of this association to Stuart conceptions of sacred kingship after the monarch's death, is suggested by the ceiling panels of the Whitehall Banqueting House, painted by Peter Paul Rubens in 1637.[61] Here James' unification of the kingdoms of Scotland and England is remembered as Solomon presiding over the case of the two mothers in I Kings 3 in a typology that celebrates the Stuart king's commitment to peace and praises his wisdom.[62]

The use of Solomonic images to celebrate the supremacy of Tudor and Stuart monarchs elucidates the importance of typology's theory of historical progress to constructions of sacred and political authority, as well as to the broader formulation of Protestant history. The proliferation of biblically inflected royal iconography certainly testifies to the cultural and political impact of this reading practice, but it also points up typology's figural nature and venerating potential. The Protestant radar for the idolatrous—what Thomas Becon terms 'the payntynge of tabernacles gylddynge of Images, settynge vp of candles... & such other idle inuencions of [Catholicism]' which 'obscured... the glory of God'—was undoubtedly strong.[63] But the erection of Israelite-royal iconography on church buildings, stained glass, and religious texts demonstrates that Protestants did not entirely abandon visual signifiers in sacred spaces. In fact, the reformed emphasis on reading and applying the scriptures could lead to the erection of alternative, physical things.

Although popular, the intensive application of Solomon's reign to that of Tudor and Stuart monarchs required some exegetical writhing. For although Solomon was a ruler famed for wisdom, wealth, and global renown, as well as the completion of the Temple, he was a king who, according to I Kings 11, ended his days in idolatry. The Solomon who appears in the images discussed earlier is one whose image has been whitewashed, and whose narrative has been truncated in an effort to purge the seven hundred wives and three hundred concubines who, with their shrines and incense, 'turned his heart from the Lord God of Israel' (I Kings 11:9). Yet, the troubled end of this biblical king, as the following examples attest, is rarely fully erasable.

[61] For more on the analogy between Solomon and James drawn in the Banqueting House see Per Palme, *The Triumph of Peace: A Study of the Banqueting House* (London: Thames & Hudson, 1957), 22–5; Guibbory, *Christian Identity*, 53–4.

[62] For more on the symbolism of this panel, as well as the others, see Roy Strong, *Britannia Triumphans: Inigo Jones, Rubens and Whitehall Palace* (New York: Thames & Hudson, 1981).

[63] Thomas Becon, *The iewel of ioye* (London: J. Daye and W. Seres, 1550), n.p.

SAPIENTIA SOLOMONIS

On 17 January 1565 the boys of Westminster school performed a play called *Sapientia Solomonis*, or The Wisdom of Solomon, before Queen Elizabeth and her royal visitor, Princess Cecilia of Sweden. This play, originally written by the German dramatist Sixt Birck, was overhauled for the royal occasion by an unknown English adapter, who, as Ruth Blackburn has noted, added a new Prologue and Epilogue, extended the comic scenes featuring the character of Marcolph, and added the allegorical figures Sapientia, Justitia, and Pax.[64] The play recounts the most celebrated moments of King Solomon's reign and frames these with a Prologue and Epilogue that establish clear connections between Queen Elizabeth and her Old Testament predecessor. The play's biblically derived royal iconography is made all the more extravagant by the occasion of its performance before Elizabeth, for the queen's presence allows her identification with Solomon to be more forcefully realized. The Prologue, addressed to the queen, visually and ideologically connects the two monarchs promising that 'Blessed Solomon will see presently another ruler greatly blessed by the same tokens'.[65] The lines of the Prologue reinforce the monarchs' shared attributes of wisdom, mercy, and justice, but, as the opening progresses, it works to conflate these two rulers through language that renders the intended subject uncertain. The closing lines of the Prologue are suggestive of this emergent ambiguity: 'Not unwillingly like will see like; a queen will see a king, a prudent ruler will see a most prudent. Solomon with his wisdom will be here among us' (Pro. 27–9). This promise of an embodied Solomon registers a double meaning, referring to Queen Elizabeth, the physically present addressee of the Prologue, as well as anticipating the arrival of the actor playing the Old Testament king. Allowing biblical king and royal queen to bleed into each other at its close, the Prologue positions the main body of the play, which recounts Solomon's prayer for wisdom, judgement of the two mothers,

[64] Ruth Blackburn, *Biblical Drama under the Tudors* (The Hague: Mouton, 1975), 143–4. Blackburn describes Birck as a 'Protestant dramatist... a student of political theory and of Renaissance ideas of kingship' (142). For more on the English adapter's changes see Payne's 'Introduction' to *Sapientia Solomonis*, 27–9, and for discussion of the play in relation to England's colonial goals see William Tate, 'Solomon, Gender and Empire in Marlowe's *Doctor Faustus*', *Studies in English Literature, 1500–1900, Tudor and Stuart Drama* 37.2 (Spring 1997): 257–76 (257–60).

[65] Birck and English adapter, *Sapientia Solomonis*, 53, Prologue: 23–6. All further references will be given in the main body of the chapter. It should be said that the original performance was given in Latin but, for the purposes of this chapter, Payne's English translation has been used.

construction of the Temple, and visit of the Queen of Sheba (I Kings 3–10; II Chronicles 1–9), as a sustained celebration of Queen Elizabeth's Solomonic virtues and the pair's typologically shared heritage.

Although these instalments are described confidently to the audience before the play begins as 'the whole story' of great Solomon's life (Arg. 18–19), the drama, unsurprisingly, cuts short the biblical account of Solomon's life, suspending the narrative at the triumphant visit of the Queen of Sheba. Yet, although the play appears straightforwardly to dislocate Solomon's virtues from his disgraced end, the exiled conclusion of the biblical narrative hovers around the periphery of this blanched dramatization. The fissures in the play's refitted narrative appear subtly, as the drama ideologically evokes its biblical source. In Act One, Scene Three, during a conversation on kingship, Achisar, an overseer in the palace, and Adoniram, a superintendent, give thanks that they are not ruled by 'a tyrant' but by the 'pious' and 'clement' Solomon (1.3.6–8). While Adoniram passively accepts that even tyranny is 'predestined and brought to pass by God's providence' (1.3.17–19), Achisar undercuts this rather Calvinist view of history by suggesting that 'the course of providence may be thwarted, changed by the wilfulness of men' (1.3.20–1). Solomon's entry at this precise moment is evocative given that in the biblical narrative his wilful rebellion against God shifted the course of Israelite history. In I Kings 9, God appears to Solomon reiterating his providential plan to 'establish the throne of thy kingdom vpon Israel for ever' (v.5); after Solomon's lapse into idolatry, however, God punishes him by saying 'Thou hast not kept my couenant . . . I wil surely rent the kingdome from thee, and wil giue it to thy seruant' (I Kings 11:11). In light of the consequences of Solomon's idolatry, his entry amid Achisar's comment on the providential significance of men's actions becomes ideologically redolent of his disobedience and punishment. The scene's discussion of tyranny further calls Solomon's disgraced end to mind given that his son and successor, Rehoboam was, as Killeen has shown, 'the epitome of oppressors', and perhaps the period's most discussed and infamous biblical tyrant.[66] Indeed, it was the tyrannical rule of Rehoboam that directly precipitated the promised division of Israel after Solomon's death and the loss of most of the kingdom to Solomon's servant, Jeroboam.

While subsequent scenes work to showcase how Solomon 'persevere[d] in the footsteps of [David]' by exercising wisdom, overseeing the construction of the Temple, and magnificently receiving the awe-filled Queen

[66] Killeen, 'Chastising with Scorpions', 498. For more on readings of Rehoboam see Killeen, *The Political Bible*, 135–55.

of Sheba, the play is at other moments similarly troubled by the seams in its refitted narrative (1.4.14–15). Shadows of the end of Solomon's reign are cast subtly in the scenes involving Marcolph—a figure drawn from medieval legends—whose comic effect is achieved by consistently undermining the king's authority.[67] In Act Three, Scene Four, for example, Marcolph attempts to usurp Solomon's position as judge in the case of disputed maternity boasting 'I myself will end this grave dispute' (3.4.7). The comment is made during Solomon's retreat to consider his judgement. Marcolph amplifies the significance of Solomon's deliberation, which is not present in the biblical narrative, when he observes: 'In this case of yours he is hesitating, unable to make up his mind. He stays at home, in hiding. He leaves me here as judge. I, Marcolph, will say which of you may claim the living baby' (3.4.51–5). This inserted scene involving Marcolph undermines the attempt in this Act to praise Solomon's supernaturally derived wisdom which, on his return to pronounce judgement, he declares has been specially revealed to him through 'infallible signs' (3.5.90). For Marcolph's comic provocations, and the subsequent time they afford to Solomon for consideration, showcase a prevaricating monarch exercising a distinctly human brand of wisdom. Marcolph's speech alone on stage after Solomon has concluded the case further undercuts the sacred origins of the king's renowned wisdom by suggesting that he is duped easily by the appearances of women:

> The King does not know the deceitfulness of women. Because a woman weeps—sheds many tears and sobs bitterly—he thinks her sighs are genuine and judges women by himself and his own standards. Fie, even a King is a mere laughing stock if he does not know that there is no faith in women, whose tongues belie their thoughts.[68] (3.5.87–94)

This is a comment that not only undermines Solomon's divine gift of wisdom, but points up the very weakness that leads to his disobedience and idolatry in the final years of his reign. It is, I Kings 11 reveals, because Solomon cannot resist the allure of 'many outlandish women' that he defies God's instruction to marry within Israel (v.1). The roots of this failure are, Marcolph's misogynistic attack on women implies, visible earlier in his reign.

Given the royal occasion, it seems unlikely that these subtle allusions to Solomon's disgraced end are part of any deliberate strategy, but rather are a natural consequence of engaging with a biblical narrative that is complex

[67] For more on Marcolph see Payne, 'Introduction', *Sapientia Solomonis*, 30.

[68] According to Blackburn, Marcolph's attack on women was added by the English adapter who greatly enlarged this scene for comic effect: *Biblical Drama*, 143.

and contested. A narrative which, in a biblically saturated society, does not operate in isolation, but always has the potential to conjure ideologically a network of biblical intertexts. As Solomon's disobedience and punishment briefly move into view, the play exposes how the process of exegetically shoehorning Elizabeth into a Solomonic mould was not only tricky, but symbolically problematic. Yet, in spite of these fleeting moments when the play seems to possess the potential to divulge the inherent instability of typologically infusing this biblical king with England's queen, *Sapientia Solomonis* remains an important example of the extent to which biblical typology could facilitate, and encourage, extended veneration of England's monarchs. The Epilogue reiterates the connectedness of biblical and contemporary history, and Israelite and English monarch, by offering an exegetical summary of their parity: 'A Queen is given to us who is a rival of illustrious King Solomon . . . Solomon was just; our Queen is unjust to no man. Solomon was merciful, our Queen is mercy itself' (Epi. 13–15). There is at the close little scope for missing the political application of the biblical episodes that have been presented. The Epilogue recaps for viewers how Solomon's giving of the baby to its true mother and erection of the Temple foreshadow Queen Elizabeth's commitment to the 'true Church' and support of reformed principles more generally (Epi. 19). The Epilogue's final parallel reinforces Elizabeth's position as an antitype of Solomon by casting the diplomatic visit of Princess Cecilia with that of the Queen of Sheba who was similarly delighted to enjoy his regal countenance. Yet the positive tone of the Epilogue, which concludes by describing Solomon, like Elizabeth, as a 'bright ornament', one who is 'pious and wholly dedicated to God', is ultimately strained by the very biblical text that it seeks to recapitulate (Epi. 10, 4–5). Because although the play suspends Solomon's narrative at its peak, the unspoken biblical ending of this Old Testament king's reign nags at the closing attempt to glorify the watching Elizabeth. This is perhaps because, unlike pictorial images, such as Holbein and Morton's, which statically capture the Old Testament king in a moment of time, *Sapientia Solomonis*' dramatic, linear movement across Solomon's reign involuntarily gestures towards the alternative, excised ending that exists outside the boundary of the play. In doing so, it reminds that the legacy of England's new Solomon remains to be written.

GREAT BRITAINS SALOMON

Sixty years later, a similarly selective reading of the biblical account of Solomon's reign was used on a royal occasion to celebrate the sacred reign of another English monarch—Williams' *Great Britains Salomon*, which, as noted earlier, was preached to commemorate King James' death. In a sense, the sermon was, like *Sapientia Solomonis*, performed before the honoured Stuart king, for the congregation's attention is repeatedly drawn to the '*liuely Statue*', or funeral effigy, of the recently deceased king that stood at the centre of the Abbey's choir.[69] In the vein of earlier sermons that drew political parallels between the early modern present and the reign of this Old Testament king, Williams emphasizes that the monarchs' typological connection is not arbitrary. Williams' opening lines assert that the historical moment dictates that 'no *Booke* will serve this turne, but the Book of the *Kings,* no King but . . . onely *Salomon*' (1). The confidence with which Williams declares his chosen biblical passage depends on a specifically typological understanding of the coherence of scripture and history: the text presented does not, he explains, 'hang together like a rope of sands, but the *parts* thereof are chained, and linked very fast, in a mutuall cohaerence one with another' (5). The precise biblical passage to which Williams attends is I Kings 11:41–3, and these verses appear in the printed edition of the sermon as follows:

> *And the rest of the words of* Salomon, *and all that he did, and his wisedome, are they not written in the Booke of the Acts of* Salomon?
> *And the time that* Salomon *raigned in Jerusalem ouer all Israel, was forty yeares.*
> *And* Salomon *slept with his Fathers, and was buried in the Citie of* Dauid *his Father.* (A2v)

This reprinted portion of text is revealing for it captures how the process of tracing Solomon's biblical narrative in the present demanded a truncated reading of the scriptural account. Verse 43 is stopped midway and in its entirety should read: 'And Salomon slept with his fathers, and was buried in the Citie of Dauid his Father: and Rehoboam his sonne reigned in his steade' (I Kings 11:43). Given that Rehoboam was, as mentioned above, one of the period's best known tyrants, and that it was during his reign that God fulfilled his promise to give the kingdom to Jeroboam as punishment for Solomon's disobedience (I Kings 11:11), it is perhaps understandable that the negative legacy of Solomon's reign was trimmed from view for the royal occasion. More broadly, Williams unsurprisingly overlooks the broader context of these verses which sit, as the Geneva

[69] Williams, *Great Britains Salomon*, 35. All further references to this work will be given in the main body of the chapter. For a discussion of the effigy used during the funeral of King James, and where it was placed, see Jennifer Woodward, *The Theatre of Death: The Ritual Management of Royal Funerals in Renaissance England, 1570–1625* (Woodbridge: Boydell Press, 1997), 175–87.

headnote to I Kings 11 affirms, amid a chapter that recounts Solomon's spectacular fall into disobedience: 'Salomon hathe a thousand wiues and concubines, which bring him to idolatrie. His God raiseth up aduersaries against him. He dyeth'. Instead, from this excerpt of I Kings 11 Williams seeks to 'obserue three parts, the *Happy life*, the *Happy Raigne*', and, most pointedly, 'the *happy end* of this great King *Salomon*' (3).

After considering the successes of Solomon's reign in the first portion of the sermon, Williams offers his congregation a rather Foxean historical comparison of the life and reigns of Solomon and James. He notes how both were, for example, the only sons of their mothers and childhood kings, and traces how Solomon's commitment to the development of shipping, building works, and national peace prefigures the activities of James' reign. And, just as '*Salomon* of all the Kings of *Israel*' was committed to God's church, 'So', Williams declares, 'our Late Soueraigne of all *Christian Kings*, that euer I read of, was the most constant *Patron, of Churches,* and *Church-men*' (38). Of course this comparison in particular reveals the problematic nature of comparing Solomon's reign with James'. Because, although Solomon may have given Israel a permanent Temple in which to worship, his commitment to God ultimately faltered—a failure that was manifested tangibly in his erection of multiple shrines to foreign gods. While the problematic nature of this analogy is not registered by Williams, there is an earlier moment in the sermon when he seems compelled to acknowledge, albeit briefly, the murky final years of Solomon's reign. Before embarking on the detailed paralleling of the histories of these two kings, Williams, in what is essentially an aside, vaguely notes that 'in the full portion... [Salomon] would proue, but a foile, a *shadow*, and not a liuely *image*, and representation to decke, and adorn these present *Funeralls*' (3). It is a comment that acknowledges the slipperiness of the entire typological project, and one that Williams rather lamely recovers from by declaring that James 'resemble[s] [Salomon] only in his choisest *Vertues*' (3).

Williams' glancing defence of his exegesis is important because it reveals that a desire to craft a suitable 'liuely *image*' for the dead King James is what spurs his selective reading of Solomon's biblical narrative. But the comment also illuminates how reading James as an antitype of Solomon participates directly in the period's monarchical image making. Indeed, Williams' sermon is rather obsessed with images, both symbolic and tangible. He notes that 'King *Salomon* in his Funeralls... had no *Statue* at all carried before him. That was peraduenture scarce tolerable amongst the *Jews*', and evocatively extends James to his listeners as a physical model of the biblical king: 'A *Statue* God Almightie hath this day prouided for him... King *Iames* shall lend unto [*Salomon*] a *Statue*'. The elision of James' body, or effigy in the visual context of the sermon, with Solomon's powerfully reinforces the typological connection for which Williams makes a case. James is, or was, Solomon embodied: '*King IAMES* shall first die in *Salomons* Text, and *Salomon* shall then arise in King IAMES his VERTUES' (7–8). As this comment suggests, Williams' typology works backwards as well as forwards as the biblical text foreshadows the majesty of King James' reign, and the living James was an incarnation of the deceased Solomon. But the sermon's typologies, and their involvement in fashioning the monarchical image, extend further still. At the close, Williams concedes that the funeral effigy of King James that has been the sermon's visual centre is but an 'Artificiall *Repraesentation*' of his sovereignty and depicts 'no more than his outward Bodie, his cloathes and Ornaments' (75). As such, Williams calls the congregation to turn to view 'another *Statue*', one 'God hath prouided', that is, the newly crowned Charles (75). Significantly, at this moment, Charles is not simply cast as the inheritor of the mystical body politic but the symbolic body of Solomon: 'For as [God] hath made a liuely *Representation* of the *Vertues* of *Salmon*, in the person of *King Iames*: so hath he done a like *Representation* of the *Vertues* of King *Iames* in the Person of King *Charles*' (76). Gaze shifts from James' effigy, the past, to the body of Charles, the future. James, antitype of Solomon, becomes Charles, antitype of the Solomonic James.

The complexity of these typological layers is suggested in the final line: 'Though his *Father* be dead, yet is he, as though hee were not dead, for he hath left *One* behinde him most like himselfe' (76). At this moment, the regal identities of Solomon, James, and Charles coalesce as Williams works to entrench the sacred heritage of England's new king. Solomon's image, typologically excavated from its biblical context and trimmed into a suitable 'liuely *image* . . . to decke, and adorn' James, becomes a means of charting and representing the relocation of the body politic to his successor. This use of Solomon's image naturally demands a selective reading of the biblical text, one that severs the early years of Solomon's majestic reign from the geographic and political fracture of Israel that occurred after his death. But Williams' extended adulation of Stuart Solomons, and celebration of the progression of an Anglo-Israelite line of kings, demonstrates the difficulty of occluding fully the biblical account of Solomon's reign.

THE LOVE OF KING DAVID AND FAIR BETHSABE

Early modern sermons and royal iconography illuminate a trend in editing, amending, and reimagining Solomon's biblical narrative, and this active readerly process can also be detected in the period's commercial theatre. Although not performed on any royal occasion, George Peele's *The Love of*

King David and Fair Bethsabe, first performed in 1593/4 and played 'diuers times' in subsequent years, attests to a sustained public demand for visual representations of Old Testament kingship.[70] As the title suggests, the play primarily addresses the reign of David and, depicting the Old Testament king's adultery with Bathsheba, Tamar's rape, and his indecision during Absalom's rebellion, is certainly not guilty of expunging David's failings as recounted in II Samuel 11–18. Although Peele offers his audiences an unusually frank rendering of II Samuel's account of David's kingship, he does insert a fictional exchange that neutralizes ambiguity surrounding Solomon's succession to the Israelite throne in the opening chapter of I Kings.[71]

I Kings begins by detailing how David, infirmed by illness and age, is usurped by his fourth son Adonijah. Although aware of Adonijah's actions, David refuses to act, an inertia that prompts the prophet Nathan and Bathsheba, mother of Solomon, to collude to convince David of the right of his younger son. Nathan counsels Bathsheba to 'Go, and get thee in vnto King David, & say vnto him, Didest not thou, my lord, O King, sweare vnto thine handmaide, saying, Assuredly Salomo[n] thy sonne shal reign after me, & he shal sit upon my throne? Why then is Adoniiah King?' (I Kings 1:13–14). This apparent recollection of the past, which moves David to pronounce publicly Solomon as his successor, piqued the interest of early modern exegetes. Typically, biblical commentators and sermonizers worked to smooth over the possible suggestion in the biblical text that Bathsheba's claim was fabricated.[72] The marginal note for I Kings 1 in the Geneva Bible, for example, disallows reading David's naming of

70 Peele, *The Love of King David*, 189. All further references will be given in the main body of the chapter. Peele's reimagining of Solomon comes amid a flurry of dramas addressing biblical kings. The Stationers' Register lists, for example, *Hester and Ahasuerus* (1580–94), *Nebuchadnezzar* (1596–7), *Darius* (1603), *Solomon and the Queen of Sheba* (1606), *The Tragedy of Mariam* (1613), *Herod and Antipater* (1622), and *King Solomon's Wisdom* (*c.*1650). For more on the dating and structure of Peele's play see: A. R. Braunmuller, *George Peele: Criticism and Interpretation* (Boston: Twayne Publishers, 1983); Carolyn Blair, 'On the Question of Unity in Peele's *David and Bathsabe*', in *Studies in Honor of John C. Hodges and Alwin Thaler*, ed. Richard Beale Davis and John Leon Livesay (Knoxville: University of Tennessee Press, 1961), 35–41.

71 Retellings of David's reign tended to focus on his divine selection as king, his authorship of the Psalms, and his repentance, rather than dwell on the sins themselves. This emphasis is unsurprising given David's association with Tudor monarchs. See Osherow's assessment of the early modern approach to David's failings in *Biblical Women's Voices*, 135–9.

72 For more on the textual ambiguity of I Kings 1, see Tomoo Ishida, 'Solomon's Succession to the Throne of David: A Political Analysis', in *Studies in the Period of David and Solomon and Other Essays*, ed. Tomoo Ishida (Winona Lake, IN: Eisenbrauns, 1982), 179–80. This questionable succession narrative is not present in I Chronicles 23 where David pronounces Solomon king before his own death. Because Peele includes David's adultery and Absalom's rebellion, his account of David's reign seems to draw on II Samuel, rather than I Chronicles which does not record these episodes. Furthermore, the

Solomon as motivated by his wife's persuasions, and instead explains that David was 'moued by the Spirit of God... because he foresawe that Salomon shulde be the figure of Christ' (I Kings 1:30, note).[73]

Peele's play similarly offsets the implication that Solomon's succession in I Kings was secured through political manipulation. This comes towards the end of the play, when David is mourning the rebellion of his third son, Absalom. Bethsabe, attempting to comfort David in his distress, asks if 'That Salomon, whom Israels God affects, / ... Should be no salve to comfort David's soule?' (H1v–H2). To which David responds: 'Salomon ... is Davids lord, / Our God hath nam'd him lord of Israel: ... / And he shall surely sit upon my throne' (H2). David reiterates his selection of Solomon a few lines later to Nathan saying 'I promise thee, and louely Bethsabe, / My son Salomon shall gouern after me' (H2). This solemn declaration, alongside the previous exchange with Bethsabe, works to corroborate the claim in I Kings 1:14 that David had indeed named Solomon as his successor earlier in his reign. These moments explain Nathan and Bethsabe's collusion in the opening of I Kings by suggesting that the pair are not attempting to manipulate the succession, but acting to protect the throne from a usurper.

The play's interest in the process of succession is important given the historical context. By the time *David and Bethsabe* was entered into the Stationers' Register in 1594, Elizabeth, popularly celebrated as a new David as well as a new Solomon, was sixty years old, her ageing body a symbol of the succession crisis she was by now unable to avert.[74] By subtly plugging the narrative gap in the opening of I Kings, Peele's play seems to fantasize about an heir, and a clear line of succession, that the England of the 1590s obviously lacked. Indeed, David's direct naming of Solomon offers a striking contrast to Elizabeth's refusal to address the question of succession. The queen not only refused to name a successor but, in the latter years of her reign, banned discussion of the succession entirely.[75] Performed in a decade when questions of succession were increasingly negotiated by the clandestine political manoeuvres of Elizabeth's Privy

involvement of Nathan and Bathsheba in the succession of Solomon also suggests that Peele was drawing on the account of Solomon's reign in I Kings rather than I & II Chronicles.

[73] For a similar reading of this biblical narrative see John Merbecke, *The holie historie of King Dauid* (London: Henrie Middleton, 1579), 68–9.

[74] For Elizabeth as Solomon, see p. 53–7, 67–70, and for an account of her comparison with David see Michele Osherow, 'A poore Shepherd and his sling', in *Elizabeth I: Always Her Own Free Woman*, ed. Carole Levin, Debra Barrett-Graves, and Jo Eldridge Carney (Aldershot: Ashgate, 2003), 119–30.

[75] For more on how the succession question influenced the period's dramatic output see Marie Axton, *The Queen's Two Bodies: Drama and the Elizabethan Succession* (London: Royal Historical Society, 1977).

Council, Peele's play offers a compelling alternative—a succession secured by hereditary right and royal endorsement.[76]

Tweaking the biblical text to represent an alternative to the political uncertainty of the 1580s and 1590s, the play's idealized succession sequence culminates with a quasi-coronation of the heir-apparent. David, after naming Solomon as his heir, asks his son to confirm his suitability for leadership:

> Tell me my Salomon, wilt thou imbrace
> Thy fathers precepts graved in thy heart,
> And satisfie my zeale to thy renowne,
> With practice of such sacred principles
> As shall concerne the state of Israel? (H2v)

The triumphant tone that this oath, and the scene generally, strive towards is, however, undercut by the kingly example David extends to Solomon. The scenes preceding this one have traced a reign blighted by poor decisions. David has been exposed as an adulterer and murderer, and his failure to punish Ammon for Tamar's rape is the direct cause of Absalom's rebellion. In light of this prior behaviour, David's request that Solomon accept 'thy fathers precepts' is troubling. Peele's David is an exemplar of divine disobedience whose reign has been marred by political instability. The suggestion that Solomon's rule might be blemished by similar personal failings emerges in his response to David—'[I] feed upon your soule'—a comment that reinforces that father and son possess a shared nature (H2v). This affirmation opens into a long speech which reveals Solomon's unhealthy obsession with obtaining divine knowledge and power. Amid this speech, Solomon ominously pledges to 'learne the skill / And holy secrets of [God's] mightie hand', to discern how 'How th'eternall fram'd the firmament', and questions 'for what time shall this round building stand? / What Magistrates, what Kings shall keepe in awe / Mens mind with bridles of th'eternall law?' (H2v–H3). Although a typically celebrated aspect of his character, Solomon's learning and wisdom acquire a more threatening edge in these lines as he embodies, what Michael Hattaway terms, the perceived 'danger [of] learning without piety' in the period.[77] Indeed, in this moment, the play illuminates that the aspects of

[76] For an assessment of the Privy Council's involvement in the succession see Stephen Alford, *The Early Elizabethan Polity: William Cecil and the British Succession Crisis, 1558–1569* (Cambridge: Cambridge University Press, 2002); Jean-Christophe Mayer, ed., *The Struggle for the Succession in Late Elizabethan England: Politics, Polemics and Cultural Representations* (Montpellier: University Press Paul-Valéry, 2004).

[77] Hattaway, 'Paradoxes of Solomon', 515. This use of Solomon is interesting as his narrative was sometimes invoked to warn of the relationship between acquisition of

Solomon's character that cause him to be hailed as a regal exemplar, possess, when unchecked, dangerous potential.

The aspirations towards divinity that Peele's Solomon exhibits prompt a warning from his father that 'things to come exceed our human reach' and an urging to avoid the rather Faustian use of 'conjectures of inferior signs' or 'the figures of some hidden art' (H3).[78] Yet, in spite of this caution, the play reveals a Solomon initially unable to grip the divine focus his father encourages, one who almost gives way to his unnatural desires. In language that anticipates Marlowe's later vision of embodied obsession in Faustus, Solomon describes how a 'secret fury ravisheth my soule, / Lifting my mind above her humane bounds' with 'violent hunger' (H3v).[79] Although Solomon's escalating aspirations are eventually tempered by a glimpse 'of zeale devine' (H3v), his outburst ominously foreshadows the divine disobedience that leads him into idolatry in I Kings 11. Revealing a mind distracted from its creator and turned to Creation, Peele's Solomon points to the alternative, biblical ending of scripture's wisest king.

In undercutting the established representation of this biblical king as a model statesman, *David and Bethsabe* offers a more ambiguous vision of Solomon's kingship that resonates with the context of unsecured succession. Because, although the inserted extra-biblical scene works to smooth over the ambiguity surrounding Solomon's ascension in I Kings, the representation of the future monarch is less than reassuring. Indeed, as the play hints at Solomon's interest in magic and unhealthy desire for power it raises the spectre of a successor not firmly committed to orthodoxy, one who would have reverberated with contemporary fears surrounding the rival claimants, Isabella, Infanta of Spain, and the son of Mary Queen of Scots, James, who jostled for the English throne. Coming towards the end of Queen Elizabeth's reign, *David and Bethsabe* taps more ambivalent readings of this Old Testament king than those circulating in the period's political theology and Tudor iconography. In Peele, the

knowledge and vanity. See, for example, Fulke Greville, *Certaine learned and elegant vvorkes* (London: E[lizabeth] P[urslowe], 1633), 48.

[78] In this section of text Peele's Solomon begins to share an affinity with the medieval Solomon who was capable of magic and in command of demons. The association of Solomon with magic in Western tradition was made through the attachment of his name to a number of magical books, including *Clavis (Clavicula) Salomonis* and *Ars Notoria*. For an overview of the extra-biblical texts centring on Solomon see M. D. Conway, *Solomon and Solomonic Literature* (London: Kegan Paul, 1899).

[79] Two scholars have suggested reading Faustus as an inverted figure of King Solomon. See Hattaway, 'Paradoxes of Solomon', and Tate, 'Solomon, Gender and Empire'. See also Hattaway's brief, alternative reading of Peele's Solomon, in which he argues that 'the prince's virtue sanctifies his Faustian vision': 'Paradoxes of Solomon', 525.

Israelite line yields promises of disobedience, political instability, and flawed leaders, rather than paragons of kingly virtue.

In allowing a more equivocal reading of Solomon's narrative to surface, Peele's play exposes the inherent instability of covenantal identification with Israel and its rulers by English monarchs. Albeit more subtly, *Sapientia Solomonis* also demonstrates that, although drama could, like paintings and sermons, be deployed to celebrate the typological connections between biblical king and England's queen, the movement from page to stage can be strained by the ideological presence of excised sections of scripture's narrative. Despite selective readings, and even blatant additions to the scriptural account, early modern reimaginings of Solomon's narrative are, it seems, often unable to erase fully the unfavourable aspects of his reign from view. While *Sapientia Solomonis* and Williams' sermon are subtly problematized by the existence of the Bible's alternative account of Solomon's reign, *David and Bethsabe*, uninhibited by a royal audience, illuminates the spectrum of negative, as well as positive, associations that must be confronted if Solomon is to be read typologically within the early modern present.

Given Solomon's instability as a biblical type of secular kingship it is perhaps surprising that Tudor and Stuart monarchs turned so frequently to this biblical king to endorse their authority and legitimacy. Those who sought to harness Solomon's wisdom, wealth, and global renown for political purposes were, however, rarely deterred by his disgraced end. Indeed, Solomon's sacerdotal kingship became integral to the biblically inflected iconography of the Tudors and Stuarts, and, more specifically, to conceptualizations of sacred authority after the Reformation. Typological readings of Solomon advanced, then, beyond political flattery. They fostered a form of national homage of the royal body that bordered on veneration. Solomonic royal iconography affirms that, in spite of Protestantism's commitment to words rather than images, there remained, on some level, a need for tangible expressions of the sacred. Moreover, the rich symbolism on which images such as Holbein and Morton's rely captures the extent to which the reformers depended on highly figural readings of the Bible to establish England as an elect, covenantal nation, and affirm its monarch as head of Christ's true church. Unmoored from their scriptural contexts and transformed for transposition into the early modern present, biblical figures like Solomon were incorporated within a vast repository of figurative images that, as Chapter 3 also attests, literally minded reformers continued to generate.

3

A Tale of Two Jobs

Reading Suffering, Providence, and Restoration in King Leir *and* King Lear

The Book of Job begins by introducing an 'upright and juste' protagonist who 'feared God, & eschewed euil' (Job 1:1). Having established the spiritual credentials of the book's central figure, the narrative then moves to reveal Job to be a man of significant means. With seven sons and seven daughters, seven thousand sheep, three thousand camels, as well as hundreds of oxen and asses, Job is 'the greatest of all the men of the East' (Job 1:3). This brief account of fervent piety, familial blessing, and material wealth gives way, however, to the Bible's most protracted example of bodily suffering and mental anguish.[1] Across forty-two chapters, the deteriorating Job narrates the human response to loss, despair, and chronic physical affliction. Job's protracted bodily misery follows the theft of his livestock, slaughter of his servants, and death of his children. Job 2:7–8 vividly notes that he developed 'sore boyles, from the sole of his fote vnto his crowne. And he toke a potsharde to scrape him, and he sate downe among the ashes'. Images of fleshly suffering like this one recur frequently in this biblical book and, scattered throughout the central dialogues, each example reinforces a body in pain.[2]

[1] While the Book of Job is the Bible's most extended account of human suffering, examples of suffering appear in a variety of other biblical books. Many of the Psalms address mental anguish (see, for example, Psalm 22, 73, and 119) and the suffering of Jesus is the centre point of the Gospels. Jesus also spoke about suffering in Matthew 17:12; Mark 8:31, 9:12; Luke 9:22, and many of the New Testament letters reference the trials of the first Christians (Acts 5:41, 9:16; Romans 8:17; I Corinthians 12:26; Philippians 1:29, 3:10; I Thessalonians 1:5, 3:4; II Timothy 1:8; I Peter 3:14–17, 4:13–19). For other examples of biblical suffering, see the history of the Israelites, their slavery and wanderings in the wilderness, as detailed in Exodus; the image of the suffering servant in Isaiah 53, and the suffering of individuals and churches throughout the Book of Revelation.

[2] See, for example, the description of Job's 'corrupt' breath in 17:1, and the momentary relief provided by 'flesh in my tethe' (Job 13:14).

The intense physical suffering endured by this biblical body is, importantly, not the result of illness or accident but the working of an external agent. In thirteen verses, recorded in chapters one and two, the narrative action relocates to a heavenly setting where the reader witnesses a conversation between God and Satan. During this exchange, Satan, who surmises that Job's faith is dependent on his earthly prosperity and bodily health, makes a wager with God that positions suffering as a means of assessing Job's faith:[3]

> Skin for skin, and all that euer a man hath, will he giue for his life. But stretch now out thine hand, and touch [Job's] bones and his flesh, *to see* if he will not blaspheme thee to thy face. Then the Lorde said vnto Satan, Lo, he is in thine hand, but saue his life. So Satan departed from the presence of the Lord, and smote Job. (Job 2:4–7)

These verses transform the reader's understanding of the remainder of the book. They transpose Job's subsequent physical suffering from an arbitrary occurrence into a litmus test for spiritual authenticity. In the context of this heavenly conversation, Job's affliction becomes, as Page duBois has said of torture, a 'guarantor of truth', with his divinely sanctioned pain engaged in a similar 'process of truth-making'.[4] The proximity of the suffering body to revelations of truth, in this case, the truth of genuine faith, is the starting point of this chapter's interest in Job. Tying the suffering of an individual to a cosmic struggle between good and evil, this biblical book imbues bodily pain with a higher, divine purpose, and, for many early modern readers, demonstrated how trials of the flesh operated within providential patterns.

Although the penitential Psalms of David and Passion narratives were regularly cited in early modern discussions of suffering, Job's protracted pain ensured that this biblical account of anguish accrued particular resonance for the bodies that suffered across Europe in the wake of the Reformation. In this climate of pain, Job's story was mined for practical advice on the appropriate response to suffering, and, read typologically, was mobilized to reassure individuals that deliverance awaited those who remained constant like Job. The dialogue between God and Satan that begins the narrative—proving as it did that suffering befell the godly with God's foreknowledge—ensured that this biblical book became embroiled in what continues to be Christianity's most difficult theological question:

[3] This wager is the second made by Satan. The first occurs in Job 1:11, and results in the loss of Job's material wealth and the death of his children. Job's refusal to 'sinne' and 'charge God foolishly' (1:22) for his changed circumstances precipitates the second wager which allows Job's body to be afflicted.

[4] Page duBois, *Torture and Truth* (London: Routledge, 1991), 47.

why does a God who is entirely good and completely sovereign permit suffering? Amid the multiple, lengthy, and contested answers that circulated in response to this question in the sixteenth and seventeenth centuries, Job emerged as an important proof-text, and not just for theologians. *The True Chronicle History of King Leir* (*c.*1594, published 1605) and Shakespeare's *King Lear* (*c.*1606) probe the problem of suffering and the ensuing question of how to respond to affliction through the Book of Job, and the answers these plays offer are radically different. Unlike previous scholarly discussions that have made a case for the influence of Job on Shakespeare's play alone, this chapter posits that *Leir*, Shakespeare's primary source, is also indebted to this biblical book.[5] An awareness of how both plays navigate the topic of suffering through a Joban paradigm alters how we understand the fundamental differences in these retellings of the reign of an ancient British king. For although *Leir* finds in Job the promise of final delivery from hardship—a providential pattern popularized by early modern sermons—*Lear* reads the Old Testament text more sceptically, discrediting the exegetical tradition that works to prove suffering pointful. By the conventions of popular interpretation of Job, the suffering in *Lear* eventually should find meaning. By typological standards it should foreshadow the conclusion of suffering at the Second Coming of Christ, which promised restoration of the body as well as the soul for the faithful. But the apocalyptic moment that brings significance to pain never materializes in *King Lear* and, rather than an indicator of faith or promise of hope, the afflicted body is an empty sign—a physical proof that 'nothing will come of nothing'.[6]

JOB AND PROVIDENTIAL SUFFERING IN POST-REFORMATION EUROPE

Although the problem of suffering was by no means a new question in the sixteenth century, theologians tackled the issue with renewed verve amidst the fallout of the Reformation. Large parts of Europe were affected by religious violence, and in some countries this violence persisted for two centuries.[7] Brad S. Gregory has identified the burning of two Augustinian

[5] For Shakespeare scholars who have considered the relationship between *Lear* and Job, and Shakespeare's familiarity with *King Leir*, see the discussion and notes on p. 94.

[6] William Shakespeare, *The Tragedy of King Lear* (Conflated Text), *The Norton Shakespeare*, ed. Stephen Greenblatt, Walter Cohen, Jean E. Howard, and Katharine Eisaman Maus (New York and London: W. W. Norton, 1997), 1.1.89. All further references will be given in the main body of the chapter.

[7] Simpson, *Burning to Read*, 17.

monks in Brussels in July 1523 as the 'beginning' of a wave of martyrdom, after which executions continued with 'shifting rhythms' and 'varying intensities, in different towns and countries across Europe into the seventeenth century'.[8] It has been estimated that in Europe between 1523 and 1600, 4,400 Protestants and Anabaptists were executed for heresy, with a further 300 Catholics executed in England between 1536 and 1680.[9] While the religious martyrdoms that followed in the wake of the Lutheran challenge provide the most systematic example of suffering in this period, thousands of others experienced hardship as a result of famine, plague, war, and religious exile.[10]

For those in Europe facing physical affliction the Bible's pages reminded that the people of God had long been plagued by adversity. Accounts of displacement, disease, poverty, and massacre appear in both Testaments making clear, as Luther put it, that 'the Gospel... speaks of [Christian] life in the world in terms of suffering, injustice, the cross, patience, and contempt for this life and temporal wealth'.[11] The life of Christ clearly exemplified this expectation. John Calvin repeatedly stressed that because Christ's kingship was spiritual and involved bodily suffering and relative poverty 'the disciples of Christ must walk among thorns, and march to the cross amidst uninterrupted afflictions'.[12] For many biblical commentators, Christ's death—and the suffering faithful across the scriptures generally—announced physical affliction, rather than material blessing, to be a mark of spiritual authenticity and election. In this regard, the plight of the protagonist in the Book of Job proved to be a particularly poignant example for sufferers. The dialogue between God and Satan reveals that Job's emotional and bodily suffering arises not as a result of

[8] Brad S. Gregory, *Salvation at Stake: Christian Martyrdom in Early Modern Europe* (Cambridge, MA: Harvard University Press, 1999), 1.

[9] Figures noted by Gregory, *Salvation at Stake*, 6; William Monter, 'Heresy Executions in Reformation Europe', in *Tolerance and Intolerance in the European Reformation*, ed. Ole Peter Grell and Bob Scribner (Cambridge: Cambridge University Press, 1996), 48–65.

[10] See the overview of suffering in Europe in this period in Simpson, *Burning to Read*, 17–19, and Diarmaid MacCulloch, *Reformation: Europe's House Divided* (London: Penguin, 2003), 311–13, 485.

[11] Luther, *Luther's Works*, 46:35. See also Luther's reading of Psalm 22: *Luther's Works*, 12:131. For discussion of Luther's *theologia crucis* see Alistair McGrath, *Luther's Theology of the Cross: Martin Luther's Theological Breakthrough* (Oxford: Blackwell), 149; and for a summary of the reformers' views about temporal wealth see Bonnie L. Pattison, *Poverty in the Theology of John Calvin* (Eugene, OR: Pickwick Publications, 2006), 81–122.

[12] John Calvin, *Commentary on... Matthew, Mark and Luke*, trans. William Pringle (Edinburgh: Edinburgh Printing Company, 1845), 1:388. For a fulsome discussion of Calvin's views on suffering and poverty see Pattison, *Poverty*, esp. 151–203, as well as Ronald S. Wallace, *Calvin's Doctrine of the Christian Life* (London: Oliver & Boyd, 1959), 68–75.

wickedness but because his fear of the Lord is exceptional—'none *is* like him in the earth' (Job 1:8).

The Book of Job's importance to early modern conceptions of suffering is captured in the titles of many publications that address the narrative. Works such as Richard Humfrey's *Iob's pietie, or, The patterne of a perfect man* (1624), Antony Fawkner's *Comfort to the Afflicted* (1626), Henry Rogers' *Balm for the bruised: Job 5:18–19* (1631), and Manley Thomas' poem *The affliction and deliverance of the saints or, The whole booke of Iob* (1652) illustrate that preachers, biblical commentators, and poets were attracted to Job's exemplary function.[13] The steady and varied stream of publications on Job that emerged during the sixteenth and seventeenth centuries attests to public interest in this biblical book more broadly.[14] There were paraphrases of the text, such as George Abbot's *The whole booke of Iob paraphrased* (1640), commentaries, like Théodore Beza's *Job expounded* (1589), lengthy poetic narratives, as in Francis Quarles' *Job Militant* (1623), dialogues like Richard Humfrey's *The Conflict of Job* (1624), and even a play, now lost, by Robert Greene simply entitled *Job* (1587).[15]

One of the most extensive and popular considerations of the Book of Job in this period was Calvin's sermon series which, translated by Arthur Golding, appeared in English in 1574 and was reissued again in 1580 and 1584. Calvin's exposition of Job—which is broken into 159 sizeable instalments each addressing just one or two verses—elucidates how this biblical narrative was understood to resonate with the ongoing assault on Protestants across Europe.[16] Susan E. Schreiner has even suggested that Calvin undertook the sermons on Job after personally 'experienc[ing] the

[13] Richard Humfrey, *Iob's pietie, or, The patterne of a perfect man* (London: George Norton, 1624); Antony Fawkner, *Comfort to the Afflicted* (London: H. Lownes, 1626); Henry Rogers, *Balm for the bruised: Job 5:18–19* (London: Robert Allot, 1631); Manley Thomas, *The affliction and deliverance of the saints or, The whole booke of Iob* (London: W.H., 1652).

[14] For Job's importance to theologians before the sixteenth century, and for a discussion and overview of works on Job in the Middle Ages, particularly Gregory the Great's *Moralia in Job*, see Laurence L. Besserman, *The Legend of Job in the Middle Ages* (Cambridge, MA: Harvard University Press, 1979), esp. 44–114.

[15] George Abbot, *The whole booke of Iob paraphrased or, made easie for any to understand* (London: Edward Griffin, 1640); Théodore Beza, *Job expounded... partly in manner of a commentary, partly in manner of a paraphrase* (London: John Legatt, 1589); Francis Quarles, *Militant Job with Meditations Divine and Moral* (London: Felix Kyngston, 1624); Richard Humfrey, *The Conflict of Job by Way of a Dialogue* (London: William Jaggard, 1607). Greene's play was entered into the Stationers' Register in 1587: Harbage, *Annals*, 51.

[16] John Calvin, *Sermons of Master Iohn Caluin, vpon the booke of Iob*, trans. Arthur Golding (London: [Henry Bynneman], [1574]). Editions of Calvin's sermons in languages other than English were also published in 1563, 1569, and 1611. For more on the immense popularity of Calvin's text see Susan Elizabeth Schreiner, *Where Shall Wisdom Be Found?*

painful reality of religious persecution and exile'.[17] Whatever Calvin's personal experience of suffering, the sermons are inflected by an awareness of the circumstances of religious violence in early modern Europe. The opening address to the reader broadly alludes to 'the state of this present time', and notes that the sermon series has been motivated by an acute sense that now is the time 'if euer men needed too learne what patience is' from Job.[18] More precise references to the violence stirred by religious changes in Europe emerge in the main body of the sermons. In sermon twenty, the fourth on Job chapter five, Calvin notes that the 'little flock' of believers is under attack by 'an infinite number of woolues', and a more direct reference to the suffering experienced by Protestants is made when he laments 'they are not satisfyed with putting of vs to single death: but the[y] ... seeke nothing but to destroye vs and to make cleane riddance of vs'.[19] More specifically, the graphic descriptions of Job's 'pierce[d]' bones and 'blacke' flesh in Job 30:17, 30 prompt recollection of the methods of torture and execution that inflict pain on Protestant bodies. Just as Satan tormented Job, 'the enimies of the truth do now adayes condemne the faithfull to be burned', and mention is also made of the 'gallowes', 'gibbet', and the 'stake ... set vp for a childe of God to be turned'.[20]

Beza's exposition of the Book of Job in *Job expounded* (1589) similarly demonstrates that sixteenth-century interpretation of the Book of Job was bound up with the historical circumstances of suffering in Europe. He declares that 'this is the time, if euer, in which we haue but small cause to reioyce' due to the suffering inflicted by 'horrible famine, warre and pestilence ... vpon the whole earth'. These circumstances are cited as a direct motivation for his work on Job:[21]

> We are fallen into those times in which the Lord ... to sift, exercise, and trie his children, hath, if ever at any time, now let loose the raynes to the devill and his angells. I haue not without great cause among the other parts of holie Scripture, chosen and taken in hand to interpret this booke.[22]

Calvin's Exegesis on Job from Medieval and Modern Perspectives (Chicago: University of Chicago Press, 1994), 7.

17 Schreiner, *Where Shall Wisdom Be Found?*, 6. After the outbreak of persecution under Francis I, Calvin was forced to flee to Basel and, while in Geneva, witnessed social and political unrest as well as serious bouts of plague, particularly in 1542–5.

18 Calvin, *Sermons ... vpon the booke of Iob*, 'To all Gentle Readers', n.p.

19 Calvin, *Sermons ... vpon the booke of Iob*, 101. This reference to 'wolves' draws on other parts of scripture where the analogy is used to refer to those outside the true church who attempt to destroy it. See the teachings of Jesus in Matthew 7:15 and Acts 20:29.

20 Calvin, *Sermons ... vpon the booke of Iob*, 608–9; Schreiner, *Where Shall Wisdom Be Found?*, 6.

21 Beza, *Job expounded*, C4v.

22 Beza, *Job expounded*, B3v.

Beza's comments pinpoint the contemporary appeal of this Old Testament book. Job retains relevance because, then as now, suffering is used by God to 'sift, exercise and trie' the faithful, and for the rare insight it offers into divine governance of the universe. The Book of Job's affirmation that suffering occurs with God's foreknowledge and according to a higher, spiritual purpose is similarly important to Calvin's exegesis. He assures his readers that Job's suffering was precipitated by God's 'owne purpose . . . [He] was minded to punishe his seruaunt, and he minded it for just cause.'[23] Evidently, as Calvin and Beza suggest, the Book of Job was a key means of substantiating the doctrine of providence and asserting that God's choices, however perplexing or arbitrary they might appear by human standards, have cause.

The doctrine of providence—which in essence asserts that God governs everything—was not 'a marginal feature' of early modern religious culture but, as Alexandra Walsham's work has shown, 'enjoyed near universal acceptance'.[24] Certainly, a providentially orientated worldview underpinned Protestant understanding of the relationship between biblical and contemporary history, and the universe as a whole, and this doctrine had a profound impact on reformed attitudes towards suffering. As previous chapters have noted, a God who was in control of past, present, and future enabled the entirety of Christian history to be viewed as one cohesive structure that built towards the fulfilment of a higher, divine plan.[25] Calvin draws on this unified theory of history when he explains that if Job, 'a sound and rightuouse man', was 'handled so straungely at Gods hand' it is 'no maruell th[at] we now in these latter dayes . . . haue now and then many crosses to beare . . . at the hand of the liuing God, who notwithstanding loueth vs, for the seruing of whom according to his word, we be turned from ydolls vnto him'.[26] Job's narrative affirmed, then, that the affliction of the believer does not only occur with God's

[23] Calvin, *Sermons . . . vpon the booke of Iob*, 23.

[24] Walsham, *Providence*, 2. Walsham reminds that belief in the divine ordering of the universe was not a new concept with the Reformation. It was central in the narratives of the Old Testament prophets, as well as in the writings of Church Fathers, such as Saint Augustine's *De Civitate Dei*, and Thomas Aquinas' *Summa Theologica*. While the concept may not have been original, the reformers placed renewed emphasis on the sovereignty of God, focusing afresh on his intervention in the world. See, for example, the prominence afforded to providence in Calvin's *Institutes*. For analysis of the historical development of providence see Walsham, *Providence*, 8–32; Michael J. Langford, *Providence* (London: SCM Press, 1981), esp. Chapter 2.

[25] For the importance of providential thought to biblical typology, see Chapter 1, pp. 30–3.

[26] Calvin, *Sermons . . . vpon the booke of Iob*, 'To all Gentle Readers', n.p.

foreknowledge but within a providential plan specifically designed to bring about spiritual good.

Although belief in an all-knowing God who governed the universe was generally used to offer reassurance to suffering individuals, the doctrine of providence raised a number of troubling questions for early modern Christians about the existence of evil and the suffering of the innocent. The believer who accepted a God who was both fully omniscient and omnipotent must logically question if this God is the author of sin.[27] Reformed theologians worked tirelessly to manoeuvre a space that allowed God to be at once wholly powerful and completely good; yet, they disagreed over the extent to which God was involved in the creation and operations of evil in the world. Although Calvin insisted that God could will evil without being the author of sin, some later reformers offered more radical assessments of God's relationship to evil.[28] Beza, for example, seems to attribute the creation of evil to God when he claims by God's will 'all things are made, yea euen those things which are euill' because 'before all beginning . . . [he determined] to create all things, in their time, for his glory'.[29] Whatever God's precise involvement in the existence of evil, on this latter point of glorious end-purpose theologians tended to agree. Even the direst circumstances could be used to further the plan and magnificence of God.

It is, then, a firm belief in the continual operation of a divine plan that enabled theologians like Beza to speak of suffering positively. Because 'the Lord fetcheth Light out of Darkness', suffering experienced as a result of 'Plague . . . Famine, Pestilence, War, and such like' may, Beza asserts, be termed 'Good'.[30] Whatever providence might logically imply about the nature of God, the emphasis this doctrine placed on a deity who participated in the day-to-day enabled human suffering to be recast as something greater. In the case of Job, Beza states that God 'justly use[s] . . . the life of Jobs children and also of his servants to overcome Satan . . . [and] declare his power'.[31] Calvin reads Job's suffering in a similar vein explaining that

[27] Walsham, *Providence*, 14.

[28] See Paul Helm, *John Calvin's Ideas* (Oxford: Oxford University Press, 2004), 112, for analysis of Calvin's distinction.

[29] Théodore Beza, *A briefe declaration of the chiefe points of Christian religion set forth in a table*, trans. William Whittingham (London: Tho. Man, 1613), 9–10. See also William Perkins' comments in *A golden chaine, or The description of theologie containing the order of the causes of saluation and damnation* (London: John Legat, 1600), 244, and *A Christian and plaine treatise of the manner and order of predestination and of the largenes of Gods grace*, trans. Francis Cacot and Thomas Tuke (London: F. Kingston, 1606), 49–50.

[30] Théodore Beza, *A Learned Treatise of the Plague wherein the Two Questions . . . are resolved* (London: Thomas Ratcliffe, 1665), 14–15.

[31] Beza, *Job expounded*, F2v.

'the afflictions of Gods children' likewise 'serue them for [salues &] medicines: and [moreouer] the end of them is alwayes happie: insomuch that they haue euer cause to glorifie God'.[32] Because God governed all things the believer could be certain that, however unfathomable by earthly standards, suffering would ultimately have a 'happie' end. Calvin's comment illuminates that Job's appeal in many senses hinged on the narrative's positive trajectory of suffering. Beginning with an affirmation that suffering operates according to a higher plan and for a greater purpose, and ending with the cessation of Job's pain and his restoration, this biblical book not only offered assurance of God's omniscience but hope.

A JOBAN MODEL OF SUFFERING

If the structure of the Book of Job reassured readers that suffering always had a higher meaning and point, the person of Job was used to illustrate the appropriate response to suffering. In considering Job's example it was generally felt that individuals could not only better understand the purpose of their affliction, but learn how to bear their circumstances properly. For Calvin, Job's suffering was not, as some thought, a precursor of Christ's, but foreshadowed the suffering of subsequent generations: 'the prayses whyche the holye Ghoste gaue vnto Iob [were] not so muche for himselfe as for our instruction, to the end we should know how we ought to rule our life'.[33] Indeed, Calvin repeatedly affirms the text's omnipresent relevance stating more than thirty times that it has been preserved for 'our instruction'.[34] In *The whole booke of Iob paraphrased* George Abbot similarly foregrounds Job's exemplary function and, like Calvin, Abbot advises that the narrative might be 'well ... applied to all such as read it'.[35] In Job's story readers will find a 'principall pillar to support a Christian in strong trials', and a 'paterne and precept of faith and patience, as any the whole Bible affords'.[36] It is, then, Job, rather than Christ, who Abbot looks to for an example of suffering to extend to his readers. Christ's willingness to die for the furtherance of God's salvation plan certainly made him the Bible's ultimate ideal sufferer, and a template for many afflicted individuals; yet, for some interpreters, Christ's divinity meant

32 Calvin, *Sermons ... vpon the booke of Iob*, 819.

33 Calvin, *Sermons ... vpon the booke of Iob*, 6.

34 See, for example, Calvin's insistence in sermon 31 on Job 8: *Sermons ... vpon the booke of Iob*, 155–60.

35 Abbot, *The whole booke of Iob*, 'To the Reader', n.p. Calvin also calls the reader to 'apply' Job's example: Calvin, *Sermons ... vpon the booke of Iob*, 701.

36 Abbot, *The whole booke of Iob*, 'To the Reader', n.p.

that his actions could not be equated fully with the suffering of individuals. The suffering of Job, on the other hand, could.

For many commentators Job's applicatory appeal rested on his bodily and emotional frailty which rendered him a suitable 'type' of the suffering individual. Job was, as Humfrey assures, a man 'of the same mould and temper that wee are, and was liable to all our infirmities'.[37] Unlike Christ, Job did not endure his afflictions perfectly or, as the proverbial saying coined from the Epistle of James suggests, patiently.[38] In Job 19:7, for example, Job rails against the injustice of his suffering ('Beholde, I crye out of violence, but I haue none answere: I crie, but there *is* no iudgement'), and later he laments that God has abandoned him: '*If* I go to the East, [God] is not there: if I go to the West, yet I cannot perceiue him: *If* to the North where he worketh, yet I cannot see him: he will hide himselfe in the South, and I cannot beholde him' (Job 23:8–9). Amidst Job's passionate, human, response to pain biblical commentators located a useful and believable exemplar for contemporary sufferers. As Calvin explains, 'it is good for vs' to have the example of Job to 'shewe vnto vs howe there haue bin other men as fraile as wel, who neuertheless haue resisted temptations, and continued stedfastly in obedience vnto God, although he haue scourged them euen with extremitie'.[39] Although Job's pain caused him to cry out against his affliction and even question divine justice, early modern commentators found his resolute refusal to 'blaspheme God, and dye' exemplary (Job 2:9). In the midst of adversity Job continues to acknowledge the existence of a God who is faithful, rebutting the logic of his friends with hopeful declarations such as 'Thogh he slay me, *yet* wil I trust in him' (Job 13:15) and 'I am sure, that my Redemer liueth, and he shal stand the last on the earth' (Job 19:25). It is, then, Job's faithful perseverance that readers are to emulate when they face trials; as Humfrey extols: 'looke to the Actions of this great man, this humble man, and by it so modell out all your liues and affections . . . [hold] his godly constancie as a Mirror ever before you'.[40]

While individuals were to imitate Job in constancy of faith they were to learn from his shortcomings. Readers were encouraged to recognize that Job's impassioned response to his affliction was at times intemperate. Job

[37] Humfrey, *Iob's pietie*, B1v.
[38] See pp. 96–8 for further consideration of Job's patience. For the biblical association of Job with patience see James 5:11, and for the proverbial popularity of this idea see Morris Palmer Tilley, *A Dictionary of the Proverbs in England in the Sixteenth and Seventeenth Centuries* (Ann Arbor: University of Michigan Press, 1950), J59, 348, as well as Hamlin, *The Bible in Shakespeare*, 319–26.
[39] Calvin, *Sermons . . . vpon the booke of Iob*, 1.
[40] Humfrey, *Iob's pietie*, B1v.

'being ouercharged both with the greatnesse of his griefe and the despite-full dealing of his friendes' is, in Beza's view, 'nowe and then carried too farre in approving his owne innocencie'. As a result he falls to questioning 'the vnsearcheable deapth of Gods judgements . . . bewray[ing] mans frailite and corruption'.[41] The frailties of Job's temper by no means gave present-day sufferers leave to rail against God. Instead, as Calvin suggests, readers must learn from Job's outbursts how to check their passions:

> Job were a mirror of pacience, yet nothwithstanding he was not so well stayed as to ouermayster himselfe when hee spake of God. For he proceeded not with such a reuerence as hee ought to haue done, but ranne hedlong into this temptation, wherof he was not ouercome, but resisted it although with much ado. Se[e]ing then that the passions which are in vs are so farre out of square: let vs learne to hold them as it were in prison: and when we haue well fought to tame our selues.[42]

An appropriate response to suffering is one in which the individual learns to 'tame' their natural compulsions and chooses not to 'resist' the trials imposed. According to the logic of Calvin's advice, an intemperate reaction is an admission of unwillingness to submit fully to God's will. The need for the believer to submit to suffering is a keynote of Calvin's sermon series on Job. Readers are urged to 'kepe [your]selues from quarrelling with God' and 'learne to submit . . . vnto his hande', for God must be a 'rough ryder' to a 'rough horse' who, 'stubborne and stiffenecked', must be taught to 'bowe' to that which refines.[43]

Of course the narrative arc of the Book of Job also could be deployed to encourage sufferers to look beyond their immediate circumstances. Abbot explains to his readers that the example of Job has been left 'in respect of after-times, to leave upon record a paterne of patience, and a seale of Gods power and faithfulnesse in upholding the righteous, and in delivering them out of all their troubles'.[44] The applicatory power of Job is, for many interpreters, intimately bound up with the figure's eventual deliverance from pain. Yet, the promise of liberation which Job was understood to extend to successive generations is typically spiritual, rather than temporal, in nature. While Job's riches and bodily health are restored at the end of the narrative, the early modern individual was taught to hope

[41] Beza, *Job expounded*, B1l–r.
[42] Calvin, *Sermons . . . vpon the booke of Iob*, 565.
[43] Calvin, *Sermons . . . vpon the booke of Iob*, 607, 28, 817. It should be said that Calvin's use of Job to insist on strict submission chimes with his theory of passive political obedience. For more on this theory, see Quentin Skinner, *The Foundations of Modern Political Thought*, vol. II (Cambridge: Cambridge University Press, 1978), 193.
[44] Abbot, *The whole booke of Iob*, A1r–A2v.

only in a spiritually good end. Humfrey's application of the conclusion of the Book of Job is revealing in this regard: '[Job] euer before you, fight out the Lords Battaile couragiously: and when Sinne and Satan are trodden downe, you shall be sure to reigne with God for euer and euer.'[45] Herein lies the crux of Job's typological promise for reformed commentators—at the end of time God will make restitution, evil will be defeated, and the elect will exist forever in a world where suffering and death are absent.

Job's centrality to early modern expectations of future, final deliverance is affirmed clearly in martyrological writings that emerged across Europe in response to religious persecution. In John Foxe's *Actes and Monuments* (1563) the Joban promise of eventual restoration finds resonance in prison cells and among individuals for whom earthly restitution seemed unlikely. In addition to marginal references, the Book of Job is invoked in the accounts of several martyrs whose stories and letters are recorded by Foxe.[46] James Bradshaw, for instance, commends Job as 'an exampl of holy suffering fliction' to his imprisoned and later martyred friend, George Marsh. Similarly, Laurence Saunders—who, with heaven-raised arms, goes to the stake exclaiming 'welcome lyfe'—writes to assure his wife that he 'with godly Iob conclude[s] . . . *Euen though he kill mee, yet will I put my trust in him*' (Figure 3.1).[47] By identifying with Job, the suffering individual could, according to the principles of biblical typology, hope for similar restitution. It is for this reason that the imprisoned John Bradford urges his fellow suffers to 'forget [not] the end that happened to Iob: for as it happened to him, so shall it happen vnto you'.[48] A typological understanding of the unity of biblical history and the present—over which a never-changing God presides—meant that the conclusion of suffering was never in doubt; as Bradford reassures prisoner Richard Fleet: 'trust in [God] wyth Iob, and you shall perceiue that the ende will be to finde him mercyfull & full of compassion: for he will not breake promise with you'.[49] Read typologically, Job's one-time deliverance spoke of deliverance for all time, for all who continued to trust in God.

[45] Humfrey, *Iob's pietie*, B1v.

[46] Foxe's work draws on a range of biblical texts but makes particular use of the Psalms, Job, Isaiah, Daniel, Matthew, and Romans. The various editions, missing volumes, and pages make it difficult to arrive at a stable number of biblical references to Job in Foxe's work. That said, Volume 2, part one of the 1583 edition references Job twenty-nine times, and there are a further twenty references in the second part of Volume 2.

[47] John Foxe, *Actes and monuments of matters most speciall and memorable, happenyng in the Church with an vniuersall history of the same.* Vol. 2 (first half) (London: John Daye, 1583), 1573, 1497.

[48] Foxe, *Actes and Monuments*, Vol. 2 (first half), 1632.

[49] Foxe, *Actes and Monuments*, Vol. 2 (first half), 1649.

Figure 3.1. 'The burning of Martyr Laurence Saunders at Couentry', from John Foxe, *Actes and Monuments* (RB 59843). By permission of the Huntington Library, San Marino, California.

Such readings of Job's narrative illuminate how this biblical book could be deployed to substantiate the connection between suffering and restitution espoused by sixteenth-century martyrologies. In detailing the deaths of Christianity's first martyrs, as well the fate of believers in sixteenth-century Germany, France, and England, works such as Ludwig Rabus' *The History of God's Chosen Witnesses, Confessors and Martyrs* (1552), Jean Crespin's *History of the Martyrs* (1554), Adriaen van Haemstede's *History and Deaths of the Devout Martyrs* (1559), and Foxe's *Actes and Monuments* positioned suffering as a marker of faithfulness.[50] As they drew together accounts of men and women from across history for whom faith was worth more than life, Protestant martyrologies, as Gregory has shown, bolstered a sense of cohesion between nations and individuals who no longer identified with the Roman Catholic Church.[51] Certainly, as the

[50] For more on the historical development of these martyrologies see Gregory, *Salvation at Stake*, 165–97; Thomas S. Freeman and Thomas F. Mayer, *Martyrs and Martyrdom in England c.1400–1700* (Woodbridge: Boydell Press, 2007).

[51] See Gregory, *Salvation at Stake*, 183–7. As the Introduction mentions (p. 10), although Protestants may have agreed on the principles of *sola fide* and *sola scriptura* they

imprisoned and tortured look towards future restoration, such as that purportedly promised in Job, martyrological works—like the biblically inflected royal iconography of the Tudors and Stuarts—wrote Protestants within the history of God's chosen people and announced the victims of persecution to be members of Christ's true church.[52]

The martyrological tradition illustrates, then, how the suffering body could function as an ideological signifier in post-Reformation Europe, but not expressly in the Foucauldian sense. In *Discipline and Punish: The Birth of the Prison* (1979) Foucault argued that the publicly punished body is 'directly involved in a political field; power relations have an immediate hold upon it; they invest it, mark it, train it, torture it, force it to carry out tasks, to perform ceremonies, to emit signs'.[53] Works like Foxe's suggest, however, that martyred bodies may have the inverse ideological function—that the suffering body can become a means of empowering the targeted group. In these instances, the 'sheer material factualness of the human body', which Elaine Scarry describes, lends an 'aura of "realness" and "certainty"' to Protestantism.[54] Certainly, images of martyrs who are prayerful or rejoicing mark the body in pain as a visible locus of spiritual selection and authority. John R. Knott comments on this phenomenon in his study of reformed discourses of martyrdom: victims 'gain [new] voices through suffering, as pain becomes a source of enhanced spiritual power'.[55] In this tradition, rather than entrenching the authority of those who inflict suffering, public punishment becomes a sign that marks the suffering individual as victor rather than victim.

This reversal undergirds the advice John Bradford pens to other 'godly men' suffering during the Marian persecutions. Here, the narrative of

disagreed over finer points of doctrine such as the nature of the communion elements and freedom of the will.

[52] Foxe connects sixteenth-century martyrs to the first Christians who were killed, and figures Elizabeth as a new Constantine. For further consideration of suffering as a mark of the true church see Catherine Davies, 'Poor Persecuted Flock', in *Protestantism and the National Church in Sixteenth Century England*, ed. Peter Lake and Maria Dowling (London: Croom Helm, 1987), 78–102.

[53] Michel Foucault, *Discipline and Punish: The Birth of the Prison* (New York: Vintage Books, 1979), 25. On the usefulness of Foucault's understanding of punishment in a martyrological context see John R. Knott, *Discourses of Martyrdom in English Literature, 1563–1694* (Cambridge: Cambridge University Press, 1993), 9.

[54] Elaine Scarry, *The Body in Pain: The Making and the Unmaking of the World* (Oxford: Oxford University Press, 1985), 14. Knott states that, unlike the victims Scarry describes, those depicted in martyrologies did not lose their voices in suffering: *Discourses of Martyrdom*, 9, 33–84.

[55] Knott, *Discourses of Martyrdom*, 9.

Job—understood providentially and applied typologically—enables the individual to approach present suffering according to its end:

> You haue heard of the pacience of Iob, (sayth S Iames) and you haue seene the end how that God is mercifull, pacient and long suffering: euen so I say vnto you that you shall find accordingly, if so be you be pacient, that is, if so be you feare hym, set his word before you, serue him thereafter, and if he lay his crosse on you, you beare it with pacience: the which you shall do when you consider it not according to the present sense, but accordyng to the end.[56]

Viewed from the vantage of this promised end the suffering body emits an ideology other than punishment, and declares pain to have a higher meaning. Suffering becomes 'Gods gyfe', as Tyndale put it, and martyrdom is, what Luther terms, 'the most precious, most noble death, one which is granted only to God's children, to those of God's spirit'.[57] In this tradition, the body that is hanged, burned, drowned, and imprisoned is, like Job's blackened and worm-eaten form, a symbol of spiritual authenticity, a conduit of providence, and, most importantly, a harbinger of the coming defeat of suffering and evil.[58]

Early modern application of the Book Job turned, then, on the fact that the narrative's structure endorsed reading present suffering in light of future restitution—a progressive schema that similarly preoccupies the account of human suffering detailed in *King Leir.* The display of suffering in this play, much like the rejoicing bodies of burning Christians captured in martyrologies, attests to a continuing need to visualize the Bible's restorative promises long after reformers had cleansed their churches of images of the suffering and crucified Christ. In *King Leir*, a recapitulation of Christian expectations of future deliverance, as well as linguistic allusions to the Book of Job's narrative and exegetical framework, visually reinforce the promised arrival of divine justice at the Second Coming. Endorsing the notion that future deliverance gives meaning to everything that has gone before, *King Leir* adheres to a typological schema of historical progress. Indeed, the play's engagement with the Book of Job, much like contemporaneous exegesis, contends that the present is made bearable by virtue of the promised future.

[56] Foxe, *Actes and Monuments*, Vol. 2 (first half), 1650.

[57] Tyndale, *The Obedie[n]ce*, viii; Luther in Robert Kolb, 'God's Gift of Martyrdom: The Early Reformation Understanding of Dying for the Faith', *Church History* 64.3 (1995), 402.

[58] Job's body is described in this way in Job 7:5 and Job 30:30.

SUFFERING IN HOPE OF JOB'S 'GOOD END'

Scholars have long noted that Shakespeare's dramatic retelling of the reign of the ancient British king, Lear, is indebted to the Book of Job. Harold Bloom, for example, suggested that *King Lear* is 'manifestly influenced' by Job, Frank Kermode said that Shakespeare 'makes Lear like Job', and John Holloway observed a 'clear parallel' between the texts' central figures.[59] More recently, Steven Marx revived critical interest in the connection between the Book of Job and *King Lear* by suggesting that the two works recall one another 'through verbal echoes, thematic parallels, and similarities in plot', and Hamlin, whose study *The Bible in Shakespeare* (2013) offers the most sustained consideration of the narratives' association to date, has shown the extent to which Shakespeare's play wrestles with the text of its biblical precursor.[60] That there are commonalities between Shakespeare's *King Lear* and the Book of Job is clear, and it is assumed these similarities are original to Shakespeare's dramatization of the Lear narrative. As Hamlin states, 'Shakespeare's is the only version of the Lear story that alludes to Job'.[61] Scrutiny of *King Leir*—a play scholars accept was Shakespeare's primary source—suggests, however, that this may not be the case.[62] Albeit in alternative ways to *King Lear*, and

[59] Harold Bloom, *Ruin the Sacred Truths: Poetry and Belief from the Bible to the Present* (Cambridge, MA: Harvard University Press, 1989), 19; Frank Kermode, 'Introduction', in *Shakespeare: King Lear A Casebook*, ed. Frank Kermode (London: Macmillan, 1969, rpt. 1992), 18; John Holloway, *The Story of the Night: Studies in Shakespeare's Major Tragedies* (London: Routledge, 1961, rpt. 2005), 85. Other scholars who have noted a connection between these texts include G. Wilson Knight, *The Wheel of Fire: Interpretations of Shakespearean Tragedy* (London: Methuen, 1930; rpt. 1964), 191; Jan Kott, *Shakespeare Our Contemporary*, trans. Boleslaw Taborski (Bristol: Methuen, 1965/1986), 100–33; Rosalie L. Colie, 'The Energies of Endurance: Biblical Echo in *King Lear*', in *Some Facets of King Lear: Essays in Prismatic Criticism*, ed. Rosalie L. Colie and F. T. Flahiff (Toronto: University of Toronto Press, 1974), 117–44; W. R. Elton, *King Lear and the Gods* (San Marino, CA: Huntington Library, 1966), 30; Kenneth Muir, *King Lear: Critical Essays* (New York and London: Garland Publishing, 1984), 289–90; Peter Milward, *Biblical Influences in Shakespeare's Great Tragedies* (Bloomington: Indiana University Press, 1987), 157–7, 163, 167, 173–91, 197; Robert Pack, *The Long View: Essays on the Discipline of Hope and Poetic Craft* (Amherst: University of Massachusetts Press, 1991), 251–76.

[60] Marx, *Shakespeare and the Bible*, 59; Hamlin, *The Bible in Shakespeare*, 304–33. See also Robert Pack, *Willing to Choose: Volition and Storytelling in Shakespeare's Major Plays* (Sandpoint, ID: Lost Horse Press, 2007), 127–47.

[61] Hamlin, *The Bible in Shakespeare*, 308.

[62] For Shakespeare's familiarity with, and use of, *King Leir* see Geoffrey Bullough, ed., *Narrative and Dramatic Sources of Shakespeare*, 8 vols. (London: Routledge & Kegan Paul; New York: Columbia University Press, 1957–75), 7: 269–308; Richard Knowles, 'How Shakespeare Knew *King Leir*', *Shakespeare Survey* 55 (2002): 12–35; Hamlin, *The Bible in Shakespeare*, 308. For a broader discussion of the story of King Lear in oral and written tradition prior to Shakespeare see Alan R. Young, 'The Written and Oral Sources of *King*

certainly to a different end, *King Leir* is preoccupied with a model of suffering that is inflected by the Book of Job.[63] Read in relation to this biblical book and its wider interpretative iterations, the plot and language of *King Leir* may be understood to offer Joban-inspired answers to questions of theodicy, suffering, and divine justice circulating in the later part of the sixteenth century.

King Leir recalls the Book of Job in narrative episodes and through its central figure. The play opens with a test in which the king, 'resolv'd . . . to try' which of his daughters loves him most, engages in an assessment comparable with the wagers made to test Job's faith.[64] The outcome of this love test is reminiscent of the consequences of the wagers in the biblical source, for Leir, like Job, loses his authority and social position. Metaphorically, the old king loses his children who 'reject, contemn, despise, abhor [him]' (3.3.87)—an abandonment that resonates with Job's desertion by his brethren and neighbours (Job 19:13–18) and the mocking scorn of his wife (Job 2:9). Just as Job's lament for his predicament is uttered from a scrap of desolate ground—sometimes termed a dunghill—Leir is forced to languish beyond the confines of his kingdom as he wanders in a 'strange country' (5.3.48).[65] Furthermore, for both men, suffering is first emotional and then physical, and its increasing intensity is manifested visibly through bodily deterioration. Over the course of the play, Leir's cheeks become 'hollow, spare and leane', and, by the final Act, he is declared 'full weak . . . ill apaid' and is on the verge of physical collapse: 'Oh, I do faint' (4.3.37; 5.3.94–5; 5.4.22). But Leir, like his biblical precursor, is importantly not left to suffer indefinitely or allowed to perish. Restored in the final scene to his former wealth and position, Leir's suffering is brought to a similarly 'good end' at the hands of a just God.[66]

Although *Leir* structurally invokes the Old Testament's most sustained narrative of suffering, the play's indebtedness to the Book of Job is revealed more subtly, and specifically, at the level of language

Leir and the Problem of Justice in the Play', *Studies in English Literature 1500–1900* 15.2 (Spring 1975): 309–19.

[63] For a general overview of the biblical and religious references in *King Leir* see Naseeb Shaheen, *Biblical References in Shakespeare's Tragedies* (Newark: University of Delaware Press, 1987), 144–5; Elton, *King Lear*, 63–72.

[64] Anon., *The Chronicle History of King Leir and his Three Daughters*, ed. Sidney Lee (London: Chatto & Windus, 1909), 4, 1.ii.75–7. All further references will be given in the main body of the chapter. For the biblical wagers see Job 1:11; 2:4–5. In relation to Shakespeare's *King Lear*, see Marx's Joban reading of the opening test: *Shakespeare and the Bible*, 62.

[65] A hill of dung is mentioned in Wycliffe's Bible: Job 2:8.

[66] Job 23:13, marginal note.

and verbal allusion. When Leir laments, for example, that his suffering has left him a 'shaddow of my selfe' (4.2.17) his description has echoes of Job's declaration that 'my strength is like a shadowe' (17:7). For both figures, this physical depletion of the body prompts repeated cries for death. Leir implores death to bring an end to his suffering, pleading 'Ah, gentle Death . . . / Then come, I pray thee, even with all my heart, / And end my sorrows with thy fatal dart', and elsewhere admits that he 'doth desire his troubled dayes had end' and 'I / Would wish no longer life, but craue to dye' (3.3.45–8 / 3.3.8 / 4.7.182–3). These exhortations reverberate, in tone and sentiment, with Job's recurrent longings for death, such as when he exclaims 'Oh that I might haue my desire, and that God wolde graunt me the thing that I long for!' (6:8), and elsewhere 'my soule chuseth rather to be strangled *and* to dye, then *to be in* my bones' (7:15). The climax of Leir's suffering also visually evokes one of the most disturbing images of physical anguish in the Book of Job. In chapter thirteen, Job, seeking to communicate the extent of his bodily pain to his friends, reveals that he has been moved to 'take my flesh in my tethe' in order to find relief (13:14). The anonymous play may recall this lurid moment when Perillus extends his arm to Leir and encourages him to 'feed on this flesh' (5.4.34).

The play's ideological engagement with the narrative of Job extends beyond the biblical text, in that the language recapitulates the central tenets of Joban exegesis more broadly. Perhaps the most striking evidence of *King Leir*'s engagement with the wider interpretative framework surrounding the Book of Job in this period is Perillus' description of Leir as 'the mirror of mild patience' (3.1.12). This comment aligns Leir with Job's most well-established quality as a sufferer. As the Geneva headnote documents, Job had been extolled as an 'example of singular pacience' since the apostle James commended him to the dispersed Jews: 'Ye haue heard of the pacie[n]ce of Job and haue known what end the Lord *made*' (James 5:11).[67] Although the description of Leir as a 'myrrour of mild patience' broadly resonates with Job's proverbially famous patient suffering, the phrase operates more specifically as a declaration of the drama's Joban heritage.[68] The phrase 'myrrour of mild patience' directly recalls Calvin's description of Job as a 'mirrour of patience', an expression that is

[67] The Geneva headnote to the Book of Job also mentions that Job is commended as a 'juste man' in Ezekiel 14:14. For consideration of Job's patience in the biblical text, and its proverbial history, see Hillel A. Fine, 'The Tradition of a Patient Job', *Journal of Biblical Literature* 74:1 (1955): 28–32.

[68] For the proverbial association of Job with patience see Tilley, *A Dictionary of the Proverbs in England*, J59, 348.

repeated more than ten times across his sermons on Job.[69] Given that Calvin's sermon series was by the play's performance in 1594 in circulation in six editions, the unknown dramatist could have gleaned the phrase through direct reading. Even if this was not the case, the two decades between Golding's first translation of Calvin's work in 1574, and the play's performance at the Rose, was enough time for the expression to develop an established association with the suffering Job. In fact, from the 1590s onwards, the phrase 'mirrour of patience' was regularly used by a variety of writers when commenting on Job. George Abbot, Philip Stubbes, and Richard Greenham, for example, in writings published within a few years of *King Leir*'s first performance, each label Job a 'mirrour of patience', attesting to the popularity of this Joban axiom in the contemporary lexicon.[70] Because of this specific tradition of referring to Job as a 'mirror', and because Job is so tied to patient suffering generally in this period, the description of Leir as a 'myrrour of mild patience' affirms that the play ruminates on the Christian tradition of extolling Job as a longsuffering exemplar.

The impact of a Joban model of suffering on the anonymous *King Leir* is important given that King Lear's desire to be 'the pattern of all patience' has been used to corroborate the connection between Shakespeare's play and the Book of Job (3.2.36).[71] Hamlin has persuasively argued that 'Shakespeare connects Job and Lear through allusions involving patience', specifically noting that Lear's description of himself as a 'pattern of all patience' (3.2.37) appears to echo Golding's reference to Job as 'a perfect patern of patience' in the dedication to Calvin's sermons.[72] While this may be the case, the association of Leir with a Job who is patient does precede Shakespeare's drama, and it is possible that the earlier play's engagement with a patient-in-suffering Job informs the correlation between Job, patience, and Shakespeare's Lear which Hamlin has observed. Given that both plays engage with a Joban model of suffering, the dissonance of *King Lear*—which as subsequent discussion suggests is not so out of line with the biblical text—does not simply challenge the

[69] Calvin, *Sermons... vpon the booke of Iob*, 57, 93, 107, 152, 177, 189, 264, 458, 565, 729. As noted below, Hamlin connects the description of Lear's patience in Shakespeare's play to Golding's dedication in Calvin's *Sermons*: *The Bible in Shakespeare*, 319.

[70] George Abbot, *An exposition vpon the prophet Ionah Contained in certaine sermons* (London: Richard Field, 1600), 242; Philip Stubbes, *A motiue to good workes Or rather, to true Christianitie indeede* (London: Thomas Man 1593), 188; Richard Greenham, *A fruitful and Godly sermon containing necessary and profitable doctrine, for the reformation of our sinfull and wicked liues* (Edinburgh: Robert Walde-graue, 1595), B6l.

[71] See, for example, Naseeb Shaheen, *Biblical References in Shakespeare's Plays* (Newark: University of Delaware Press, 1999), 611; Hamlin, *The Bible in Shakespeare*, 319.

[72] Hamlin, *The Bible in Shakespeare*, 322, 319.

conclusory righting of wrongs in *Leir.* It quarrels with an exegetical tradition of aligning Job's apparently patient suffering with regeneration, which the source play recapitulates.

While *King Leir* and *King Lear* are both influenced by the popular notion of Job's patience, only in the anonymous play does the central figure assume an archetypal function reminiscent of Job in early modern exegesis. Perillus' soliloquy in Act Three, Scene One announces Leir to be an exemplary sufferer: 'He the mirror of mild patience, / Puts up all wrongs, and never gives reply' (3.1.12–13). Leir's silent, submissive suffering marks him as a model to mirror, and suggests that he is more of the tempered subject that reformed commentators sometimes desire Job to be.[73] Not only is Leir devoid of Job's questioning impulse, he observes the common instruction to avoid grumbling against apparent injustices, as Calvin reminded in one of his Job sermons: 'Then if it please God to visit vs with rigour, and wee see not why hee doth it: yet must wee keepe our mouth shet that we murmur not agaynst him, and neuerthelesse haue it open still too glorifie him.'[74] Prayer, as Calvin explained elsewhere in his exposition of Job, is the only appropriate vocal response to suffering. This 'true remedy' for crisis is a cure that Leir similarly recommends in time of trial: 'Even pray to God, to bless us from their hands: / For fervent prayer much ill hap withstands' (4.7.16–17).[75] Leir is not the only figure in the play to adhere to the suffering ideal espoused in commentary on the Book of Job. Cordella also assumes an exemplary function, particularly in choosing to accept that her hardship is divinely determined. When tempted to question why she suffers, Cordella reminds herself that it is at 'the pleasure of [her] God', and, as such, resolves to 'willingly embrace the rod' (2.4.27–8). The words and imagery Cordella uses are redolent of the advice Calvin derives for sufferers from Job's questioning in chapter 31: 'Let us kepe our selues from quarrelling with God when he stryketh vs with his rods.'[76]

The play's effort to extol the merits of acceptance and submission in the face of suffering is bound up with its broader interest in the question of why suffering occurs. For this question was asked not only by early modern sufferers, but in the Book of Job itself. It is because Job's friends

[73] See the discussion of Calvin and Beza's warnings to sufferers to avoid Job's questioning of God on pp. 88–9.

[74] Calvin, *Sermons . . . upon the booke of Iob*, 606.

[75] Calvin, *Sermons . . . upon the booke of Iob*, 13.

[76] Calvin, *Sermons . . . upon the booke of Iob*, 607. Leir and Cordella's refusal to question and willingness to suffer is, more broadly, a practical demonstration of what Ewan Fernie refers to as Christianity's 'extraordinary reversal of values' in which 'shame and humiliation . . . become divine, and are mingled and equated with love, with triumph and with glory': *Shame in Shakespeare* (London: Routledge, 2002), 31.

are unable to reconcile the suffering of the virtuous with a God who is just that they repeatedly assume that Job's affliction is a punishment for sin. Eliphaz, for instance, rails 'who euer perished being an innocent? Or when were the upright destroied?' and Bildad declares that, if innocent, Job's circumstances are a perversion of divine justice: 'doeth God peruert iudgement? Or doeth the almighty subvert iustice?' (Job 4:7; 8:3).[77] In keeping with this concern in the dialogues of Job, *King Leir* affords space to questioning how a just God can allow the innocent to suffer. At the moment of expected death, Perillus exclaims:

> O just Jehovah, whose almighty power
> Doth govern all things in this spacious world,
> How canst thou suffer such outrageous acts
> To be committed without just revenge? (4.7.205–8)[78]

Perillus' acceptance of God's providential sovereignty ('[God] doth govern all things') is perforated by the reality of his contingent predicament. His admission that 'outrageous acts' occur under the watch of an all-powerful God elucidates a weak spot in the reformers' theology of suffering, for an insistence that suffering operates according to a providential pattern must, logically, make God a tyrant responsible for evil.

Although the play briefly vocalizes this unsettling possibility, the implications of Perillus' question remain unexplored as Leir responds with a reminder of the futility of questioning God's motivations: 'Let us submit to the will of God: / Things past all sense, let us not seek to know; / It is God's will, and therefore must be so' (4.7.212–14). While the internal rhymes create a rather glib tone, and suggest that Leir's response does little to salve the sting of Perillus' question, the advice Leir offers once again chimes with early modern applications of Job's narrative. As the Geneva headnote to Job makes clear, 'Job helde that God did not always punish men according to their sinnes, but that he had secret judgments, whereof man knewe not the cause, and therefore man co[u]lde not reason against God'.[79] Instead of questioning God, the sufferer must, as Leir suggests to

[77] Albeit more indirectly, Job also questions the justice of God when, in chapter 24, he notes the prosperity of the unrighteous, and notes that the deeds of the wicked go unpunished by God. For more on Job's questioning, see the discussion on p. 106.

[78] Perillus' reference to Jehovah, the common European representation of the Old Testament divine name Yahweh, calls to mind the history of the people of Israel, who, although chosen by God, were forced to endure hardship and trial before reaching the Promised Land. Interestingly, the sixteenth century was the first recorded instance of the term Jehovah being used. For more on the term's etymology see 'Jehovah, n', *Oxford English Dictionary Online* (Oxford: Oxford University Press, March 2017), <http://www.oed.com/view/Entry/100996?redirectedFrom=jehovah>, accessed 19 Apr. 2017.

[79] 'Preface', the Book of Job, *Geneva Bible.*

Perillus, be comforted by the knowledge that their suffering operates within God's mysterious divine plan.[80] Leir's entreaty to Perillus to accept their predicament passively is bolstered through the elision of the old king's impending death with Christ's. In what Leir expects to be his final words, he prays a prayer remarkably similar to that prayed by Jesus in Luke 23:46 ('Father, into thine hands I commend my spirit'): 'Now, Lord, receive me, for I come to thee' (4.7.226). Leir's association with Christ at this moment is not incompatible with his Joban identity. Some commentators read Job as a 'type' of Christ, as well as the suffering Christian, a typological reading that commonly emerges in commentary on Job 42:8, which records Job's intercession on behalf of his friends. A typological connection was also suggested by writers who compared Job's acceptance of his suffering to Christ's yet more perfect example of submission in the Garden of Gethsemane (Matt. 26:37–9).[81]

Leir's identification with Christ prior to his assumed death is reinforced by an earlier moment when he likens himself to the 'pelican, / That kills itself, to save her young ones' lives' (2.3.43–4). This analogy is important because the pelican's supposed sacrifice for her young had an established connection with Christ's death in Christian history—an association which, as Hamlin notes, has a bearing on a reference to the bird in Shakespeare's *King Lear*.[82] The pelican, who was believed to wound itself to revive its young, exemplified a willingness to endure bodily pain for greater good that was comparable to Christ's. Heinrich Bünting, commenting on the views of Saint Jerome, elucidates how the behaviour of a bird that revived its chicks on the third day evoked Christological comparisons:

> Pellican[s] . . . kill their young ones vpon their beake, and then leaue them lying in their neast for three daies; at the end of which time, the female grieuously wounds her selfe vpon the breast, and pouring her bloud vpon her young ones, reuiues them againe. This bird may very well be a type and figure of our blessed Sauiour, who . . . poureth out his bloud vpon vs, whereby we are made capable of eternall life.[83]

[80] For a contemporary discussion of why believers should never question God see William Perkins, *The Workes of that famous . . . Mr. William Perkins*, 3 vols. (Cambridge: John Legatt, 1612–13), I.415.

[81] For Job as a type of Christ see Beza, *Job expounded*, 11–26; Humfrey, *The Conflict of Job*, 23; Joseph Caryl, *An exposition . . . upon the thirty-eighth, thirty-ninth, fortieth, forty-first, and forty-second, being the five last, chapters of the book of Job* (London: M. and S. Simmons, 1653), 889; Arthur Jackson, *Annotations upon the five books immediately following the historicall part of the Old Testament* (London: Roger Daniel, 1658), 298.

[82] Hamlin, *The Bible in Shakespeare*, 326.

[83] Heinrich Bünting, *Itinerarium totius Sacrae Scripturae. Or, the trauels of the holy patriarchs, prophets, iudges, kings, our sauiour Christ, and his Apostles* (London: Adam Islip, 1636), 78.

While the pelican imagery used in *King Leir* speaks to the play's reading of suffering as regenerative and bolsters Leir's association with Christ, the reference to this bird in Shakespeare's play is used to different effect entirely. Lear terms his children 'pelican daughters' (3.4.74). For Hamlin this phrase affirms Lear's connection to Christ but it does so in a way that is 'mainly contrastive. Lear does not willingly feed his daughters with his own blood... rather they are devouring him.'[84] By the time *Lear* was written the pelican was an established symbol of Christological sacrifice and, as Hamlin reminds, Shakespeare 'would have seen [the "pelican-in-her-piety"] in any number of places' including 'on a carved and painted boss in Southwark Cathedral, then St Saviour's, where [his] brother was buried'.[85] While Shakespeare likely encountered the 'pelican-in-her-piety' in multiple places as Hamlin suggests, the presence of this allegory of Christological sacrifice in *King Leir* may specifically inform its alternative use in *King Lear*. In replacing an image of messianic self-sacrifice with one of consumptive offspring, *King Lear* enacts a disturbing reversal that is in keeping with its wider repeal of Christian expectations and providential frameworks discussed below.

The regenerative and Christological imagery threaded throughout *King Leir*, as well as the message of passive acceptance of adversity, rests—much like early modern applications of Job's narrative—on the Christian expectation of divine justice. Throughout the play the operations of a God who is just are affirmed repeatedly. Cordella, for example, declares that she has 'put her trust' in 'Him which doth project the just', and Leir asserts that the 'just heavens' will not forgive Gonorill and Ragan (1.3.129–32; 5.4.59). Belief in a just God also informs the Ambassador's confident declaration that Ragan's crimes will be punished, 'God... ere it be long, / Will find a mean to remedy this wrong' (5.2.89–90), and underpins Cambria's assertion that a higher justice awaits those who have wronged Leir:

> The heavens are just, and hate impiety,
> And will, no doubt, reveal such heinous crimes:
> Censure not any, till you know the right:
> Let him be judge that bringeth truth to light. (5.2.30–3)

Even the play's wicked characters articulate a belief that God eventually will administer justice for evil deeds. Before agreeing to Gonorill's request to kill the king, Skalliger declares her 'viperous woman, shame to all thy sex: / The heavens, no doubt, will punish thee for this' (3.2.38–9). The play's repeated expectation of the administration of divine justice chimes

[84] Hamlin, *The Bible in Shakespeare*, 326.
[85] Hamlin, *The Bible in Shakespeare*, 326.

with the typological arc of historical progress which biblical narratives like Job's were considered to espouse. This particular biblical book reminded, as the marginal note to Job 23:13 reiterates, that Job 'at length had good successe' because '[God] had appointed him to a good end'.

King Leir does not frustrate this expectation of a 'good end'. The play closes with the triumph of the forces of good and the old king's restoration, outcomes which are attributed to the workings of a just God. The Gallian king declares 'God protected [Leir] from all their spite, / And we are come in justice of his right', and Leir too attributes his deliverance 'First to the heavens' (5.10.51–2; 5.12.3). While the play may, albeit momentarily, confront the difficulty of Christianity's most vexing question, the trajectory of suffering, like that in the Book of Job, ultimately affirms the operation of divine justice as the wicked are punished and the godly are restored. In *King Leir* temporal suffering continues to be a reminder—as it was in early modern exegesis of Job and the martyrological tradition—that under the direction of a sovereign God a providential plan of eternal victory was being issued forth. In dramatizing this hope, as well as exemplary suffering, the play offers practical advice, if no definitive answer, to the problematic question of the suffering of the faithful. While *King Leir*'s display of suffering works to provide ocular proof of the progressive workings of typology's structure of promise and fulfilment, Shakespeare's *King Lear* exposes a shocking rupture in this divine pattern. In this sense, if *King Lear* is accepted, to use Jan Kott's phrase, as 'a new book of Job' then it is Job read from an alternate vantage point to that of the anonymous play that was Shakespeare's source.[86] In *King Lear* the pain of the isolated sufferer remains disconnected from a biblical and exegetical tradition that reiterated causality and regeneration. In this Joban tale, the Christian promise of future restoration is spectacularly frustrated.[87]

IS THIS THE PROMISED END?

Unlike its biblical and dramatic sources which acknowledge the existence of a Christian deity amid their accounts of suffering, *King Lear*, as has often been noted, is located in a more uncertain polytheistic setting where

[86] Kott, *Shakespeare*, 104.

[87] The structural and verbal allusions to the Book of Job in *King Lear* have, as mentioned earlier (pp. 94–5), been noted by a variety of scholars and, as such, will not be retraced in what follows. For an overview of the works' textual connections, see in particular Hamlin, *The Bible in Shakespeare*, 304–33.

the only gods acknowledged are pagan.[88] In Act One, Scene One Lear reveals himself to be dependent on what William R. Elton terms a variety of 'higher powers', rather than the Christian God specifically, swearing by 'the sacred radiance of the sun' and 'the mysteries of Hecate' (1.1.109–10).[89] Cordelia also appeals to a rather general grouping of 'kind gods', Kent swears 'by Juno', and Lear refers to 'Apollo', 'Jupiter' and cries out to 'great gods' (4.7.14; 2.4.21; 1.1.159; 2.4.20; 1.4.252; 3.2.47). The relocation of Lear's narrative from the broadly Christian setting of *King Leir* to this polytheistic environment does not, however, signal a loss of interest in the earth's supernatural governance. While the register might differ in Shakespeare's retelling, the relationship between earthly events and the workings of higher powers remains a central concern in Shakespeare's play. There are references to the 'operation of the orbs' and the 'late eclipses in the sun and moon' (1.1.111; 1.2.96–7)—the belief that the movement of the stars or planets determines earthly events—as well as to the goddess Fortuna whose spinning wheel or turning ball was thought to determine earthly circumstances.[90] The Fool refers to 'Fortune, that arrant whore' and attributes the shift in Kent's circumstances to the goddess whose 'great wheel runs down a hill' (2.4.50, 66–7). Kent himself notes Fortuna's power to reverse the conditions she delivers when he says 'Fortune, good night; smile once more; turn thy wheel!', and Edgar and Cordelia similarly attribute shifts in circumstances to 'fortune's blows' (2.2.165; 4.6.216; 5.3.6). Importantly, the play's pagan descriptions of earthly governance are not incompatible with the popular Christian doctrine of providence.[91] In the sixteenth and seventeenth centuries there was, as Walsham has shown, a 'widespread tendency to personify earthly instability and attribute the vicissitudes of one's existence to the fickle goddess Fortuna'.[92]

Images of Fortuna with her ball or wheel, or references to the more general cosmic movement of the planets, were by no means erased by the reformers'

[88] See especially Elton, *King Lear*, 68, 172, as well as the following works which note the absence of divine voices: Stephen Greenblatt, 'Shakespeare and the Exorcists', in *Shakespeare and the Question of Theory*, ed. Patricia Parker and Geoffrey Hartman (London: Methuen, 1985, rpt. 2005), 177–80; Marx, *Shakespeare and the Bible*, 75; Hamlin, *The Bible in Shakespeare*, 330–1.

[89] Elton, *King Lear*, 172. The subsequent discussion of the play's invocations to pagan deities and principles is indebted to Elton's observations of the play's polytheism, see especially 172–6.

[90] For an overview of Fortuna's significance in this period see Helen Cooper, *Shakespeare and the Medieval World* (London: A & C Black, 2010), 143–56.

[91] For a detailed overview of the ways in which other ideas of earthly governance overlapped with providence see Elton, *King Lear*, esp. 9–33; Walsham, *Providence*, 8–32.

[92] Walsham, *Providence*, 21.

renewed emphasis on a sovereign God who intervened in the day-to-day circumstances of the world. Indeed, Golding acknowledges the tenacity of these older ideas when, in his preface to Calvin's sermons on Job, he addresses those who wrongly attribute their 'perils and crosses' to 'the influence of the skies, or father them vpon fortune'.[93] While reformed writers discouraged such conceptualizations of earthly circumstances, their discussions often acknowledge the broad ideological proximity of Christian and pagan notions of supernatural governance. Thomas Gataker, for instance, quips that 'Fortune is no other than but God nicnamed', and Richard Hooker observes that 'God's own knowledge and will is rightly termed by the name of Providence. The same being referred... by the ancients to be called *natural destiny*.'[94] These comments affirm that older, pagan imagery could be invoked in discussions of the earth's governance, and in explanations of the doctrine of providence until well into the seventeenth century.

For this reason, the allusions to multiple deities and planetary movements in *King Lear* are not insignificant. Indeed, the sole invocation of pagan concepts of governance may pass comment on the vagaries of earthly events. For unlike providence, which was predicated on the faithfulness of an eternally constant God, Fortuna—whom Cordelia pointedly terms 'false' (5.3.6)—was renowned for fickleness; as Helen Cooper puts it, 'instability was part of the very definition of Fortune'.[95] This instability is implicit in the popular term of address 'blinde Fortune', and in Calvin's description in the sermons on Job of Fortune's wheel, on which individuals are precariously 'hoysed up alofte: and afterward let fall agayne' by the happening of 'aduenture'.[96] While pagan and Christian imagery could sometimes overlap in discussions about the cause of earthly happenings, Calvin's reminds that the believer must think differently to 'the children of this world... whiche imagin a wheele of Fortune'. 'The chaunges and returnings which we see in the world, are not things that happen by aduenture', he asserts, but the result of 'the hand of God'.[97] In light of this distinction, references to Fortune in *King Lear* point up that, at best,

[93] Arthur Golding, 'The Epistle Dedicatorie', in Calvin, *Sermons... vpon the booke of Iob*, n.p.

[94] Thomas Gataker, *Of the nature and vse of lots a treatise historicall and theologicall* (London: Edward Griffin, 1619), 21; Richard Hooker, *The works of Mr. Richard Hooker in Eight Books of the Laws of Ecclesiastical Polity* (London: William Baynes and Son, 1822), 132. See also the examples noted in Elton, *King Lear*, 9–63; Walsham, *Providence*, esp. 2–26.

[95] Cooper, *Shakespeare*, 143.

[96] Edward Leigh, *Annotations on five poetical books of the Old Testament (viz.) Job, Psalmes, Proverbs, Ecclesiastes, and Canticles* (London: A.M., 1657), 166; Calvin, *Sermons... vpon the booke of Iob*, 516.

[97] Calvin, *Sermons... vpon the booke of Iob*, 516.

the action of the play takes place in a world where only inconstant forces of governance are operational, a world whose polytheistic deities do not necessarily promise the eventual deliverance or restorative justice in which Christians hope.

The play's setting in a polytheistic environment that calls into question typological understanding of historical progress is in keeping with the representation of a Joban protagonist who amplifies the frustrations and isolation of the central figure in the biblical narrative. Job, at several points during the dialogues with his friends, passionately cries out against his circumstances. Job 3:1–7, for example, reveals that Job 'cursed his day', and rails 'Let that day bee darkenesse, let not God regarde it from aboue, neyther let the light shine vpon it, *But* let darkenesse, & the shadowe of death staine it: let the cloude remayne vpon it, and let them make it fearefull as a bitter day . . . Yea, desolate be that night, and let no ioy be in it'. This Job—embittered, despairing, and hopeless—is not the exemplary 'mirrour of patience' that biblical commentators commended to suffering individuals, but he does, as Marx has noted, resonate with the disaffected Lear who, amid the storm, issues a similarly destructive cry:[98]

> Blow, winds, and crack your cheeks! rage! blow!
> You cataracts and hurricanoes, spout
> Till you have drenched our steeples, drowned the cocks!
> You sulphurous and thought-executing fires,
> Vaunt-courier to oak-cleaving thunderbolts,
> Singe my white head! And thou, all-shaking thunder,
> Smite flat the think rotundity o' the world!
> Crack Nature's molds, all germens spill at once,
> That make ingrateful man! (3.2.1–9)

Lear's bodily anguish, like Job's, prompts an appeal to the calamitous force of nature, one that is tied, as Marx reminds, to an expectation of material annihilation.[99] The emphasis on disintegration and disorder in these lines is significant, for it suggests a lack of purpose and hopelessness that decries the expectation of future regeneration that dominated exegesis of Job and underpinned the doctrine of providence. This sense of futility is compounded when Lear subsequently resigns himself to the elements: 'Then let fall / Your horrible pleasure. / Here I stand, your slave, / A poor, infirm, weak, and despised old man' (3.2.17–20). Evidently, while the suffering

[98] Calvin, *Sermons . . . vpon the booke of Iob*, 57; Marx, *Shakespeare and the Bible*, 68. On the broader popularity of Job's patience see pp. 96–8, and Hamlin, *The Bible in Shakespeare*, 319–26.

[99] Marx, *Shakespeare and the Bible*, 68.

Job considers himself to be at the mercy of an omnipotent God who 'hath giuen, and . . . hath taken' (Job 1:21), Lear understands himself beholden to the 'servile ministers' of nature who 'have with two pernicious daughters joined' against him (3.2.20–1). For Shakespeare's 'pattern of all patience' (3.2.36), there is no 'Almightie' against whose ways to protest (Job 6:4).[100]

Job's acceptance of the sovereignty of God does not prevent questioning why God forces him to endure suffering. Job queries the purpose of his existence when he cries 'why died I not in the birth? or why dyed I not, when I came out of the wombe?', and later asks 'Wherefore is the light giuen to him that is in miserie? and life vnto them that haue heauie hearts?' (Job 3:11, 20). He also reminds his sceptical friends that '[God] destroyeth the perfite and the wicked' (Job 9:22), notes that 'the tabernacles of robbers doe prosper, and they are in safetie, that prouoke God' (Job 12:6), and observes that 'the rod of God is not vpon [the wicked]' (Job 21:17). Although these outbursts were often excised from early modern writings that sought to deploy Job as an exemplar, or were used by commenters to encourage individuals to moderate their passions more strictly than Job, their presence in the biblical text meant that the narrative could be turned to question providentialism and divine justice. *King Lear*'s engagement with the Book of Job certainly hones in on the expressions of injustice contained in this biblical book as Lear too observes that the wicked go unpunished. Marx finds Lear's exclamation 'See how yond justice rails upon yond simple thief. Hark, in thine ear. Change places and, handy-dandy, which is the justice, which is the thief? Thou hast seen a farmer's dog bark at a beggar?' (4.6.147–50) particularly reminiscent of Job's queries, as is the shout over Cordelia's lifeless body 'Why should a dog, a horse, a rat have life, / And thou no breath at all?' (5.3.305–6).[101] While such cries resonate with Job's questioning of the wisdom and the justice of a God who allows him to suffer, in *King Lear* there is, as Hamlin states, 'no voice from the whirlwind' who eventually responds.[102]

In the absence of such a voice *King Lear* offers a more chilling response to the inquiries that are levelled at the gods. Appeals for justice and divine rescue frequently are met with further revelations of injustice. Albany's insistence that the Heavens will correct Goneril's wickedness ('If that the heavens do not their visible spirits / Send quickly down to tame these

[100] For Lear's invocations to higher authorities see pp. 102–3, as well as Elton, *King Lear*, 172–6.

[101] Marx, *Shakespeare and the Bible*, 68, 75. The closest parallel to Job's outcries in *King Leir* is Leir's somewhat wistful appeal for death in 3.3.45–8 which is discussed earlier, p. 96.

[102] Hamlin, *The Bible in Shakespeare*, 330. In Job 37, God answers Job from the whirlwind.

vild offenses, / It will come' (4.2.47–9)), for example, is answered by her denouncement of him as a 'milk-livered man! . . . a moral fool' (4.2.52/58), and followed by a messenger who enters with news of the loss of Gloucester's eyes. The subsequent proclamation of justice—'This shows you are above, / You justicers, that these our nether crimes / So speedily can venge'—is similarly frustrated when Albany's follow-up question—'Lost he his other eye?'—receives the reply 'Both, both, my lord' (4.2.79–81, 82). As relief perpetually fails to arrive the play reveals the inhabitants of Lear's world to be at sea in a universe that not only lacks providential patterns, or where divine beings are stubbornly silent, but where their existence is never verified. Unlike the Book of Job, there is in *Lear* no opening or closing dialogue to affirm the existence of heavenly powers and suggest that the suffering endured has a higher, spiritual purpose. While questions about the purpose and justice of suffering eventually receive a divine response, if not a direct answer, in the conclusion of anguish and restoration of the afflicted in both Job and *Leir*, in *King Lear* divine silence proliferates.[103] As Stephen Greenblatt puts it, 'nothing answers to human questions but human voices'.[104] In this Joban tale, the unanswered longing of the protagonist proves appeal to the heavens to be futile.

There are, it seems, no omnipotent beings in Lear's world. And yet the play does in Edmund represent a puppet master of sorts. The Machiavellian plotting of Edmund—which is unique to Shakespeare's *Lear*—is the cause of much of the suffering witnessed on stage.[105] The estrangement of Edgar and Gloucester, Gloucester's capture and torture, and the deaths of several figures, including Lear and Cordelia, are directly traceable to Edmund's 'villainous melancholy' (1.2.124). As such, Edmund's invocation to the gods to assist the advancement of his schemes—'Now, gods, stand up for bastards' (1.2.22)—is not so much an acknowledgement of divine efficacy, but proof of the impotence of belief, for only Edmund will stand up for Edmund. Edmund's later insincere petition to the gods before his father further affirms their ineffectuality, and instead marks Gloucester's bastard son an unseen manipulator of earthly events. Seeking to persuade Gloucester of Edgar's murderous intentions, Edmund declares 'I told him, the revenging gods / 'Gainst parricides did all their thunders bend; / Spoke, with how manifold and strong a bond / The child was

[103] Discussing the absence of divine answers in *Lear*, Hamlin reminds that God's response to Job is a 'non-answer': *Shakespeare and the Bible*, 330. Other scholars who have remarked on the gods' silence in the play include Jay L. Halio, 'Introduction', in *Critical Essays on Shakespeare's King Lear*, ed. Jay L. Halio (New York: G. K. Hall, 1996), 1; Marx, *Shakespeare and the Bible*, 61, 75; Hamlin.

[104] Greenblatt, 'Shakespeare and the Exorcists', 177.

[105] The Gloucester plot is adapted from a story in Philip Sidney's *Arcadia*.

bound to the father' (2.1.46–9). This is, as Elton notes, a comment that works to dupe Gloucester by appealing to 'the traditional notion of thunder as the divine voice'.[106] Yet, because the anticipation of divine 'thunders' summons a Jovan god—and Jove is a parricide—Edmund's solicitation of the gods is a revelation of his own speciousness, as well as a comment on the futility of expecting divine vengeance.

Lear who, like Gloucester, is a victim of Edmund's workings as well as his daughters', articulates a similarly barren hope in the operations of the gods while he wanders on the heath. In his Joban desolation he becomes aware of the 'poor naked wretches' whom he has 'ta'en / Too little care of' while king (3.4.29, 34–5). Importantly, Lear marks his new-found desire to assist the 'houseless heads' that with him endure the 'pelting of this pitiless storm' as an effort to 'show the heavens more just' (3.4.30–1, 37). That Lear's personal suffering makes him more attuned to the plight of others appears to imbue suffering with regenerative capacity. Yet, given that Lear is, as Jonathan Dollimore, Linda Woodbridge, and Marx have observed, by this point in the play similarly destitute, the suggestion that human effort can precipitate change when heavenly intervention has failed is shown to be equally ill-founded.[107] The reformative potential of pain is extinguished by the absence of agency—Lear's and the heavens'—and hopeless anguish. The climax of this grief in Act Five elucidates the futility of hoping in a just end to the suffering experienced in the play. For although the arrival of the bodies of Goneril and Regan appears to give rise to the advent of divine justice, Albany's announcement of the long-awaited 'judgment of the heavens' is succeeded by the play's clearest affirmation of its absence as Lear enters with Cordelia dead in his arms (5.3.230).

This tragic outcome confounds audience expectations of a restorative end to suffering and suggests that affliction is not, as commentators on Job frequently claimed, spiritually efficacious.[108] Calvin, concerned to emphasize that suffering has a higher purpose in his Job sermons, goes as far as to claim that 'when a Martyr and a childe of God bringeth a good conscience thither, and suffereth there in a good quarrell: he sanctifieth the same which was after a sorte cursed', and Tyndale, commenting on suffering more generally, declares that it is a 'happy thinge' to suffer because in doing so 'paciently' one is 'sure that thou arte sealed with Gods spirite

[106] Elton, *King Lear*, 134.

[107] Jonathan Dollimore, *Radical Tragedy: Religion, Ideology, and Power in the Drama of Shakespeare and His Contemporaries* (Chicago: University of Chicago Press, 1984), 193–4; Linda Woodbridge, *Vagrancy, Homelessness, and English Renaissance Literature* (Urbana: University of Illinois Press, 2001), 205; Marx, *Shakespeare and the Bible*, 75.

[108] See discussion on pp. 89–93, for the importance of Job's ending to conceptions of suffering in this period.

vnto everlasting lyfe'.[109] The expectation that suffering should be pointful also informs the alternative, restorative ending for *King Lear* that Nahum Tate devised, and inflects the work of Shakespeare scholars who find Lear's anguish atoning. John M. Lothian considers the play's 'spire of meaning' to be the 'spiritual history or regeneration of King Lear', while Paul N. Siegel suggests that the suffering of Lear and Cordelia precipitates the release of their souls 'from the prison of their bodies' and enables them to be 'reunited in eternal bliss'.[110] While these readings attest to a desire to make the play's suffering meaningful, *King Lear* does little to suggest that this is the case. Instead of precipitating his salvation, Lear understands his experiences to have left him in hell or purgatory—both recognized places of punishment and spiritual alienation—when he says to Cordelia: 'You do me wrong to take me out o' the grave. / Thou art a soul in bliss; but I am bound / Upon a wheel of fire, that mine own tears / Do scald like molten lead' (4.7.45–8). Lear, it seems, does not anticipate the imminent conclusion of his pain or the arrival of divine deliverance.

Lear's growing spiritual desolation is in keeping with the overall frustration of redemption in the play through the character of Cordelia.[111] As several scholars have noted, Cordelia absorbs much of the play's Christian imagery and, in Shakespeare's retelling, it is she, rather than Lear, who is marked as a figure of Christ.[112] In Act Four, Scene Four Cordelia's words echo Christ's explanation of his purpose in Luke 2:49 ('I must go about my fathers busines'), 'O dear father, / It is thy business that I go about' (4.4 24–5), and the analogy is further suggested when the Gentleman reminds Lear 'Thou hast one daughter, / Who redeems nature from the general curse / Which twain have brought her to' (4.6.199–201). Cordelia's presumed ability to rectify the errors of her sisters mirrors Christ's

[109] Calvin, *Sermons...upon the booke of Iob*, 609; Tyndale, *The Obedie[n]ce*, vii–viii. Knott has also shown that this sentiment pervades the martyrological tradition, which articulates the belief that 'the greater the physical abuse the victims of persecution endure, the more impressive their spiritual victory': *Discourses of Martyrdom*, 10.

[110] John M. Lothian and Paul N. Siegel, quoted in Elton, *King Lear*, 4. For an overview of tenacity of Christian readings of the play see Hamlin, *The Bible in Shakespeare*, 327. See too the alternative reading of audience experiences of *Lear*'s tragedy in A. D. Nuttall, *Why Does Tragedy Give Pleasure?* (Oxford: Clarendon Press, 1996), 81–106.

[111] In what follows I build on Greenblatt's arguments concerning empty redemption and failed resurrection in the play: 'Shakespeare and the Exorcists', 180–1.

[112] This is in contrast to *King Leir* where, as noted earlier, Leir is represented as a type of Christ. For Shakespeare's Cordelia and Christ see: Paul N. Siegel, *Shakespearean Tragedy and Elizabethan Compromise* (New York: New York University Press, 1957), 186; John Reibetanz, *The 'Lear' World: A Study of King Lear in Its Dramatic Context* (Toronto and Buffalo: University of Toronto Press, 1977), 120–2; Katharine Goodland, 'Inverting the Pietà in Shakespeare's *King Lear*', in *Marian Moments*, ed. Buccola and Hopkins, 47–74; Hamlin, *The Bible in Shakespeare*, 324–5.

redemption of the sins of Adam and the Christological allusion is, in the view of Siegel, 'made unmistakable'.[113] But the specifics of the biblical analogy are perhaps less important than the general expectation it generates. Cordelia's apparent ability to atone for an historic curse adheres to a typological structure of promise and fulfilment and appears to affirm history's progressive movement. Yet the typological expectation Cordelia arouses as a figure of Christ is ultimately thwarted by the trajectory of her life, which discredits a regenerative view of historical progress. For unlike Christ's death and resurrection which point towards the resurrected bodies of all of the faithful at the Second Coming, Cordelia's body promises a resurrection that fails to materialize. Lear's declaration that Cordelia is 'gone forever' (5.3.258) is succeeded by a glimmer of expectation that a redemptive conclusion may yet arrive: 'This feather stirs, she lives! If it be so / It is a chance which does redeem all sorrows / That ever I felt' (5.3.264–6). As Greenblatt observes, the hope expressed in such lines embodies the culmination of the characters' and audience's expectation that 'Cordelia would not die, that the play will build toward a revelation powerful enough to justify Lear's atrocious suffering, that we are in the midst of what the Italians called *a tragedia di fin lieto*, that is, a play where the villains absorb the tragic punishment while the good are wondrously restored'.[114] *King Lear* provides no such resolution.

Although the wicked die, Cordelia's death and lack of resurrection powerfully frustrates audience anticipation of a familiar visual testimony of the redemptive process. Lear's suggestion that Cordelia may rise ideologically taps a long tradition of staging Christ's resurrection in mystery plays, a dramatic spectacle that the play's audiences could have witnessed first-hand in the Cycles and religious drama that played around the country during Elizabeth's reign.[115] Commenting on the influence of mystery plays on the resurrection that occurs in *The Winter's Tale*, Groves reminds that 'in a culture in which the primary myth of faith centred on someone rising again, [the scene of Hermione's statue coming to life] is parasitic upon the wonder that the Resurrection generates'.[116] With this in mind, Lear's announcement—'she lives!'—invites the expectation of bodily revival only to assert the impossibility of such a phenomenon: 'she's gone for ever!' (5.3.264, 269). Lear's later question as he hovers disbelieving over

[113] Siegel, *Shakespearean Tragedy*, 186.

[114] Greenblatt, 'Shakespeare and the Exorcists', 180.

[115] Groves, *Texts and Traditions*, esp. 33–59; Whitfield White, *Drama and Religion.* Greenblatt also connects this audience expectation to medieval Resurrection plays: 'Shakespeare and the Exorcists', 181. For an overview of the popularity of resurrection as a trope in medieval plays and Mystery Cycles see O'Connell, *The Idolatrous Eye*, 63–88.

[116] Groves, Texts and Traditions, 187.

Cordelia's body 'thou no breath at all?' is met only by his own hopeless response, which eradicates any remaining expectation that there will be a resurrection analogous to Christ's: 'Thou'lt come no more, / Never, never, never, never, never!' (5.3.305–7).[117] With each repeated 'never' the play extinguishes hope in the immortality of the soul, and disavows the Joban-derived expectation that eternal bliss (for)ever awaits the sufferer.[118] The frustration of these biblically and culturally established expectations in the play is articulated by Kent, whose chilling question 'Is this the promised end?' (5.3.263) points to the falsification of eschatological hope and failure of typological progress.[119] The limp body of Cordelia offers a visual answer to this question, for it affirms that there will be no subsequent revelation of meaning and verifies death as the end of life. By evoking expectation of a bodily restoration that it ultimately denies, *King Lear* spectacularly reveals typology to be a perpetuating process of disappointment, and suggests that its providential assurance of future restoration is illusory.

In rupturing Christian expectations of historical progress, *King Lear* drains suffering of its expected spiritual significance. Instead of a marker of the true church, mechanism for enhancing faith, or means of accessing eternal bliss, affliction has become a signifier of spiritual hopelessness and perpetual death. In this sense, *King Lear* inverts a Joban exegetical tradition that worked to prove that suffering was no arbitrary occurrence, but part of a preordained providential plan that culminated in the conclusion of pain and spiritual restoration. Read typologically, Job's eventual deliverance was typically understood by early modern biblical readers to issue a promise of rescue for all sufferers for all time. While *Lear* might thwart this celebrated trajectory of suffering, *Leir* attests to how powerful this biblical paradigm could be. For Leir, in the familiar mould of Job the 'mirrour of patience', responds to questions of innocent suffering with soundbites affirming the faithfulness and constancy of a God who will eventually deliver justice. Leir's providentially rooted worldview is shown to underpin his acceptance of, and submission to, the will of God, and it is an attitude that the play's restorative ending ultimately affirms is well-founded. In this sense, the play's suffering bodies continue, as in the martyrological tradition,

[117] Interestingly, Shaheen connects Lear's cry at this moment with Job 7:9–10: *Biblical References in Shakespeare's Tragedies*, 156.

[118] As mentioned earlier, pp. 89–90, Job's restoration was usually applied spiritually to the lives of early modern sufferers. The Geneva gloss on Job 19:26, which points readers towards heavenly restoration, is typical in this regard: '[Job] had a ful hope, that bothe the soule and body shulde enjoye the presence of God in the last resurrection'.

[119] As discussed in Chapters 1, pp. 32–3, and 6, pp. 174–5, apocalypse is fundamentally a typological idea because the Second Coming is understood to be the final fulfilment that gives meaning to everything that has gone before.

to function as emblems of the outworking of providence. Moreover, in providing sustained ocular proof of the operations of a providential pattern, *Leir* affirms Protestantism's ongoing need for visual, as well as figural, signs of future hope.

As they respond in different ways to the dominant interpretative tradition of the Book of Job in the sixteenth and early seventeenth centuries, *King Leir* and *King Lear* demonstrate how alternative biblical readings and theologies could be disputed on stage as well as page. These related plays illuminate how drama could perpetuate and confound biblical narratives in perceptible, yet subtle, reimaginings that endorse and undermine established exegetical frameworks. An awareness of how drama interacts with biblical narratives, reading practices, and interpretative traditions elucidates that the relationship between Job and *King Lear* transcends verbal echoes and textual allusions. For in taking Job's outcries of injustice to their logical conclusions, and representing hope frustrated and deities who are permanently absent, *King Lear* subverts established expectations of narrative progression and inverts familiar exegetical and providential patterns. At a time when suffering and conflict persisted in Europe, and when the Second Coming seemed overdue, Shakespeare's *Lear* spectacularly unmoors Joban desolation from biblical and exegetical promises of coming restitution. Cut loose from a typological framework of historical progress, suffering in *King Lear* is no prelude to a revelation of higher purpose, but a harbinger of 'nothing' (1.1.86). It is not inappropriate that this crucial word in Shakespeare's play, which appears more than thirty times, is used in Job as a sign of God's power—God 'hangeth the earth upon nothing' (Job 26:7).[120] But to Job's affirmation of the creation of something from nothing, *King Lear* terrifyingly retorts 'nothing will come of nothing' (1.1.89).

[120] For discussion of the repetition and significance of 'nothing' in *King Lear* see, for example, Robert F. Fleissner, 'The "Nothing" Element in King Lear', *Shakespeare Quarterly* 13.1 (1962): 67–70; Elton, *King Lear*, 184–8; Emily Sun, *Succeeding King Lear: Literature, Exposure, and the Possibility of Politics* (New York: Fordham University Press, 2010), 33–6.

4

'By moste sweete and comfortable allegories'

Discerning Spiritual Signs in the Song of Songs

In his preface to Henry Finch's 1615 biblical commentary on the Song of Songs, William Gouge states what 'A Great priuiledge it is, that the Lord hath committed vnto vs his diuine Oracles'.[1] This confident declaration that the words of God, in the form of the Bible, are the possession of 'vs', the community of believers, rests on the Reformation ideal that scripture was for everyone, not simply those within the ecclesial hierarchy. While Gouge's opening lines chime with the early reformers' commitment to the 'Bible for all', the remainder of the preface expresses unease over the practicalities of this injunction.[2] The Bible contains 'mysteries' and 'strange' parts, Gouge concedes, and as such is as a 'sealed book' to some readers.[3] This acknowledgement reverses the collective 'vs' of the opening line and places the lay reader within an interpretative hierarchy. Because it is 'needfull that the letter of the Scripture bee interpreted . . . euery booke . . . requireth a faithfull and learned interpreter'. The words of caution Gouge extends to biblical readers is in large part driven by the subject of Finch's *Exposition*; some biblical books need interpretation 'more then other[s]', Gouge admits, 'among and aboue those some, this *Song of Solomon*'.[4]

The Song of Songs is a biblical book that demonstrates the reformers' capacious and flexible understanding of scripture's 'one sence, which is the literall sence'.[5] For as Gouge acknowledges, this biblical text exemplifies

1 William Gouge in Henry Finch, *An exposition of the Song of Solomon: called Canticles* (London: John Beale, 1615), A3r.

2 For the qualifications added to this ideal see Chapter 1, pp. 37–40, as well as Simpson, *Burning to Read*, 106–41, and Narveson, *Bible Readers*, 22–30.

3 Gouge in Finch, *An exposition*, A3r. This assessment of the Bible contrasts, for example, with that of Cranmer who suggested in the introduction to the Great Bible (1540) that scripture's pages were understandable by 'euery reader': *The Great Bible*, i–r.

4 Gouge in Finch, *An exposition*, A3r.

5 Tyndale, *The Obedie[n]ce*, R2v.

that there were parts of scripture where it was difficult to discern meaning; the literal or 'tongue' sense is, Gouge explains, 'obscure and hard to be understood' in some places.[6] Biblical writers frequently communicated through figurative language and sustained metaphors, as in portions of Hosea, the Gospel accounts of Jesus' parables, sections of Paul's letters, and most of the Book of Revelation. While the presence of these writings in scripture contributed to the reformers' conception of a literal sense that transcended the immediate implication of the Bible's words, the Song of Songs posed a thornier exegetical problem for literally minded interpreters. This poetic dialogue between two lovers was entirely devoid of any textual reference to God or clear historical basis, and nowhere indicated that its account of human intimacy was to be read symbolically rather than literally. As such, the Song presented readers with an uncomfortable choice: either accept the presence of a purely erotic text within divinely inspired scripture, or make the case for a literal reading that was figural. For the reformers, as for centuries of Christian commentators on this biblical book, the former was more unpalatable than the latter.

Protestant interpretation of the Song of Songs challenges many of our assumptions about biblical reading in this period. Allegorical as well as typological reading practices were essential to the reformed effort to legitimize an alternative spiritual reading of the Song's erotic contents. Indeed, a complex amalgam of figural methodologies was used to translate, or more accurately transpose, the book's erotic words into divine signs. Discussing the relationship between hermeneutics and semiology in the sixteenth century, Foucault explains how the biblical interpreter must use 'the totality of learning and skills' to 'make . . . signs speak and discover their meaning'.[7] Given that the Song's status as scripture declared its pages to be spiritually relevant, the exegetical process of making this book's 'signs speak' was clearly an important, yet complex, one. For the task of imbuing the Song's erotic words with spiritual signification was not simply dependent on figural reading practices but on human words. Because the Song itself did not substantiate a spiritual reading of its narrative, the reformers were forced to rely on extra-biblical texts, such as commentaries, sermons, and verse paraphrases, to disavow a literal reading and illuminate spiritual meaning. But this process of relying on human words to secure the relationship between sign and spiritually signified was, as this chapter explores, impaired by the reformers' view of the inherently fallen and

[6] Gouge in Finch, *An exposition*, A3r. In this case, Gouge, like Whitaker, understands the literal or 'tongue' sense to be the intended meaning. See Chapter 1, p. 46.

[7] Michel Foucault, *The Order of Things: An Archaeology of the Human Sciences*, trans. A. Sheridan (London and New York: Routledge Classics, 2002), 33.

inadequate nature of language. 'We lack the natural ability', Calvin declares, for 'pure and clear knowledge of God', a failing that ultimately warps the potential of human discourse.[8]

The reformed understanding of the limitations of language emerges within a long tradition of Christian semiotics which, as Brian P. Copenhaver and Charles B. Schmitt note, placed 'God at one extreme and matter or non-being at the other'.[9] This notion is bound up with the nominalist division between '*res*' and '*verba*'. The split between '*res*' and '*verba*' problematizes, as Chapter 1 considers, any confluence between speech and thought because 'words are signs which signify secondarily what the impressions of the mind import primarily'.[10] This logic undermines the entire process of human representation as it creates a fissure between the thought ('*res*') and the written word ('*verba*').[11] Interestingly, a number of early modern biblical commentators on the Song allude to this fracture in the representative process, and, more specifically, to the deficiencies of the written word. In doing so, they point up how nominalism's influence on reformed theology placed biblical expositors in something of a bind. According to the Calvinist conception of humanity's fallen and distorting mind, the erotic content of the Song of Songs was inherently dangerous for biblical readers; yet, the only way to overcome the book's eroticism, and assert a higher, divine meaning, was through writing, a process that, by reformed logic, is intrinsically deficient.

Poetic recapitulations of the Song that emerge in the sixteenth and early seventeenth centuries acknowledge this tension in different ways. Although separated by more than seven decades, the verse paraphrases of William Baldwin (1549) and Francis Quarles (1625) draw upon similar methodologies to neutralize the Song's eroticism for their readers. Both works exemplify how the sensuality of this poetic and literary biblical text ironically induced lumpen commentary.[12] In a different vein, Robert Aylett's allegorical epic, *The Song of Songs, which was Salomons metaphrased in English heroiks* (1602), which offers a poetic rumination on the Song's

8 Calvin, *Institutes*, 68, 1.5.15.

9 Brian P. Copenhaver and Charles B. Schmitt, *A History of Western Philosophy: 3. Renaissance Philosophy* (Oxford: Oxford University Press, 1992), 152.

10 William of Ockham, *Summa totius logicae*, in *Philosophical Writings*, ed. Boehner, 48. For more on the nominalist heritage of the Reformation see McGrath's discussion of Luther, *Intellectual Origins*, 74–80; Charles B. Schmitt and Quentin Skinner, eds., *The Cambridge History of Renaissance Philosophy* (Cambridge and New York: Cambridge University Press, 1996), 162, 72; Streete, 'Reforming Signs', 3–5.

11 See Trousdale, *Shakespeare and the Rhetoricians*, 31.

12 William Baldwin, *The canticles or balades of Salomon* (London: William Baldwin, 1549); Francis Quarles, *Sions Sonets. Sung by Solomon the King* (London: W. Stansby, 1625). All further references to these texts will be made in the main body of the chapter.

central themes and tropes, figuratively testifies to the interpretative challenge the Song presented to early modern readers.[13] Indeed, these poetic reimaginings of the Song of Songs reveal how the exegetical attempt to elucidate the spiritual significance of this biblical book was hobbled by the inadequacies of the writerly process, and deficiency of human language more generally.

BIBLICAL EROTICA

The question of why the Song of Songs is included in the biblical canon and, more specifically, the spiritual relevance of this book's erotic words, has provoked scholarly interest since the early Christian Church. Origen wrote ten volumes of commentary on the Song, and his protracted study of the book's dialogue marks the beginning of a flurry of scholarship that extended from Christianity's earliest writers to the millenarians of the seventeenth century.[14] E. Kallas and Temper Longman note that between the fourth and eleventh centuries, thirty-two commentaries on the Song of Songs are recorded in *Patrologia Latina*, a sizeable number considering that there were six commentaries on Galatians and nine on Romans.[15] Records suggest that exegetical interest in the Song escalated during the medieval period, particularly from the twelfth century onwards, with, according to E. Ann Matter, almost one hundred commentaries produced on the Song between the fifth and fifteenth centuries.[16] More specifically, the Song was among the most commonly transcribed manuscripts of the Middle Ages, and is thought to have been preached more frequently than any other Old Testament text during the thirteenth century.[17] The depth

[13] Robert Aylett, *The Song of Songs, which was Salomons metaphrased in English heroiks* (London: William Stansby, 1621). All further references to this text will be made in the main body of the chapter.

[14] Origen, *The Song of Songs*, trans. R. P. Lawson (Westminster: Newman Press, 1957). For discussion of Origen and other patristic commentaries on the Song see J. P. Tanner, 'The History of the Interpretation of the Song of Songs', *Bibliotheca Sacra* 154.613 (1997): 23–46.

[15] Endel Kallas, 'Martin Luther as Expositor of the Song of Songs', *Lutheran Quarterly* 2 (1988): 323–42 (323); Temper Longman III, *Song of Songs* (Grand Rapids, MI: Eerdmans, 2001), 30. See the works on the Songs of Songs by Allan of Lille, Gilbert of Hoyland, Hugh of Saint Victor, and Honorius Augustodunensis in *Patrologia Latina*, ed. J. P. Migne, 217 vols. + 4 index vols. (Paris: Garnier, 1841–61), respectively 210: 51–110; 184:11–252; 177:1209–22; 172: 295–518.

[16] See E. Ann Matter, *The Voice of My Beloved: The Song of Songs in Western Medieval Christianity* (Philadelphia: University of Pennsylvania Press, 1990), 8.

[17] David Carr, 'Gender and the Shaping of Desire in the Song of Songs and its Interpretation', *Journal of Biblical Literature* 119.2 (Summer 2000): 233–48 (247–8).

of interest in this biblical book during the medieval period is captured in the painstaking exegesis of Bernard of Clairvaux who wrote eighty-six sermons on the first two chapters and opening verse of chapter three.[18]

Theological interest in the Song did not abate with the advance of religious reform in Europe in the sixteenth and seventeenth centuries. In fact, more commentaries on the Song were produced in this period than on any other biblical book apart from the Psalms, an unsurprising output given that the Reformation ideal of the 'Bible for all', coupled with the onset of mass printing across Europe, handed the Song's explicit pages to the laity.[19] The early reformers expressed interest in this biblical text, as Luther's lecture series on the Song of Songs, completed at Wittenberg in 1530, attests. Indeed, across the continent a healthy number of publications on the Song were printed during the sixteenth century, particularly, as Elizabeth Clarke has shown, in the cities of Basle, Lyon, Venice, and Paris, with eighty-two commentaries printed in the French capital alone.[20] In England, interpretative work on this biblical book was similarly intensive. Sermon series on the Song, such as those by Thomas Drant, Bartimaeus Andrewes, Théodore Beza, and Richard Sibbes, were popular, as were treatises and prose paraphrases, and Francis Quarles' emblem book, which drew extensively on the biblical text, was reproduced eleven times between 1635 and 1696.[21] It was also common to use portions of the Song of Songs as hymn text. Writers such as William Loe and George Wither set the Song's words to music for use in church worship, while the text's poetic qualities attracted the interest of a variety of poets including

[18] Figure noted in Longman III, *Song of Songs*, 32. For consideration of this sermon series see D. Robertson, 'The Experience of Reading: Bernard of Clairvaux's *Sermons on the Song of Songs*', *Religion and Literature* 19 (1987): 1–20. A list of medieval works on the Song of Songs is provided in E. Ann Matter's Appendix in *The Voice of My Beloved*, 203–10. See also Ann W. Astell, *The Song of Songs in the Middle Ages* (Ithaca: Cornell University Press, 1990).

[19] See figures in George L. Scheper, 'Reformation Attitudes toward Allegory and the Song of Songs', *Publications of the Modern Language Association* 89.3 (May 1974): 551–62 (555).

[20] Clarke, *Politics, Religion and the Song of Songs*, 12. For Luther's lectures see *Luther's Works*, 15:191–264, and for a discussion of these see Kallas, 'Martin Luther as Expositor', 323–41.

[21] Thomas Drant, *Two sermons preached the one at S. Maries Spittle* (London: John Daye, 1570); Bartimaeus Andrewes, *Certaine verie worthie, godly and profitable sermons, vpon the fifth chapiter of the Songs of Solomon* (London: Robert Waldegraue, 1583); Théodore Beza, *Master Bezaes sermons vpon the... canticles* (Oxford: Joseph Barnes, 1587); Richard Sibbes, *Bovvels opened... divers sermons on the fourth, fifth, and sixth chapters of the Canticles* (London: W. Godbid, 1658); Jude Smith, *A misticall deuise of the spirituall and godly loue betwene Christ the spouse* (London: Henry Kirckham, 1575); Joseph Hall, *Salomons diuine arts... With an open and plaine paraphrase* (London: H[umphrey] L[ownes], 1609); Francis Quarles, *Emblemes* (London: G.M., 1635).

Edmund Spenser and Michael Drayton.[22] Broadly speaking, during the sixteenth and seventeenth centuries, the Song prompted more theological writings in England than all of Paul's Epistles and the Gospels, a point illustrated by the production of some 500 commentaries in the seventeenth century alone.[23]

The exegetical questions that sustained scholarship on the Song centred on reading; chiefly, how to read the text correctly and, consequently, ensure that it was read appropriately by others. This concern over right reading was bound up with a longstanding attempt by biblical interpreters to restrict, or delay, ordinary readers' access to the Song. St Jerome, for example, advised that the Song be read only by those who had been schooled in the entirety of scripture. Yet a closer look at the directions he gives for a young woman's study, detailed in a letter to his disciple, Paula, suggest that the level of schooling required was unachievable. Indeed, as Longman suggests, the scheme of study outlined seems designed to ensure that the Song's contents would never be read:

> Let her begin by learning the psalter, and then let her gather rules of life out of the Proverbs of Solomon. From the Preacher let her gain the habit of despising the world and its vanities. Let her follow the example set in Job of virtue and patience. Then let her pass on to the Gospels... Let her also drink in with a willing heart the Arts of the Apostles and Epistles. As soon as she has enriched the storehouse of her mind with these treasures, let her commit to memory the prophets, the heptateuch, the Books of Kings and of Chronicles, the rolls of

22 For music see William Loe, *Songs of Sion Set for the ioy of gods deere ones* (Hamburg: S.n., 1620), and George Wither, *The hymnes and songs of the Church diuided into two parts* (London: [John Bill], 1623); for poetry see: Drayton, *The harmonie of the church*, as well as the following discussions of Spenser's engagement with the Song: Israel Baroway, 'The Imagery of Spenser and the Song of Songs', Journal of English and Germanic Philology 33.1 (January 1934): 23–45; Leigh Deneef, *Spenser and the Motives of Metaphor* (Durham, NC: Duke University Press, 1982), 70–6; L. Staley Johnson, 'Elizabeth, Bride and Queen: A Study of Spenser's April Eclogue and the Metaphors of English Protestantism', *Spenser Studies: A Renaissance Poetry Annual*, Vol. 2 (Pittsburgh: University of Pittsburgh Press, 1981), 75–9; Noam Flinker, *The Song of Songs in English Renaissance Literature* (Cambridge and New York: D. S. Brewer, 2000), 66–87, 100–19. For an overview of poetry addressing the Song, see Campbell, *Divine Poetry*, 60–6; Scheper, 'Reformation Attitudes toward Allegory', 556. It is also worth noting Lewalski's assessment that the Song was 'second only to the book of Psalms in the frequency with which it was rendered into verse': *Protestant Poetics*, 53.

23 Figure noted in Scheper, 'Reformation Attitudes toward Allegory', 556. Popular early modern commentaries include: Dudley Fenner, *The Song of Songs* (Middelburgh: Richard Schilders, 1594); Henoch Clapham, *Three partes of Salomon his Song of Songs* (London: Valentine Sims, 1603); Thomas Brightman, *A commentary on the Canticles... the allegories explained* (London: John Field, 1644); Nathanael Homes, *The Works of Dr. Nathanael Homes. A Commentary Literal or Historical and Mystical or Spiritual on the Whole Book of Canticles* (London: J. Legate, 1652); William Guild, *Loves entercours between the Lamb & his bride* (London: W. Wilson, 1658).

> Ezra and Esther. When she has done all these she may safely read the Song of Songs but not before: for, were she to read it at the beginning, she would fail to perceive that though it is written in fleshly words, it is a marriage song of a spiritual bridal. And not understanding this she would suffer from it.[24]

Writing centuries later, a similar unease over readers' reception of the Song's erotic imagery motivates the advice given by Théodore Beza. He too suggests that the Song only be read by the most spiritually mature, as he draws a parallel between Solomon's biblical writings and the areas of the Israelite Tabernacle.[25] Proverbs is 'the vtter common court for the people', while Ecclesiastes is the 'inner place, prouided for the Priestes'. The Song, however, is the 'Sanctuarie called the holy of Holies' and, as such, is unsuitable for approach by the laity.[26] Gouge, writing almost three decades after Beza's sermons on the Song were published, invokes the same cautionary analogy explaining that 'the Jews' termed this book 'the holy of holies', and 'permitted none to read it alone till he were thirty yeere olde'.[27]

The longstanding desire of biblical scholars to restrict the Song's readership to a tiny minority of learned and spiritually mature readers is motivated by a fear that the unwitting reader would become preoccupied by the text's erotic imagery. A number of the Song's early modern commentators acknowledge this potential. George Wither notes that the Song of Songs is 'often abused' and, in *Hymns and Songs* (1623), he cautions 'no man [to] presume to sing, or repeat, in a carnall sense, what is here spiritually intended'.[28] What Wither is alluding to is a fear that the words of the Song, some of which were included in his hymns for Church worship, might be used in songs or poems exchanged by lovers. This anxiety that the words of God could be debased by the fleshly impulses of their readership also emerges in Richard Sibbes' *Bowels Opened* (1639). Sibbes acknowledges that there are 'diverse things in this *Song*, that a corrupt heart' may 'take offense' but stresses that 'to the pure all things are pure'. For him, lustful readings of the Song would be imperceptible to minds governed by the Holy Ghost who, Sibbes assures, will 'carrie up the Soule to things of a Heavenly Nature'.[29] Nathanael

[24] Jerome, *Nicene and Post-Nicene Fathers (St Jerome: Letters and Select Works)*, Vol. 6, ed. Philip Schaff and Henry Wace (Grand Rapids, MI: Eerdmans, 1996), 194. Longman III, *Song of Songs*, 32. On Jerome, see also Marvin H. Pope, *Song of Songs* (New York: Doubleday, 1977), 119.

[25] Lewalski, *Protestant Poetics*, 54.

[26] Beza, *Master Bezaes sermons vpon the... canticles*, 12.

[27] Gouge in Finch, *An exposition*, A4v.

[28] George Wither, *The schollers purgatory discouered* (London: G. Wood, 1624), 56; Wither, *The hymnes*, 31.

[29] Sibbes, *Bovvels opened*, 2–3.

Homes' commentary similarly addresses the need for the human mind to be directed away from its natural inclinations towards a 'higher spiritual' understanding of the text; he charges his readers: 'away . . . with all carnal thoughts, whiles [sic] we have heavenly things presented us under the notion of *Kisses, Lips, Breasts, Navel, Belly, Thighs, Leggs*. Our minds must be above our selves'.[30] In calling for the mind to be 'above' its natural inclinations, Homes draws, like the other writers cited, on a Calvinistic understanding of humanity's weakened comprehension as a result of the Fall. Calvin had examined this deficiency at length in chapter five of the *Institutes*, where he explained that 'although the Lord represents both himself and his everlasting Kingdom in the mirror of his works with very great clarity, such is our stupidity that we grow increasingly dull towards so manifest testimonies, and they flow away without profiting us'.[31] Calvin suggests that it is because the mind is unable to comprehend the mysteries of God that it begins to 'privately forge' its 'own particular error . . . one and all, we forsake the one true God for prodigious trifles'.[32] It is, it seems, humanity's specific inclination towards idolatry that concerns biblical scholars of the Song, for this predisposition amplified the potential for readers to become transfixed by the Song's erotic imagery. Sibbes in particular is mindful of this inherent tendency when he cautions his readers that 'we cannot so directly conceive of [the Song of Songs]. Onely our care must be, not to looke so much on the *colours*, as the *Picture*: and not so much on the Picture, as on the *Person* it selfe represented: that we looke not so much to the *resemblance*, as to the *Person resembled*'.[33] Unable to comprehend the divine, and innately prone to idolatrous distractions, Sibbes' caution elucidates how the Song's readers were perennially deemed to be in danger of mistaking the book's fleshly signs for the spiritual thing they signified.

ALLEGORY VERSUS TYPOLOGY

The primary way in which biblical commentators worked to offset the captivating potential of the Song's erotic language was through a vigorous insistence that the book's words be read figuratively, rather than

[30] Homes, *The Works of Dr. Nathanael Homes*, 469; Scheper, 'Reformation Attitudes toward Allegory', 558.

[31] Calvin, *Institutes*, 63, 1.5.11.

[32] Calvin, *Institutes*, 64, 1.5.11.

[33] Sibbes, *Bowels opened*, 4.

literally.[34] When it comes to the language of the Song, there is little trace of the reformed celebration of the 'Holy Spirit [a]s the very simplest writer and speaker'; instead, writers reiterate the linguistic complexity and abstruse meaning of this biblical work.[35] William Baldwin and Bartimaeus Andrewes are typical in their insistence that the Song's meaning is 'more darkely hyd than other partes of Scripture' and 'displayed in figures and presented . . . in darke speeches'.[36] The suggestion that the book's true meaning resides beyond the surface of its erotic words is further reinforced by the poetic and rhetorical terms that commentators frequently used to describe the Song's language. Beza, for example, describes the Song as filled with 'similitude and figure' and written in a 'stile and phrase . . . altogether allegoricall', and Gouge similarly notes that the work has 'manie Rhetoricall allegories, and hyperbolicall metaphors'.[37] By emphasizing the figurative nature of the Song's language in this way, reformed writers sought to neutralize the erotic intimacy literally implied by its words. The reader was to look to the book's higher, and hidden, symbolic meaning. This alternative layer of meaning for which commentators on the Song argued, rested on a fundamental exegetical principle of the reformers. That is, the belief, as Henoch Clapham put it, that scripture everywhere 'teacheth . . . Christ Iesus and him crucified'.[38] It was this conviction that, hermeneutically speaking, legitimized the transposition of the Song of Songs from an account of erotic love into a narrative of divine devotion. Reformers argued that from a Christological vantage, the book's human relationship spoke of the love between Christ and the Church, or Christ and the individual soul.[39]

[34] There are two notable instances in the history of Christian exegesis of insistence upon a literal interpretation of the Song of Songs. Theodore of Mopsuestia (AD 350–428) understood the biblical text as simply a passionate love poem between Solomon and his wife. For more on his views see Longman III, *Song of Songs*, 38–9. A similar reading was also suggested during the Reformation period by Sebastian Castellio who, on the basis of the Song's lack of spiritual significance, said it should be discounted from the biblical canon. For further discussion of his views see Han R. Guggisberg, *Sebastian Castellio, 1515–1563*, trans. Bruce Gordon (Aldershot: Ashgate, 2003).

[35] Luther, *Luther's Works*, 12:51–2. See also Luther's comments on the simplicity of the Bible's language in 4:439.

[36] Baldwin, *Canticles*, A2v; Andrewes, *Certaine verie worthie, godly and profitable sermons*, n.p.

[37] Beza, *Master Bezaes sermons vpon the . . . canticles*, 2; Gouge in Finch, *An exposition*, A4v; Lewalski, *Protestant Poetics*, 67.

[38] Clapham, *Three partes of Salomon*, A5v. Luther did much to popularize this principle, regularly affirming that Christ was 'the goal of all things and the thing signified through all other things': Luther, *Dictata super Psalterium*, in Lewalski, *Protestant Poetics*, 118.

[39] While this was the most popular reading of the Song during the sixteenth and seventeenth centuries, variations of this spiritual reading were present in early Jewish

The intrinsic problem with a literally literal reading of the Song's contents from the reformers' point of view seems to have been that it implied a connection between the divine and the erotic. Any such association was unthinkable, and firmly denied by commentators. The strength of feeling stirred by this suggestion is implicit in some expositors' rejection of a typological approach to the text. In this regard, the problem with typology was that it stressed the historical basis of the Song's contents, and therefore called readers to accept human love as a similitude or type of the love of Christ. As George Scheper and Barbara Lewalski note, for many exegetes this was an unsavoury idea made intolerable by the fact that it required accepting Solomon's marriage to the daughter of Pharaoh as the historical relationship that inspired the Song.[40] The clear rebuke of Solomon's marriage, as well as his sexual practices more generally, in I Kings 11 meant that this human relationship could not be taken to shadow forth divine love. As Beza asserts at the beginning of his sermons: 'farre it is from all reason to take that alliaunce & marriage of [Solomon's] to haue bin a figure of so holy and sacred a one as that which is proposed vnto us'.[41] As a work of fiction, the Song, Beza explains, must be treated as an 'allegory', and interpreted according to 'a spirituall sense'.[42] A similar discomfort with the carnal implications of a typological interpretation prompts James Durham to stress that the 'Song is not Typical, as being made up of two Histories, to wit, *Solomon's* Marriage, and Christ's... But it is Allegorick, not respecting *Solomon*, or his Marriage, but aiming to let out spiritual Mysteries.'[43] In the case of the Song of Songs, allegory, relying as it did on invented fictions to represent spiritual truth, was for many Protestant commentators a less problematic alternative

readings of the text, where the Bridegroom was interpreted as God and the Bride as Israel. For an overview of this Jewish usage see Gerson D. Cohen, 'The Song of Songs and the Jewish Religious Mentality', *The Samuel Friedland Lectures 1960–1966* (New York: The Jewish Theological Seminary, 1966). Patristic and medieval Christian commentators frequently added a third Marian layer of interpretation to their reading of the Song as a narrative of Christ and the Church. For discussion of this development see Matter, *The Voice of My Beloved*, 151–71; Susan L. Smith, 'The Bride Stripped Bare: A Rare Type of the Disrobing of Christ', *Gesta* 34.2 (1995): 126–46. This three-fold method of reading the Song was also the mark of sixteenth-century Catholic exegesis. See, for example, the preface to the Song of Songs in *The Holie Bible faithfully translated into English, out of the Authentical Latin... By the College of Doway* (Doway: Laurence Kellan, 1609–10), 2.

40 Scheper, 'Reformation Attitudes toward Allegory', 557; Lewalski, *Protestant Poetics*, 60.

41 Beza, *Master Bezaes sermons vpon the... canticles*, 1r. See also Lewalski for the opposition of Beza and others to a typological reading of the Song: *Protestant Poetics*, 59–60.

42 Beza, *Master Bezaes sermons vpon the... canticles*, 1r, 'The Argument', n.p.

43 James Durham, *Clavis Cantici: Or, an Exposition of the Song of Solomon* (Edinburgh: George Swintoun and James Glen, 1668), 10.

to typology. This reading practice denied the account of human love any historical reality, and enabled the Song's contents to be understood as a literary vehicle through which spiritual truth was communicated; as Beza emphasizes: the book 'delieuereth to our vnderstanding things heavenly and spirituall, by a similitude and figure of things natural and corporall'.[44] It is, then, because allegory was understood to separate the Song's perceived account of spiritual intimacy from the unseemly throes of an erotic encounter that many commentators favoured this interpretative practice.

What is interesting about the reformed use of allegory in the case of the Song of Songs is that here, when faced with the text's eroticism, this figurative reading practice is not the dangerous 'cobweb' or 'beautiful harlot' that reformers elsewhere charged detracted from scripture's true meaning.[45] Rather, as the Geneva Preface to the Song suggests, allegory is embraced as the means by which the Song's spiritual significance might be realized: 'by moste swete and comfortable allegories and parables [the Song of Songs] describeth the perfect love of Jesus Christ . . . and the faithful soule or his Church . . . his spouse'.[46] Evocatively termed by the Geneva editors as 'sweet and comfortable', allegory is in much reformed exegesis of the Song not only used willingly, but celebrated for its revelatory potential. The reformers' ready dependence on allegory prompted Lewalski to conclude that both medieval and reformed exegetes interpreted the Song in 'allegorical rather than typological terms'.[47] While this assessment broadly is true, closer scrutiny of reformed approaches to the Song illuminates exegetical methodologies that are often more contested. There are commentators who, perhaps mindful of the apparently arbitrary nature of allegorical readings, remain committed to typology as a means of ascertaining the Song's spiritual meaning. The Prologue to the Song of Songs in Taverner's 1539 edition of the Bible, for example, seems to advocate a typological interpretation when it suggests that Solomon wrote the work to celebrate his marriage: 'Salomon made this Balade or songe by him selfe and his wyfe the daughter of Pharao, under the shadowe of him

[44] Beza, *Master Bezaes sermons vpon the . . . canticles*, 2. See Chapter 1, pp. 44–6, for discussion of the reformers' distinction between allegory and typology and the inherent difficulties of this division.

[45] John Donne, *Essays in Divinity*, ed. Evelyn M. Simpson (Oxford: Clarendon Press, 1952), 40; Luther, *Luther's Works*, 5:347.

[46] 'Preface', The Song of Songs, *The Geneva Bible*.

[47] Barbara K. Lewalski, 'Typology and Poetry', in *Illustrious Evidence: Approaches to English Literature of the Seventeenth Century*, ed. Earl Miner (Berkeley: University of California Press, 1975), 41–69 (58). It should be said that elsewhere Lewalski makes a similar claim but goes on to note Taverner's Bible (discussed below) and *Dutch Annotations* as exceptions: *Protestant Poetics*, 59–60. See also Scheper's assessment of allegorical readings of the Song: 'Reformation Attitudes toward Allegory', 555.

selfe fyguryinge Christ, and under the person of his wife the Church'.[48] What is more common than this typological approach, however, are the many instances when writers seem unwilling, or unable, to commit fully to reading the Song of Songs as an allegorical fiction or typological history, and instead make contradictory claims for both interpretative practices.

The 1583 sermons of Bartimaeus Andrewes exhibit this confused exegetical approach. The opening lines root the Song's contents in Israelite history, suggesting that the book concerns 'a wise and excellent man *Solomon* king of Peace . . . who was a figure of Christ', and, in doing so, imply a typological approach to the text.[49] Yet, despite this initial acceptance of an historical Solomon as a type of the Christological Bridegroom, Andrewes later claims that the Song's account of the 'eternall and constant love of Christ Jesus towards his Church' is told through 'alligoricall, and parabolicall speeches'.[50] Within a few lines, Andrewes retreats once more to a typological reading of the biblical text when he notes that '*Solomon* in his marriage with the daughter of *Pharaoh* . . . supported the person of Christ Jesus: as in the 45 Psalm'.[51] This unstable exegetical footing can also be discerned in the biblical annotations compiled by John Downame. Downame seems at the outset of his work to make a case for a 'spiriutall', or allegorical, reading of the Song, but his commitment to this reading is less than constant:

> Generally it is acknowledged, that is, not as an history, or prophecy (as some conceive it) but as a divine Parable, wherein naturall and visible things allegorize things supernaturall, and under the figures of Solomon and his Love, is shadowed the true Prince of peace and his rich affections to his Church and people. And this is that genuine and spiritual explication.[52]

Although Downame acknowledges the rationale for rejecting the Song's historicity, his comments reveal that he is unable to accept the book entirely as a work of fiction. Traces of a typological approach emerge as he references the human relationship of 'Solomon and his Love', and are further implied by the description of the Old Testament king as a 'shadow' pointing forward to the 'true prince'.[53]

These examples demonstrate that pinpointing the interpretative methodology used by reformers in exegesis of the Song is not straightforward

48 Richard Taverner, *The most sacred Bible, whiche is the Holy Scripture* (London: John Byddell, 1539), 'Preface to the Song of Songs', CCXXIX; Lewalski, *Protestant Poetics*, 60. See also the influence of typology on Quarles' *Sions Sonets* discussed below, pp. 130–6.

49 Andrewes, *Certaine verie worthie, godly and profitable sermons*, 5.

50 Andrewes, *Certaine verie worthie, godly and profitable sermons*, 5.

51 Andrewes, *Certaine verie worthie, godly and profitable sermons*, 5–6.

52 John Downame, *Annotations upon all the books of the Old and New Testament* (London: Evan Tyler, 1657), 7Gr.

53 Downame, *Annotations*, 7Gr.

Many commentators had difficulty accepting the carnal suggestiveness of a typological reading, yet remained unwilling to embrace the work as an allegory. Indeed, the examples cited illustrate how, in the case of the Song of Songs, the clear division that Protestant scholars such as Whitaker attempt to draw between allegory and typology is in practice much less distinct. In fact, writers such as Downame and Andrewes make little attempt to differentiate between the figurative reading practices they use, reiterating that a mixed exegetical mode continued to hold sway among literally minded reformers.[54] Recognition of this incongruity and acknowledgement that Protestant exegesis of the Song relied on an interpretative methodology characterized in the reformed tradition as both corrupting and Catholic, registers in some commentaries on this biblical book. It is implicit in the distinction Clapham draws between 'making Religion an Allegorie', as the Catholics have done, and insisting on 'hau[ing] Religion without all Allegorie'.[55] Durham similarly works to justify the use of allegory in the case of the Song when he posits that:

> There is a great difference betwixt an Allegorick Exposition of Scripture, and an Exposition of Allegorick Scripture: The first is that, which many Fathers, and School-men fail in, that is, when they Allegorize plain Scriptures and Histories, seeking to draw out some secret meaning, other than appeareth in the words; and so will fasten many senses upon one Scripture. This is indeed unsafe, and is justly reprovable; . . . An Exposition of an Allegorick Scripture, is, the opening and expounding of some dark Scripture . . . making it plain and edifying.[56]

Revealingly, Durham's defence of allegory illustrates that a figurative reading of a 'dark' text like the Song of Songs was not considered to be a renunciation of the literal sense. An allegorical reading of the Song is instead termed 'plain', affirming that the reformers accommodated spiritual readings of the Song within their understanding of scripture's literal sense.

LITERAL INTENTION(S) IN THE SONG

In the case of the Song of Songs, the reformers' enlarged understanding of scripture's literal sense generated similar contradictions to those outlined previously.[57] Gouge articulates an enriched definition of the literal or, as he terms it, 'letter' sense, when he asserts that in the case of the Song of

[54] Tyndale, *The Obedie[n]ce*, R2v. See Chapter 1, p. 46, for a discussion of Whitaker and an overview of reformed distinctions between allegory and typology.
[55] Clapham, *Three partes of Salomon*, A6r.
[56] Durham, *Clavis Cantici*, 22–3.
[57] See Chapter 1, pp. 45–8.

Songs it is 'needfull' that this sense be 'interpreted, so the mystery thereof vnfolded'.[58] A literal reading is not the text's obvious meaning but is in need of interpretation. Durham's lengthy commentary further elucidates the complexities of the interpretative methodology required to locate the Song's 'literal' meaning:

> I grant it hath a literal meaning, but I say, that literal meaning is not immediat, and that which first looketh out, as in Historical Scriptures, or others which are not figurative, but that which is spiritually and especially meant by these Allegorick and Figurative speeches, is the Literal meaning of this Song: So that its Literal sense is mediat, representing the meaning, not immediatly from the Words, but mediatly from the Scope, that is, the intention of the Spirit, which is couched under the Figures and Allegories, here made use of: For, a Literal sense . . . is that which floweth from such a place of Scripture as intended by the Spirit in the words.[59]

The idea that the literal sense is not necessarily that 'which first looketh out', and the suggestion that a figurative reading could, in some instances, be the literal sense, was a complex notion for the common reader to grasp. Indeed, this logic destabilizes the entire interpretative process as the means of discerning those portions of biblical text where the meaning is 'not immediate' relies, as the earlier consideration of Whitaker and Donne suggested, on the reader's ability to understand the 'intention' of the Spirit.[60] Durham's defence of a figurative interpretation of the Song problematically makes access to scripture's truths dependent on humanity's inherently compromised perceptive abilities. But 'Dull', as Calvin put it, to heavenly mysteries, the mind's capacity for discerning the intended 'literal' meaning of scripture must, by reformed logic, be destined to fail.[61]

A natural consequence of unmooring literal meaning from what was obviously implied by the scripture's words was that there was no means of circumscribing how the Song's dialogue should be read. Unsurprisingly, this led to variation in interpretation as reformers' readings were inflected by personal circumstances and doctrinal convictions, as was common in medieval exegesis of the Song. Bernard of Clairvaux, like many of his contemporaries, read the Bride as a monastic penitent longing for spiritual union with Christ, while some commentators in the reformed tradition identified her as a symbol of the repentant sinner.[62] In keeping with this

[58] Gouge in Finch, *An exposition*, A3r. [59] Durham, *Clavis Cantici*, 6.

[60] See Chapter 1, pp. 46–8. Durham expresses a similar logic again later: see *Clavis Cantici*, 23.

[61] Calvin, *Institutes*, 63, 1.5.11.

[62] For an extensive discussion of this popular interpretation, and of Bernard of Clairvaux specifically, see Matter, *The Voice of My Beloved*, 123–55. For a detailed overview of

reading, Finch understands the Bride's description of herself as 'blacke' (1:4) as an allusion to the Calvinist doctrine of depravity.[63] He notes in his *Exposition* (1615) that this description is an affirmation that 'sinne is in vs as the spots are in the Leopard, not by accident, but by nature, which no art can cure, no water wash off, because they are in the sinowes & in the most inner parts'.[64] George Gifford's sermon series also demonstrates that, when freed to interpret the literal sense as the intention of the Holy Spirit, commentators frequently found evidence of key reformed doctrines in the Song's words. Gifford suggests that Song of Songs 2:10–12 ('Arise, my loue . . . For beholde, winter is past: the raine is changed, and is gone away. The flowers appeare in the earth: the time of the singing of the birdes is come, and the voyce of the turtle is heard in our land') speaks of the spiritual growth of God's elect:

> The alleogrie . . . is taken from the time of the yeare . . . that is, what the state of all the Elect was before their calling, and then what it is after they be called of the Lord and regenerate. Before they bee called, their hearts bee euen like the earth in winter, vnder the colde frost, & stormes of sinne: For there can no sweete thing grow vp, there is an utter barrenness. After that the Lord hath called them, and that they be regenerate, there is an heavenly warmth of his spirit, and the sweete dew of his graces, and then sweet flowers appeare, and then the wholesome fruites doe budde forth.[65]

Gifford's augmentation of a description of the changing seasons into a symbolic reading of the spiritual development of the believer suggests that the reformers, like their accused Roman Catholic counterparts, could with the aid of figural methodologies find any belief hidden within scriptures. Indeed, the Song's erotic account of human intimacy was found by some to speak of the circumstances, as well as the doctrine, of Protestants. Thomas Bentley affirms England's position as an elect nation when he reads Queen Elizabeth as the 'spouse' of Christ whose earthly 'authoritie . . . familie and spirituall societie' is part of the kingdom of the 'heauenlie Bridegroome'.[66] Martin Luther also posited a political interpretation of the Song. Uniquely, Luther understood the text as an allegory of the 'sublime peace' of

divergences in Protestant and Catholic readings of the Song see Scheper, 'Reformation Attitudes toward Allegory', 557–9; Lewalski, *Protestant Poetics*, 60–8.

[63] For more detailed discussion of doctrinal readings of the Bride's blackness see Stanley Stewart, *The Enclosed Garden: The Tradition and the Image in Seventeenth-Century Poetry* (Madison: University of Wisconsin Press, 1966), 64–7.

[64] Finch, *An exposition*, 79.

[65] George Gifford, *Fifteene sermons vpon the Song of Salomon* (London: Barnard Alsop, 1620), 112–13.

[66] Bentley, *The monument of matrones*, 308. See also Johnson's discussion of Elizabeth as the Bride: 'Elizabeth, Bride and Queen', 78–80.

Solomon's reign, describing it as 'an encomium of the political order', and celebration of 'the greatest of all human works . . . government'.[67] Thomas Brightman's *A Commentary on the Canticles* (1644) was yet more speculative. Brightman read the Song apocalyptically, much in the vein of his understanding of the Book of Revelation, finding in its pages an elaborate historical prophecy stretching from the Old Testament rule of King David to the seventeenth century.[68] Such diverse readings of the Song suggest how the need to offset the text's eroticism, and proclaim a 'literal' meaning that was figural, sparked an interpretative endeavour that destabilized the process whereby biblical truth could be known. The Reformation had positioned scripture as the only secure path to truth, but as exegesis of the Song of Songs suggests, ascertaining what this truth was, or how to be certain of it, was a deeply subjective process.

MAKING MEANING IN THE SONG

Perhaps the greatest practical difficulty for the reformers' symbolic readings of the Song of Songs was that, unlike the parables of Jesus, this biblical text did not suggest, even implicitly, that its words had a higher meaning and should be treated figuratively. Biblical commentators worked to plug this exegetical fault line through writing, producing expositional works disproportionate in size to the eight-chapter Song. Clapham's commentary takes the reader through 298 pages of painstaking exposition, while John Collinges, as Scheper notes, produces a staggering 1,500 pages on the Song's opening two chapters.[69] Written interpretation of the Song also tended to be typographically dense. Dudley Fenner begins his commentary, *The Song of Songs* (1594), by praising scripture's 'shining simplicitie'; yet, the words of the biblical text are deemed sufficiently complex as to require a heavily glossed poetic paraphrase, prose paraphrase of each chapter, and lengthy commentary.[70] Fenner's work attests to the intense exegetical endeavour to define and delimit how the Song's erotic

[67] Luther, *Luther's Works*, 15:195–6.

[68] See Brightman, *A commentary on the Canticles.* For discussion of Brightman's historical reading see Jeffrey A. Hammond, 'The Bride in Redemptive Time: John Cotton and the Canticles Controversy', *The New England Quarterly* 56.1 (March 1983): 78–102. See Clarke's *Politics, Religion and the Song of Songs* for an assessment of the diverse political uses to which the Song was put in seventeenth-century England.

[69] Clapham, *Three partes of Salomon*; John Collinges, *The intercourses of divine love . . . expressed by Solomon* (London: A. Maxwel, 1676): Scheper, 'Reformation Attitudes toward Allegory', 556.

[70] Fenner, *The Song of Songs*, A4r. See, for example, B2r–B3v.

contents were understood by lay readers. It is one of a number of commentaries that contain multiple readings of every chapter of the biblical book.

William Baldwin's *The Canticles or Balades of Salomon phraselyke declared in English metres* (1549) is more deliberate in its effort to restrict independent lay reading of the Song.[71] Baldwin's readers are urged towards a symbolic understanding of the biblical text through strict adherence to the commentary's interpretative machinery: 'thou must reade them well . . . & in reading note the sentence more than the time, with the argumentes whiche go before and after the songes. And reade them orderly, so shall the proces of the matter helpe the muche' (A2v). Although Baldwin's title promises a 'phraselyke' rendering of the biblical text into metre, his work, as the address to the reader suggests, is a complex medley of exegetical formats within which the verse paraphrase is, proportionally, only a tiny part. Each chapter of the Song is summarized, after which, verses are grouped into smaller sections and a more detailed prose explanation is given under the title 'Argument'.[72] Only then does the reader arrive at the verse translation of the corresponding portion of the biblical text.

This series of repetitive layers is constructed to outline, affirm, and reaffirm a spiritual reading of the Song's words, and the cumulative effect of these exegetical manoeuvres is a repackaging of the Song's erotic signs as theological signifiers. As Noam Flinker describes, Baldwin constructs the work so that 'one set of significations supplants another'.[73] This is certainly the case in the 'Argument' given for the suggestive 'My loue put in his hand at the hole, and my herte was moued within me' (Songs 5:4):

> Thus is the poore churche deceyued through frayltie of the flesh: whiche he consyderyng and seyng the dore shut, that is the spirite so hyndred in carnal iudgement, that she can not receyue hym, thrusteth in his hande, that is his power, grace, and helpe, through the hole of the dore, that is the eleccion whiche remayneth in olde Adam the dore of the flesshe, whiche through his grace he openeth. (G4r).

This exposition works to neutralize the eroticism of the biblical text by recontextualizing its words within a theological discussion of divine grace

[71] Baldwin's work was the earliest published collection of English poetry and Noam Flinker has shown how *Canticles* had 'direct influence on the work of later poets such as Spenser, Shakespeare, Donne, Herbert, Milton and Marvell': *The Song of Songs*, 32, 31–100.

[72] For the accuracy of Baldwin's biblical translation see John N. King, *English Reformation Literature: The Tudor Origins of the Protestant Tradition* (Princeton: Princeton University Press, 1982), 367–8.

[73] Flinker, *The Song of Songs*, 32.

at work. The symbolic reading of 'hole' is influenced by Revelation 3:20 ('Behold, I stand at the doore, & knocke. If any man heare my voice & open the doore, I will come in vnto him, and will suppe with him, & he with me'), as an act of 'grace' enables the (key) 'hole' of the Church or believer's soul to be opened, allowing the Bridegroom, Christ, to gain entry. This alternative, spiritual reading of Song of Songs 5:4 subtly inflects the corresponding verse paraphrase:

> MY Loue dyd put his hande of myght,
> In to my hole of fleshly sence:
> Whereby myne inwarde partes outryght
> Dyd swel and ryse, through influence
> Of grace. (H1v)

By this third interpretative stage, the 'phraselyke' verse has acquired a direct reference to man's 'fleshly' desires and divine 'grace', allusions which, in the context of the preceding discussion, seek to diffuse the Song's erotic intimacy by recasting it as an analogy for a divine process.[74] With the lengthy Argument typographically looming over this comparatively brief section of verse, Baldwin's *Canticles* works to offset the apparent failings of the biblical text by textually substantiating the relationship between the Song's erotic words and what they spiritually signified.

The sheer verbosity of Baldwin's *Canticles*, like similarly constructed commentaries on this biblical book, suggests an uneasiness that the Song of Songs does not speak more directly, or more literally, of its spiritual significance. This anxiety is traceable in interpretative engagements with the Song across the sixteenth century, and identifiable in the exegetical works produced well into the seventeenth century. Indeed, in spite of a lapse of several decades, Francis Quarles' versified 'periphras' of the biblical text, *Sions Sonets* (1625), reveals a similar dis-ease to Baldwin's *Canticles* over the lack of textual evidence for a figural reading of the Song as a narrative of Christ's love for the Church.[75] Quarles' text confronts this

[74] Flinker argues that Baldwin's commentary on this verse 'reinscribes the sexual as an aspect of the spiritual', and suggests that the fleshly focus of this section of Baldwin's work ensures that the 'project of providing "suche songes [that] might once drive out of office the baudy balades of lecherous loue" is fundamentally threatened': *Song of Songs*, 50, 52. See also Clarke who argues that the residual eroticism of Baldwin's verse more generally 'is an important signifier of the completeness of the love of Christ for the soul': *Politics, Religion and the Song of Songs*, 17, 15–18.

[75] *Sions Sonets* was one of a number of biblical verse paraphrases that Quarles published in the 1620s; these works included *A Feast for Wormes* (1620), which addressed the narrative of Jonah, *Hadassa: Or, The History of Queene Ester* (1621), *Job Militant* (1624), and *The Historie of Samson* (1630).

exegetical dilemma rather differently though.[76] Instead of a compendious layering of commentary, Quarles creates a version of the Song infused with the divine signifiers that the biblical text was thought to lack. The work begins with a clear affirmation that the Song's 'Speakers' are 'CHRIST, the *Bridegroome*; the CHVRCH, the *Bride*' (A4r), and then moves to unravel a version of the Song in which these symbolic identities are readily discernible.[77]

This clarity of meaning is primarily achieved by interlacing the biblical narrative with New Testament imagery that affirms the Bridegroom's Christological identity. The opening verse 'periphras' draws, for example, on the shepherding analogy of John 10:11–16, where Christ describes himself as the 'good shepheard' who 'giueth his life for his sheepe' (John 10:11). Quarles' Bride pointedly addresses her lover as 'gentle Shepherd', and the Bridegroom responds with a promise to 'make thee mistris of my Flocks' (1:6; 2:1).[78] These shepherding references work to affirm the Christological identity of the Song's male voice. More broadly, they recast the Bridegroom as a caring pastor of his spiritual flock, as opposed to the desiring lover of the opening chapters of the biblical text. Allusions to the Cross further emboss Quarles' 'periphras' with Christological signifiers. The Passion narrative is invoked implicitly, for example, in the Bridegroom's depiction of his lover as the 'dearest off-spring of my dying blood', and re-emerges again later when the Bride describes finding her lover 'lowly laide / Beneath the tree of Loue' (2:1; 21:9). These references to the crucifixion are significant because they replace the biblical text's focus on the sexual potency of the male lover's body (for example, 'his mouth *is as* sweete things, and hee is wholy delectable' (Songs 5:16)) with images of its physical suffering. *Sions Sonets* further works to offset the sexual appeal of the male voice's body by foregrounding

[76] *Sions Sonets* was extremely popular during the period going through eight editions after 1625 as part of the larger work *Divine poems containing the history of Ionah. Ester. Iob.* (London: Miles Flesher, 1630). *Sions Sonets* has, however, generated little recent scholarly interest, and attention to Quarles' biblical paraphrases more generally has been limited. Notable exceptions include Streete, 'Frances Quarles' Early Poetry', and Ross, 'Epic, Meditation, or Sacred History?'.

[77] Although the Song implied neither directly or indirectly that it should be read as a narrative of divine love, the nuptial metaphor discerned in the text was described elsewhere in scripture. See Israel's description as a Bride in Hosea 1–2, as well as Exodus 34:12, Leviticus 17:17, Isaiah 54:5, and I Chronicles 5:25. This marriage metaphor also occurs in the New Testament. Christ is described as a Bridegroom in John 3:29; Mark 2:19–20; Matthew 9:14–15, 25:1–13; Romans 7: 1–6; II Corinthians 11:2–3, Ephesians 5:22–33, and Revelation 21:2, 9.

[78] This statement also resonates with Jesus' three-fold instruction to Peter 'fede my shepe': John 21:15–17.

his divine perfection: 'his body is Heauen, for in his brest / The perfect Essence of a God doth rest' (17:1).

The Bridegroom's purity is also stressed when he is described as 'Vnblemisht, vndistayned with a spot', 'a *Nazarite*, on whom ne're Rasor came' (17:3, 2). The latter description of the Bridegroom as a 'Nazarite' is particularly evocative as it signals his adherence to the vow of consecration outlined in Numbers 6:1–21. It is an identification that affirms the male lover's spiritual distinction, for as Ainsworth explains in *Annotations*, 'a Nazarite hath his name of *Separation*' and refers to 'a choise and chiefe man, separated of God unto excellencie above his brethren'.[79] While the Bridegroom's description as a 'Nazarite' affirms his spiritual purity generally, it also signals his Christological identity. The Geneva marginal note to Numbers 6:2 defines a Nazarite as one 'which separated them selues from the worlde, and dedicated them selues to God: which figure was accomplished in Christ'. More specifically, the particular description of the Bridegroom as a Nazarite 'on whom ne're Rasor came' recalls the description of the Bible's most notable Nazarite, Samson, who was famed for his uncut hair: 'There neuer came razor vpon mine head: for I am a Nazirite vnto God from my mothers wombe' (Judges 16:17). Samson was frequently linked to Christ typologically because of similarities in the narratives of their births and deaths. Guild explains to his readers that an annunciation preceded Samson and Christ's births, and notes that both men were sold for money, and bound and led away by their captors. Most important to this typological comparison is the fact that Samson and Christ used their deaths as a means of defeating their enemies.[80] Indeed, according to clergyman Edmund Bunny, Samson's life and death mark him as 'a figure of that most holy *Nazarite* to come', Christ, 'that onely true *Nazarite*'.[81] By invoking the purity and significance of the Nazarite vow, and linking the Bridegroom typologically to Samson and to Christ, Quarles' *Sonets* disallows understanding the Bridegroom as merely a besotted human lover.

Typology appears to be central to the attempt in *Sions Sonets* to substantiate the Song's spiritual significance poetically. The Bride is described as 'Faire Daughter of the highest King', suggesting that Quarles accepts the relationship between Solomon and Pharaoh's daughter as the work's historical basis (20:11). A typological interpretation is further

[79] Henry Ainsworth, *Annotations upon the five bookes of Moses, the booke of the Psalmes, and the Song of Songs, or, Canticles* (London: [M. Flesher and J. Haviland], 1627), 169.

[80] Guild, *Moses vnuailed*, 156–9.

[81] Edmund Bunny, *Of the head-corner-stone: by builders still ouer-much omitted that is; a forme of teaching Iesus Christ, out of all the Holy Scriptures* (London: W. Iaggard, 1611), 245.

implicit in the way in which Quarles paraphrases a biblical reference to the Israelite king in Song of Songs 3:11 ('Come forth, ye daughters of Zion, and behold the King Salomon with the crowne'):

> A greater Prince, then *Solomon*, is here,
> The beautie of whose Nuptials, shall appeare
> More glorious farre, transcending his, as farre
> As heauens bright Lamp out-shines th' obscurest Starre. (11:5)

This section of the verse paraphrase accepts the typological trajectory of promise and fulfilment, in that it directs readers from the historical type, Solomon, towards his 'greater' successor, or antitype, Christ. This forward movement is also suggested in the description of the 'greater Prince's' impending 'Nuptials', an allusion to the marriage feast of the Lamb in Revelation 19:7: 'Let vs be glad and reioyce, and give glorie to him: for the marriage of the Lambe is come'. Quarles' 'greater' Prince, termed as 'glorious' and a vision of 'heauens bright lamp', further resonates with John's vision in the Book of Revelation of the 'Sonne of man' with a 'head, & heares . . . white as wooll' and eyes as a 'flame of fire' (Rev. 1:13, 14). By translating the Song's glancing reference to Solomon in 3:11 into a recognizable type of Christ, *Sions Sonets* offers readers both a vision of the Christological antitype and a glimpse of the moment of final fulfilment in his Second Coming.

Having transposed the Song's male lover into a type of the Bridegroom promised by the Book of Revelation, *Sions Sonets* reiterates a typological understanding of historical progress in the closing lines. The final poems draw extensively on the pastoral images and symbolism of John 15:1–6, where Christ describes himself as a vine and God as a 'husband man' (15:1), and the most direct invocation of this biblical intertext is found in the Bridegroom's affirmation: 'I Am thy Gard'ner, Thou my fruitfull Vine' (24:1). As Quarles' Bridegroom paraphrases the words of Christ in John 15, his divine identity is once again affirmed. Yet, these words also signal the beginning of a section where Christ supersedes Solomon as the Bridegroom in Quarles' text. This reading is strongest when the Bridegroom declares to the Bride: 'The vines of *Solomon* were not so faire, / His Grapes were not so precious, as thine are' (24:1). This implied division of the persons of Christ and Solomon is reinforced a line later when the Christ-Bridegroom addresses the figure of Solomon directly: 'O Princely *Solomon*, thy thriuing vine / Is not so faire, so bountifull as mine' (24:2). In this configuration, Quarles' text goes further than implanting textual signifiers that enable the Bridegroom of the Song to be read as Christ. Instead, the closing lines of *Sions Sonets* offer a direct revelation of the spiritually signified, an image of the speaking Christ.

In *Sions Sonets*, the attempt to plug the textual lacuna that exists in reading the Song as a narrative of divine love produces a version of the Song that is less problematic than the biblical source. For in Quarles' work, the reader progresses through a text where the relationship between the Song's erotic words and what they spiritually signify has been made obvious by the insertion of familiar Christological imagery from the New Testament. But the creative effort in *Sions Sonets* to align the Song's signs with what they are assumed to signify has the potential to muddy the divine truth that the work is so concerned to uphold. Because in over-writing the biblical text, Quarles shifts the reader's focus away from the divinely ordained words of scripture towards an alternative version where the Song's erotic signs have been made to 'speak'.[82] The reliability of this speaking version is thrown into doubt when, at various points, *Sions Sonets* involuntarily discloses the incapability of human language to convey divine truth, or capture the reality of spiritual experience. In poem fifteen, for example, Quarles' Bride admits that the depth of her feelings cannot be communicated through writing: 'What curious Pen, what Artist can define / A matelesse sorrow; Such, ah, such was mine' (15:5). In this moment, the impossibility of linguistic precision is captured in the emotive non-word 'ah'. It is an expression that suggests a disparity between what is inwardly felt and what can be outwardly communicated, and, as such, resonates with the nominalist assertion that speech and thought are, as Elsky puts it, 'at odds'.[83]

Sions Sonets points up a fracture in the revelatory process again later in the verse paraphrase of Song of Songs 5:10–16. In this portion of biblical text, the female voice offers an exhaustive description of her lover's body which concludes with an affirmation of her satisfaction with the account: 'this is my wellbeloued, and this is my louer, O daughters of Ierusalem' (Songs 5:16). In *Sions Sonets*, however, the Bride's description of the Bridegroom falters, suggesting a breakdown in the representative process. This failure is encapsulated in the aborted praise of the Bridegroom's body. Quarles' Bride stops before she gets to the final description in the biblical text, her lover's mouth ('his mouth *is as* sweete things' (Songs 5:16)):

> His Mouth-But stay; What need my lips be lauish,
> In choice of wordes, when one alone will rauish?
> But shall, in briefe, my ruder tongue discouer
> The speaking Image of my absent Louer? (17:7)

[82] Foucault, *The Order of Things*, 33. [83] Elsky, *Authorizing Words*, 33.

In these lines, the Bride articulates a frustration that the 'speaking image', or what Elsky terms, 'mental language', cannot be distilled into words.[84] Indeed, she seems to experience how 'the act of speech is a moment of struggle between the mental articulation of a thought and its expression in the sounds of convention-bound speech'.[85] In her overt expression of the failure of words to capture the mental image, Quarles' Bride wrestles with the consequences of the separation between *res* and *verba*. As language is no longer understood to be a transparent signifier of things, human representation of the divine is forever destined to fall short.[86] In many senses, the Bride's verbal struggle in *Sions Sonets* becomes emblematic of the challenges facing Quarles as a biblical interpreter. Like his Bride, Quarles too must confront the inadequacy of language to capture, and human paraphrase to contain, the magnitude of divine truth.

It is perhaps because of the intrinsic insufficiency of words that Quarles' text periodically leans towards a more mystical revelation of Christ. This tendency emerges most forcefully in the moments when the Bride of *Sions Sonets* ruminates on the sensory appeal of her lover. She explains that he 'enrich[es] the aire' with 'delitious sweetnesse' and notes how virgins are overwhelmed by seeing him: 'Virgins fixe their eyes vpon thee, / And all that view thee, are enamour'd on thee' (1:2). This latter description is important because it implies a link between sensory stimulation and experiencing Christ. This notion re-emerges more overtly in the Bridegroom's account of the effect of his body on his lover:

> I am Hee, whom thy chaste soule admires;
> The Rose, for smell; the Lily, to the eye,
> Is not so sweet, is not so faire as I;
> My vailed beautie's not the glorious prize
> Of common sight. (6:1)

In these lines, Quarles' Christological Bridegroom comes into view through sensory contemplation of the components of his body, and the emotional response stirred by this meditation is connected to a spiritual, rather than physical arousal, that of the 'chaste soule'. The efficacy of the meditative process is affirmed more directly by the Bride, who elsewhere pleads 'O, Let the beautie of thy Sunne-like face / Inflame my soule' (1:3). In suggesting that contemplation of this Bridegroom-Christ has spiritual consequences, *Sions Sonets* garners, at this juncture at least, a more Catholic aesthetic.

[84] Elsky, *Authorizing Words*, 32. [85] Elsky, *Authorizing Words*, 33.
[86] See Foucault's discussion of this shift in relation to Babel in *The Order of Things*, 40–1.

This confessional ambiguity does not necessarily suggest that Quarles had covert Catholic sympathies; rather, these mystical moments seem to be precipitated by the text's inherent struggle with the deficiencies of the interpretative process.[87] As the paraphrasing process is perforated intermittently by a realization of the limitations of language for articulating the divine, *Sonets* briefly seeks hermeneutic refuge in the experiential. In these instances, the visual and sensory seem more attainable, or at least more straightforward, than verbal or written expressions of the divine. More broadly, Quarles' *Sonets* illuminates how reformed exegesis on the Song could resonate with the common medieval conception of the work as, what Lewalski terms, a 'paradigm of the contemplative life or of the mystical experience'.[88] Indeed, by embracing a figural interpretation of the Song, Quarles' *Sonets* further demonstrates that the reformers produced exegesis that, in essence, had much in common with their allegorizing predecessors.

Nevertheless, despite this dalliance with an alternative representative system, Quarles' text ultimately retreats to a more conventional, reformed reliance on words. In the end, the alignment of sign and spiritually signified in the Song must depend on words, and so the lengthy interpretative process continues. The closing admission of Quarles' Bride is suggestive of this perpetuating cycle: 'My heart's the vowed Seruant of thy Word' (25:1). While it is out of 'service' to the Word that *Sions Sonets* works to substantiate the Song's spiritual signification textually, the paraphrase suggests that the Word is not enough. Stuffed with the divine signifiers that the Song of Songs so obviously lacks, *Sions Sonets* fantasizes about a world, and a biblical text, where words and truth resemble one another and provide a straightforward revelation.[89] The illusory nature of such a world is revealed when the paraphrase is forced to acknowledge the innate insufficiencies of language. In these brief moments, *Sions Sonets* concedes that representation and divine truth are inherently incompatible.

[87] For consideration of Quarles' Protestantism see Streete, 'Frances Quarles' Early Poetry', 88–108.

[88] Lewalski, 'Typology and Poetry', 59. See, for example, Francis de Sales, *The Mystical Explanation of the Canticle of Canticles*, trans. Henry B. Mackay (London: Burns & Oates, 1908). For consideration of the medieval contemplative approach to scripture more generally see John C. Hirsh, *The Boundaries of Faith: The Development and Transmission of Medieval Spirituality* (Leiden: E. J. Brill, 1996). For a popular Catholic text that encouraged using the senses to understand the scriptures see *Ignatius Loyola: The Spiritual Exercises and Selected Works*, ed. G. E. Ganss (London: Paulist Press, 1991).

[89] See Foucault, *The Order of Things*, 40–6.

TRUTH AND THE WORD

Many of the interpretative paradoxes at play in reformed exegesis of the Song of Songs are encapsulated in the allegorical quest of the wandering soul in Robert Aylett's *The Song of Songs, which was Salomons metaphrased in English heroiks by way of dialogue. With certayne of the brides ornaments* (1621). Although Aylett's 'English heroik', which is written in an allegorical style similar to Edmund Spenser's *The Faerie Queene* and John Bunyan's *Pilgrim's Progress*, is, in form and concept, rather different to the works considered earlier, its engagement with the Song of Songs reveals a similar concern with the instability of the representative process.[90] The work opens with a verse translation of the eight-chapter Song refiguring it as a dialogue between Christ and the Church, after which Aylett begins an epic charting the expedition of the poem's male speaker to the Court of Heavenly Love. The male voice records how, over the course of his journey, he meets a series of women, such as Humilitie and Courage, who aid his progress towards the Queene of Heavenly Love. This spiritual quest for religious salvation is, as Flinker observes, achieved 'by means of feminine figures who appeal to [the] narrator as attractive women before he can learn anything of their allegorical import'.[91] For example, the lady Humilitie illuminates the speaker's pride and ambition, thereby enabling him to conquer these vices and continue his journey towards the lady Repentance.[92] The journey and experiences of Aylett's narrator reverberate with the lovers' concerns in the Song. The Bride's search 'in the citie, by the strets & by the open places' to seek him who her 'soule loueth' (Songs 3:2) is amplified in the lengthy expedition of Aylett's narrator to the Queene of Heavenly Love. He begins the opening Proem with the admission: 'Long time I sought Loues Court most carefully.'[93] In many senses the speaker's quest for salvation, or Christ, in the poetic narrative embodies the struggle of

[90] For parallels between Aylett's work and the *Faerie Queene* see Flinker, *The Song of Songs*, 100–20.

[91] Flinker, *The Song of Songs*, 103.

[92] See Flinker, *The Song of Songs*, 100–20, for more on the significance of these allegorical women. The development of the narrator in Aylett's epic is in keeping with reformed readings of the Song that, as Lewalski suggests, understood the book as a 'paradigm of the typical Christian life from the time of effective calling or regeneration . . . through the uneven course of spiritual triumphs and failure which mark the process of sanctification': 'Typology and Poetry', 59. See, for example, John Dove's *Conversion of Solomon* which claims that the Song provides 'the direction to holinesse of life' (t.p.).

[93] Aylett, *The Song of Songs*, 21, Proem 4. Subsequent references to the epic are given in the main body of the chapter and have been formatted according to the book, meditation, and verse numbers provided in Aylett's published work.

the interpreter tasked with locating spiritual truth in the Song of Songs. Indeed, the uncertainty of interpretative processes gives rise to the poem's internal commentary on the efficacy of writing in the speaker's quest for salvation.

The first hint of the spiritual significance of the writerly process emerges at the end of the opening verification of the Song, the conclusion of which prompts the speaker to praise his 'Maker' for 'this holy Meditation / Of heau'nly Loue' (1.1.75–6). It is unclear, however, whether the object of this praise is the Song of Songs, or the poetic rewriting of the biblical text that has just been concluded. This ambiguity intensifies in the following stanza when the speaker prays that he might 'not become a reprobate' and asks:

> But grant that as this Song I doe relate
> Of heau'nly Loue, it may my Soule here moue
> To be as true as Turtle to her Mate:
> That neuer worldly cares my heart remoue
> From this most precious Pearle. (1.1.77)

Once again, the speaker's words have two possible meanings. On the one hand, 'this Song' may refer to the Song of Songs, extended to encompass Aylett's own versification of the scriptural text. On the other, it may describe the poetic work alone, and particularly the forthcoming epic, which subsumes the identity of the biblical Song. Both readings, however, imbue the act of writing with spiritual significance, presenting it as a means of anchoring the soul in the face of worldly trials. The suggestion that the process of writing has some degree of spiritual efficacy returns again in the fourth meditation, when the speaker's contemplation of the lady Faith provokes a physical reaction: 'My ioynts doe tremble, and mine heart doth quake, / When I Faiths wondrous works begin to write' (1.4.58). The connections implied between body, soul, and pen are affirmed in subsequent lines when the act of writing gives rise to an alteration in the speaker's spiritual state: 'Shee from the sleepe of sinne doth me awake' prompting 'Sinnes fogs and mists of errour . . . away' (1.4.58), and later, in Meditation Five, where writing is credited with the solidification of hope: 'First of Hope Faiths daughter next in sight: / And make my Hope stand stedfast whilst of Hope I write' (1.5.4).

These brief suggestions that the writerly process is spiritually effectual open out into a more sustained evaluation of language itself in Book Two of *The Brides Ornaments*. Here, when attempting to describe Mercy, the speaker pointedly laments: 'But ah! no pen is able' (2.3.32). This exclamation is part of the speaker's growing frustration that the poetic product cannot attest to the reality of what he seeks to communicate; he concedes:

But vaine it is to thinke by likelinesse
Of earthly things, to type out things Diuine,
Since none her heau'nly Nature can expresse,
But who the God-head can aright define. (2.1.48)

These lines acknowledge the flawed capacity of the human mind to comprehend, and express, 'things Diuine', a sentiment which resonates strongly with the Christian doctrine that after the Fall humanity will, as Calvin states, 'lack the natural ability' to ascertain 'clear knowledge of God'.[94] As Aylett's work accepts the impossibility of bringing definition to the divine through earthly comparisons, it, much like Quarles' *Sonets*, articulates a gap between verbal and written expression and God. In doing so, Aylett's *Song* affirms that the division of *res* and *verba*, as Shuger explains, 'distance[s] text from reader' and parallels 'a separation of sign from signified dividing visible form from spiritual substance'.[95] Aylett's speaker, in suggesting that the divine and earthly are two extremes or, as Copenhaver and Schmitt term, 'at two end points', identifies an unbreachable divide. And it is a recognition of this fault line that forces the speaker to confront the flaws in the representative process, and the futility of his own writing, more overtly in the remaining account of his journey.[96] The speaker's realization of the deficiency of words prompts a poetic crisis, somewhat aptly, in the meditation dedicated to the lady Truth. Almost immediately, he bemoans the impossibility of describing Truth in words: 'My bounded Muse here dareth not define / Of boundlesse Truth from all Eternitie, / Which as impossibles to mete by Line' (2.2.7). The enormity of the task forces the speaker to conclude that his poetic endeavour is futile because Truth, he explains, resides not in matter but in the divine: 'Truth in all's compar'd to God alone, / And none but God her glorie can declare' (2.2.42). Yet, in spite of this admission, Aylett's narrator continues to cling to the flawed vehicle of language, producing a further five stanzas that work to define truth as manifest in 'Iudgement, Action, Speech and... Heart' (2.2.9). Clearly, truth must be comprehensible, tangible, and expressible for the salvific journey to progress. The speaker's continuing attempt to describe truth gives rise to a further acknowledgement of the insurmountable nature of the task. Taking the reader back to the Fall and to the actions of 'Our two first Parents', he reminds that only 'Corrupted words and actions' are possible from the human heart (2.2.19). Language, as an

94 Calvin, *Institutes*, 68, 1.5.15.

95 Shuger, *Habits of Thought*, 37. For further discussion of debates about the nature of language in the early modern period see Pendergast, *Religion, Allegory, and Literacy*, 102–15.

96 Copenhaver and Schmitt, *Renaissance Philosophy*, 152.

expression of humanity's corrupt perception, is once more deemed to be innately incapable of embodying divine truth.

Having accepted the impossibility of accurately conveying truth in words, the speaker's profound discomfort with the consequences of this reality moves into view. Indeed, a recognition of the unreliability of language causes his spiritual progress to falter momentarily when he pauses to reflect on a time when truth resided not in words, but within the confines of the Church its 'carefull Keeper' (2.2.20). In this moment, the narrative ruminates on the repercussions of the religious Reformation of the sixteenth century which shifted the locus of truth away from a visibly unified church with centuries of tradition.[97] While the speaker initially finds refuge in the thought that truth may reside within the perimeters of an ecclesiastical institution, he soon recalls that the 'false Ornaments of the Church of Rome, / Like painted Harlot, shuns the open Light' (2.2.22). This supposed rejection of 'light', or truth, is, in line with conventional reformed opinion, attributed to a lack of dependence on the Bible. For as he goes on to explain, under Rome 'poore Laiks' are prevented from having 'sight / of holy Writ, to frame their judgement by' (2.2.22). It is, then, after consideration of an alternative locus of truth that the speaker retreats to his search for truth in the 'certayne ground' of scripture (2.4.5). Yet this search ground is not as 'certayne' as Aylett's speaker anticipates. Indeed, only a few stanzas later, he stumbles upon the weak spot in ascertaining truth from the scriptures—the human interpreter:

> Truth hath not so many Friends,
> ... For Satan all his malice 'gainst her bends,
> Supplanting Her by force or subtilties.
> ... And therefore they maliciously deuise
> Interpretations false, and glosses vaine,
> Traditions, mens inuentions, 'gainst her to maintaine. (2.2.29)

While this attack on 'interpretations false' and 'glosses vaine' is aimed at the Roman Catholic Church with its doctrines of 'Puragorie' and 'Limbo', it is difficult not to read in these lines a critique of exegetical processes more generally (2.2.29–30). Irrespective of confessional identity, truth may be bent by 'mens inuentions'. Indeed, as an imaginative '[re]inuention' of the Song of Songs, Aylett's work stands accused of many of the interpretative crimes the speaker cites. Both the poetic verification of the Song and allegorical epic function as an extended 'gloss' on the biblical text—at times becoming indistinguishable from it—as Aylett, like Baldwin and

[97] On the broader significance of this loss see Shuger, *Habits of Thought*, 122–3.

Quarles, works to 'supplant' the eroticism of the Song's words. Furthermore, in censuring Catholicism's interpretative dependence on 'mens inuentions' the speaker problematically suggests that reformed exegesis is, conversely, objective, or unmediated. In reality, however, the literal readings of the reformers are, as Durham's commentary on the Song acknowledges, equally reliant upon the perceptive abilities of the biblical commentator. Interpretation, whether Catholic or Protestant, will always be mediated by the writer's intention.

The intention of Aylett's speaker is, he explains in the closing stanza, the embellishment of the Bride: 'I to adorne the Bride doe offer here / These Ornaments' (2.5.52). What this poetic work and others like it on the Song seeks to accomplish is the textual adornment of the biblical narrative with signifiers of spiritual meaning. The ornamentation Aylett constructs for this purpose is considerable—two books of poetry, each containing ten meditations comprised of an average of seventy-five, nine-line verses, a total of 320 pages. The inference of Aylett's offering is clear; the Song of Songs, problematic as it is, necessitates human interpretation and compels textual embellishment. The result, as the speaker's closing remarks suggest, is that Aylett's *Song* comes to embody the textual impasse the reformers faced. Insufficient though they are, words are the only means available to clarify biblical truth.

Poetic responses to the Song of Songs like Aylett's illuminate how the apparent absence of divine meaning in this biblical text presented reformed exegetes with a number of interpretative challenges. For not only was God's message to the faithful uncertain, but problematically hidden in a sensual account of human intimacy. Unwilling to accept the presence of a purely erotic text in scripture, and fearful of the distracting potential of the Song's sensual imagery, the literalist reformers retreated from the meaning obviously implied by the Song's words. The spiritual meanings they espoused point up the complexity, but also the malleability, of the reformers' literal sense, for in the case of the Song, reformed 'literalism' was readily expanded to accommodate highly figurative readings of the text's erotic contents. Indeed, in this biblical text, Protestant interpreters seem to embrace allegory willingly as a means of sanitizing the Song's contents. In the case of the Song of Songs, allegory is no longer the distorting methodology that, for many reformers, encapsulated the hermeneutic failings of the medieval and Roman Catholic Church, but an interpretative conduit through which the Song's erotic signs could be aligned with the divinely signified. Yet in the process of justifying the discretionary use of an exegetical methodology that they elsewhere maligned, reformed biblical commentators expose the subjective nature of the entire interpretative process. The certitude of the Song's meaning problematically relies, to use Durham's term, on 'similitudes'. As such, the process of ascertaining the Song's spiritual truth, that which is divinely 'intended', always remains reliant on the perceptive capabilities of the fallen human mind. This instability manifests itself in elaborate, textually tenuous readings, wherein it is difficult to discern how the exegetical outworking of the reformers' broadened literal sense is anything other than semantically different from figurative interpretations.

By obsessively overwriting and rewriting the biblical narrative, writers such as Baldwin and Quarles worked to remove space for individual interpretation of the Song, and produce versions of the biblical text suited to the carnally inclined minds of their readers. Yet the process of producing these safeguarded versions of the Song demonstrates, as Foucault explains, that 'commentary resembles endlessly that which it is commenting upon and which it can never express'.[98] As interpreters strived to provide the appropriate number and combination of words to fix the Song's spiritual message textually, they are ultimately forced to confront the incapacity of words to embody, or even reflect, the gravity of what they seek to communicate. But the failure of language to elucidate the Song's signs also illuminates a larger flaw in the reformed reliance on words. Language, as Quarles and Aylett's poetry affirms, stands at an extremity from thought, and therefore is perpetually incapable of capturing the meaning to which it is directed. For reformed commentators, however, the word remains the only acceptable source of consolation and truth. As such, the endless textual attempt to connect sign and signified emerges from a hope that one day the stream of textual similitudes will give way to the thing itself, an authoritative 'literal' meaning.

[98] Foucault, *The Order of Things*, 46.

5

Typologies of Marian Maternity

Literal and Spiritual Birth in Seventeenth-Century Women's Writing

In the set of prayers dedicated for use during childbirth in Thomas Bentley's *Monument of Matrons* (1582) the woman experiencing the 'nips, pinches, and pangs' of labour is encouraged to ruminate on the words spoken to 'Our grand-mother Eue, and in hir to vs all; I will increase thy sorowe, when thou art with child: with paine shalt thou bring foorth thy children'.[1] Within these prayers, Eve alone is the antecedent of the expectant mother and it is significant that biblical matriarchs such as Sara, Hannah, Bathsheba, and Christ's mother, Mary, who are elsewhere commended to the reader as exemplars of 'motherlie and carefull affection', disappear from view.[2] As the sorrowing mother experiences the legacy of Eve's sin in Genesis, she has, according to the schema of the prayers, cause to reflect on her own transgression: 'our sins ... hath made [labour] to be dangerous, painefull, and full of perill, which thou didst laie vpon our grand-mother Eue, and vpon all vs hir posteritie, as a correction and punishment for sin: and therefore I confesse deere God, that through my manifold sins, I haue not onlie deserued this thy rod of correction, but far sorer, and more greeuous punishment'.[3] Recollection of the Bible's first mother drives the sorrowing woman to claim Eve's sin as 'our sin', and induces a moment of confession that accepts the pains of labour as a deserved punishment for personal wrongs. As the bequest of a guilty foremother, labour pain becomes in these prayers evidence of women's continuation in sin.

Bentley's elision of labour pain with female sin both past and present is by no means exceptional.[4] In her study of early modern attitudes towards

[1] Thomas Bentley, *The fift lampe of virginitie conteining sundrie forms of christian praiers and meditations* (London: H. Denham, 1582), 96.

[2] Bentley, *The monument of matrones*, B2r.

[3] Bentley, *The fift lampe*, 102.

[4] For additional examples, see Henry Ainsworth, *The orthodox foundation of religion* (London: R.C., 1641), and John Hamilton, *A Facil traictise ... Dedicate to his soverain*

reproduction, Mary E. Fissell notes that, after the Reformation, women were regularly called to 'identify with Eve' whereas in the medieval period, they commonly 'identified themselves with the Virgin by going to Mass, praying specifically to her, and wearing relics or sanctified objects related to her'.[5] While totalizing assessments that suggest an acute pre-/post-Reformation shift in Mary's significance have been shown to be problematic, Fissell is one of a number of scholars who continue to suggest that the importance of Mary's motherhood, and more specifically, the processes of her maternal body, was reduced in the wake of the Reformation.[6] The intense theological speculation on the significance of anatomical changes to Mary's birth canal or the mystical properties of her breast milk that characterized medieval and later Roman Catholic writings,[7] gave way to a denial of the efficacy of the physical processes of the Marian body, and a more general praise of her piety and faith in the work of reformists.[8] And, as the miraculous connotations of Mary's pregnancy and labour faded, there were consequences for female bodies more generally; in essence, as Fissell quips, 'the womb went bad'.[9]

Prince, the Kings Majestie of Scotland, King James the Saxt, in *Catholic Tractates of the Sixteenth Century, 1573–1600*, ed. Thomas Graves Law (Edinburgh: W. Blackwood & Sons, 1901), 226.

[5] Mary Fissell, *Vernacular Bodies: The Politics of Reproduction in Early Modern England* (Oxford: Oxford University Press, 2004), 46.

[6] Recent studies that have illuminated Mary's continuing importance among reformers, and disavowed any straightforward erasure of her presence in early modern England and those parts of Europe that accepted religious reform, include: George Henry Tavard, *The 1000 Faces of the Virgin Mary* (Collegeville, MN: Liturgical Press, 1996); Bridget Heal, *The Cult of the Virgin Mary in Early Modern Germany: Protestant and Catholic* (Cambridge: Cambridge University Press, 2007); Gary Waller, *The Virgin Mary in Late Medieval and Early Modern English Literature and Popular Culture* (Cambridge: Cambridge University Press, 2011). For scholarship beyond Fissell that suggests that the significance of Marian motherhood was reduced by religious reform see Tina Beattie, *God's Mother, Eve's Advocate: A Marian Narrative of Women's Salvation* (London: Continuum, 2002); Donna S. Ellington, *From Sacred Body to Angelic Soul: Understanding Mary in Late Medieval and Early Modern Europe* (Washington, DC: Catholic University of America Press, 2001).

[7] For an example of this manner of reading Mary's body see Gaspar Loarte, *Instructions and aduertisements, how to meditate the misteries of the rosarie of the most holy Virgin Mary* (London: W. Carter, 1597), and for an overview of Roman Catholic understanding of the Virgin's body see Ellington, *From Sacred Body*, 48–59; Waller, *The Virgin Mary*, 33–5; Julia Kristeva, 'Stabat Mater', in *The Female Body in Western Culture: Contemporary Perspectives*, ed. Susan R. Suleiman (Cambridge, MA: Harvard University Press, 1986), 99–118.

[8] It is not, then, that Protestants abandoned discussion of the biological processes of Mary's body but that attention to them became part of a rejection of Roman Catholic emphasis on the miraculous nature of the Marian body. For more on this distinction see Heal, *The Cult of the Virgin Mary;* 64–115; Waller, *The Virgin Mary*, 55–79.

[9] Fissell, *Vernacular Bodies*, 54. Other scholars have similarly noted that reformed attitudes towards Mary had consequences for women. See Beattie, *God's Mother*, 131; Patricia Crawford, *Women and Religion in England 1500–1720* (London and New York:

Bentley's prayers for the labouring woman are suggestive of the way in which readings of Eve, cursed in Genesis 3:16 to bear children 'in sorowe', contributed to a souring of the maternal functions of the female body.[10] An emphasis on Eve's maternity renders the womb a site of sin, rather than salvation, and its denigrated position is a concern of female writers who sought to reconceive the status of women and motherhood in early seventeenth-century England. Aemilia Lanyer, in her prefatory letter to the reader in *Salve Deus Rex Judaeorum* (1611), chastises those men who 'doe like Vipers deface the wombes wherein they were bred, forgetting that they were borne of women, nourished of women, and that if it were not by the means of women they would be quite extinguished out of the world'.[11] In *The Mothers Blessing*, which went through twenty-three editions after its publication in 1616, Dorothy Leigh suggests a similar depreciation of the maternal body. She reminds her readers that, although Eve was a mother who brought 'great and wofull shame' to all women, Mary's maternity 'broght vs a Sauiour'.[12] As Leigh's comparison suggests, an assessment of motherhood that is properly orientated in scripture will acknowledge the historic importance of Mary's maternal contribution as well as Eve's sin. For both Lanyer and Leigh, a re-evaluation of the female body turns on the Marian body because it alone facilitated Christ's humanity. Mary, without man, provides the material substance necessary for redemption and her fleshly contribution is found to mark the maternal body as a site of spiritual significance. Reading the Bible, Lanyer and Leigh determine that Mary's material labour has spiritual consequences, because, in delivering Christ, she delivers God's plan for salvation to the earth and inaugurates the new covenant. Because this covenant fulfils that which was promised in the Old Testament, it must, according to biblical typology,

Routledge, 1993), 47; Dolan, *Whores of Babylon*, 121–2; Christopher Hill, *Society and Puritanism in Pre-Revolutionary England* (New York: St. Martin's Press, 1997), 389.

[10] It should be said that Eve's actions in the opening chapters of scripture made Genesis a central proof-text in debates on gender in the early modern period. This biblical book became, as Barbara McManus explains, 'the foundation of Renaissance discourse about the essential nature and function of women': 'Eve's Dowry: Genesis and Pamphlet Controversies about Women', in *Women, Writing, and the Reproduction of Culture in Tudor and Stuart Britain*, ed. Mary Burke, Jane Donawerth, Linda Dove, and Karen Nelson (Syracuse: Syracuse University Press, 1999), 193–4. For more on how Eve was read in the period see Philip Almond, *Adam and Eve in Seventeenth-Century Thought* (Cambridge: Cambridge University Press, 1999), 143–209.

[11] Lanyer, *Salve Deus Rex Judaeorum*, ed. Woods, 48. As the dedicatory poems are numbered separately in this edition of *Salve Deus*, poetic references cite the page number followed by the line number. All further references to this text will be given in the main body of the chapter.

[12] Leigh, *The mothers blessing*, 35–6. All further references to this text will be given in the main body of the chapter.

atone for Eve's sin. But these writers also suggest that the new covenant initiates a form of maternity that has, within the Christological dispensation, profound spiritual resonance.[13] For if, as *Salve Deus* and *The Mothers Blessing* advocate, the Bible is read typologically, Marian maternity becomes a mechanism of deliverance, and the inheritance of the 'Mother of our Lord' becomes a motherhood rich in spiritual issue and consequence (95: 1031).

MARIAN TYPOLOGIES AND THE LABOUR OF FEMALE FLESH

As an interpretative practice, typology was, from its New Testament inception, bound up with ideas about the maternal body. In Galatians, the apostle Paul supports his rebuke of those Christians who insisted that observance of the law was necessary for salvation with a re-reading of the Old Testament narratives of Hagar and Sarah (Gen. 16–18).[14] For him,

[13] Although a number of scholars have referenced Lanyer's use of biblical typology within larger considerations of her engagement with the Bible's contents (Micheline White, 'A Woman with Saint Peter's Keys?: Aemilia Lanyer's *Salve Deus Rex Judaeroum* (1611) and the Priestly Gifts of Women', *Criticism* 45.3 (2003): 323–41; Theresa M. DiPasquale, 'Woman's Desire for Man in Lanyer's *Salve Deus Rex Judaeorum*', *Journal of English and Germanic Philology* 99.3 (2000): 356–78; Marie H. Loughlin, '"Fast ti'd unto them in a golden chain": Typology, Apocalypse and Women's Genealogy in Aemilia Lanyer's *Salve Deus Rex Judaeorum*', *Renaissance Quarterly* 1 (2000): 133–79), there has not been a sustained interrogation of how the structures of this exegetical practice underpin the poem's conception of literal and spiritual maternity, and facilitate the relationship constructed between the Old and New Testaments. Other scholars who have more broadly considered how the Bible shapes Lanyer's poetic project include: Kari Boyd McBride and John C. Ulreich, 'Answerable Styles: Biblical Poetics and Biblical Politics in the Poetry of Lanyer and Milton', *Journal of English and Germanic Philology* 100. 3 (2001): 333–53; Patricia Phillippy, 'Sisters of Magdalen: Women's Mourning in Aemilia Lanyer's *Salve Deus Rex Judaeorum*', *English Literary Renaissance* 31.1 (2001): 78–106; Erica Longfellow, *Women and Religious Writing in Early Modern England* (Cambridge: Cambridge University Press, 2004), 59–91; John Rogers, 'The Passion of a Female Literary Tradition: Aemilia Lanyer's "Salve Deus Rex Judæorum"', *Huntington Library Quarterly* 63.4 (2000): 435–46. Leigh's work has been considered in relation to genre and female writing (Valerie Wayne, 'Advice for Women from Mothers and Patriarchs', in *Women and Literature in Britain, 1500–1700*, ed. Helen Wilcox (Cambridge: Cambridge University Press, 1996), 56–79; Kristen Poole, '"The fittest closet for all goodness": Authorial Strategies of Jacobean Mothers' Manuals', *Studies in English Literature* 35.1 (1995): 69–88) but discussion of how the Bible is read in *The mothers blessing* remains limited. Notable exceptions include sections of Catherine Gray's 'Feeding on the Seed of the Woman: Dorothy Leigh and the Figure of Maternal Dissent', *English Literary History* 68 (2001): 563–92, and Elaine V. Beilin's *Redeeming Eve: Women Writers of the English Renaissance* (Princeton: Princeton University Press, 1987), 177–207, although neither addresses typology directly.

[14] For more on the history of typology, and the understanding of the place of the Old Testament within this interpretative framework, see Chapter 1, pp. 28–37, 42–6. For

the maternity of these women proves that to continue in the law is to misinterpret its announcement of the new covenant under Christ:

> Tell me, ye that will be vnder the Law, doe ye not heare the Lawe? For it is written, that Abraham had two sonnes, one by a seruant, and one by a freewoman. But he which was of the seruantt, was borne after the flesh: and he which was of the free woman, *was borne* by promes. By the which things another thing is ment: for these *mothers* are the two testaments, the one which is Agar of mount Sina, which gendereth vnto bondage. (For Agar *or* Sina is a mountaine in Arabia, and it answereth to Hierusalem which nowe is) and she is in bondage with her children. But Hierusulem, which is aboue, is free: which is the mother of vs all. For it is written, Reioyce thou barren that bearest no children: breake forth, & cry, thou that trauailest not: for the desolate hath many moe children, then she which hath an husband. Therefore, brethren, we are after the manner of Isaac, children of the promes.
> (Gal. 4: 21–8)

Read in light of Christ, Paul finds 'another thing is ment' by the Genesis narrative and understands Hagar and Sarah as figures for the old and new covenants, here termed 'testaments'. Sarah, understood as a figure of the New Jerusalem that is a spiritual, heavenly community, gives birth to a child of 'promes', Isaac, who is a type of those who are born according to the spirit, rather than 'the flesh'. The analogy between that which was promised by the law and that which was fulfilled by Christ turns, then, on a distinction between flesh and spirit, and it is one that teaches, as John Calvin explained in a comment on this passage, that children of the new covenant do not hope in 'carnal, earthly, and temporal things, but in ... spiritual, heavenly and eternal benefits'.[15] According to Paul's exegesis, living under the law is akin to being born of the flesh; both are merely a shadow, or a type, of spiritual rebirth.[16]

For many sixteenth- and seventeenth-century commentators, however, Paul's understanding of the hermeneutic relationship between Old Testament shadow and Christological fulfilment did more than authorize a reciprocal reading of scripture's two Testaments. Commenting on Galatians 4:22–8, William Perkins explained that Paul speaks of those in his time who 'went about to establish their owne righteousnesse by the

Paul's understanding of the law beyond Galatians 3–4, see Colossians 2:17, the letter to the Romans, as well as II Corinthians 3:13–18 and Hebrews 10:1.

[15] Calvin, *Institutes*, 459, 2.11.10. For a detailed consideration of how this passage from Galatians was interpreted by reformers, and on Paul's reading of this passage of Genesis more generally, see Luxon, *Reforming Figures*, 16, 77–96.

[16] Before Paul, the distinction between a birth of the flesh and that of the spirit was made by Jesus who explained to Nicodemus the need to be 'born again' to 'see the kingdom of God': John 3:3.

lawe . . . And the Papists of our time, who will not be subiect to the iustice of God, but set vp their owne iustice in the keeping of the law'.[17] Following the apostle's example, Perkins finds that 'another thing' is meant by Paul's words; the enslavement of Hagar and the Galatians foreshadows those who continue to live in bondage in 'our time'. Perkins' expansion of Paul's typology of Genesis to include the early modern present speaks to the inclusion of contemporary history within a continuing process of typological fulfilment, a firmly established practice by the early seventeenth century.[18] While the extended application of this reading practice was commonplace among clerics like Perkins, understanding the present as part of the Bible's omnipresent history was by no means confined to the work of churchmen and theologians, or indeed the lay writings of men. Female readers without formal training in hermeneutics responded to the typologizing imperative, and Molekamp's study of *Women and the Bible in Early Modern England* (2013) has demonstrated the extent to which women, with varying levels of education, engaged 'in non-linear modes of reading the scriptures. These included typological readings of the Bible, liturgical readings, and repetitive, meditative readings'.[19] Among their female contemporaries, Lanyer and Leigh's awareness of the central tenets of biblical typology may not, then, be considered exceptional. Yet, both writers' sustained application of this knowledge to produce readings that are as sophisticated as they are innovative is certainly remarkable, and has much to say about the way in which typology underpinned the alternative biblical readings and altered theologies that emerge in female exegesis of the seventeenth century.

For Dorothy Leigh in *The Mothers Blessing*, typology facilitates an intricate reinterpretation of scripture that is to the advantage of mothers as well as her own writing project. The centrality of the Bible to Leigh's conception of her work is declared on the title page with the words of King Solomon in Proverbs 1:8: 'My sonne, heare the instruction of thy father, and forsake not the lawe of thy mother.' Quoting from a biblical book that, as this verse and the later inclusion of Bathsheba's instructions to Lemuel (Prov. 31:1–9) suggest, affords space and significance to maternal, as well as paternal, wisdom, Leigh begins the work of aligning her maternal advice with biblical models of motherly instruction. Within this endeavour, Christ's mother, Mary, is paramount. Leigh arrives at her consideration of Marian maternity via a discussion of the exemplary

17 Perkins, *A Commentarie or Exposition*, 342.
18 For an overview of typology's expansion to include the present see Chapter 1, pp. 30–4.
19 Molekamp, *Women and the Bible*, 15.

chastity of Susanna whose story is told in Daniel 13.[20] Readers are encouraged to 'bee, as [Susanna] was, chaest, watchfull, and wary' and it is this initial concern for the preservation of female chastity that prompts a recollection of that 'woman vertuous aboue all other women', Mary (33–4). While Leigh wishes that 'all women . . . woule learne of this blessed Virgin to bee chaste', it becomes clear that Mary's significance extends beyond her suitability as the archetypal female exemplar when she is declared a site of 'blessing . . . to vs women' (37).

Leigh understands Mary to be a source of 'blessing' specifically because her contribution to biblical history absolves women from the legacy of Genesis: 'through that gracious Virgin . . . it pleased GOD to take away the shame, vvhich EVE our Grandmother had brought vs to' (35). In this reading, Mary functions as a typological counterbalance to Eve's sin and, her position as such, permanently alters how the Genesis narrative is to be interpreted: 'For before, men might say, The woman beguiled me, and I did eate the poysoned fruit of disobedience, and I dye. But now man may say, if he say truly, The woman brought me a Sauiour . . . *The seede of the woman hath taken downe the Serpents head*; and now whosoeuer can take hold of the seed of the woman by faith, shall surely liue for euer' (35–6). Offsetting Eve's provision of sin with Mary's provision of a Saviour, Leigh stresses that the connections she discerns in these women's narratives is biblically inscribed. Her paraphrase of Genesis 2:15 ('I will also put enimitie between thee and the womá, & between thy sede and her sede. He shal breake thine head, & thou shalt bruise his heele') is a sharp reminder that God not only appointed a woman to a seminal role in his plan for salvation, but chose to reveal this at the beginning of biblical history.

Unsurprisingly, this biblical verse was important to other women writers who similarly sought to ground a reconsideration of Eve's sin in wider biblical readings. For Rachel Speght, writing in response to Joseph Swetnam's attack on women through Eve, Genesis 2:15 points to an alternative biblical legacy for women and shifts attention away from Eve's punishment towards that which absolves it: 'the first promise that was made in Paradise, God makes to woman . . . that as the woman had beene an occasion of his sinne, so should woman bring foorth the

[20] Daniel 13 was included in the Apocryphal section of the Geneva Bible and King James Bible, and appeared in the Vulgate as well as the Douay Rheims translation. Leigh and her readers would also have been familiar with Susanna because she was popularly invoked in discussions of female behaviour, commonplace books, and conduct manuals, as well as sermons and art. Several stanzas in *Salve Deus* are also devoted to Susanna. For consideration of these verses, and how Susanna is positioned as an antecedent of the Countess of Cumberland, see DiPasquale, 'Woman's Desire for Man', 365–9.

Sauiour'.[21] Writing later, Alice Sutcliffe's lengthy admonishment of Eve's disobedience gives way to an acknowledgement of the significance of this promise: 'Yet courage Woman, . . . / thy Seed / . . . shall Sathan deadly wound.'[22] As these examples attest, a right reading of Eve's punishment will include Genesis 2:15. But, more specially as Leigh's lines suggest, it will precipitate a recognition of that which was promised to Eve reaching fruition in the body of Mary. Drawing a distinction between 'before' and 'now', Leigh reminds her readers that they are witnesses of the new covenant and must read scripture as such. To continue to focus on Eve's damnation is to read the Bible according to the old covenant; to be, as Calvin said of the enslaved Galatians, 'blind and accursed' and 'content with present shadows' because of a refusal to 'stretch their minds to Christ'.[23] If scripture is read 'truly', Leigh asserts, and rooted in the 'now', exegesis will acknowledge the significance of Mary's contribution and accept her, as 'I.B.' claimed in *Virginalia* (1632), as 'that instrument of ioy / Which Eue's sad curses did to blessings turne'.[24] According to the terms of Leigh's exegesis, a refusal to accept Mary's maternity as a fulfilment of Eve's legacy effectively denies the New Testament revelation of the Saviour.

While Genesis 2:15 is used to substantiate biblically the typological connectedness of Eve and Mary, Leigh's subsequent move to explore how the Virgin is prefigured by five Old Testament women is a more speculative endeavour. These women, selected because 'the first letters of [their] names doe make [Mary's] whole name', are presented to the reader as follows:

Michal,
Abigail,
Rachel,
Iudith, &
Anna (41).[25]

[21] Rachel Speght, *A mouzell for Melastomus, the cynicall bayter of, and foule mouthed barker against Euahs sex* (London: Nicholas Okes, 1617), 6. See also Joseph Swetnam, *The araignment of leuud, idle, froward, and vnconstant women or the vanitie of them, choose you whether: with a commendation of wise, vertuous and honest women* (London: George Purslowe, 1615).

[22] Alice Sutcliffe, *Meditations of man's mortalitie* (London: B[ernard] A[lsop] and T[homas] F[awcet], 1634), 150.

[23] Calvin, *Institutes*, 460, 2.11.10. For further discussion of the reformed understanding of Jewish 'blindness' see Preus, *From Shadow to Promise*, 16–20, 268.

[24] 'I.B.', *Virginalia. or Spirituall sonnets in prayse of the most glorious Virgin Marie* (Rouen: the widow of N. Courant, 1632), 26.

[25] It should be noted that, in this section of *The mothers blessing*, Leigh claims to draw on a list of names compiled by 'godly and reuerend men of the church' (41).

This typesetting literalizes the perceived connections between scripture's two Testaments in a way that positions Mary as the fulfilment of the five Old Testament women named.[26] According to typological standards, Mary becomes the antitype of these women because their qualities are found to coalesce and reach fruition in her body; their 'vertues', Leigh explains, are 'wholly combined in her' (41). The way in which Leigh visually conjoins Mary with her Old Testament antecedents is especially important because, as Gary Waller explains, 'the Old Testament heroines were dissociated from Mary by the reformers and seen rather as exempla of heroic, obedient and faithful women, virtuous Protestant witnesses for the faith'.[27] Indeed, the last woman on Leigh's list, Hannah, was regularly championed in reformed writings as the ideal biblical mother and, as Michele Osherow has shown, in many senses 'replaces the Virgin Mary in Protestant considerations of a motherly figure'.[28]

By interweaving the names of popular Old Testament exemplars like Hannah with Mary's name, Leigh re-conjoins Christ's mother to her biblical predecessors and suggests a biblical omnipresence more commonly found in medieval and Roman Catholic readings.[29] The teachings of the sixteenth-century Jesuit scholar Peter Canisius, recalled in *The widdoves mite* (1619), for example, find Mary in 'the *woman whose seed was promised in Paradise*' but also claim her as '*the true Rebecca; The true Iudith; The true Esther; The true temple and Sanctuary of God prophesied by* Ezechiel, *and the very way of Saints* . . . *She was that which* Moyses *saw in the bush and fire; the mysticall Arke of the Testament* . . . Now in the new Testament, behold that vnited which before you saw scattered.'[30] While Leigh might not go as far as to suggest that Mary, rather than Christ, enables the full meaning of the Old Testament to become clear, her typology, which similarly outlines how various Old Testament narratives foreshadow Mary, is no less evocative: '[Mary] was as faithfull to her husband, as *Michal*, who saued her husband *Dauid* from the fury of *Saul*, although hee were her father and her King, not preferring her owne life before the safety of her husband. She was as wise as *Abigail*, who is highly commended for her wisdome: amiable in the sight of her

[26] In this point, I build on Gray's observation that Leigh uses this 'miniature acrostic' to evoke a 'biblical master narrative' that 'testifies to a wide sphere of female activity and public piety': Gray, 'Feeding on the Seed', 575.

[27] Waller, *The Virgin Mary*, 56.

[28] Osherow, *Biblical Women's Voices*, 74.

[29] See Waller for a discussion of Marian omnipresence in medieval readings of scripture: *The Virgin Mary*, 56.

[30] 'A.G.', *The widdoves mite cast into the treasure-house of the prerogatiues, and prayses of our B. Lady* (Saint-Omer, 1619), 66–7.

husband, as *Rachel*: stout and magnanimous in the time of trouble, as *Iudith*: patient and zealous in prayer, as *Anna*' (42). Evidently, Leigh intends 'MARIA' to conjure a series of biblical intertexts which attest to the Virgin's significance and, by following the acrostic of Mary's name with this explanatory note, she pinpoints the precise qualities and narratives she seeks to arouse.

Significantly, these lines credit Mary as the antitype of a series of women whose narratives challenge the masculinity and authority of men. A glimpse of Rachel, perhaps the most conventional of the biblical women Leigh names, moves the Israelite leader, Jacob, to weeping (Genesis 29:11), while Hannah's zeal causes her to reject Elkanah's acceptance of her barren state (1. Sam. 1:8) and entreat God to give her a son in the Bible's first prayer to God (by an individual other than a prophet) in the sanctuary.[31] Michal, Abigail, and Judith are each praised by Leigh for acts of autonomy with political consequences. The praise of Michal originates in I Samuel 19:11–17, where she is found engineering the escape of her husband, and the deception of her father, in a narrative which is marked by David's silence in the midst of his wife's ingenuity.[32] The subsequent commendation of Abigail's wisdom is similarly rooted to a biblical text that is celebratory of female single-mindedness. Abigail's reparations to David and his army for Nabal's churlishness are explicitly devised and conducted without her husband's consent (I Sam. 25:19), and news of her resourcefulness is cited as a direct cause of Nabal's death (I Sam. 25:37). Abigail's delivery of her household chimes with Leigh's praise of Judith's bravery which, in the face of the ineptitude and weak faith of city officials, saves a city from the Assyrian army. Beheading their general, Holofernes, with his own sword, the biblical book devoted to her industry and valour marks her as a political liberator of the Israelite nation. What is notable in Leigh's invocation of the narratives of Michal, Abigail, and Judith in particular to praise Mary is that, in each case, God chooses to bring victory 'by the hand of a woman' (Judith 13:25).

[31] Osherow notes the seminal importance of this first prayer by an individual, and terms it 'a critical episode in the Bible': *Biblical Women's Voices*, 45–6. Osherow also discusses how the biblical text emphasizes Hannah's independence from Elkanah: see 47–8.

[32] See Osherow who notes that all the active verbs in the biblical text are attributed to Michal and reminds that, typically, Michal was chastised for the lies she tells in this passage, as well as her later derision of David's celebration before the Ark of the Covenant (II Sam. 6): 'Wives, Fears and Foreskins: Early Modern Reproach of Zipporah and Michal', in *Biblical Women in Early Modern Literary Culture*, ed. Brownlee and Gallagher, 84. In light of this common denigration of Michal's narrative, Leigh's selection of Michal, instead of Miriam, for example, is unusual and may be understood as a reclaiming of her significance in biblical history.

These independent women of the Old Testament, celebrated for unfeminine and perhaps even unsavoury traits, seem curious forerunners to Mary who was typically praised by reformers for her piety and maternal affection.[33] Yet, the very peculiarity of these antecedents is revealing because they suggest that the significance of Marian maternity surpasses exemplarity. As the mother of Christ, Mary too engages in an act of deliverance, but it is one that marks her as a spiritual, rather than political, rescuer of God's people; as Leigh explains: 'now man may say . . . I feede of [the Sauiour] by faith and liue . . . by God, working in a woman: man can claime no part in it' (35). As Leigh foregrounds the divine importance of Mary's maternity for salvation and celebrates the exclusion of men from the incarnational plan, her selection of Old Testament women who are praised for autonomous acts of deliverance seems appropriate. Her Marian acrostic reveals, then, that true appreciation of Mary, and an understanding of the significance of her maternity, logically emerges from a hermeneutic appreciation of the relatedness of both Testaments.

A typological reading of the Old Testament in light of the New reveals a Mary who embodies, both in person and name, the variety of important roles women have played across biblical history. This lineage of providentially important women is found, however, to have significance beyond Mary when Leigh suggests that her inheritance of virtues is available to all women: 'Seeing then, that by this one name [Maria], so many vertues are called to remembrance, I thinke it meete, that good names be giuen to all women, that they might call to minde the vertues of those women whose names they beare' (42–3). Here, Mary's name, and naming women more generally, functions as a signifier of the latent potential of women. The implication is that, as individuals are given biblical names, such as 'Abigail' or 'Judith', they accrue a figurative connection to a host of biblical predecessors (41).[34] Because all the virtues of biblical women are encapsulated in 'one name', 'Marie', the process of naming illuminates, and expands, a typological network of virtuous women across Christian history (41). According to Leigh's exegesis, in giving birth to the Saviour, Mary exonerates women from Eve's legacy, but she also reconnects contemporary women to their virtuous biblical predecessors whose faithful, brave, independent, and zealous examples they are authorized to follow.

[33] For an overview of reformed readings of Mary see Heal, *The Cult of the Virgin Mary*, 64–115.

[34] For further discussion of the attention given to naming children in *The mothers blessing*, see Jennifer Louise Heller, *The Mother's Legacy in Early Modern England* (Farnham: Ashgate, 2011), 73–8.

By reading Mary typologically, Leigh uncovers a network of women across biblical history whose alternative virtues foreshadow the spiritual and political impact of Mary's maternity and, consequently, the significance of contemporary women. It is an exegetical strategy deployed to similar effect at the beginning of Lanyer's *Salve Deus Rex Judaeorum*. While the opening prose address to the reader likewise works to establish a biblical community of virtuous and powerful women, Lanyer is more pointed in her assessment of the collective significance of the Old Testament women she chooses. The women she names are each used by God to bring down the 'pride and arrogancie' of men: 'As was cruell *Cesarus* by the discreet counsel of noble *Deborah*, Judge and Prophetesse of Israel: and resolution of *Jael* wife of *Heber* the Kenite: wicked *Haman*, by the divine prayers and proceeding of beautifull *Hester*: blasphemous *Holofernes*, by the invincible courage, rare wisdome, and confident carriage of *Judeth*: & the unjust Judges, by the innocency of chast *Susanna*: with infinite others, which for brevitie sake I will omit. As also in respect it pleased our Lord and Saviour Jesus Christ . . . to be begotten of a woman' (41). The structure of Lanyer's exegesis, moving as it does from Old Testament to New, emphasizes women's providential contribution across biblical history, but it also suggests, by the standards of typology, that the most significant created being used by God was a woman and mother. By placing Mary at the end of a list of faithful Old Testament women, Lanyer demonstrates that her celebration of Marian maternity is not born from a belief in Mary's intercessory abilities but is based on a form of biblical reading authorized by reformers.

The inclusion of Mary within a list of powerful women who undo the evil plans of men also marks Marian maternity as a mechanism that offsets specifically male-authored sin, a suggestion that anticipates the later poetic emphasis on the catalogue of male wrongs that drive the Passion narrative and contribute to Christ's death. In the address to the reader, Mary inherits a biblical lineage which, with the exception of Susanna, is notable in its political and providential resonance. Through the actions of Deborah, whose speech mobilizes the Israelite army whom she accompanies into battle against the Canaanite army (Judges 4), and Jael, who brings an end to the conflict by hammering a tent peg into the temple of their General, *Cesarus*, God fulfils the prophecy to deliver Israel's enemy 'into the hand of a womá[n]' (Judith 4:9) and saves the nation; and Esther and Judith's contribution to the respective downfalls of Haman and Holofernes similarly results in the rescue of their peoples from death.

In grouping Mary alongside a series of women whom God uses to save his chosen people, motherhood is transposed from womanly convention into a divinely ordained act of rescue: 'it pleased our Lord and Saviour

Jesus Christ, without the assistance of man... from the time of his conception, till the houre of his death, to be begotten of a woman, borne of a woman, nourished of a woman, obedient to a woman; ... yea, even when he was in his greatest agonie and bloodie sweat, going to be crucified, and also in the last houre of his death, tooke care to dispose of a woman' (49–50). According to this description, Mary's significance hinges on her maternal body because, as a woman, she had the biological capacity to facilitate the incarnation. Indeed, the maternal functions of the female body are understood here to be central to Mary's divine selection for this historic task. Tying Christ's conception, birth, and sustenance to Mary's maternal body, Lanyer showcases how pregnancy, labour, and breastfeeding are intrinsic to the Bible's ultimate act of salvation. Her Jesus is a fleshly one, and readers are reminded that the sweating and suffering Christ on his way to the cross was made human through the physical processes of a labouring and nourishing female body. Physically bringing God to earth, Christ's humanity is the direct inheritance of his mother, and here, the relationship between mother and son, rather than father and son, takes precedence.[35] The bond between Christ and Mary importantly turns on their fleshly connection as Christ's physical 'agonie' opens into a remembrance of his mother before his death. By emphasizing that Mary's centrality extends beyond the birth, nurture, and obedience of the Christ child and into salvific narratives of the Christ man, Lanyer locates the tasks of mothering alongside the conclusion of the divine plan for salvation through the cross.

Foregrounding how the atonement is dependent on an intermingling of the material processes of maternity with the divine plan of incarnation, Lanyer is, like Leigh, at pains to assert that this salvific act is accomplished 'without the assistance of man' (49). As such, the Marian body, as a site where God meets female flesh, is marked as the location of a birth unlike any other. Thomas Adams makes this clear when, contemplating the creation of Adam, Eve, and their descendants, he notes that Christ's origin 'was of a different maner from all these. 1. not of no precedent flesh, as *Adam.* 2. Not of a man without a woman, as *Eue.* 3. Not of man and woman, as all we. 4. But after a new way; of a woman, without a man'.[36] While Christ's creation from female flesh marks his birth as unique, the Marian body, facilitating as it did a meeting of flesh and spirit, inaugurates

[35] See Naomi Miller's discussion of Lanyer's representation of Christ's obedience to his mother: '(M)other Tongues: Maternity and Subjectivity', in *Aemilia Lanyer: Gender, Genre and the Canon*, ed. Marshall Grossman (Lexington: University Press of Kentucky, 1998), 143–66.

[36] Thomas Adams, *The happiness of the church* (London: G.P., 1619), 288.

the possibility of an alternative, spiritual birth. German theologian Jakob Böhme elucidates this additional importance: Mary was 'highly *blessed among* and above all *women* Ever since Eve; for the Covenant opened it selfe in her'.[37] Although Mary gave birth to God in flesh, in doing so, her womb also becomes the origin of the new covenant, that which was, according to Paul in Galatians 4:22–8, spiritual matter. By reminding that Christ's physical suffering, on which the salvation plan hinged, was dependent upon female flesh, Lanyer affords Mary a role in spiritual, as well as physical, formation. As such, her address to the reader begins the work of translating the significance of Marian motherhood from the domestic and physical, to the spiritual and historical that characterizes the later poetic sections addressing Mary.

Lanyer's alignment of Mary's maternity with the activities of female rescuers who overthrow men, and attribution of Christ's material body to woman alone, heralds the important distinction drawn between the spiritual substance of male and female flesh in the poem proper. The poetic narrative opens on the night of Christ's betrayal in the garden of Gethsemane and begins its cataloguing of male wrongs with the sleeping disciples. This retelling of the disciples' inconstancy, as detailed in the synoptic Gospels, is, however, shot through with a remembrance of the Genesis account of creation and the Fall. It is, Lanyer suggests in the poem's first direct use of a biblical intertext, specifically because the disciples are 'Scorpions bred in *Adams* mud' that they fail in their duties towards Christ (67: 381).[38] This allusion to man's creation in Genesis 2:7 from 'the dust of the grounde' lays blame for the disciples' deficiencies firmly at Adam's feet but it is also suggestive of a broader concern to illuminate the separate origin and, consequentially, intrinsic flaws, of male flesh in particular. The New Testament men, whose sins Lanyer exposes in 'Salve Deus', pointedly have their substance in 'dust and earth', a composition that marks them as Adam's sons in character as well as form (80: 675). As Adam's heirs, the men possess 'great weakenesse in the Flesh' and are given to sin (70: 426).

Lanyer's interest in the sinful legacy of Adamic flesh is specifically suggested in her assessment of Petrine conceit. Peter's show of loyalty to Christ was stimulated, Lanyer interprets, by a conviction that he was 'above' his companions, and his arrogance prompts a declaration that, of

[37] Jakob Böhme, *The fifth book of the authour, in three parts the first, Of the becoming man or incarnation of Jesus Christ* (London: J.M., 1659), 62.

[38] Lanyer's account of the failings of the sleeping disciples in the Garden of Gethsemane is interspersed with references to the sins of a series of Old Testament men including David, Solomon, the Israelites' Egyptian oppressor, Pharaoh, as well as Adam.

all the disciples, 'he was most too blame' (66: 355–6). This evaluation of Peter is interesting because it directly echoes the later assessment of Adam in 'Eves Apologie': '[Eve's] fault, though great, yet he was most too blame' (85: 778).[39] The exact repetition of this phrase positions Peter as an antitype of Adam and, in doing so, reiterates that the sins of Adamic flesh stretch from Genesis to the Gospels. The subtle allusions to Genesis that intersperse Lanyer's Passion suggest that Gethsemane, that 'blessed Garden' beset by 'Vipers', is a second Eden (67: 363, 365). Understood as such, the catalogue of male failure that stretches from the disciples to Christ's executioners operates, in many senses, as an alternative to Genesis 3, a point made clear when Lanyer urges in the verse preceding 'Eves Apologie': 'Let not vs Women glory in Mens fall' (84: 758). Evidently, it is 'Mens fall', rather than Eve's fall, that begins *Salve Deus.*

It is significant that within Lanyer's retelling of this New Testament fall, women are excluded from the fleshly weakness that cripples men. In fact, Lanyer has it so she has to read the Bible backwards, to Eve, to locate a female sin of similar magnitude and even then, this sin is not consummate with the male wrongs previously considered: '[Eve's] sinne was small, to what you doe commit' (86: 818). Importantly, Lanyer claims the sins of New Testament men to have hermeneutic significance beyond the Gospels; reading Genesis from the vantage point of the Passion 'makes our former fault muche lesse appeare' (84: 762). Once again, Lanyer's exegesis pivots here on a clear understanding of the typological relationship the two Testaments of scripture share, and it is an understanding that enables her to position male betrayal of Jesus as a fulfilment of Eve's betrayal of God in the Garden. In keeping with the trajectory of typological exegesis, where that which is promised is merely a shadow of what is to come, the sins of New Testament men exceed, not only those of the Genesis Fall, but 'All mortall sinnes' collectively: 'This sinne of yours, surmounts them all as farre / As doth the Sunne, another little starre' (87: 823–4). These stanzas reinforce that sound exegesis is that which reads the whole Bible and informs a change of behaviour, a point made clear when men, having recognized their responsibility for Christ's death, are called to alter their attitudes towards women:

> Then let us have our Libertie againe,
> And challendge to your selves no Sov'raigntie;
> You came not in the world without our paine,
> Make that a barre against your crueltie. (87: 825–8)

[39] For a detailed consideration of Lanyer's re-reading of Genesis 1–3 and how it can be read as a response to the contemporary *querelle des femmes* see Beilin, *Redeeming Eve*, esp. 177–207.

As Lanyer makes a case for a shift in male perception of women based on right biblical reading, she also explicitly calls for a shift in attitudes towards motherhood reminding that men are dependent on the 'pain' of childbirth for their continuation. Although, as Bentley's prayers suggest, childbirth pain had become a marker of women's fault in the Genesis Fall, in Lanyer's reading, the travails of female flesh are cited as a 'barre' to male cruelty and that which demand respect.

This alternative view of labour and motherhood is underpinned by a reading of Mary's relationship with Eve, and Lanyer's understanding of the significance of Marian motherhood more generally. That Lanyer positions Mary as Eve's antitype is clear, but she also situates her pain-free birth as the fulfilment of the curse of pain Eve bequeathed to all women when she describes the Virgin as: 'A maiden Mother, subject to no paine . . . / Making thee Servant, Mother, Wife, and Nurse / To Heavens bright King, that freed us from the curse' (97–8: 1083, 1087–8).[40] Deftly shuttling between New Testament and Old, Lanyer claims the birth of Christ as the typological fulfilment of the Genesis curse. Her Mary suffers 'no paine' and is therefore exempt from the Genesis promise that women would bear children 'in sorowe' (Gen. 3:16).[41] Lanyer's conception of a Marian labour that is pain free chimes with a reading of Mary's childbirth that predominantly concerned Roman Catholic writers.[42] The Spanish Jesuit Gaspar Loarte reminded readers of his *Instructions and aduertisements, how to meditate the misteries of the rosarie of the most holy Virgin Mary* (1597) of the distinction between Mary's disposition during labour and that of other women: 'Thou shalt finde, howe in counter change of griefes which other women feele in child-birth, she felt a strange and ineffable solace, a singuler ioy and diuine consolation.'[43] 'A.G.', writing in 1619 in response to those reformers who, in seeking to stress Mary's humanity, asserted that she experienced the normal processes of labour, rebukes those that 'thinke, & often say, *That she was deliuered of our*

[40] Beilin, for instance, refers to Lanyer's Mary as a 'second Eve': *Redeeming Eve*, xix.

[41] For discussion of the ideas surrounding Mary's pain-free childbirth see Beattie, *God's Mother*, esp. 100–3.

[42] It should be said that although this chapter demonstrates how Lanyer's Mary accrues a rather Roman Catholic aesthetic in some places of the poetic narrative, it is not concerned with assessments of Lanyer's confessional position. Scholarship has shown that Lanyer's text is dedicated to eminent Protestant women and noted that, although of Jewish decent and married to an Italian Catholic, Lanyer socialized at court and in largely Protestant circles. See, for instance, Leeds Barroll, 'Looking for Patrons', in *Aemilia Lanyer*, ed. Grossman, 29–48; Gray, 'Feeding on the Seed', 563–92. For a detailed discussion of Lanyer's awareness of other aspects of Roman Catholic theology see Gary Kuchar, 'Aemilia Lanyer and the Virgin's Swoon: Theology and Iconography in *Salve Deus Rex Judaeorum*', *English Literary Renaissance* 37.1 (2007): 47–73.

[43] Loarte, *Instructions*, 23.

Sauiour after the same labourious, vulgar, and vncomly manner to which other women are subiect by their descende[n]ce from Eue'.[44]

While the distinction between Eve and Mary's labouring may be drawn more forcefully by 'A.G.', Lanyer's assessment of Mary's painless childbirth nonetheless insists that Marian maternity marks a change from the Genesis 'curse'. In representing a Mary whose labour is untainted by the Fall, Lanyer's vision of Marian maternity resonates with that of John Pettus who, in his 1674 commentary on Adam and Eve, explained that Mary's painlessness was what God had intended for all women: '*Mary* without fraction of any Membranes, which causeth that virginate effusion of bloud, and consequently pain; and also without pain . . . brought forth a child: so should every woman ('tis suppos'd) have enjoyed the like benefit, had not this curse come upon them.'[45] While Pettus continues to conceive of labour pain as a sign that women remain under the Genesis curse, God's raising of Mary from 'poore degree' to 'Mother . . . To Heavens bright King' is, according to Lanyer, an act that alters the significance of childbearing for all women. It is deemed that which 'freed us from the curse' (98: 1087–8). The 'us' here is significant because through it the narrative claims Mary's painless labour as an outward sign of the new covenant's significance for labouring women; in giving birth to the Saviour, Mary fulfils God's promise of deliverance through woman's 'seede' and renders the curse obsolete (Gen. 3:15). Although women may continue to experience labour pain, after Mary, this pain has, according to the exegetical programme of 'Salve Deus', altered significance for all time. It is now a 'barre' to male cruelty.

The insistence in these lines that Mary's painless labour has consequences for women who live under the new covenant once again renders Marian motherhood as a task that has a spiritual, and figurative, significance that transcends the historic moment of Christ's birth. The divine importance of Marian maternity beyond the birth narratives is registered again later in the poem when Lanyer represents a Mary who physically reacts to Christ's death; she writes: 'Her griefes extreame . . . / To see his bleeding body oft shee swooned' (94: 1011–12). Gary Kuchar's discussion of 'Salve Deus' has shown that this specific description of a swooning Mary engages with the *lo spasimo* controversy which broke out in the medieval period over representations of Mary at the cross.[46] The crux of

[44] 'A.G.', *The widdoves mite*, 82.

[45] John Pettus, *Volatiles from the history of Adam and Eve containing many unquestioned truths* (London: T. Bassett, 1674), 136.

[46] Kuchar, 'Aemilia Lanyer and the Virgin's Swoon', 47–73. In what follows I build on Kuchar's observations of Lanyer's swooning Mary who, he argues, is 'at the center of Lanyer's project of imagining women in clerical roles' (44).

the matter was whether or not Mary watchfully stands by the cross or swoons and actively suffers alongside the crucified Christ.[47] It is the doctrinal implications of the latter which are of course significant, because a physical response from Mary under the cross functions as an admission that she is a participant in the redemptive process.[48] Yet, Lanyer's representation of a swooning Mary does not simply suggest the poem's endorsement of a woman's involvement in redemption.

According to the depiction common in medieval paintings, a swooning Mary was one who was experiencing the pains of childbirth, and therefore is a description which specifically marks her maternity as that which enables her to be cooperative with Christ.[49] Within the swoon, as Amy Neff explains, '[Mary's] childbirth pain, like Christ on the cross . . . pays the price required for mankind's salvation' and becomes indicative of her position as spiritual mother of believers.[50] The suggestion that Mary became a mother again at the foot of the cross has a scriptural basis in John 19:26–7, when Jesus commends Mary to John as 'thy mother', and the disciple to his mother as a 'sonne'. As Neff notes, this new maternity was read by a number of early Church Fathers, including Ambrose, as an analogy for Mary becoming mother to those who, through the crucifixion, become sons and daughters of the Church.[51] By representing a Mary who swoons, then, the poem infuses maternity with spiritual, and indeed redemptive, efficacy, and it does so in a way that begins to distinguish between literal and spiritual motherhood. Mary's swoon under the cross arises from 'griefes extreame . . . but new begun' suggesting that she now suffers those pains Lanyer claims she had avoided in physical childbirth (94: 1011–12).[52]

[47] Amy Neff explains that the suggestion that Mary swooned under the cross first gained traction in the thirteenth century and could be seen 'countless times' by the fourteenth and fifteenth centuries: 'The Pain of Compassio: Mary's Labor at the Foot of the Cross', *The Art Bulletin* 80 (1998): 254–73 (254).

[48] In reformed thought, Mary was not engaged in the redemption process. She was merely a witness to the atonement. For a discussion of Mary's passivity see Ellington, *From Sacred Body*, 50–1, as well as Prudence Allen, *The Concept of Women: The Aristotelian Revolution, 750 B.C.–A.D. 1250* (Grand Rapids, MI: Eerdmans, 1985), 383–97.

[49] For a detailed discussion of artistic representations of the swoon as childbirth see Harvey E. Hamburgh, 'The Problem of Lo Spasimo of the Virgin in Cinquecento Paintings of the Descent from the Cross', *Sixteenth Century Journal* 12.4 (1981): 45–75; Neff, 'The Pain of Compassio'.

[50] Neff, 'The Pain of Compassio', 267.

[51] Neff, 'The Pain of Compassio', 255.

[52] Ellington traces the 'public portrayal' of Mary's labour at the cross in sixteenth-century art and sermons and describes it during this time as 'popular': *From Sacred Body*, 192–3. For an overview of attitudes towards Mary's labour pain in Christian history, see Neff, 'The Pain of Compassio'; Kuchar, 'Aemilia Lanyer and the Virgin's Swoon', 57–8. See also Kuchar, 57–71, for further consideration of how Lanyer's representation of Mary's

Just as the crucifixion inaugurates Mary's maternal suffering, so too it begins the travails of the female flesh she has bequeathed to her son. Christ's inherited female flesh is foregrounded because his pain is reminiscent of the travails of maternal labour; his suffering, unlike his birth, rends the material body resulting in an emission of 'His blood, his teares, his sighes, his bitter groanes' and physical rupture as 'his members' are 'torne' (91: 926; 101: 1162). Yet, it is at the moment of death that Lanyer's Christ is figured most clearly as a labouring mother whose pains bring forth spiritual life: 'With sharpest pangs and terrors thus appailde, / Sterne Death makes way, that life might giue him place' (101: 1157–8). Christ's body undergoes the pangs, groans, and sighs of a physical travail which, like Mary's swoon, produces spiritual issue. The poem, having earlier denigrated male flesh as inherently sinful, continues here to reiterate the redemptive properties of female flesh. Christ's suffering is made possible because of the flesh he inherited from a woman 'without . . . man', and it is an inheritance that continues in Lanyer's retelling of the crucifixion to be exclusively female and maternal (49).

The suffering of Mary's flesh in the redemptive process signals how her role as biological mother, foregrounded earlier in 'Salve Deus', is superseded by a maternal role that is spiritual during the Passion. As she labours alongside Christ for salvation, Mary is, as a number of scholars have observed, represented in an active, nurturing role that announces the inauguration of a maternity that figuratively extends beyond physical, or literal, biological processes, to include the spiritual nurture of future generations. Her body is seen producing 'tears' that 'wash away [Christ's] pretious blood' that 'sinners might not tread it under feet', and, as these tears prevent the desecration of Christ's blood, they perform, as Theresa M. DiPasquale argues, 'the work of the new Covenant' (95: 1017–18).[53] Set apart from 'sinners', Mary is also later found '[u]pon her knees' tending to that which 'must be gath'red' (95: 1020–2).[54] Physically nurturing this salvific balm, the material body of Lanyer's swooning Mary facilitates the process of redemption beyond the stable, this time enabling it to be completed. In representing Mary in this way, *Salve Deus* carves out a central position for childbirth and motherhood in the Passion narrative as well as the birth narrative.

swoon, and activity during the Passion generally, suggest that she 'give[s] birth to the redemption' (58).

[53] Theresa M. DiPasquale, *Refiguring the Sacred Feminine: The Poems of John Donne, Aemilia Lanyer, and John Milton* (Pittsburgh: Duquesne University Press, 2008), 136.

[54] Kuchar reads Mary's actions here in connection with Isaiah 11:1 and teases out how her representation as a spiritual gardener can be read in relation to the poem's concern with the clerical authority of women: 'Aemilia Lanyer and the Virgin's Swoon', 58–61.

FIGURATIVE MATERNITY AND THE LABOUR FOR SPIRITUAL REBIRTH

The way in which *Salve Deus* represents a maternal body that shifts to perform spiritual tasks under the new covenant resonates with the extension of Mary's significance beyond the birth narratives in *The Mothers Blessing*. Leigh's praise of Marian maternity suggests a Mary who, in nourishing the infant Christ physically, becomes involved in the sustenance of believers across Christian history. Readers are forced to recall how the provision of spiritual food was dependent on the Marian body ('The woman brought me a Sauiour, and I feede of him by faith and liue') and, later, Leigh more directly implicates Mary in the nourishing process when she declares: 'except they feed of the seed of the woman, they haue no life' (35, 36). The recurring emphasis on Mary's provision of Christ's body on which believers 'feed' is significant because it seems to draw on an understanding, common in the medieval period, of her body as the site of a banquet, or wedding feast for believers.[55] Figuring Mary's womb as such a dining chamber, Parisian Chancellor Jean Gerson, in a sermon on the Annunciation, termed her as a 'hostess' who provided 'dishes' through which her guests could be 'nourished by [Christ's] fullness'.[56] But a Mary whose (breast)feeding sustains the believer, as Leigh suggests, is one who also resonates with the redemptive significance afforded to Marian lactation in Roman Catholic thought.

Within the broader medieval 'fetishization' of the Marian body, Mary's breast milk became, what Waller terms, 'a major . . . relic' and, assumed to have redemptive properties, continued to be a source of fascination into the seventeenth century.[57] Writing in 1610, William Crashaw explains in *The Jesuites Gospel* (1610) that Mary's breast milk was embroiled in the Roman Catholic equation of Virgin Mother with Son with the result that 'the pappes of a Woman [are] equalled with the *wounds* of our *Lord*, and her *milke* with his *bloud*'.[58] Although Leigh steers clear of any doctrinal suggestion that Mary participates in the redemption of humankind from sin, she does position Christ's mother as a redemptress of women when she claims: 'except they feed of the seed of the woman, they haue no life.

[55] See Ellington, *From Sacred Body*, 49–51.

[56] Gerson in Ellington, *From Sacred Body*, 49. The connection between Mary's body and banqueting has been said to have scriptural basis in the Song of Songs and Revelation. See Waller, *The Virgin Mary*; Ellington, *From Sacred Body*.

[57] Waller, *The Virgin Mary*, 33, 45. See also Ellington, *From Sacred Body*, 59.

[58] William Crashaw, *The Iesuites gospel* (London: E, [sic] A[llde], 1610), 32; Waller, *The Virgin Mary*, 20.

Will not therefore all women seek out this great grace of God, that by *Mary* hath taken away the shame, which before was due vnto vs euer since the fall of man?' (36). In giving birth to the Saviour, Mary is found to eradicate Eve's legacy but also to inaugurate a new, grace-filled dispensation which permanently alters the position of women. Because of Mary's maternity, a spiritually enriched conception of motherhood is now divinely permissible for all women.

Leigh identifies a spiritual dimension within her own maternal role when, defending *The Mothers Blessing*, she asks: will not a mother 'blesse [the child of her wombe] euery time it suckes on her brests, when shee feeleth the bloud come from her heart to nourish it?' (10). Here, breastfeeding is credited with a spiritual outcome—blessing—an indicator that, as a mother, she is naturally equipped to nurture her children spiritually and physically. While Catherine Gray suggests that this comment mobilizes 'seventeenth-century medical theories regarding mother's milk as a concoction of the blood' to create 'a continuity between the role of the mother and that of spiritual guide',[59] Leigh's conflation of the biological and spiritual is perhaps better understood in relation to the redemptive potential of Marian lactation. A mother who can spiritually 'blesse' her child through nursing is akin to a Marian mother who literally nourishes Christ but also spiritually nourishes believers. Leigh more clearly positions herself as the typological fulfilment of this spiritually nourishing Mary with the claim that she too provides 'spirituall food of the soule' (10).

Leigh is not alone in her conception of a Mary whose divine contribution is found to elide flesh with spirit and body with soul, or in reading herself as the typological fulfilment of a Marian mother with a spiritual remit. In a meditation on 'the soules affinitie with Christ' in Bentley's *The Monument of Matrons* (1582), the speaker contemplates Mary's bond with Christ resolving that 'as thou art his corporall mother, so art thou through faith his spirituall mother: and I following thy faith with all humblenesse, am his spirituall mother also'.[60] Here identification with Mary allows the speaker to claim her position as a spiritual mother and, in doing so, evidences the existence of a thought process that understands Mary's material motherhood to shade into a powerful model of spiritual parentage. While in Bentley's meditation, this outward movement enables the soul to realize fully its kinship with Christ, in *The Mothers Blessing* this typological trajectory facilitates a move from the conflation of flesh and

[59] Gray, 'Feeding on the Seed', 572.
[60] Bentley, *The monument of matrones*, 5, 8.

spirit to the resolution of flesh as spirit.[61] This shift becomes apparent when, in a schema redolent of Mary's sorrowing under the cross, the fleshly pains of childbearing are positioned as a prelude to the spiritual labour for souls by Leigh: 'My deare Children . . . *Can a Mother forget the child of her wombe?* . . . Is it possible, that shee, which hath carried her child within her, so neere her hart, and brought it forth into this world with so much bitter paine, so many grones and cries, can forget it? nay rather, will shee not labour now till Christ be formed in it?' (9–10). Over the course of these lines, the responsibilities of material motherhood give way to spiritual concerns, a movement that is authorized biblically by Isaiah 49:15, some of which is quoted directly: 'Can a woman forget her childe, and not haue compassion on the sonne of her wo[m]be? though they shulde forget, yet will I not forget thee'. The entirety of this verse illuminates an important distinction between material and spiritual parentage because, although God initially uses the bonds between mother and son to communicate his commitment to the people of Zion, the literal mother is, ultimately, superseded by the more constant, divine parent. Leigh's citation and exegesis of this biblical text suggests, then, that literal and spiritual maternity are not equivalent: material labour—that is, giving birth to flesh—is understood as a figure, or type of a maternity that is spiritual.

Leigh's understanding of her place within this hierarchy of maternity allows her to designate the writing of *The Mothers Blessing*, like the apostle Paul's letter to the church in Galatia, as a natural, maternal compulsion:

> Could Saint *Paul* say vnto the *Galatians*, that were but strangers to him concerning the flesh . . . *My little children, of whom I doe trauaile againe in birth, vntill Christ be formed in you?* . . . And can any man blame a mother (who indeed brought forth her childe with much paine) though she labour againe till Christ bee formed in them? . . . Therefore let no man blame a mother, though she something exceede in writing to her children, since euery man knowes, that the loue of a mother to her children, is hardly contained within the bounds of reason. (9–10)[62]

[61] In this point I expand Gray's argument that Leigh's concept of motherhood 'slides between the spiritual and material', a rhetoric that Gray contends facilitates Leigh's political and religious critique and justifies the spiritual nurture of her sons: 'Feeding on the Seed', 572–3, 576–80.

[62] Kirsten Poole explains that Leigh's discussion of her labour, and the representation of her text as a child, is part of an authorial strategy that allows her to claim 'a position and authority which men cannot hold, and cannot easily refute': '"The fittest closet for all goodness"', 75. See also Poole, '"The fittest closet for all goodness"', 82; as well as Heller, *The Mother's Legacy*, 57–8, for more on how Leigh authorizes her writing.

Conceiving of himself as a spiritual mother, Paul's words in Galatians 4:19 underpin a typology of maternity that positions the figurative ability to give birth to Christ in the soul as the natural fulfilment of the literal labours of the female body.[63] Because Paul is compelled by metaphoric 'trauaile' to write to the Galatians then a mother, connected by 'flesh', as well as spirit, must likewise 'labour' in written text to deliver Christ to her children.

Leigh's figurative use of the term 'labour' reminds her readers that she is, like Sarah, a mother of the 'promes', or the new covenant, and therefore labours for children of the spirit, rather than the flesh (Gal. 4:28). As is made clear elsewhere in the text, she is engaged in a 'labour for the spirituall food of the soule' and explains to her readers that 'you may see it is a labour: but what labour? a pleasant labour, a profitable labour: a labour without the which the soule cannot liue' (5). Just as literal labour has been replaced with a labour that is spiritual, so too has the material nourishment of the maternal body been replaced by the spiritual food provided in *The Mothers Blessing*. Her textual labour delivers the body of Christ to her readers, without which they will, like the children of Israel without provision of manna, 'starve' (5).[64] In literally giving birth to sons and figuratively giving birth to a text which she understands will facilitate spiritual rebirth, Leigh's motherhood follows the trajectory of Marian maternity. Reading the Bible typologically, Leigh finds that she too is a mother whose flesh resolves itself as spiritual matter.

While Leigh's suggestion that she is a spiritual mother in the tradition of Mary, as well as the apostle Paul, makes a bold statement about the providential importance of her work, Lanyer's conception of her place within biblical matrilineage is yet more audacious. Early in *Salve Deus*, Lanyer invokes the Old Testament tradition of barrenness when, in apparent deprecation of her skill, she refers to her 'barren Muse', 'barren Braine', and 'barren skill' (10: 155; 63: 276; 64: 313). But the barren women of the Old Testament are, importantly, not childless for long: Sarah, the barren wife of Abraham, was used to establish the Israelite nation when she bore Isaac in her nineties (Gen. 17:17–19); Rebecca, whose barrenness is revealed in the prayers of her husband, Isaac, later

[63] Paul's figurative understanding of himself as a mother opens out into his later reading of Sarah as a spiritual, rather than a literal mother. For discussion of Paul's figural motherhood, and how it was read in this period, see Luxon, *Reforming Figures*, esp. 80–96.

[64] See Edith Snook, *Women, Reading and the Cultural Politics of Early Modern England* (Aldershot: Ashgate, 2005), 65, for further discussion of how Leigh understands the manna provided by the Israelites in relation to the nourishment provided by mothers. See also Gray's analysis of Leigh's understanding of the spiritual provision she offers to her children: 'Feeding on the Seed', 571–3.

gives birth to Jacob and Esau (Gen. 25:21–6); Rachel, beloved, yet barren, wife of Jacob, eventually gives birth to her husband's favoured sons Joseph and Benjamin (Gen. 29:31; 35:24), and the prayer of the barren wife, Hannah, leads to the birth of the Israelite judge, Samuel (1 Sam. 5–28). These narratives reveal that, in the Old Testament, acknowledgements of barrenness regularly herald a birth of considerable consequence.[65]

In light of this tradition, Lanyer's representation of herself as a barren mother may be read as a bold announcement of a birth of substantial magnitude: that of 'our Lord Iesus himself' (34). Lanyer's presentation of *Salve Deus* to her readers as the textual body of Christ is, as a number of scholars have noted, a recurring concern. Patricia Phillippy suggests that 'the *corpus Christi* is literalized in Lanyer's literary corpus' and, more recently, Femke Molekamp has traced how 'her book is constructed of the materials of Christ's body' to reveal Christ 'not merely represented but actually incarnated' in the text .[66] If Lanyer claims Christ to be incarnated in 'Salve Deus', her deliverance of this body to the reader must logically declare her to be the embodiment of his mother. Her position as a second Mary is strongly suggested at the close of 'Salve Deus' when she reveals that, like Christ's mother, who was informed of her motherhood in a visit from the angel, Gabriel, and following the convention of the annunciation to the barren wives of the Old Testament, she received news of her divine nomination to deliver a sacred body of text into the world; in a dream, she was 'appointed to performe this Worke' (139).[67] Her position as Mary's successor is further encapsulated in the repeated insistence that, in penning *Salve Deus*, she too gives birth to that which will provide spiritual nourishment; her poem is frequently termed a sacred 'Feast' wherein her readers may receive the 'Paschal Lambe' she has 'prepar'd' for them to 'feed upon' (7: 83, 85–9).[68] The recurring use of images of feeding and

[65] For barrenness in the Old Testament, see Osherow, *Biblical Women's Voices*, 47; Robert Alter, *The Art of Biblical Narrative* (New York: Basic Books, 1981), 85.

[66] Phillippy, 'Sisters of Magdalen', 101; Femke Molekamp, 'Reading Christ the Book in Aemilia Lanyer's *Salve Deus Rex Judaeroum* (1611): Iconography and the Cultures of Reading', *Studies in Philology* 109:3 (2012): 311–32 (312).

[67] Lanyer also figures herself as a sorrowing mother in the 'preamble of the Author before the Passion' by referring to the pursuit as her 'Labour' for 'Infant Verse': 62–3: 269, 279.

[68] Lanyer's repeated use of feasting imagery has been a point of interest in scholarship of her work. Other scholars have noted the connection between Lanyer's feast and the celebration of the Eucharist (Michael Schoenfeldt, 'The Gender of Religious Devotion: Amelia Lanyer and John Donne', in *Religion and Culture in Renaissance England*, ed. McEachern and Shuger, 209–33; Kari Boyd McBride, 'Sacred Celebration: The Patronage Poems', in *Aemilia Lanyer*, ed. Grossman, 60–82; Molekamp, 'Reading Christ the Book') and preaching (White, 'A Woman with Saint Peter's Keys?') but not, as suggested here, with the medieval tradition of Marian nourishment. It is also worth noting that, elsewhere in the text, Lanyer's patrons are informed that this feast will deliver 'health of the soule' (34), and

banqueting across *Salve Deus* is reminiscent of the symbols of eating and sustenance that proliferate in Marian writings, meaning that it is not necessary to understand this imagery, as Micheline White does, as Lanyer's performance of an exclusively male 'priestly task of "feeding" her readers with the Word'.[69] Rather, within the context of the work's broader interest in Mary, Lanyer's provision of spiritual nourishment lays claim to a typological inheritance of Marian maternity that is spiritual, one that illuminates a female tradition of spiritual nurture that originates in the birth narratives but stretches across time.

Lanyer's celebration of Mary's exegetical significance from Genesis through to the Gospels and into the present age demonstrates the symbolic tenacity of Marian maternity into the seventeenth century. For her, as well as Leigh, Mary's example transposes childbearing from a curse into a crown for all women, for all time, and becomes central to the formulation of the spiritual motherhood that authorizes their works. Although Mary might be the only one who literally gives birth to Christ, Lanyer and Leigh, with varying degrees of directness, understand themselves as the typological fulfilment of that mother. Their attempt to elevate, as well as extend, the remit of motherhood in *Salve Deus* and *The Mothers Blessing* relies on the typological structure of shadow and fulfilment, a trajectory which facilitates the transposition of literal maternity into figural maternity and allows flesh to resolve itself as spirit: Mary's physical maternity gives way to a spiritual maternity because, in giving birth to God in flesh, her body facilitates spiritual rebirth under the new covenant. Mary's provision of spiritual nourishment is fulfilled in the provisions of the authorial mother within whose work the fleshly birth of Christ becomes a textual rebirth of divine truth. Read typologically, the Marian body, with

the healing properties afforded to *Salve Deus* further align its author with Mary who, in medieval tradition, was regularly associated with spiritual healing. For a seventeenth-century example, see the medical imagery used in Antony Stafford, *The femall glory: or, The life, and death of our Blessed Lady* (London: Thomas Harper, 1635), 17–18.

[69] White, 'A Woman with Saint Peter's Keys?', 331. See also DiPasquale who connects Mary to ideas of female priesthood: *Refiguring the Sacred Feminine*, esp. Chapter 2. It is not incompatible to view Lanyer in both a clerical and maternal role. Acknowledgement of how the text's feasting imagery resonates with Marian nourishment illuminates that Lanyer is the inheritor of a powerful medieval tradition of maternal importance. Reading Lanyer's feast in relation to the Marian tradition of feeding and banqueting also adheres to White's understanding of the representation of the Marys in *Salve Deus* as Christ's true disciples in the tradition of the Song of Songs (see White, 'A Woman with Saint Peter's Keys?', 334–6). It should be said that the feast in *Salve Deus* is further tied to Mary in the work's evocation of the Song of Songs and Revelation, suggested when Lanyer calls her readers 'To enter with the Bridegroom to the feast' (41: 15). Mary was frequently associated with the Bride of the Song and the Book of Revelation. For more see Astell, *The Song of Songs*, 42–72.

its womb, birth canal, blood, pain, and breast milk, is always fulfilled by *spiritual* matter.

Consequently, the effort to elevate motherhood by illuminating the interconnectedness of physical and spiritual maternity involves, by typological standards, the resignation of its materiality, its realness, to the realm of the shadow. Leigh's physical labour for her children is fulfilled by her 'traualie' for their spiritual rebirth, a 'labour' for 'Christ [to] be formed' (11). This spiritual maternity is deemed a truer labour than labour of the flesh; the 'best labour is for the foode of the Soule', because it is 'a labour without which the soule cannot liue' (7, 5). For Lanyer, the process of poetic labour has produced a 'figure' of Christ's dying body; *Salve Deus* is termed 'my Paschal Lambe, / The figure of that living Sacrifice' (7: 85–6). Material labour is a figure of spiritual maternity that generates only spiritual matter. According to this trajectory, literal maternity must be a type, which is superseded, fulfilled, rendered obsolete, like the Old Testament law, by its promised antitype of spiritual maternity.[70] In the end, Lanyer and Leigh celebrate the mother who is, as Luxon says of Paul's interpretation of Sarah, 'not a mother in any fleshly sense'.[71] Inferring that true motherhood is spiritual rather than physical, *Salve Deus* and *The Mothers Blessing* ultimately retreat from the materiality of the maternal. To become a spiritual mother, the literally pregnant, birthing, and lactating female body must be relinquished.

[70] This trajectory chimes with Luxon's discussion of the implications of Paul's distinction between the birth of the Old Testament mothers Hagar and Sarah: *Reforming Figures*, 89–95.

[71] Luxon, *Reforming Figures*, 78.

6

Reading Revelations

Figuring the End in Post-Reformation Literary Culture

In a biblical commentary called *A reuelation of the reuelation* published in 1615 the Protestant writer Thomas Brightman declared the last book of the Bible to be '*a Revelation made by God* from which all the vayles of obscurity are taken away'. This new clarity of vision is possible because, as Brightman later marvels, readers of this biblical book see 'the whole garment displaied... at once'.[1] Brightman's comments are indicative of reformed understanding of biblical apocalypse—the Second Coming of Christ gives meaning to the entirety of history because it is the ending towards which everything moves. As the final ligature in history's preordained, progressive structure, Christ's return is time's defining moment. Hermeneutically speaking, it is the final antitype. Previous chapters of this book have identified Christ's victorious Second Coming as a determining framework for Protestant conceptions of history and identity, and suggested how this promised end inflected early modern Bible-reading more generally.[2] This chapter brings these wider discussions, and this book, to a close by considering how scripture's most sustained account of the end-point of history was read and applied in the early modern present.[3]

The Book of Revelation records how the return of Christ will be preceded by the persecution of Christ's true church at the hands of Satan's forces. This vivid account of a cosmic struggle for souls acquired new resonance in the decades after the Reformation as Protestants and

[1] Thomas Brightman, *A reuelation of the reuelation that is, the reuelation of St. Iohn opened clearely With a logicall resolution and exposition* (Amsterdam: [s.n.], 1615), 2, 3[9]7.

[2] See especially Chapters 2, pp. 49–78, and 3, pp. 79–112.

[3] Although the Book of Revelation is scripture's longest account of last days, the return of Christ is addressed in Daniel 7–12; Mark 13; Matthew 24; Luke 17:22–37; Luke 21; I Corinthians 15:20–8; II Corinthians 5:1–31; I Thessalonians 4:15–18; II Thessalonians 2:1–12.

Roman Catholics made counter-claims of spiritual authenticity.[4] Although the precise application of Revelation's prophecies varied, reformed commentators generally associated the persecuted faithful of Revelation with Protestantism, and looked forward to the defeat of an antichristian enemy who was invariably Catholic.[5] As Katharine R. Firth observes, 'on one thing both English and the continental Protestants agreed: the *revelation* of Antichrist was a historical event embodied in their own movement for reformation'.[6] The popularity and importance of apocalyptic theology in England during the sixteenth and seventeenth centuries has been demonstrated by scholars such as Firth, Brian Ball, Richard Bauckham, and Paul Christianson, but the hermeneutic principles that facilitated viewing the Reformation, and its subsequent religious and political fallout, through an eschatological lens warrant further scrutiny.[7] Because although early modern scholarship regularly acknowledges the popular invocation of Revelation's narrative in discourses of anti-popery, and cites the reformers' association of the Antichrist and Whore of Babylon with the pope and Roman Catholic Church, it has frequently neglected to examine the exegetical practices, and paradoxes, that underpin these readings.[8] A typological reading of the

[4] The tendency among reformers to read the present eschatologically was not a new phenomenon. A number of studies have demonstrated the importance of apocalyptic theology in the medieval period. See in particular: Norman Cohn, *The Pursuit of the Millennium: Revolutionary Millenarians and Mystical Anarchists of the Middle Ages* (London: Pimlico, 1957, rpt. 2004); Marjorie Reeves, *The Influence of Prophecy in the Later Middle Ages: A Study in Joachimism* (Oxford: Clarendon Press, 1969); Bernard McGinn, *The Apocalypse in the Middle Ages* (Ithaca: Cornell University Press, 1992). For consideration of the apocalypse in Jewish and early Christian writings see D. S. Russell, *The Method & Message of Jewish Apocalyptic, 200 BC–AD 100* (Philadelphia: Westminster Press, 1964); John Joseph Collins, *Apocalypse: The Morphology of a Genre* (Missoula: Scholars Press, 1979).

[5] By comparison, as Stuart Clark notes, Catholic eschatology in this period is 'less insistent': *Thinking with Demons*, 340, 341–7. That said, some Catholic commentators did associate Protestantism with the Antichrist. See Katharine R. Firth, *The Apocalyptic Tradition in Reformation Britain, 1530–1645* (Oxford: Oxford University Press, 1979), 111–13, 161.

[6] Firth, *The Apocalyptic Tradition*, 29.

[7] See Firth, *The Apocalyptic Tradition*; Brian W. Ball, *A Great Expectation: Eschatological Thought in English Protestantism to 1660* (Leiden: E. J. Brill, 1975); Richard Bauckham, *Tudor Apocalypse: Sixteenth Century Apocalypticism, Millenarianism, and the English Reformation from John Bale to John Foxe and Thomas Brightman* (Oxford: Sutton Courtenay Press, 1978); Paul Christianson, *Reformers and Babylon: English Apocalyptic Visions from the Reformation to the Eve of the Civil War* (Toronto: University of Toronto Press, 1978). For apocalyptic theology in Europe see Robin Bruce Barnes, *Prophecy and Gnosis: Apocalypticism in the Wake of the Lutheran Reformation* (Stanford: Stanford University Press, 1988); Irene D. Backus, *Reformation Readings of the Apocalypse: Geneva, Zurich, and Wittenberg* (Oxford: Oxford University Press, 2000).

[8] It should be said that Warren Johnston has considered applications of biblical apocalypse in a period beyond the scope of this book, 1660–1700 (*Revelation Restored: The Apocalypse in Later Seventeenth-Century England* (Suffolk: Boydell Press, 2011)), and elsewhere I have considered how the Whore of Babylon was read and used by Protestants

scriptures legitimized filtering the present through the future promised in the Book of Revelation, and this theory of history undergirds the interpretative hubris that characterizes Protestant exegesis of this complex biblical text.

Reformed scholars frequently claimed that understanding the Book of Revelation's meaning was predicated on the possession of accurate sight—a faculty with which the biblical book is itself concerned. Biblical commentators, sermonizers, and literary writers who engaged with Revelation's narratives warned that the eyes of the faithful could be duped by the illusory tactics of the Antichrist's forces. Edmund Spenser's 'The Legend of Holiness' (1590), Thomas Dekker's *The Whore of Babylon* (1607), and Thomas Middleton's *A Game at Chess* (1624) represent revelations that occur in the early modern present, and in elucidating the deceptiveness of the antichristian enemy these works cohere with the concerns of popular Protestant exegesis. Yet, these literary reimaginings of Revelation's cosmic battle point up the intrinsic difficulty of reading apocalypse in relation to the present—the progression of time.

READING A REVELATION

Protestant commentators who wished to assert the Book of Revelation's relevance to the struggle of reformed churches across Europe against the Roman Catholic Church faced a hermeneutically tricky task. For this biblical book, the product of a series of visions delivered to the apostle John by an angel, spoke symbolically about future events. Revelation comprises, what Richard Bernard terms, 'certain forms, shapes, and figures,

*c.*1590–1620 (Brownlee, 'Imagining the Enemy'). Esther Gilman Richey has also shed light on the range of literary writings that engage with Revelation, but her study does not consider biblical hermeneutics at length: *The Politics of Revelation in the English Renaissance* (Columbia and London: University of Missouri Press, 1998). More broadly, Alison Shell and Frances E. Dolan have addressed the Whore of Babylon in broader discussions of the tropes of anti-Catholic writing, respectively: *Catholicism, Controversy, and the English Literary Imagination, 1558–1660* (Cambridge: Cambridge University Press, 1999), 41–8; *Whores of Babylon: Catholicism, Gender, and Seventeenth-Century Print Culture* (Ithaca: Cornell University Press, 1999) 6–9. Studies that have considered the Whore in early modern drama include: Julia Gasper, *The Dragon and the Dove: The Plays of Thomas Dekker* (Oxford: Clarendon Press, 1990), 62–75; Barbara L. Parker, 'The Whore of Babylon and Shakespeare's *Julius Caesar*', *Studies in English Literature, 1500–1900* 35.2 (1995): 251–69; Adrian Streete, '"An old quarrel between us that will never be at an end": Middleton's *Women Beware Women* and Late Jacobean Religious Politics', *Review of English Studies* 60.244 (2009): 230–54; Adrian Streete, *Apocalypse and Anti-Catholicism in Seventeenth-Century English Drama* (Cambridge: Cambridge University Press, 2017).

as it were Images and pictures'.[9] De-coding the meaning of the apocalyptic disclosures that Revelation recounts became a major task for reformed biblical scholars. Indeed, the book became one of the most frequently interpreted scriptural texts in the sixteenth and early seventeenth centuries. As Bauckham notes, at least eighteen full commentaries addressing Revelation were published in the Tudor period, many of which, including John Bale's influential *The Image of Bothe Churches* (1545), received multiple republications.[10] John's prophecy garnered a similar level of exegetical attention during the reign of England's first Stuart monarch, with expositors such as Hugh Broughton, Patrick Forbes, Thomas Mason, William Cowper, Richard Bernard, and Arthur Dent each producing substantial commentaries on this complex book.[11] Treatises scrutinizing the operations of the Antichrist and Whore of Babylon were also readily available from England's booksellers and pamphleteers, and the contemporary relevance of Revelation's prophecies were expounded in sermons series, such as those by Heinrich Bullinger and George Gifford, and examined in a special course of lectures delivered by William Perkins at Cambridge in 1595.[12]

The tide of expositional writings published on Revelation during the sixteenth and early seventeenth centuries suggests that ascertaining this book's meaning was interpretatively demanding. Many of these works record a concern that Revelation's perplexing style would deter lay reading. Augustin Marlorat, a French Augustinian monk and later pastor at Rouen, counters readers' apprehension at the beginning of his commentary with a caution: 'the thinges, that are sette foorth in this prophecie

[9] Richard Bernard, *A key of knowledge for the opening of the secret mysteries of St Iohns mysticall Reuelation* (London: Felix Kyngston, 1617), 130.

[10] Bauckham, *Tudor Apocalypse*, 137. Bale's work was first published in 1545 and was reissued in 1550, 1555, and 1570: *The image of bothe churches after reulacion of saynt Iohan the euangelyst* ([Antwerp]: S. Mierdman, 1545).

[11] Hugh Broughton, *A reuelation of the holy Apocalyps* (Middelburg: Richard Schilders, 1610); Patrick Forbes, *An exquisite commentarie vpon the Reuelation of Saint Iohn* (London: W. Hall, 1613); Bernard, *A key*; William Cowper, *Pathmos: or, A commentary on the Reuelation of Saint Iohn* (London: John Buge, 1619); Thomas Mason, *A revelation of the Revelation . . . whereby the pope is most plainely declared and proued to bee Antichrist* (London: G. Eld, 1619); Arthur Dent, *The Ruine of Rome . . . Written especially for the comfort of Protestants, and the daunting of Papists* (London: Nicholas Okes, 1624).

[12] See, for example, George Downame, *A Treatise concerning the Antichrist* (London: Cuthbert Burbie, 1603); George Abbot, *The Reason with Doctor Hill hath brought for the vpholding of Papistry* (Oxford: Joseph Barnes, 1604); J. Paul Parrin, *Luthers Fore-Runners*, trans. Samson Lennard (London: Nathanael Newbery, 1624); Heinrich Bullinger, *A Hundred Sermons vpon the Apocalips of Jesu Christe*, trans. John Day (London: Iohn Day, 1561); George Gifford, *Sermons vpon the whole booke of Revelation* (London: Thomas Man, 1599); William Perkins, *Lectures vpon the three first chapters of the Reuelation* (London: Thomas Purfoote, 1604).

darkly, and in manner riddlelyke muste not hinder the godlie from readyng of it'.[13] In many cases, charges to read revelation open into reminders that this prophetical book warrants a distinctive interpretative approach. Refuting the advice of 'the Papists' who claim that Revelation was too 'full of darkeness and obsuritie . . . for the common people' to read, Dent stresses that 'there is nothing in this Prophesie, which study and diligence, with prayer and humility, may not ouercome. True . . . the shell is thicke, and hard to breake: but being broken, the kernell is most sweet and pleasant.'[14] Dent's encouragement to his readers is both an entreaty to study Revelation's narratives and a declaration of hermeneutic methodology. The text's 'kernell'—or true meaning—is not that which is immediately implied by the words but resides within a figurative 'shell'. Donne is similarly anxious to press Revelation's exegetical peculiarity in a sermon delivered at St Paul's in 1624. He notes that unlike other parts of scripture where there is 'danger in departing from the letter', in Revelation 'there is . . . danger in adhering too close to the letter'—in this biblical book the 'figurative sense is the literall sense'.[15] Donne's explanation reminds that reformed readers did not abandon their commitment to scripture's 'literall sense' when interpreting Revelation. Instead, commentary on this biblical book frequently illustrates the reformers' attempts to hold fast to a brand of literalism that accommodated figural readings.[16] Unsurprisingly, Protestant commentators tend to evade the interpretative convolutions that facilitate mapping Revelation's narrative onto the present. Instead, they assert, as Marlorat puts it, that the meaning of 'this booke shall be simple, playne and cleare to the faythfull'.[17]

The confidence with which Protestants interpreted Revelation was predicated on the belief that the events John foretold were being fulfilled in the present. Dent notes the significance of the historical juncture at the outset of his expositional work, *The Ruine of Rome* (1603): 'we liue in an age wherein the most of the things prophesied in this booke are fulfilled . . . many things which vnto [the Fathers] were very obscure, are vnto vs most cleare and manifest'.[18] Readers of Perkins' 1606 commentary likewise are reminded of their privileged position in history. Unlike earlier generations, Perkins' readers are witnesses to the disclosures this biblical book describes: 'so many things being fulfilled which were foretold in this booke, we may

[13] Augustin Marlorat, *A Catholike exposition vpon the Reuelation of Sainct Iohn* ([London]: H. Binneman, [1574]), A2v.

[14] Dent, *The ruine of Rome*, AA2r–AA3v.

[15] Donne, *Sermons*, 6:62.

[16] I have discussed the reformers' understanding of the literal sense of Revelation and the influence of the present moment on Protestant readings of John's prophecy in brief elsewhere: see Brownlee, 'Imagining the Enemy', 214–15.

[17] Marlorat, *A Catholike exposition*, A2v.

[18] Dent, *The ruine of Rome*, A3r.

easily see what is meant by it'.[19] The break from Rome, and the legacy of this division, was understood to fulfil particular aspects of John's vision. Bale, for instance, described the exile of 'purgatory, pilgrimages, & other peltries' in many parts of Germany and England as 'a deadly wounding of one of the beastes heads' (Rev. 13), and, writing later, Bernard declared the prophecy concerning the sixth church of Philadelphia (Rev. 3:7–13) to be 'now... where we doe liue, and shall continue to the ouerthrow of Rome'.[20] By the early decades of the seventeenth century historical readings of Revelation's pages were commonplace—an interpretative methodology that owed no small part to the approaches popularized by the works of Bale and Foxe. Bale's *The Image of Bothe Churches* advocated combining biblical exegesis with scrutiny of history, for by 'conferring the one with the other' it was possible to 'perceyue most wonderfull causes. For in the text are they onely proponed in effecte... but in the cronicles they are euidently seene by all ages fulfilled'.[21] Foxe's *Actes and Monuments* was, as the earlier discussion of the Book of Job suggested, similarly influential in the development of an apocalyptically inflected Protestant historiography.[22] In fact, as Firth notes, Foxe was 'the first British author to write a Protestant apocalyptic history that attempted to explain changes in time in terms of an unfolding pattern of events'.[23] For Foxe, Revelation compelled such an approach for it 'conteineth a Propheticall history of the Church: so likewise it requireth by histories to be opened'.[24] Through this associative reading Foxe recorded a Christian history that, since the earliest days of the Church, moved towards the rescue of truth from a corrupt Roman Catholic Church.[25]

In using current circumstances to interpret Revelation's prophecies Protestant commentators relied on a typological understanding of history's unity. The proximity of apocalyptic and typological modes of thought is suggested in Brightman's commentary on Revelation. Using an architectural metaphor, Brightman marvels that John's 'Historye... compacteth all into one, & setteth the whole building before our eyes, that we might see to what perfection that singular frame doth at length come... The events came forth by litle and litle, and point by point... to make vp the whole frame of the building together & at once.'[26] For

[19] William Perkins, *A godly and learned exposition or commentarie vpon the three first chapters of the Reuelation* (London: Adam Islip, 1606), A1v.

[20] John Bale, *The image of both Churches after the most wonderfull and heavenly Reuelation* (London: Thomas East 1570), 2:59v; Bernard, *A key*, D4v.

[21] Bale, *The image of both Churches* (1570), 1:A4r.

[22] See Chapter 3, pp. 90–3.

[23] Firth, *The Apocalyptic Tradition*, 110.

[24] Foxe, *Actes and Monuments*, 'Foure Questions propounded to the Papists', n.p.

[25] For more on Foxe and Bale's historical reading of Revelation see Bauckham, *Tudor Apocalypse*, 140, and Firth, *The Apocalyptic Tradition*, 110–15.

[26] Brightman, *A reuelation of the reuelation*, 3[9]7.

Brightman, Revelation verifies the forward advancement of a 'singular frame' of history, but, as a prophecy, it also catapults its readers outside of time. Readers of John's vision are spectators of the 'whole'—witnesses to the end in the here and now. In revealing the end-point towards which all of time moves, the Book of Revelation celebrates what Bale terms as the 'complet summe' as well as 'whole knitting vp' of history.[27] Christ's return and defeat of Satan is the ultimate antitype, the end-point in a chain of meaning that encompasses both Testaments of scripture and stretches across present and future ages.[28]

A PROTESTANT REVELATION

For biblical scholars in the sixteenth and seventeenth centuries, Revelation's disclosure of a definitive end to time was both ideologically compelling and hermeneutically significant. One of the benefits of reading Revelation was, according to the German Professor of Divinity Franciscus Junius, that readers could 'distinctly see to what part of the storie of the Church, and to what point of time, eueriething is to be referred'.[29] For just as this biblical book made knowable the trajectory of history, so too it verified the eternal vindication of Christ's true church. Reformed commentators express little doubt over the identity of the church whose victory is promised in Revelation—as Bernard confidently declares: 'by this booke may we, the reformed Churches, the true members of Christs Church, know . . . our promised future happinesse'.[30] Indeed, so clearly does Bernard find the Book of Revelation to speak of the current conflict between Protestantism and Catholicism that his 1617 commentary, *A key of knowledge*, painstakingly catalogues those verses that prove 'John for the

[27] Bale, *The image of both Churches* (1570), 1:A3v. For a more detailed discussion of the way in which reformed understanding of the relationship between past, present, and future influenced apocalyptic thinking see Frank Ardolino, *Apocalypse & Armada in Kyd's Spanish Tragedy* (Kirksville: Sixteenth Century Essays & Studies, 1995), 46.

[28] As Chapter 1 notes, Frye describes typology as 'a theory . . . of historical process': *The Great Code*, 80. For more on the relationship between typological thought and history see Chapter 1, pp. 31–3, as well as Frye, *The Great Code*, 80–1.

[29] Franciscus Junius, *Apocalypsis. A briefe and learned commentarie* (London: Richard Field, 1592), 'An admonition vnto the reader', n.p.

[30] Bernard, *A key*, E8v. Dent's work makes a similar claim of Protestant victory through reading Revelation when, in the subtitle, it claims that through this book it is 'plainly shewed and proued, that the popish religion' will 'come to an vtter overthrow' for this work has been 'written especially for the comfort of Protestants, and the daunting of papists': Dent, *The ruine of Rome*, title page.

Protestants' and 'John against the Papists'.[31] The exegetical effort to trace present circumstances onto Revelation's narratives was, then, bound up with the future its prophecies were understood to promise the Protestant faithful. Irrespective of current circumstances, Protestants—the true church of Christ—awaited 'the most happie condition'.[32]

The claim of apocalyptic victory for Protestantism was a bold one, and reformed biblical scholars acknowledged that this interpretation of Revelation would not be accepted universally. Interpretative deviation was, however, afforded little sympathy. Failure to accept that Revelation's prophecies spoke of the fall of the Roman Catholic Church was typically credited to spiritual blindness, for, as Bale put it, there is 'nothing more manifest, vnless we haue eies & will not see'.[33] A similarly confident declaration is made by Mason: 'none except the diuell blinde his eyes, but may see the Pope' in John's prophecy.[34] As these remarks suggest, the language of seeing pervades reformed exegesis of this biblical book. This preoccupation with sight was arguably precipitated by Revelation itself, which persistently reminds readers of the falsity of the antichristian figures it represents. The prophecies disclose how the Antichrist's agents will dupe the earth's inhabitants through false appearances (Rev. 13:13–16; 17:3–7) and 'signes, and lying wonders' (II Thess. 2:9). According to John's vision of the future, only those with the ability to discern the authenticity of what is seen will avoid false worship in the last days. Given this assessment, reformed claims of accurate vision could function to affirm Protestants as members of Christ's true church to whom the spurious workings of the false church had been made known.

A sense of heightened and privileged perception underpins the opening address to 'the watchfvll eyes in this ovr State' who 'search out . . . walking spirits of Antichrist' in Bernard's *A key of knowledge*, and is suggested in the distinction Dent draws between blindness and sight in his exegesis of Revelation 13.[35] The 'eares & eies [of al papists and worldlings] are sealed and shut vp' to the mysteries of the Beast. The meaning of this passage

[31] Bernard, *A key*, F4r. [32] Bernard, *A key*, E4v–r.

[33] Bale, *The image of both Churches* (1570), 2:58v–59v.

[34] Mason, *A revelation of the Revelation*, 63.

[35] Bernard, *A key*, B1r. It should be said that the accusation that the pope was the Antichrist was not distinctive to the Reformation period. John Wyclif made this claim in *De Papa* (1379). For more on the popularity of this idea before the Reformation see Richard K. Emmerson, *Antichrist in the Middle Ages: A Study of Medieval Apocalypticism, Art, and Literature* (Seattle: University of Washington Press, 1981), 204–37. For the spread and development of this association in the sixteenth and seventeenth centuries see Christopher Hill, *Antichrist in Seventeenth Century England* (Oxford: Oxford University Press: 1971), 9–13.

may be 'vnderstood of none but those onely, whose eares and eies God openeth to heare, & see, and vnderstand, that is, the very elect of God'.[36] As the recipients of a special revelation, the identity of the Antichrist's agents would not only be recognizable to reformed readers but 'most euident'.[37]

That the meaning of this complex book is apparent to the elect is suggested in the descriptions of Revelation's plainness that recur in Protestant exegesis. Foxe notes that the book uses 'playne woordes' to announce the Whore of Babylon as 'the City of Rome', Marlorat describes the prophecies as 'playne and cleare', and David Pareus quips that Revelation 17 confirms that 'two nuts are not more alike, then is the *Beast and Purpled Whore* to the Papacy'.[38] The stress on Revelation's clarity of meaning is also indicative of the wider need to reconcile figural readings of this symbolic book with the Protestant commitment to hermeneutic literalism. To this end, the insistence that Revelation revealed its meaning typically, rather than allegorically, was similarly important.[39] Pareus reassures his readers that 'in many Types ... the signification is plaine, and the Analogie with the things signified not obscure: as the Analogie of the *seven Candletickes*, with the *seven Churches* ... of the *Locusts* with the *devouring Monkes*, of *Babylon* and the *Great Whore* with *Rome*'.[40] Bernard similarly affirms the apparent simplicity of Revelation's typology when he remarks that 'there is such answerablenes of the Antitype to the type' in this biblical book.[41] The confidence with which reformed commentators approach Revelation reminds that applying John's prophecies to the present was by no means considered to be an interpretative leap. Instead, because type and antitype were perceived to 'follow so cleerly one vpon another' in Revelation, commentators express little hesitation in declaring '*the Pope in his Pontificalitie and Popedome is the Antitype and the beast here meant*'.[42]

36 Dent, *The ruine of Rome*, 180.

37 Gifford, *Sermons vpon the whole booke of the Revelation*, 340.

38 Foxe, *Actes and Monuments* (1583), 1778; Marlorat, *A Catholike exposition*, A2v; David Pareus, *A commentary upon the divine Revelation of the apostle and evangelist, Iohn* (Amsterdam: C.P., 1644), 10. See also similar comments in William Fulke, *Praelections vpon the sacred and holy Reuelation of S. John*, trans. George Gifford (London: Thomas Purfoote, 1573), 112; Cowper, *Pathmos*, 12; Forbes, *An exquisite commentarie*, A4r.

39 Reformers typically vilified allegory but they accommodated biblical typology within their definition of scripture's literal sense. See Chapter 1, pp. 41–5.

40 Pareus, *A commentary upon the divine Revelation*, 10. See also the emphasis on a typological reading in Forbes, *An exquisite commentarie*, A1r, and Thomas Taylor, *Christs victorie over the Dragon* (London: M[iles] F[lesher], 1633), 1.

41 Bernard, *A key*, C7r; H2r/51.

42 Bernard, *A key*, C7r; H2r/51.

Even when typological methods are not cited directly in Protestant exegesis the influence of the core principles of this reading practice is discernible in the fluid shift from sacred history to the present. Shorthand phrases such as 'Romishe Antichrist'—repeatedly used by the Swiss reformer Heinrich Bullinger—or Perkins' warnings against 'that purple whoore of Rome' and 'the sea of Antichrist at Rome', draw on a typological understanding of the unity of history to announce Revelation's antichristian forces to be fulfilled by Roman Catholicism.[43] This reading practice similarly informs visual representations of Revelation's figures which were included in some expositional works and Bibles.[44] In Luther's 1522 New Testament the text of Revelation was supplemented with twenty-one explanatory woodcuts produced by Lucas Cranach the Elder.[45] Among this series was an image of the Whore of Babylon wearing the papal tiara (Figure 6.1).[46] This illustration was, as Natasha and Anthony O'Hear explain, provocative and influential: 'The image of the Whore of Babylon as the pope . . . set in motion centuries of anti-Catholic polemic . . . creating an unmistakable identification of the office of the papacy with a character from Revelation widely regarded as a symbol of evil'.[47] In suggesting that Revelation's prophecies could be

[43] Heinrich Bullinger, *A confutation of the Popes bull . . . with a defence of the sayd true Christian Queene* (London: Iohn Day, 1572), A1r; Perkins, *Lectures vpon . . . the Reuelation*, 354–5. See also the examples used in Parrin, *Luther's Fore-Runners*, 70.

[44] See, for example, the images contained in Bale, *The image of both Churches*, 58; Martin Luther, *Das Newe Testament Deutzsch* (Wittenburg: M. Lotter, 1522); Forbes, *An exquisite commentarie*, 249. For a discussion of visual representations of Revelation, including in-depth discussion of Luther's text, see: Natasha O'Hear, *Contrasting Images of the Book of Revelation in Late Medieval and Early Modern Art: A Case Study in Visual Exegesis* (Oxford: Oxford University Press, 2011), 135–98; Robert Scribner, *For the Sake of Simple Folk: Popular Propaganda for the German Reformation* (Oxford: Clarendon Press, 1994), 169–75.

[45] Luther, *Das Newe Testament*. It should be said that elsewhere the richly symbolic nature of Revelation prompted Luther to query the book's canonicity. See the comments in his Preface in *Luther's Works*, 35:400. Yet, as Craig R. Koester notes, Luther did eventually become persuaded of a historical approach to Revelation: *Revelation and the End of All Things* (Grand Rapids, MI: Eerdmans, 2001), 11. Luther's caution towards the Book of Revelation was shared by Calvin. Revelation was among the few books of scripture for which Calvin did not produce a commentary, although he did posit that the pope was the Antichrist in his commentary on II Thessalonians 3:3–12: John Calvin, *Commentaries on the New Testament*, ed. D. W. Torrance and T. F. Torrance, 12 vols. (Edinburgh: Oliver & Boyd, 1959–65), 4:339. For a discussion of Calvin's apocalyptic theology, and a comparison with Luther, see Barnes, *Prophecy and Gnosis*, 32–3.

[46] Cranach also depicted the Beast of Revelation 11 wearing the papal tiara.

[47] Natasha O'Hear and Anthony O'Hear, *Picturing the Apocalypse: The Book of Revelation in the Arts over Two Millennia* (Oxford: Oxford University Press, 2015), 168. Luther's apocalyptic theology grew in popularity due to the widespread adoption of Lutheranism as the state religion in many countries across Europe. See R. Po-Chia Hsia, *Social Discipline in the Reformation: Central Europe 1550–1750* (London: Routledge, 1989), 112–13; Hill, *Antichrist*, 9–13.

Figure 6.1. The Whore of Babylon, from Martin Luther, *Das Newe Testament Deutzsch*. Herzog August Bibliothek Wolfenbüttel: Bibel-S. 4 257a.

decoded through scrutiny of current political and religious circumstances, the visual exegesis that accompanied Luther's first vernacular translation of Revelation encouraged readers towards a typological interpretation of John's prophecies. The clash between Protestantism and Catholicism was marked as an apocalyptic event—a battle between good and evil.

That Protestant readings of the conflict between Revelation's true and false churches were bound up with an attempt to legitimize and delegitimize Christianity's factions in the wake of the break with Rome is clear. By identifying Protestantism as Christ's true church the reformers laid claim to the history and future of God's chosen people, and announced the Roman Catholic Church to be false. The reformed association of Revelation's false figures with the Roman Catholic Church illustrates how Protestantism, despite its literalist claims, was reliant upon figurative definitions of identity. Yet, as Luxon's discussion of reformed hermeneutics reminds, figural identifications have a much longer history in Christian tradition. Since the apostolic period, Christianity has been 'committed to an allegorical ontology . . . [Christianity] others the self and the world into God's allegory of himself and his kingdom. . . . And Christianity's names for the other, whether it be the old self, the other of the past, or the other of the present (as viewed from eternity) are the Jew, the Synagogue, the "carnal" Jerusalem, the whore, the flesh, and the world.'[48] For Protestants in the sixteenth and seventeenth centuries, the Book of Revelation was replete with vocabulary and imagery useful for delineating the reformed Church from the Church of Rome, and the names and workings of Revelation's Beasts, Antichrist, Whore of Babylon, Satan's forces and false church quickly became established synonyms for the Roman Catholic Church and its officials (Figure 6.2). The extent to which literally minded reformers were compelled by Revelation's figurative ontology is keenly felt in literary reimaginings of the biblical narrative that strive to reveal Revelation's contemporary import using figural means. Spenser's 'The Legend of Holiness', Dekker's *The Whore of Babylon*, and Middleton's *A Game at Chess* allegorically cast historical events and circumstances as the apocalyptic battle between good and evil. In doing so, these works not only demonstrate the extent to which Protestantism was figuratively inclined, but elucidate the intrinsic problems associated with reading the Reformation as a decisive apocalyptic moment.

[48] Luxon, *Reforming Figures*, 26.

Figure 6.2. The Pope on the seven-headed beast, from Patrick Forbes, *An exquisite commentarie vpon the Reuelation of Saint Iohn* (RB 20180). By permission of the Huntington Library, San Marino, California.

GOODLY WOMEN AND SCARLET WHORES

The Protestant tendency to filter the struggle of the reformed Church against its enemies through the Book of Revelation informs Spenser's heroic poem, *The Faerie Queene*, and Dekker's commemorative drama to Elizabeth I, *The Whore of Babylon.* Since Josephine Waters Bennet argued that *The Faerie Queene* was indebted to Revelation, scholars including Florence Sadler, John N. King, Andrew Escobedo, John Watkins, and Esther Gilman Richey have demonstrated the extent to which the poem's narrative episodes and central figures are influenced by this biblical book.[49] Although an apocalyptic understanding of history undergirds all

[49] Josephine Waters Bennet, *The Evolution of 'The Faerie Queene'* (Chicago: University of Chicago Press, 1942); Florence Sadler, '*The Faerie Queene*: An Elizabethan Apocalypse', in *The Apocalypse in English Renaissance Thought and Literature: Patterns, Antecedents and Repercussions*, ed. C. A. Patrides and Joseph Wittreich (Ithaca: Cornell University Press, 1984), 148–74; John N. King, *Spenser's Poetry and the Reformation Tradition* (Princeton: Princeton University Press, 1990), 72–96; Andrew Escobedo, *Nationalism and Historical Loss in Renaissance England: Foxe, Dee, Spenser, Milton* (Ithaca: Cornell University Press, 2004), 81–140; John Watkins, 'Spenser's Poetry and the Apocalypse', in *Early Modern*

six books of the epic, it is, as Sadler notes, from Book One 'that there emerges most clearly Spenser's reading of the Johannine Apocalypse'.[50] It has become a critical commonplace that 'The Legende of the Knight of the Red Crosse or Holinesse'—which recounts the Knight's encounter with various apocalyptic figures made famous by John's prophecy—employs the imagery and topoi of the last book of scripture. Spenser's recapitulation of John's vision has been termed 'one of English Literature's most celebrated retellings of [Revelation]', and the work's influence on literary reimaginings of biblical apocalypse is traceable via verbal allusions in seventeenth-century drama as well as poetry.[51] Dekker's obligation to *The Faerie Queene* is unmistakable. A significant portion of *The Whore of Babylon* is located in a Fairie Kingdom protected by the valiant 'Fairie Queene' (1.1.46), and, as several scholars have observed, the play reuses names from Spenser's work such as Florimell and Paridell.[52] The play's apocalyptic theology illustrates, however, that *The Faerie Queene*'s impact was ideological as well as linguistic. For as Dekker's *The Whore of Babylon* stages the unreliability of sight, and meditates on foiled revelatory processes, it ruminates on aspects of apocalypse that preoccupy Spenser's 'Legend of Holiness', and Protestant readers of Revelation more generally.

In *The Faerie Queene* and *The Whore of Babylon* the influence of Revelation's use of female figures to distinguish between the true and

English Poetry: A Critical Companion, ed. Patrick Cheney, Andrew Hadfield, and Garrett A. Sullivan (Oxford: Oxford University Press, 2007), 90–101; Richey, *The Politics of Revelation*, 16–35. See also John E. Hankins, 'Spenser and the Revelation of St. John', *PMLA* 60.2 (1945): 364–81; Joseph A. Wittreich, *Visionary Poetics: Milton's Tradition and his Legacy* (San Marino, CA: Huntington Library, 1979), esp. Chapter 1; Darryl J. Gless, *Interpretation and Theology in Spenser* (Cambridge: Cambridge University Press, 1994), 82–4; Richard Mallette, *Spenser and the Discourses of Reformation England* (Lincoln: University of Nebraska Press, 1997), 124–56; Anthea Hume, *Edmund Spenser: Protestant Poet* (Cambridge: Cambridge University Press, 1984), 72–106.

50 Sadler, '*The Faerie Queene*', 171.

51 Watkins, 'Spenser's Poetry and the Apocalypse', 90. For an overview of this literary influence in the seventeenth century see John Watkins, '"And yet the end was not": Apocalyptic Deferral and Spenser's Literary Afterlife', in *Worldmaking Spenser: Explorations in the Early Modern Age*, ed. Patrick Cheney and Lauren Silberman (Lexington: University Press of Kentucky, 2000), 156–74.

52 For an overview of the works' verbal parallels, and an assessment of Spenser's influence on Dekker more generally, see Cyrus Hoy, *Introductions, Notes and Commentaries to Texts in 'The Dramatic Works of Thomas Dekker'*, ed. Fredson Bowers, vol. II (Cambridge: Cambridge University Press, 1980), 300–3; Marianne Gateson Riely, 'Introduction', in *The Whore of Babylon*, ed. Marianne Gateson Riely (New York: Garland, 1980), 46–51; Susan Krantz, 'Thomas Dekker's Political Commentary in *The Whore of Babylon*', *Studies in English Literature, 1500–1900* 35.2 (1995): 271–91; Gasper, *The Dragon and the Dove*, 166; Watkins, '"And yet the end was not"', 166.

false churches is clearly perceptible. The Woman Clothed with the Sun—whose plight, pregnant and pursued by a seven-headed dragon is described in Revelation 12—had long been read as a symbol of the Church of Christ maligned by Satan's forces in the last days.[53] By contrast, the infamous harlotry of the Whore of Babylon (Rev. 17) was understood to speak of the spiritual whoredom induced by the false church. Dekker and Spenser, in different ways, develop the vivid biblical imagery of Revelation 12 and 17 into dramatic narratives that centre on the appeal of two women who allegorically represent opposing spiritual states.[54] As is well known, Spenser's Una—evocatively described as having a 'sunshyny face'—is identifiable as the shining woman of Revelation 12, and her persistent association with 'lily' whiteness further affirms her symbolic function as the one, true church, whose members are similarly characterized by their white raiment in John's visions.[55] Una's name and colourless state visually mark her as the antithesis of the duplicitous Duessa, who enters the narrative clad in the familiar costume of the Whore of Babylon: 'in scarlet red, / Purfled with gold and pearle of rich assay' (1.2.13).[56] Redcrosse's trouble differentiating between the alternative truth claims of these women 'epitomizes', what King identifies as, 'the Reformation dilemma of choosing between "images"

[53] For an overview of Christian interpretation of Revelation 12 see Joseph Rhymer, *The End of Time: Eschatology of the New Testament* (Slough: St Paul Publications, 1992), 105–9.

[54] Although a number of scholars have suggested that the oppositions drawn in Spenser and Dekker's texts might not be as absolute as the writers might wish them to be, the sustained effort to contrast the women's appearance and nature reinforces their opposition as intrinsic to the ideological programme of both texts. Critics who have questioned the binary structure of these texts include: Jean Howard, who argues that the play's theatricality undermines its ideological project: *The Stage and Social Struggle in Early Modern England* (London: Routledge, 1994), 52–60; Dolan, who suggests that Titania and the Empresse coalesce in their challenge of gender conventions: *Whores of Babylon*, 55; Regina Buccola, who explores how both Dekker's female figures are associated with the Virgin Mary: 'Virgin Fairies and Imperial Whores: The Unstable Ground of Religious Iconography in Thomas Dekker's *The Whore of Babylon*', in *Marian Moments*, ed. Buccola and Hopkins, 141–60; and Jonathan Gill Harris, who traces how the play's imagery of poison and medicine become entangled: *Foreign Bodies and the Body Politic: Discourses of Social Pathology in Early Modern England* (Cambridge: Cambridge University Press, 1998), 64–73.

[55] Edmund Spenser, *The Faerie Queene*, ed. A. C. Hamilton (London and New York: Longman, 1998), 1.12.23, 22. All further references to this text will be given in the text. The white raiment of the faithful is noted in Revelation 3:4–5; 3:18; 4:4; 6:11; 7:9–14: 19:14, and the returning Christ is also repeatedly tied to whiteness in Revelation 1:14; 6:2; 19:11; 20:11. Una's symbolic function as truth is also implied through Christological allusions. Her description in 1.1.4, for example, resonates with the imagery of John 1:29 and Revelation 19:7.

[56] Revelation 17:4 describes the Whore as arrayed in a 'skarlat' robe embroidered with 'golde, & precious stones, and pearles'. For additional consideration of the Whore's apparel in religious and popular culture see Brownlee, 'Imagining the Enemy'.

of competing churches', a contemporary application which, as John Dixon's 1597 annotations attest, was not lost on the poem's first readers.[57]

Spenser gives his readers clear cues that his apocalyptic allegory has historical resonance. As Dixon noted, Una, as a 'royall virgin' and 'goodly maiden Queene', is reminiscent of Elizabeth I as well as the Woman Clothed with the Sun (1.2.7, 1.12.8),[58] while Duessa's '*Persian* mitre' and 'triple crowne' announce her to be the pope (1.2.13; 1.7.16).[59] The apocalyptic potency of the present moment is further registered through Duessa's 'golden cup', which, as D. Douglas Waters has argued, is reminiscent of the Catholic Mass chalice (1.8.14).[60] 'Replete with magick artes' that induce 'Death and despeyre', and issuing a 'secret poison' that overwhelms the 'inner parts' (1.8.14), Duessa's cup engages with reformed suspicions of the enchanting properties of the Eucharist, which, in Bale's view, was used by the Roman Catholic Church to 'dayly ministereth . . . false religion'.[61] Spenser's anti-Catholic reading of the Whore's 'cup of golde' (Rev. 17:4) affirms the text's adherence to a typological approach to Revelation popular with Protestant commentators. Yet, the description of Duessa's potent elixir also points up how the poem amplifies the familiar

[57] King, *Spenser's Poetry*, 73; John Dixon, *The First Commentary on 'The Faerie Queene'*, ed. Graham Hough (Stansted: privately published, 1964). For a discussion of Dixon's annotations see King, *Spenser's Poetry*, 72–5; Sadler, '*The Faerie Queene*', 164–6.

[58] Dixon's poetic annotations affirm that Elizabethan readers identified Una as both the Woman Clothed with the Sun and Elizabeth I. See King, *Spenser's Poetry*, 73, 72–5, 165. For more on how Spenser represents Elizabeth throughout *The Faerie Queen* see Robin Headlam Wells, *Spenser's Faerie Queene and the Cult of Elizabeth* (London and Canberra: Croom Helm, 1983).

[59] The Whore of Babylon regularly was figured wearing the pope's triple-tiered tiara or bearing a cup resembling the mass chalice. See Figures 6.1 and 6.2 in this chapter, p. 179 and p. 181, as well as the discussion on p. 178. The reference to Duessa's '*Persian* mitre' is suggestive of her identity as both apocalyptic Whore and pope as it implies a clerical role originating in the East, and more specifically in Babylon—a geographic location that by this time, as Dolan has shown, connoted foreignness, corruption, and Catholicism (1.2.13): *Whores of Babylon*, esp. 42–4.

[60] D. Douglas Waters, *Duessa as Theological Satire* (Columbia: University of Missouri Press, 1970), 104–6. For a consideration of the cups that appear across *The Faerie Queene*, and their biblical significance, see Carol V. Kaske, *Spenser and Biblical Poetics* (Ithaca and London: Cornell University Press, 1999), 41–51. See also John N. King, who terms Duessa a 'personification of the Roman rite Mass': 'Milton's Cave of Error: A Rewriting of Spenserian Satire', in *Worldmaking Spenser*, ed. Cheney and Silberman, 148–9, and Brownlee, 'Imagining the Enemy', 220.

[61] Bale, *The image of both Churches* (1570), 2:S4v. For more on the Protestant association of the Mass—and Catholicism generally—and magic and witchcraft see Clark, *Thinking with Demons*, 360–1; Helen L. Parish, *Monks, Miracles and Magic: Reformation Representations of the Medieval Church* (New York: Routledge, 2005); Francis Young, *English Catholics and the Supernatural, 1553–1829* (New York: Routledge: 2016), 25–54.

tropes of the Whore of Babylon to warn of the susceptibility of the senses—particularly sight—to Romish spiritual attack.[62]

In Book One the debilitation of sight is often tied to Duessa's magical capabilities, a representation that speaks to the Protestant association of Catholicism with magic, and has its basis in Revelation 18:23, which notes that with the Whore's 'inchantements were deceiued all nations'. Fradubio recalls how Duessa used 'her hellish science' to raise a 'foggy mist' that made him 'dull' to Fraelissa's beauty (1.2.38), and later he recounts how Duessa 'besmeare[d]' his body with 'wicked herbes and ointments', a literal coating that clouds his perceptive faculties: 'though charmes and magicke . . . / all my senses were bereaued quight' (1.2.42).[63] The role of magic in warping perception is similarly important to Redcrosse's demise, because as Una explains to Arthur, her Knight falls into sin because of one 'Who with her witchcraft and misseeming sweete / Inueigled him to follow her desires vnmeete' (1.7.50). The use of 'Inueigled' is particularly instructive—used as it was in this period to refer to being taken 'captive by deceitful allurement' and to being 'blind in mind or judgement'—for it describes visual enthralment to be the cause, and unseeing to be the effect, of Redcrosse's encounter with Duessa.[64]

Duessa's 'misseeming' appearance is, however, not solely attributable to magic.[65] Spenser's Whore is skilled in visual artifice generally, and the narrative repeatedly reminds that Duessa 'well can faine' to 'seeme like Truth', being, as Una warns Arthur, 'Great maistresse of her art was that false Dame' (1.7.1). As one who looks like Truth, Duessa embodies what Isabel G. MacCaffrey terms 'the duplicity of seemings'—a representation that reverberates with Protestant assessments of the Whore of Babylon and her antitype, Catholicism, as but 'the shew of religion . . . a secret enemy,

62 In considering how Book One's preoccupation with seeing is an apocalyptic concern that is inflected by Protestant criticism of Catholicism I build on a body of scholarship that has considered the relationship between seeing and knowing in *The Faerie Queene*. See, for example, Joseph B. Dallett, 'Ideas of Sight in *The Faerie Queene*', *English Literary History* 27 (1960): 87–121; Theresa M. Krier, *Gazing on Secret Sights: Spenser, Classical Imitation, and the Decorums of Vision* (Ithaca: Cornell University Press, 1990); David Norbrook, *Poetry and Politics in the English Renaissance* (Oxford: Oxford University Press, 2002), 111; Jane Grogan, *Exemplary Spenser: Visual and Poetic Pedagogy in The Faerie Queene* (Farnham: Ashgate: 2009). Also, see p. 194, for scholars who have considered the importance of interpretative processes more generally in Spenser's epic.

63 For consideration of Duessa's ability to distort female beauty see Shelia T. Cavanagh, *Wanton Eyes and Chaste Desires: Female Sexuality in The Faerie Queene* (Bloomington and Indianapolis: Indiana University Press, 1994), 59–60.

64 'inveigle, v.'. *OED Online*, <http://www.oed.com/view/Entry/98950?redirectedFrom=inveigle>, accessed 1 May 2017.

65 For consideration of female duplicity in *The Faerie Queene* more generally see Helen Hackett, *Women and Romance Fiction in the English Renaissance* (Cambridge: Cambridge University Press, 2000), 135–7.

making...countenance of a friend'.[66] Typically, this shared pretence turned on interpretations of the Whore's striking apparel, which was found to speak of the 'altars copes, vestuments, miters, crosses, chalisses, books, censers, patines...a certen pompe of great riches' that, Fulke asserts, 'popish religion cannot stand w^t^out'.[67]

As Fulke's comments suggest, biblical commentators devoted much time to analysing the significance of the colour and style of the clothing John describes in Revelation. For Bale, like many of his contemporaries, the light robes of the Women Clothed with the Sun and Bride of Christ are indicative of the 'true christian church...without spot', while the 'rose-coloured whore' is portentously 'depaynted' like the 'painted chu[r]ch' of Rome which uses 'glittering colour' to 'counterfeite godlinesse'.[68] Fulke extrapolates a similar meaning from the colour of the Whore's seven-headed beast: 'the beast is paynted out to be like scarlet, which colour we knowe dothe please the court of Rome aboue all coloures'.[69] That readings of Revelation 17 commonly invoke the imagery of painting is significant, because, as Alison Shell has shown, painting—whether a face or an idol—'was a hypocritical act', and a regular trope in anti-Catholic and misogynistic writings. In both discourses, 'paint deceived the beholder into believing falsity', a representative function that appears to inform Spenser's use of a painting analogy to affirm Duessa's speciousness.[70] In Canto Seven Una states that Duessa 'cast her colours dyed deepe' to appear 'like Truth' (1.7.1), and Duessa affirms her use of coated clothing directly when, having declared to Night 'I that do seeme not I, Duessa am', she discloses that she appears in 'garments gilt' (1.5.26). This gilding is revealed elsewhere in the narrative to be highly decorative. Duessa's scarlet clothing is 'Purfled with gold and pearle' and embellished by 'crownes and owches', and her body is festooned with 'gold and jewels', 'tinsell', and 'golden bels' (1.2.13; 1.5.21). It is a glistering exterior that produces what the text pointedly terms a 'seeming glorious show', an ocular spectacle that 'much emmoue[s]' Redcrosse, and tellingly has the potential to 'bewitch all mens sight' (1.2. 21; 1.2.39).

66 Isabel G. MacCaffrey, *Spenser's Allegory: The Anatomy of Imagination* (Princeton: Princeton University Press, 1976), 154; Laurence Deios, *That the Pope is that Antichrist* (London: George Bishop and Ralph Newberie, 1590), 16.

67 Fulke, *Praelections*, 111.

68 Bale, *The image of both Churches* (1570), A2r–A3v, S4v. See also the significance of colour in Stephen Batman's *A christall glasse of christian reformation wherein the godly maye beholde the coloured abuses vsed in this our present tyme* (London: Iohn Day 1569), A2r, as well as Shell's discussion of the use of colour in anti-Catholic polemic generally: *Catholicism*, 29.

69 Fulke, *Praelections*, 110.

70 Shell, *Catholicism*, 28, see also 26–30.

Visually beguiling, the excessively ornamented Duessa becomes redolent of the spiritual dangers of that which appeals to the eye, a representative function that chimes with warnings that emerge in exegesis of Revelation 17. Fulke cautions that, like the Whore of Babylon, the 'popish religion' uses a 'glitteringe shewe of earthlye thinges' to 'dasele' the 'eies of the blockish and rude multitude', and Gifford likewise warns in his commentary on Revelation 17 that the 'pompe, glorie, & beautie' of Catholicism has 'dazzled the eyes of high and lowe' drawing them 'into superstition and idolatrie'.[71] Importantly, Redcrosse's initial encounter with Duessa registers this characteristic debilitation in perception: 'He in great passion all this while did dwell, / More busying his quicke eyes, her face to view, / Then his dull eares, to heare what she did tell' (1.2.26). Here, the impairment of sight is a trigger for wider sensory deprivation, a trajectory reiterated at other moments in the narrative. The 'mist' that Duessa 'overcast' Fradubio impedes his ability to discern Duessa's 'forged beauty', and this initial, impaired sight soon leaves 'all [his] senses... bereaued'—a paralytic state that is literalized in his entombment in a tree. The 'dimmed sight' that Duessa induces eventually causes Redcrosse to experience a comparable state of bodily paralysis (1.2.45). After bathing with Duessa, Redcrosse is described as 'lying downe' (1.7.6), a posture which, as Daryl Gless explains, has spiritual significance given the Pauline instruction to 'put on the whole armor of God, that ye may be able to stand against the assaults of the devil' (Eph. 6:11).[72] Once prostrate, Redcrosse becomes stupefied. He drinks from the enchanted stream—the effects of which 'like a feuer fit through all his body swelt'—and is 'pourd out in loosnesse on the grassy grownd' (1.7.6, 7). Given that this crippling inertia can be traced back to the moment in Canto Two when Redcrosse's 'quicke eyes' are overwhelmed by Duessa's 'tinsell trappings', it is significant that the Knight's rehabilitation begins with a restoration of Truth to his 'sad dull eyes', and a revelation of the 'sight / Of fowle *Duessa*' through stripping (1.2.13, 26; 1.8.41, 49).[73] In fact, this literalized discovery precipitates a concern in the narrative with transformed sight. Duessa is forced to fly from the 'liuing eyes' who now see her true identity, and, for Redcrosse, this realization initiates his 'celestiall discipline'—a schooling that induces the 'open[ing] of his dull eyes, that light mote in them shine' (1.8.50; 1.10.18).

[71] Fulke, *Praelections*, 111; Gifford, *Sermons vpon the whole booke of the Revelation*, 325.

[72] Gless, *Interpretation and Theology*, 123.

[73] For further consideration of Duessa's stripping see, for example, Cavanagh, *Wanton Eyes and Chaste Desires*, 28–9, 36–9; Grogan, *Exemplary Spenser*, 93–4.

The optical challenge Redcrosse faces in Book One is in some ways an imaginative microcosm of the trial faced by the last inhabitants of the earth according to the Book of Revelation. Like the faithful whom John calls to recognize the false church's imitation of the true, Redcrosse must see Duessa's 'face of falsehood' (1.8.49). The entire purpose of the Book of Revelation was, according to Bale, to teach the 'godly beleuer' to 'well knowe . . . the one church from the other', and as *The Faerie Queene* symbolically represents Redcrosse's struggle to make this distinction, it is similarly concerned to impress upon its readers the dangers of spiritual blindness.[74] Certainly, in the bedazzling Duessa Revelation's Whore of Babylon is powerfully reimagined to fuse a concern for the eye's capacity to be deceived in the last days, with a critique of Roman Catholic visual culture. For like the Church at Laodicea who are entreated in Revelation 3:18 to 'anoint thine eyes with eye salve, that thou mayest see', Redcrosse's misreading of Duessa elucidates the need for an alteration in perception—eyes must be reformed in order to see.[75]

The use of a female figure in Revelation to warn believers of the deceptive tactics of the false church of the Antichrist similarly informs the characterizations in Dekker's *The Whore of Babylon*. This apocalyptic drama, like Book One of *The Faerie Queene* and Revelation itself, uses two opposing female figures to represent the battle between good and evil and embody the difficulty of differentiating truth from falsehood in the last days. The work's indebtedness to the structure of John's prophecy is made clear in the Dramatis Personae, which lists 'TH'EMPRESSE OF BABYLON: vnder whom is figured *Rome*' and 'TITANIA the faire Queene: vnder whom is figured our late Queene Elizabeth'.[76] Titania, like Spenser's 'Fairie Queene', symbolizes both Elizabeth I and Revelation's Woman Clothed with the Sun, the latter identity, as Julia Gasper observes, etymologically suggested in her name, a derivative of Titan, the ancient sun god.[77] Although the information in Dekker's Dramatis

[74] Bale, *The image of both Churches* (1570), 3:143r.

[75] On the notion of 'reformed eyes' and early modern understanding of vision more generally see Stuart Clark, *Vanities of the Eye: Vision in Early Modern European Culture* (Oxford: Oxford University Press, 2013), 183–4.

[76] Thomas Dekker, *The Whore of Babylon*, *The Dramatic Works of Thomas Dekker*, ed. Fredson Bowers, Volume II (Cambridge: Cambridge University Press, 1964), 496, Dramatis Personae. All further references will be given in the text.

[77] Gasper, *The Dragon and the Dove*, 72. By using Elizabeth to symbolize England's status as an elect nation, Dekker's play chimes with the sentiments of earlier Tudor dramatists. Foxe's *Christus Triumphans* (*c.*1556), for example, staged how the reformed Church in England would triumph over its Roman Catholic opponents. While Dekker's play makes an effort to revive this tradition of apocalyptic stage allegory, it is worth noting that this attempt may have prompted an unenthusiastic reception among audiences (in the *Lectori* that precedes the published play Dekker suggests that the play has been unsuccessful

Personae demonstrates that he, like Spenser, typologically understood the apocalyptic battle between the forces of good and evil to be unravelling in the early modern present, the play's historical interpretation of Revelation's prophecies is much more politicized than the religious-political allusions found in 'The Legend of Holiness'.

The Whore of Babylon appeared on stage sixteen years after 'The Legend of Holiness' was first published, and in that intervening period, changes in England's political landscape led to the emergence of a more aggressive form of apocalyptic theology.[78] The new king, James I, generated anxiety among many Protestants when, in his first address to Parliament on 22 March 1603, he outlined a vision for 'a general Christian Union in religion' and hope for European peace.[79] The 1604 peace treaty with Spain was an attempt to fulfil these goals and, much to the shock of England's more militantly minded Protestants, the Gunpowder Plot of 1605 did not derail the king's commitment to conciliatory religious and foreign policies.[80] Published less than two years after this attack on Parliament, *The Whore of Babylon* voices the increasingly popular Protestant conviction that the nation and faith must guard against political and spiritual attack.[81]

The opening scene of *The Whore of Babylon* registers these Protestant fears when the play's Whore enters accompanied by religious and temporal leaders. The stage directions indicate how the costuming of the Empresse's entourage is to announce their confessional affiliation. The

(p. 497)). As Howard observes, the overtly didactic drama of the earlier Elizabethan period was no longer in fashion. Jacobean audiences 'had come to expect their edification and their politics to be more fully concealed as entertainment': *The Stage and Social Struggle*, 53.

[78] Hoy suggests that the play may have been composed in 1606: *Introductions, Notes and Commentaries*, 304. In noting the changes in England's religious politics in the period separating these works, I draw on observations I have stated elsewhere: Brownlee, 'Imagining the Enemy', 224.

[79] James I, *Journal of the House of Commons, Vol. 1: 1547–1629* (London: HMSO, 1802), 144. For a discussion of how James styled himself as *rex pacificus* see Malcom Smuts, 'The Making of *Rex Pacificus*: James VI and I and the Problem of Peace in an Age of Religious War', in *Royal Subjects: Essays on the Writings of James VI and I*, ed. Daniel Fischlin and Mark Fortier (Detroit: Wayne State University Press, 2002), 371–87.

[80] Gasper defines militant Protestants as those who 'regarded the Reformed Church as the only True Church, and conceived of it as a single, international body. They . . . thought that a unified, active defence was necessary in order to survive in the struggle against their great adversary, Rome. In practical terms, this meant seeking alliances with Protestant powers abroad . . . Alliances with Roman Catholic powers, however advantageous they might appear, were to be distrusted and shunned': *The Dragon and the Dove*, 2–3. With this definition in mind, Gasper terms *The Whore of Babylon* as 'the definitive militant Protestant play' (9).

[81] See, for example, the views articulated in Abbot, *The reasons . . . for the vpholding of papistry*, 145.

Roman Catholic clergy are readily identifiable by their '*Pontificall roabes*' (1.1), while the presence of the kings of France, Spain, and Holy Roman Empire suggests a spiritual enterprise politically supported by the powers of southern Europe.[82] Unlike Spenser, then, who in Book One of *The Faerie Queene* reimagines Revelation's Whore to speak of a spiritual threat to individual believers, Dekker conceives of an apocalyptic figure who threatens the political body of the English state.[83] If audiences fail to catch the political suggestiveness of the Empresse's entry, her opening speech, which laments that the attempt to recoup recent spiritual losses has been hampered by the impenetrable 'Fairie land' that 'weares a girdle wrought of waues' (1.1.195; 97), reiterates that the spiritual ambitions of the Roman Catholic Church will be achieved through the temporal takeover of Protestant nations by Rome's political allies. In this politicized rendering of the figure of Revelation 17, the play's opening scene resonates with the views of those seventeenth-century commentators who claimed that John's prophecy warned against attack from Spain as well as Rome. As Brightman contended, John's description of the Whore's bejewelled apparel contains 'Merchandize, by which *Spaine* is signified', a point which proves that '*Rome*... relie most of and vppon the Spaniards aid'.[84]

The familiar tropes of excessive colour and ornamentation that attach to the Empresse over the course of the play reinforce her Roman Catholic identity and affirm Dekker's location of this apocalyptic conflict in a post-Reformation context. The Empresse vividly conceives of her power as a 'Crowne' supported by a 'triple arch', 'inrich'd' with 'pretious jewels' (1.1.15–17), she is described as wearing 'carbuncles and rich stones', 'robes of purple', and 'scarlet veiles' (4.1.64; 4.4.39–40), and boasts that her kingdom is rich in 'siluer' and 'pearle' (1.1.114–15).[85] Much like Duessa, the Empresse bears a 'golden cup', the effects of which engage

[82] For an overview of the play's association of Catholicism with Spain, and how this might respond to recent episodes of English history, see Krantz, 'Thomas Dekker's Political Commentary', and Hoy, *Introductions, Notes and Commentaries*, 301.

[83] Brownlee, 'Imagining the Enemy', 226. It also should be said, as Mallette observes, that Duessa's significance modulates in *The Faerie Queene*. A seductress in Book One she is in Book Five 'a political threat': *Spenser*, 156, see also 143–68.

[84] Thomas Brightman, *The Reuelation of S. Iohn illustrated with an analysis* (Leyden: John Classm, 1616), 724. The play emphasizes the danger of an English alliance with Spain and Rome by including historical attacks, such as the Armada, as well as the supposed poisoning attempt by Rodrigo Lopez. See Gasper for a discussion of these episodes, as well as the play's other political allusions: Gasper, *The Dragon and the Dove*, 81–8.

[85] Interestingly, Sarah Scott has suggested that these pearls and stones 'function as synecdoches to signify the larger problem of acute xenophobia that surround various kinds of intercourse with the alien': 'The Empress of Babylon's "carbuncles and rich stones": The Metaphorizing of the Pox in Thomas Dekker's *Whore of Babylon*', *Early Theatre* 7.1 (2004): 67–95 (86).

with reformed attitudes towards the Mass chalice. She offers 'wine sophisticated . . . / which in taste, / Is sweet and like the neate and bolsome iuyce / Of the true grape, but tis ranke poyson' (4.4.44–8). Protestant assumptions about the bewitching capabilities of the Catholic Mass are also evoked when the Empresse is termed a 'damned sorceresse', and as her Cardinal urges a group of priests to use 'sacred drops' and 'potent Charmes' to quell and dupe Rome's enemies (4.1.59; 1.1.223–4). Tied to a familiar Catholic sacrament, and appearing in ornamented fashions that were by this time ideologically redolent of the Roman Catholic Church, Dekker's Empresse embodies the typological connectedness of sacred prophecy and Protestant history.

Of course, according to the play's apocalyptic schema, the identification of Catholicism as the antitype of the Whore of Babylon marks England as an elect nation that harbours the true, reformed, Church of Christ. The play affirms England's election most acutely through the figure of Titania, whose allegorical function as Queen Elizabeth is affirmed before the play begins. Having established Titania's political import in the Dramatis Personae, the play moves in subsequent scenes to reveal her apocalyptic identity as the Woman Clothed with the Sun. The repeated stress on a visage which 'shines . . . brightly' and emits a 'sacred light' suggests Titania's celestial nature, as does the observation that 'bright rayes . . . sparkle from [her] eyes', and her comparison to 'the Sun in heauen' (1.2.74; 4.2.85; 4.2.143; 5.1.35). By embossing Titania's identity as Queen Elizabeth with signifiers of the women in Revelation 12, Dekker's play adheres to a Protestant tradition of understanding Elizabeth to have, what Bernard Capp terms, 'a major, distinctive or even unique position in the Church's history'.[86] In *The Whore of Babylon* this expectation supports the announcement that England, and Protestantism, are biblically promised victory over their enemies.

While the representations of the Empresse and Titania suggest that Dekker, like many of his contemporaries, filtered the ongoing religious conflict in Europe through an eschatological lens, the play mobilizes the structure and concerns of the Book of Revelation to explore how a reformation of the eyes staves off the spiritual blindness induced by the antichristian workers of Rome. A connection between the religious changes of the sixteenth century and spiritual perceptiveness is forged vividly in the dumb show that precedes the main play.[87] The show begins

[86] Bernard Capp, 'The Political Dimension of Apocalyptic Thought', in *The Apocalypse*, ed. Patrides and Wittreich, 96.

[87] Howard notes that Dekker's use of dumb shows 'associates the play with the Elizabethan period' and 'with Elizabeth herself', and suggests that this opening dumb

with the '*disheueld*' and sleeping form of Truth (p. 500), before cutting to the funeral cortege of a queen who must be Mary I, as the procession is led by a group of Roman Catholic friars, bishops, and cardinals who sing in Latin. Pointedly, the mourners who follow behind the clergy are literally blinded, walking with '*scarfes before their eyes*' (p. 500). The Dumb Show casts Mary's death as a moment of apocalyptic disclosure, for as the coffin passes the slumbering Truth she wakens, dons a robe evocatively spotted with stars, and begins '*pulling the veiles from the Councellers eyes*' (p. 500). The subsequent arrival of Titania, who kisses the book Truth casts before her, unmistakably recalls the allegorical pageant *Veritas temporis filia* that marked Elizabeth's coronation, in which Truth presented the new queen with a Bible that she received and kissed.[88] Invoking a recognizable symbol of Elizabeth's commitment to religious reform, Dekker's dumb show pinpoints the queen's coronation, and the ensuing return of Protestantism to England, as an apocalyptic event that revealed spiritual truth to a nation previously blinded. It is a reading of history that confirms English Protestants to be in possession of the accurate sight that characterized the faithful in Revelation, and warns that the spiritual incursion mounted by Catholicism in England is, like the beguiling tactics of Revelation's Antichrist, specifically directed towards the eye.

The susceptibility of eyes to spiritual attack remains a concern in the play proper, where the Empresse's followers are characterized by their warped perception. In her opening speech, the Empresse boasts that her 'pomp' and 'god-like splendour' has secured the 'adoration of all dazeled eies', and elsewhere the King of France vaunts that the 'frighted people' have been 'dazled with our Cope of Starres' (1.1.1–2; 3.1.221).[89] The stunning effects of the Whore's glittering female form are also suggested by the King of Spain, who explains to the Empresse that it is commonly thought abroad that 'you can throw mists before our eyes / To make vs thinke you faire'—an accusation that strikes a chord with Fradubio's

show illuminates Dekker's effort to set up a 'dramatic conflict' which, in Howard's view, destabilizes 'the binary oppositions upon which the play's whole polemical strategy rests': *The Stage and Social Struggle*, 52, 53.

88 King notes that Dekker's *The Whore of Babylon* draws on a variety of 'well-known scenes from Elizabeth's coronation pageantry', beginning with this dumb show portraying the Queen's accession as 'a time of victory over the Church of Rome'. He also argues that the dumb show ends with a 'primal scene of Tudor iconoclasm' as Elizabeth's counsellors are seen 'driving into exile the Roman clergy, with their images, croziers, statues, and other cult objects': King, *Spenser's Poetry*, 147. For further discussion of *Veritas temporis filia* and Elizabeth's visual association with the scriptures during her reign see Molekamp, *Women and the Bible*, 3–5, and King, *Tudor Royal Iconography*, 212–14, 231–8.

89 For consideration of the reoccurring use of the word 'dazzle' in relation to the Whore of Babylon in Protestant writings see Brownlee, 'Imagining the Enemy', 217–18.

blinding at the hands of Duessa (4.4.62–3). Elsewhere, *The Whore of Babylon* affirms the difficulty of relying on visual processes to discern truth when under the Whore's influence. Plain Dealing admits that, when in Rome, the Empresse was 'in mine eye, the goodliest woman that euer wore fore part of Sattin' (4.1.62–5). But now, part of the Fairie Kingdom whose eyes are no longer 'closde vp' by the Whore's deceptive schemes, Plain Dealing declares the Empresse to be 'more vgly then a bawd' (1.2.1; 4.1.65).[90] These admissions further stress how human sight is predisposed to perversion, and reiterate the Protestant accusation that the Roman Catholic Church worked to mesmerize its followers through the aesthetic beauty of its buildings, colour of its clerical vestments, and visually evocative nature of its sacraments. Much like the 'quicke eyes' of Red-crosse which are captivated by Duessa's glinting appearance, the 'dazeled eies' that adore Dekker's Empresse remind audiences of the need to search out the authenticity of what is seen (1.1.2). Both Spenser and Dekker's apocalyptic allegories suggest that only those eyes that have been reformed to conform to truth will be able to detect the illusory tactics of the false church of the Antichrist.

THE 'TRUE-SEEMING LYES' OF ANTICHRISTIAN TRICKSTERS

Spenser and Dekker's interest in the eye's capacity to be deceived informs the theatrical abilities of other Roman Catholic aggressors who are represented in their works. This concern with performativity can be traced back to the texts' biblical source, in which the proponents of the Antichrist appear as arch-tricksters. The antichristian figures described in Revelation 13 are particularly evocative in this regard. In this chapter John outlines the activities of two Beasts who deceive onlookers with imitative spiritual power. The first Beast John foresees will dupe using language—his 'mouth, that spake great things' will prompt the 'worship' of those who listen (Rev. 13:5, 8)—while the second Beast will fool through false appearance. With 'two hornes' this Beast will look 'like the Lambe', and appear to have divine authority by performing 'great wonders' and 'signes' that will 'deceiue them that dwel on earth' (Rev. 13:11, 13–14). The ability of these Beasts to impersonate divine truth frequently prompted biblical commentators to warn that the use of holy words and a spiritual appearance were no guarantee of authenticity. Bale reminds his readers

[90] Plain Dealing, as Howard notes, 'also has some fairly comic trouble distinguishing Truth from Falsehood': *The Stage and Social Struggle*, 55–6.

that although the first Beast looks like the lamb it is 'false & cou[n]terfet', and declares that the voice of the second Beast only 'seeme[s] like Christs' but is 'a brasse pot sounding'.[91]

Unsurprisingly, Protestant interpreters tied the Beasts' acts of falsification to Catholicism. Pareus declares 'this *double bodied* and *faced Antichrist*' to be 'none other but the *Romish Pope*, clothed with the spoiles of the Romane Monarchies, and pretended *Vicarship of Christ*', and Bernard likewise connects the Beast's duplicitous nature to the pope when he explains that the Beast who 'hath *two hornes like a Lambe*' is 'the Pope' who is 'but in shewe a Lambe, he is indeed a rauening beast, hauing two hornes, a double power, Ecclesiasticall and temporall'.[92] Charges of Catholic fabrication abound in reformed readings of Revelation 13 and, as Protestant commentators work to expose the identity of these disguised tricksters they, like John, reiterate the unreliability of sight. In the last days the faithful will be witnesses to—and tested by—false signs. Scholars have often noted that *The Faerie Queene* is preoccupied with correct interpretation, and the work has been aptly described by Rufus Wood as a 'hermeneutic quest'.[93] Consideration of 'The Legend of Holiness' in relation to the Book of Revelation and its exegesis suggests that Spenser's interest in right reading is bound up with the interpretative warnings issued in the biblical source, and with the reformed effort to ascertain the meaning of John's prophecy for the present moment. In particular, Redcrosse's battles with Errour and Archimago appear to recall in structure, and essence, the spiritual attacks described in Revelation 13 in a manner that cautions against the rhetorical and verbal wiles of the Roman Catholic Church.

Early in Book One, Redcrosse and Una—who have entered a forest to seek shelter from a storm—find themselves lost. Unable to ascertain the right way among 'so many paths, so many turnings', Una, registering the danger of their predicament, urges the Knight to 'be well aware' (1.1.10; 12). Unlike Redcrosse, Una is characterized in this opening episode by her watchfulness, a state that is emphasized when Una distinguishes between the couple's perceptive abilities: 'I better wot then you . . . / I read beware'

[91] Bale, *The image of both Churches* (1570), 2:72r.

[92] Pareus, *A commentary upon the divine Revelation*, 287; Bernard, *A key*, 60/H6v.

[93] Rufus Wood, *Metaphor and Belief in The Faerie Queene* (Basingstoke: Macmillan, 1997), 29. In what follows I build on Wood's reading of the episode with Errour in particular. Other scholars who have explored the poem's interest in interpretation include: Maureen Quilligan, *The Language of Allegory: Defining the Genre* (Ithaca: Cornell University Press, 1979), 36; Jonathan Goldberg, *Endlesse Worke: Spenser and the Structures of Discourse* (Baltimore: Johns Hopkins University Press, 1981); Linda Gregerson, *The Reformation of the Subject: Spenser, Milton, and the English Protestant Epic* (Cambridge: Cambridge University Press, 1995), 62–9, 91–6; King, *Spenser's Poetry*, 73.

(1.1.13). Attentive to the 'perill' that surrounds them, Una discerns that they are in 'the wandring wood... *Errours Den*' (1.1.13). It is because Redcrosse is not vigilant, and ignores Una's observations, that he comes face to face with Errour. That this failure gives rise to a hermeneutic test of apocalyptic proportions is made clear when Errour's appearance is described. The monster, who defies clear categorization, is redolent of the first Beast of Revelation 13.[94] Just as John's account reveals an uncertainty over how to classify the Beast he sees rising from the sea, which is variously described as 'like a leopard, and his fete like a beares, and his mouth as the mouth of a lion' (Rev. 13:2), Errour can only be described by approximations. One half of her appears 'like a serpent horribly displaide, / But th' other halfe did womans shape retaine' (1.1.14). Like the apocalyptic sea-Beast, the composite nature of Errour's body renders her an interpretative challenge for the believer.

The interpretative nature of the trial Redcrosse faces is, as Wood and Hume have noted, suggested by the composition of Errour's dangerous vomit—'full of bookes and papers' it bears 'deformed monsters' as 'blacke as inke' (1.1.20, 22).[95] Redcrosse's battle with the words that Errour spews is evocative of the rhetorical threat posed by the first Beast of Revelation 13. For like Errour whose danger lies in her 'filthy maw' (1.1.20), John locates the spiritual threat posed by the Beast of Revelation 13 in its mouth, from which flows 'blasphemie against God' that elicits the worship of 'all... whose names are not writen in the Boke of life' (Rev. 13:6, 8). Unsurprisingly, the 'devilish doctrines' espoused by this Beast were, as the marginalia of the 1560 Geneva Bible affirms, commonly tied in Protestant commentary to the 'statues, ordaina[n]ces, decrees, ceremonies' of Rome (Rev. 13:4, 12, notes). Spenser's narrative ideologically reverberates with this common application of the Beast's blasphemies when Errour's young are seen 'sucking vp their dying mothers blood' (1.1.25). As an unnatural mother, Errour, as King has argued, becomes a figure of the Roman mother Church who, according to the doctrine of transubstantiation, nourishes her spiritual offspring with blood through the Mass.[96] Furthermore, given

[94] Hamilton offers an alternative reading stating that the 'source is the locusts in Revelation 9:7–10 who have the hair of women and the tails of scorpions': Note: 1.1.14: *The Faerie Queene*, ed. Hamilton, 34. Building on the observation of Josephine Waters Bennett, Hume notes the connection between Errour's vomit and the flood of the Dragon in Revelation 12:1: *Edmund Spenser*, 77–8.

[95] Wood has considered the episode's more general association with erroneous words, reading Errour's 'huge long taile' (1.1.15) as an 'an erring tale': *Metaphor and Belief*, 32. See also Hume, *Edmund Spenser*, 74.

[96] King, 'Milton's Cave of Error', 148. Gregerson also perceives an allusion to the doctrine of transubstantiation in the earlier description of 'great lumpes of flesh and gobbets raw' which appear in Errour's vomit: *The Reformation of the Subject*, 96.

that breastfeeding had, what Groves terms, 'quasi-cannibalistic' connotations in this period—breast milk was understood to be whited blood—Spenser's image of the young devouring the mother's lifeblood is all the more evocative.[97] The 'life' the progeny 'nurst' from the failing Errour is, pointedly, the cause of their deaths, as their bellies, swollen with blood, burst (1.1.26).[98] As Redcrosse observes this scene that literalizes spiritual death through the physical annihilation of monstrous bodies, the narrative signals his recognition of the erroneous nature of what he has encountered (1.1.26)—what he witnesses is a 'detestable sight' (1.1.26). In this instance, Redcrosse, like the elect in Revelation who refuse to worship the first Beast of Revelation 13, is not overcome by the wiles of his enemy.

While Redcrosse manages to defeat this first antichristian monster who embodies the apparently spurious teachings of the Roman Catholic Church, the Knight proves unable to discern the crafty tactics of a second, more subtle enemy, Archimago. As is well known, Archimago is, in name and deed, suggestive of Catholicism and its reliance on images, and references to 'his long black weedes', 'beades', and 'lowly Hermitage', as well as his tales of 'Saintes and Popes' and use of '*Aue-Mary*' specifically mark him as a member of the Roman clergy (1.1.29, 30, 34, 35).[99] Although redolent of Catholicism, Archimago's function as an image-maker also aligns him with the second Beast of Revelation 13 in the poem's wider apocalyptic schema—a connection Dixon appears to have made when, as King notes, he termed him 'a false profite'.[100] Archimago's construction of a sprite that 'imitate[s] that Lady trew' (1.1.46), Una, appears to draw upon the act of falsification described in Revelation 13:14–15. Here, the second Beast, having encouraged earth's inhabitants to set up an image in honour of the sea-Beast, gives 'spirit vnto [this] image . . . so that the image . . . shulde speake' (Rev. 13:15).[101] More broadly, Archimago's use of 'Magick bookes', 'mighty charmes', and 'spelles' to create

[97] Beatrice Groves, 'Christ's Tears and Maternal Cannibalism in Early Modern London', in *Biblical Women*, ed. Brownlee and Gallagher, 151.

[98] In Dekker's play breastfeeding is similarly tied to Catholicism and associated with infection and bodily deformity: see Scott, 'The Empress of Babylon's "carbuncles and rich stones"', 77–9.

[99] For more on Archimago's Catholic associations see King, *Spenser's Poetry*, 72–5. Richey acknowledges these Catholic signifiers but suggests that Archimago's representation also has Presbyterian connotations: *The Politics of Revelation*, 22–3.

[100] Dixon in King, *Spenser's Poetry*, 73. Other scholars who connect Archimago with Revelation's False Prophet include Sadler, '*The Faerie Queene*', 150, and Watkins, 'Spenser's Poetry and the Apocalypse', 90.

[101] The creation of this false sprite parallels the creation of False Florimell in Book Three. For more on this later falsification, see Gregerson, *The Reformation of the Subject*, 139–41.

'true-seeming lyes' (1.1.36, 37, 38) at once evokes the Beast's power to do mystical 'signes' and 'great wonders' (Rev. 13:13–14), and engages with the popular Protestant assumption that the Roman clergy relied on 'Magicke, sorcerie, or witchcraft', as Perkins charged, in their sacraments and practices.[102]

While Archimago's confessional and apocalyptic identity were, as Dixon's commentary affirms, recognizable to Spenser's biblically literate readership, Redcrosse fails to discern the dangerous nature of his attacker because the threat Archimago poses is not visually apparent.[103] Much like the second Beast who appears 'like the Lambe' (Rev. 13:11), Archimago assumes the part of 'an aged Sire', with 'feete all bare', a 'gray' beard, and eyes 'lowly bent' to the ground (1.1.29). He appears 'simple in shew', and with prayers and a breast 'often knockt' in repentance, styles himself as spiritually humble in heart (1.1.29). It is because Redcrosse fails to read the hermit as an arch-image of spirituality that he succumbs to his illusory tactics. Believing the false truth 'he saw' to be real truth (1.2.5), Redcrosse abandons Una and is led into whoredom by Duessa whose threat, like Archimago's, lies in her performative capabilities as well as mutable exterior.[104] Tricked by a series of impostors who symbolically operate as workers of the Antichrist as well as Rome, Redcrosse falls into spiritual whoredom specifically because of a catalogue of interpretative failures.

The illusory tactics that are used by the agents of the Antichrist to dupe the faithful similarly preoccupy Dekker's representation of the apocalyptic battle for souls in *The Whore of Babylon.* In line with the more politicized apocalypticism espoused by Dekker's play, the spiritual attack orchestrated by the titular Whore is, from the outset, a covert operation that is to be implemented by temporal kings. In her opening address the Empresse advises her political allies against a militaristic invasion of Fairie Land, and instead urges them towards a more clandestine infiltration of Titania's royal body. The kings of France, Spain, and the Holy Roman Empire are to 'wooe (like louers)' and gain control of Fairie Land by marrying Queen Titania (1.1.103). The Empresse's commission to the kings before their mission elucidates the art of antichristian deception.

[102] William Perkins, *A reformed Catholike: or, A declaration shewing how neere we may come to the present Church of Rome in sundrie points of religion* ([Cambridge]: Iohn Legat, 1598), 345–6.

[103] Dixon, *The First Commentary.*

[104] In addition to the performative aspects of Duessa's character noted earlier, pp. 185–7, the narrative notes how she assumes postures of 'humbleness', 'melting . . . teares', 'coy lookes', and 'seeming dead': 1.2.21, 22, 27.

They are to fashion their bodies and words to disguise their treacherous intentions:

> Draw all your faces sweetly let your browes
> Be sleekd, your cheeks in dimples, giue out great smiles,
> Your voyces string with siluer . . .
> Sweare you haue hills of pearle: shew her the world,
> And say shee will have all, so shee will kneele
> And doe vs reverence: but if shee grow nice,
> Dissemble, flatter, stoope to licke the dust
> She goes vpon, and (like to serpents) creepe
> Vpon your bellies, in humilitie;
> And beg shee would but with us ioyne a league,
> To wed her land to ours. (1.1.102–12)

This speech is loaded with suggestive biblical allusions that align the Empresse with her antichristian master. The Devil's temptation of Jesus in Matthew 4:9 ('All these [kingdomes] will I giue thee, if thou wilt fall downe and worship me') can be heard behind the instruction to promise 'all' the world if Titania 'will kneele', and Dekker seems to have the Genesis account of the Fall in mind when writing the close of this speech. Called to be as dissembling 'serpents' that 'licke the dust' and stealthily 'creepe' upon their bellies, the kings are figured as the progeny of the Genesis serpent who was condemned by God in Genesis 3:4 to crawl on its belly and eat dust. Tying the Empresse's plans for an invasion of English Fairie Land to biblical narratives where the Devil's attacks centre on seductive speech, Dekker reminds his audience that these deadly forms of covert assault continue to be implemented by the enemies of truth who, in 1607, are Spanish as well as Catholic.[105]

The Whore of Babylon explores the efforts of Revelation's antichristian forces to deceive by showcasing their use of false appearances that mask their identities and intentions. The play considers this threat literally when the King of Spain is seen dressing up in preparation to deceive the scholar, Campeius—an act that encapsulates what Jean Howard describes as the 'characters' preoccupations with artifice and shapeshifting' in this play.[106]

[105] Over the course of the play, Dekker foregrounds the conjoined Spanish–Roman threat by interweaving the struggles of Elizabeth's reign, such as the assassination attempt by William Parry and Spanish Armada, into his apocalyptic confrontation between good and evil. For a discussion of the play's representation of these historical events see Hoy, *Introductions, Notes and Commentaries*, 303–8, and Krantz, 'Thomas Dekker's Political Commentary', 273.

[106] Howard, *The Stage and Social Struggle*, 60. Howard has argued that the theatrical activities of the Empresse's forces resonate with the ideology of anti-theatrical tracts: *The Stage and Social Struggle*, 51–2.

Like Spenser's Archimago who appears as an 'aged Sire', the King of Spain ages himself theatrically in order to avoid suspicion. Addressing his footman, he asks: 'Stands my beard right? The gowne: I must looke graue, / White haires like siluer cloudes a priuiledge haue, / Not to be search'd, or be suspected fowle . . . / So: excellent: a subtile masque' (2.2.1–3, 7). The king's aptitude for multiple impersonations is affirmed later in the scene when he calls for another costume change—'Make me a courtier'—lest his 'Foxes skinne be knowne' (2.2.158, 156). Elsewhere the Empresse reveals that such use of costuming is widespread among her workers when she instructs: 'Close up your selues in artificall wals: / Or if you walke abroad, be wrapt in clouds, / Haue change of haires, or eie-brows . . . / take all shapes' (3.1.160–3).

Pointing up the Empresse's forces' predilection for dressing up, *The Whore of Babylon* draws on, and extends, metaphors of clothing that were used widely in anti-Catholic polemic to elucidate the threat posed by Catholicism.[107] Radford Mavericke, for instance, described the Roman Catholic Church as 'cloked hypocrisy', and Foxe refers to the Roman clergy as wearing 'cloak[s] of hipocrisie', phrases that speak to the imagery of shrouding which, as Shell has shown, proliferate in Protestant warnings against perceived Catholic threat.[108] Dekker's fascination with the external mutability of the Empresse's followers reverberates more specifically, though, with an exegetical tradition that, as mentioned earlier, was particularly interested in the physical descriptions of the Antichrist's workers in Revelation. The Hampshire clergyman Thomas Mason deduces that John defines the sea-Beast of Revelation 13 as 'like the Leopard' because 'no Beast is so beautifully spotted as the Leopard'. Predictably, he determines that this description points to the office of pope, for 'no Emperour or King was euer so richly or gloriously decked . . . as the Popes haue beene'.[109] William Guild similarly locates his attack on Catholic concealment in a reading of the fabricated appearances of Beasts of Revelation 13 and the Whore of Babylon when he pronounces that 'the *Romane* Church' promises 'the licentious luxurie of that lustfull Harlot, the cloaked hypocrisie of that false Prophet'.[110]

References to the false mantles of the Romanish forces of the Antichrist reinforce their tremendous skills as fraudsters, and specify the threat they

[107] Shell, *Catholicism*, 25–30.

[108] Radford Mavericke in Shell, *Catholicism*, 26; Foxe, *Actes and Monuments*, 1016. Shell states that such accusations of concealment have 'a long history in anti-Catholic polemic': *Catholicism*, 26.

[109] Mason, *A revelation of the Revelation*, 58.

[110] William Guild, *Popish glorying in antiquity turned to their shame* (London: Robert Allot, 1627), 37–8.

pose as a perversion of perception. Perkins alludes to the spiritual confusion that can ensue from this crafted corruption of exteriors when he describes how the leader of the Antichrist's forces, Satan, 'doth change himselfe into a white deuill, as though he were an angel of light, so that man can hardly distinguish his wicked suggestions, from the good motions of the spirit of God'.[111] The Church of England clergyman Laurence Deios likewise deploys the image of a whited devil in order to alert his readers to the hidden threat posed to the eyes of the faithful by the Antichrist, as well as the Roman Catholic Church. He urges readers of his 1590 treatise *That the pope is that Antichrist* against making the common 'error' in assuming

> this *beast* and *Antichrist* must be an open enemie of *Christ*... The trueth is, that the *beast* and *Antichrist*, is a descrete enemie cloked with the name of a friend... in this enemie especially, *Satan* changeth himself into an *Angell of light. Antichrist*... is a secret enemy, making shew and countenance of a friend... By this... it may sufficiently be gathered, that this *beast*, this *Antichrist*, is the Pope of *Rome*. For who is there in the Church of *Christ*, of long continuance and great authoritie, that seemeth more a friend to *Christ*, and is in trueth so sore an enemie to all that truly believe in *Christ*, as is the Pope?[112]

As *The Whore of Babylon* illuminates the illusory phenomena of the Empresse's forces it dramatizes the operations of a closeted Catholic enemy with whom Jacobean readers and audiences were clearly familiar. For like Perkins, Deios, and Spenser, Dekker urges individuals to be alert to attack from 'Angell, Deuill[s]' and cunning 'Foxes' who 'change themselues / Into the shape of Fawnes' (1.2.4; 2.1.27–8). Believing themselves living in the last days, writers of drama and poetry, as well as sermons and biblical commentaries, conceived of an apocalyptic battle within which discerning friend from foe was an uncertain process.

The perceptive difficulty that literary and biblical writers addressing the Book of Revelation warn their readers against is bound up with the clarifying potential of the Second Coming of Christ. As the final antitype, only the arrival of this moment would enable 'euery eye' to see Christ as 'the beginning and the ending' (Rev. 1:7–8). While this is the defining moment towards which Spenser and Dekker's reimaginings of Revelation look, both 'The Legend of Holiness' and *The Whore of Babylon* stop short of representing this ultimate ending, instead offering, what Watkins

[111] William Perkins, *Commentarie or exposition vpon... the Galatians* (Cambridge: Iohn Legat, 1604), 611. It should be noted that the idea of a white devil has its biblical origin in II Corinthians 11:14: 'And no marvaile: for Satan himselfe is transformed into an Angel of light'.

[112] Deios, *That the pope is that Antichrist*, 16.

terms, 'a forestalled apocalypse'.[113] Certainly, Una's stripping of Duessa before Redcrosse in Canto Eight operates as a moment of apocalyptic disclosure, in that it reveals the Whore's 'secret filth' to the duped knight (1.1.46). Yet, it soon becomes clear that this unveiling is merely a precursory disclosure, a number of which, as John explained in his prophecy, would precede the final Christological revelation at the Second Coming.

Although much anticipated, this promised end fails to arrive in Book One. The closing preparations for a 'great feast' to celebrate the 'sacred rite' that will tie Una and Redcrosse 'for euer' is not the 'Lamb's supper' given in honour of the marriage of the ecclesial Bride and Christ in Revelation 19:9 that it structurally and ideologically invokes (1.12.38). As several scholars have acknowledged, unlike this apocalyptic marriage that signals the eternal defeat of evil and the winding up of history, the concluding scene of 'The Legend of Holiness' is a betrothal.[114] In keeping with the precursory nature of these revelries, the narrative's dominant antichristian figures have been quelled rather than destroyed. Archimago has not been killed but 'layd ... lowe', the narrative's Whore has been stripped rather than burned (Rev. 18:18–21), and Redcrosse must leave Una to battle another 'monstrous beast' (1.12.36, 41). Even the revelation of the 'sunshyny' face of Una—evocatively described as a 'celestiall sight'—shades into a prefatory disclosure. Not the new dawn but a sign that 'dawning day is drawing near' (1.12.23).[115]

[113] Watkins, '"And yet the end was not"', 157. In making this point, Watkins suggests that Elizabeth's age and lack of heir informs Merlin's vision in Book Three, arguing that Merlin's admission that time continues (3.3.50) 'readmits the possibility of national tragedy' into the narrative (161). Watkins also suggests that 'Spenser draws closest to Dekker in a perpetually deferred representation of Apocalypse' (167). For further consideration of the relationship between deferral and anticipation in Spenser's work see Escobedo, *Nationalism and Historical Loss*, 81–140.

[114] In the play's historical allegory, this betrothal symbolizes the union of England and the true faith. Scholars who describe this scene as a betrothal, and acknowledge this moment's connection to the Lamb's supper, include: Douglas Brooks-Davies, *Spenser's Faerie Queene: A Critical Commentary on Books I and II* (Manchester: Manchester University Press, 1977), 111; Kenneth Borris, *Allegory and Epic in English Renaissance Literature: Heroic Form in Sidney, Spenser, and Milton* (Cambridge: Cambridge University Press, 2000), 175; Watkins, '"And yet the end was not"', 157; Gregerson, *The Reformation of the Subject*, 60.

[115] This sense that time has stalled in *The Faerie Queene* is well illustrated by the fact that the work remains unfinished. Sadler claims it was Spenser's intention to end his epic with Arthur's great battle against Paynim and his marriage with the Faerie Queen: '*The Faerie Queene*', 165. See also the discussion of endings in Andrew Hadfield, 'Introduction', *The Cambridge Companion to Spenser*, ed. Andrew Hadfield (Cambridge: Cambridge University Press, 2001), 8.

In many senses, the frustration of the decisive apocalyptic moment in Book One of *The Faerie Queene* captures the problem inherent in the apocalyptic rhetoric in the decades after the break with Rome. As Stuart Clark reminds, since Luther the Reformation had been read as a 'terminal event', but in the 1590s the Roman Catholic Church remained unbeaten, and the reformed church had yet to be vindicated as Christ's true church.[116] 'The Legend of Holiness', in postponing the apocalyptic end it repeatedly invokes, espouses an eschatology that is indicative of a Protestant faithful who continued to wait for the victorious end to their apocalyptic struggle with Rome.[117] While the emphasis on futurity at the end of 'The Legend of Holiness' points up the way in which declarations of apocalypse were redefined by Protestant commentators across the sixteenth and seventeenth centuries, it also coheres with the incremental schema of John's vision. As Richard Bauckham reminds, 'Eschatological delay is as much a feature of Revelation as eschatological imminence. It is written into the structure of the book.'[118] Amid this unspecified postponement, the conclusion of 'The Legend of Holiness' reiterates Revelation's caution that, until the End, it remains possible for the faithful to be duped by an antichristian enemy who is ever-present and evolving.

While this warning was apt for a nation whose monarch—aged and childless—was fated to leave the interests of English Protestants unprotected, Dekker's play illustrates that, even when the threat of Catholic claimants to the throne had been dispelled, Jacobean writers perceived that vigilance, even militancy, was needed to protect the nation and faith. Titania is, as Gasper observes, 'converted to militant Protestantism' over the course of the play—a development that points up the play's agitation for changes in England's religious and foreign policy to protect the faithful, and precipitate the necessary conditions for Christ to return. The play's stress on watchfulness supported by militancy is unsurprising given the new king's vision for the opposing sides of Christianity to 'meet in the Midst.'[119] In the view of many Protestants, James' conciliatory foreign policy, the advancement of Arminian-leaning clergy in the Church of England, as well as a viable attack on Parliament meant that gains

[116] Clark, *Thinking with Demons*, 340.

[117] See Watkins for more on the effect of this waiting on Protestantism and for consideration of how Spenser's stalled apocalypse might be influenced by specific questions regarding Elizabeth's succession and policies: '"And yet the end was not"', 158.

[118] Bauckham in Escobedo, *Nationalism and Historical Loss*, 81. See Richard Bauckham, *The Theology of the Book of Revelation* (Cambridge: Cambridge University Press, 1993), 1–22.

[119] James I, *Journal of the House of Commons*, 144.

made by reformers in the previous century were being eroded rather than entrenched.[120]

It is for this reason that *The Whore of Babylon* must, in the end, also reconceive its apocalyptic schema to acknowledge the evolution of an antichristian threat, and extension of time, beyond the reign of England's Woman Clothed with the Sun. The defeat of the Empresse's forces at sea—an episode that is clearly reminiscent of the English victory over the Spanish Armada in 1588—is succeeded by the birth of 'a man childe . . . a boy that looks as if he would shoote off already' (5.6.36–7). According to the play's historical allegory this birth in Titania's camp must be the successor to the Fairie throne, James.[121] A militaristic heir, Titania's successor announces the need for an active response to the perceived Spanish–Roman threat at a time when England's king was busy promoting European peace. Of course the birth of an armed child in the play's climactic scene also affirms the continuation, rather than the end, of the apocalyptic war in which, as Watkins notes, 'James—or possibly his son prince Henry' is imagined to be 'leader of a pan-European Protestant union against the Habsburgs and other Catholic powers'.[122] With this birth, the play's apocalyptic expectancy is reconceived rather than extinguished, a point reiterated by the biblical allusion to Revelation 12:5. Given that this portion of John's vision comments on the birth of a Christological 'man childe which shulde rule all the nations with a rod of yron', the delivery of a 'man childe' to Fairie Land signals that victory is imminent.[123] As such, the events of Elizabeth's reign are reformulated within the play's apocalyptic schema—they are now preparatory rather than definitive. The Empresse, while not annihilated, has been dealt an historic blow—'Great *Babylon* thus lowe did neuer fall' (5.6.126; 137)—a state that makes decisive victory probable as well as possible. While these announcements exemplify how the play strives at its close to strike a chord of hope, Titania's declaration that ends the play—'We are neere shore' (5.6.139)—cannot help but acknowledge that the terminus, near as it is, has yet to arrive.

The disconfirmation of apocalypse in Dekker's play illustrates the adverse effect of time on typological applications of Revelation's

[120] Curtis Perry discusses how these circumstances generated a literary nostalgia for Elizabeth in James' reign: *The Making of Jacobean Culture: James I and the Renegotiation of Elizabethan Literary Practice* (Cambridge: Cambridge University Press, 1997), 153–87.

[121] See Gasper for more on how this closing scene may be read in relation to James I: *The Dragon and the Dove*, 96–9.

[122] Watkins, '"And yet the end was not"', 168.

[123] Buccola notes how this allusion to Revelation 12:5 affirms the play's broader interest in Marian motherhood: 'Virgin Fairies', 157.

prophecies to the present. The invocation of a victorious moment in the English past—a moment that had been read apocalyptically—is a terrible enactment of the falsification of expectation, as the end of Dekker's apocalypse is, ironically, not-end. Given that, as Watkins states, 'time itself limits the effectiveness of apocalyptic rhetoric', *The Whore of Babylon*, much like 'The Legend of Holiness', must interrupt the process of apocalyptic uncovering that it initiates before the final revelation.[124] In doing so, both works inadvertently raise the possibility that the typological theory of historical progress might be flawed. Admitting the possibility that the final antitype might never arrive, both Dekker and Spenser's reimaginings of the cosmic battle between good and evil resist alignment with their biblical source.[125]

ENDING THE END

The repeated disconfirmation of apocalypse in reformed readings of Revelation did not, however, invalidate apocalypse as a concept.[126] While the passage of almost a century seemed to discredit the Reformation's status as a terminal event, literary and biblical commentators continually reconceived the nearness of the end, keeping apocalyptic expectations alive well into the seventeenth century. Even in the later years of James' reign, the early reformers' identification of the Roman Catholic Church with the forces of the Antichrist, and association of Protestantism with the elect of Revelation, remained central to eschatological readings of contemporary circumstances. Perhaps the most spectacular, and certainly the most politically controversial, Jacobean example of the reformulation of the clash between Protestantism and Catholicism as a conflict of apocalyptic proportions is Thomas Middleton's 1624 play *A Game at Chess*, which is discussed here by way of conclusion.

[124] Watkins, '"And yet the end was not"', 172.

[125] It should be said that the failure of Apocalypse to arrive was also problem for the Christian community who first read John's visions. See Rhymer, *The End of Time*; John M. Court, *Approaching the Apocalypse: A Short History of Christian Millenarianism* (London: I. B. Tauris, 2008), 1–51.

[126] This assessment coheres with the observations of a body of scholarship that has shown the malleability and resilience of apocalyptic thought across history. See, for example, Frank Kermode, *The Sense of Ending: Studies in the Theory of Fiction with a New Epilogue* (Oxford: Oxford University Press, 1967, rpt. 2000), 8; Stephen O'Leary, *Arguing the Apocalypse: A Theory of Millennial Rhetoric* (Oxford: Oxford University Press, 1994), 50; Escobedo, *Nationalism and Historical Loss*, 81–2.

A Game at Chess opened in the Globe theatre on 5 August 1624 and, as the title suggests, the play explores the contemporary relevance of Revelation's apocalyptic battle using the device of a chess match. Although Middleton recasts the opposing sides of good and evil as white and black 'Houses' rather than women, visual coding remains central to the construction of the play's apocalyptic allegory, just as it was in Spenser and Dekker.[127] Unsurprisingly, the black pieces work to 'dark[en] the land' spiritually, while the White House's role as protector of the 'light', that is, spiritual truth, is discernible in the whiteness of its pieces (Ind. 7, 9). As Paul Yachin notes, the metaphorical use of the delineated sides of a chess board to distinguish between good and evil had a long and established history by the time of Middleton's writing. As early as the thirteenth century, chess had been invoked to describe alternate spiritual conditions.[128] 'The world', wrote one commentator, 'resembles a chessboard which is chequered white and black, the colours showing the two conditions of life and death'.[129] Several of Middleton's contemporaries use the imagery of a chess match to similar ends. Church of England clergyman and author George Hakewill describes life as a 'great game at Chesse', and Abbot records that some liken 'our being heere in the world vnto a game at chesse'.[130] Middleton's development of this established figural trope into a five-act drama depicting the cosmic battle between the antichristian forces of falsehood and the defenders of truth results in a highly stylized rendering of the reformers' so-called literal interpretation of Revelation's meaning. The actors wear black and white costumes that speak to their spiritual conditions, but they also bear signifiers of their confessional and political identities that locate this apocalyptic battle in the early modern present. The battle between good and evil is, *A Game at Chess* declares, literally now.

The play types out the contemporary identity of the Antichrist's forces by incorporating several historical figures into the Black House. Ignatius Loyola appears in the opening 'Induction' with the monster Error—made famous by Spenser—suggestively laid by his feet.[131] The visual association of

[127] Thomas Middleton, *A Game at Chess*, ed. T. H. Howard-Hill (Manchester: Manchester University Press, 2003), Prologue 5. All further references will be given in the text.

[128] Paul Yachnin, 'A Game at Chess and Chess Allegory', *Studies in English Literature, 1500–1900* 22.2 (Spring 1982): 317–30.

[129] Anonymous in Yachnin, 'A Game at Chess', 322.

[130] George Hakewill, *King Dauids vow for reformation of himselfe* (London: [Humphrey Lownes], 1621), 68; George Abbot, *A sermon preached at Westminster May 26. 1608 at the funeral solemnities of the Right Honorable Thomas Earle* (London: Melchisedech Bradwood, 1608), 7.

[131] Michelle O'Callaghan, *Thomas Middleton, Renaissance Dramatist* (Edinburgh: Edinburgh University Press, 2009), 166–7.

Loyola—termed the 'father' and 'founder' of the Black House (Ind. 14)—with Error is allegorically instructive, as Loyola's nationality and position as the father of the Jesuit movement speak to the familiar Protestant association of Spain and Catholicism with the spiritually erroneous forces of darkness in Revelation. This application of Revelation's narrative is drawn more overtly in the play proper, in which the Black Knight is figured as the former Spanish ambassador to England, Conde de Gondomar.[132] As T. H. Howard-Hill observes, the ambassador's special chair—to accommodate a fistula—was incorporated into the performances, and effort was made to capture the particularities of his Spanish attire.[133] The effect, as John Chamberlain records in a letter to Sir Dudley Carleton, was that Gondomar was 'counterfeited . . . to the life, with all his graces and faces'.[134] The play further advances a typological reading of John's prophecy in the historical impersonations seen in the characters of the White House. Playgoer John Holles records that the episode in which the White Knight and White Duke mount an attack on the Black House clearly depicts the 'Princes cumming into Spayn' with the Duke of Buckingham.[135] Positioning the English heir to the throne in the House of 'truth and goodness' (Ind. 10), the play identifies the English as the elect of Revelation, and marks a recent episode in the country's history as an apocalyptic event.

The Spanish trip to which Holles refers took place in 1623 and was intended to finalize preparations for a marriage match, brokered by Gondomar, between the Infanta and Prince Charles. But, against expectation, Charles returned to England later that year without a Spanish bride. The protection of England and the reformed truth it sheltered from the advances of a Spanish queen was celebrated with feasting and special church services and, amid this jubilant atmosphere, the objectives of militant Protestants seemed once again to look brighter.[136] Claiming that Philip IV would never have agreed to the marriage without Charles' conversion to Catholicism, the prince and Buckingham urged war against

[132] Gondomar was the resident ambassador to James' court for almost ten years (1613–22) and a recognizable figure in England. Before his departure, he had been fundamental to the marriage negotiations for a match between the Spanish Infanta and Prince Charles, the historical episode on which the play is based.

[133] Howard-Hill, 'Introduction', *A Game at Chess*, 24. Howard-Hill has discussed the play's 'impersonations' at length and my discussion of the costumes used during the performances is indebted to his observations: *A Game at Chess*, 17–26, 192–213. See also O'Callaghan, *Thomas Middleton*, 162–7.

[134] John Chamberlain in Howard-Hill, *A Game at Chess*, 205.

[135] John Holles in Howard-Hill, *A Game at Chess*, 199.

[136] For the celebrations that took place in the wake of the prince's return see Howard-Hill, *A Game at Chess*, 13. See also Samuel R. Gardiner, *Prince Charles and the Spanish Marriage, 1617–1623* (London: Hurst and Blackett, 1869).

Spain.[137] *A Game at Chess* celebrates this brief shift in England's political winds by recasting the breakdown of the marriage negotiations as an apocalyptic victory and ending.[138] The discovery of the Black Knight's (Gondomar) plan to infiltrate the White House by the White Knight (Prince Charles) and White Duke (Buckingham) signals the end of the chess match, with the White Knight declaring: 'the game's ours—we give thee checkmate by / Discovery, King, the noblest mate of all!' (5.3.160–1). Middleton's incorporation of this historic episode, and its use to conclude the game, affirms that reformed declarations of the end of time were not necessarily discredited by repeated extensions of temporality. Instead, the apocalyptic end, continually refigured and amended, was prolonged to ensure that the Protestant faithful hovered ever on the brink of eternity.

While on the one hand the play's enmeshing of a recent episode of English history with the apocalyptic end of time speaks to the fluidity of apocalypse as a concept in the early modern period, on the other, the chess allegory used to elide biblical prophecy with the present generates expectation of a more definitive conclusion. For if a chess match is used as a metaphor for life, the end of the game must, logically, be equated with death. Abbot endorses this application of the metaphor when he declares that 'when the game is ended... Kings, and Knights and common pawnes... are swept all into the bagge' and become equal in death.[139] George Strode similarly finds the moment of 'Check-mate' to be indicative of death, but he also connects this moment to the Last Judgement—that 'vision in the booke of the Reuelation [of] the dead arraigned at the barre of the great Iudge'.[140] Middleton's *A Game at Chess* seems to invoke checkmate to announce an ending that is similarly final, as the declaration of victory by the White Knight is succeeded by the casting of the Black House into the bag.[141] The stage directions indicate that '*The bag opens,*

[137] At Buckingham's urging, the Commons devoted £300,000 to facilitate England moving on to a war footing and sent 6,000 men to fight in the Dutch Republic. See Thomas Cogswell, *The Blessed Revolution: English Politics and the Coming of War, 1621–1624* (Cambridge: Cambridge University Press, 1989), 208–56.

[138] Charles' escape from the Infanta did not signal the end of the perceived threat from a foreign bride. Indeed, almost immediately negotiations began for a match between the future king and the French princess, Henrietta Maria. Less than a year after *A Game*'s first performance, Henrietta Maria became the first official papal representative in London since Queen Mary in 1558. See MacCulloch, *Reformation*, 518.

[139] Abbot, *A sermon preached at Westminster May 26. 1608*, 7.

[140] George Strode, *The anatomie of mortalitie deuided into... eight heads* (London: William Iones, 1618), 52.

[141] Interestingly, in Abbot the sweeping into the bag is a levelling activity, but in Middleton it is only the black pieces who meet with this end, a distinction that perhaps reiterates the Black House's particular association with spiritual death.

the Black side in it' (5.3.178). The allegorical significance of this moment is explained by the White Knight who, narrating the literal descent of the black pieces/actors through the trapdoor into the stage's central 'hell', declares: 'there behold: the bag, like hell-mouth opens / To take her due' (5.3.179). Representing the spiritual damnation of the Black House in this way, Middleton's apocalyptic narrative goes much further than Spenser and Dekker's which, although willing to locate Revelation's precursory disclosures in the early modern present, ultimately stop short of announcing the final antitype. Writing amidst the jubilant celebrations that marked the return of the unwedded Prince Charles, this moment in *A Game at Chess* announces the death of spiritual darkness and the end of time itself.

Yet, the enactment of the literal and spiritual deaths of the play's Spanish and Roman antichristian forces is by no means as definitive as the chess match's spectacular conclusion allegorically implies. It soon becomes clear that the black pieces' descent into hell is no death at all, but merely an imprisonment, as their dissenting voices are heard from within the bag. The Fat Bishop ominously declares of the Black Knight (Gondomar): 'He'll peck a hole i'th'bag and get out shortly / But I shall be the last man that creeps out' (5.3.206–7). The closing speech by the White Queen's Pawn to the audience likewise works to recuperate a more mutable ending for the play's apocalyptic schema. Having commended those who are 'true friends of the White House' (Epi. 3), she turns to address those outside of this elect group: 'For any else, by envy's mark denoted, / To those night glow-worms in the bag devoted, / Where'er they sit, stand, or in private lurk, / They'll soon be known by their depraving work' (Epi. 4–8). Pointing to further revelations in the future, these closing lines work to establish an apocalyptic timeline compatible with the extension of earthly existence beyond the historical events detailed in the play. But this last-ditch effort to re-sync real time with the end of time jars against the backdrop of a chess board that literally and metaphorically disallows a mutable end. Severing the ending from the End, the final scene of Middleton's play destabilizes the progressive trajectory of history and divests apocalypse of any real meaning in the present.

As it questions the surety of historical progress *A Game at Chess*, like 'The Legend of Holiness' and *The Whore of Babylon*, casts doubt over the validity of the very reading practice that underpins the contemporary application of Revelation's last battle. For in representing revelations that are fractured, obscured, and stalled, these reimaginings of biblical apocalypse reveal the final typological uncovering to be a perennial shifting of veils, and invoke a world where the vindication of truth, like the

End itself, is always beyond reach.[142] The stripping of Duessa before Redcrosse, the sea defeat of Dekker's Whore, and declaration of checkmate in *A Game at Chess* each begin as moments of apocalyptic unveiling. Yet these conclusory revelations shade into pre-figurative events that are unable to precipitate the final antitype that would just be. In these literary reimaginings of Revelation's last battle there is no disclosure that is analogous to the Second Coming of Christ, and therefore no surety of eventual, eternal victory. The typological end-point of history that will bring meaning and clarity to everything that has gone before is, problematically, absent.

While this absence structurally and ideologically problematizes narratives that seek to celebrate the ultimate vindication of Protestantism as the true church of Revelation, 'The Legend of Holiness', *The Whore of Babylon*, and *A Game at Chess* evocatively attest to the importance of biblical typology to decoding John's prophecy and, more specifically, to Protestantism's conception of itself and its enemies. This interpretative practice facilitated the relocation of the final battle between good and evil to the early modern present and was integral to ascertaining the identity of the antichristian forces against which John warned the faithful. Proficient in a range of illusory phenomena that concealed their true nature and identity, the Beasts of Revelation 13, Antichrist and Whore of Babylon became, in Protestant thought, avatars of the false Church of Rome against whose threat individual and state must prepare.

There is, however, something inherently problematic with critiquing Catholicism's reliance on the visual and levelling a charge of false representation through the medium of a 'darke conceit' like Spenser's epic, or, as Howard acknowledges, in the theatre, which was so often criticized by reformers for being intrinsically idolatrous.[143] What Spenser, Dekker, and Middleton's apocalyptic works illuminate, then, is that in spite of anxieties over visual representation, Protestants continued to depend on visual and artistic processes to elucidate the central tenets of the faith. But the Antichrist's workers, whose images appeared in Protestant Bibles and commentaries, as well 'drawne so liuely' on stage (Dekker, Pro. 5), had themselves, as representations, the potential to distract the faithful from what they signified, and detract from the Word more generally. Given that

[142] Luxon, in his discussion of reformed attitudes towards history more generally, argues that 'the real, the true, and the literal have all been evacuated from this world and projected into the next, with the result that the Protestant Christian's grasp on reality is by way of faith (*sola fides*) and word (*sola verbo*) alone': *Literal Figures*, 66–7.

[143] Spenser, *The Faerie Queene*, 15; Howard, *The Stage and Social Struggle*, 60, as well as 47–73. On reformed attitudes towards the theatre see O'Connell, *The Idolatrous Eye*, esp. 14–28.

anti-Catholic polemic on Revelation does not acknowledge this irony, the impulse to announce Catholicism as the false church of the Antichrist evidently proved greater than reformed concerns about the allegorical and the visual. Indeed, the production of complex, imaginative apocalyptic allegories that were tailored to the Protestant struggles of the sixteenth and early seventeenth centuries illuminates the extent to which reformed Christianity remained reliant on figurative means of definition.[144] In the end, there is perhaps no other biblical book that better illustrates the capacious and contradictory nature of Protestant literalism than the Revelation of John the Divine.

[144] For Protestant reliance on figural definitions see p. 180, as well as Brownlee, 'Imagining the Enemy', 227.

Afterword

In 2015 the Hollywood star Hugh Jackman announced that he would play the apostle Paul in a forthcoming Warner Bros. film produced by Ben Affleck and Matt Damon.[1] Given that churchgoing, in the Western world at least, is in decline, one wonders that a film based on the life of a first-century missionary and apologist is an attractive venture in Hollywood. And yet *Apostle Paul* is not exceptional. Since I began writing this book there has been something of a trend towards biblically inspired films in Anglophone cinema. *Son of God* (2014), *God's Not Dead* (2014), *Exodus: God and Kings* (2014), *Noah* (2014), *Do You Believe?* (2015), *Last Days in the Desert* (2015), *Risen* (2016), and *The Star* (2017) are among the most notable titles. More high-profile biblical films are also set to emerge in coming years. *Mary, Mother of Christ*, a prequel to Mel Gibson's *The Passion of the Christ* (2004), is in production, Will Smith apparently is working on a movie about the Old Testament figure Cain, and Ridley Scott and Jeff Robinov are rumoured to be working on biblical titles. Speculation at the reasons for this cinematic trend is beyond the scope of my expertise and this book. But box office figures for recent biblical films, and studio interest in future movies, do suggest that the Bible retains interest for scriptwriters and the wider public.[2]

It seems fitting that a book examining the relationship between the Bible and early modern culture would emerge at time when the Bible's cultural impact is being felt more widely. Now, as then, the Bible's narratives are being turned into popular entertainment and reworked to resonate with contemporary concerns. In ways reminiscent of their early modern stage counterparts, these cinematic reimaginings of the Bible embed the political, social, and personal agendas of their creators. Audiences of today are, however, less likely to be attuned to the ways in which Old Testament

[1] <https://www.theguardian.com/film/2015/apr/01/hugh-jackman-apostle-paul-christian-film>, accessed 18 May 2017.

[2] Darren Aronofsky's *Noah*, which starred Russell Crowe, grossed $362,637,473 worldwide (<http://www.imdb.com/title/tt1959490/business>), while Christian Bale's appearance in Ridley Scott's *Exodus* netted $268,175,631 (<http://www.imdb.com/title/tt1528100/business>).

patriarchs like Noah and Moses are refitted for popular consumption. Some viewers may know little about the title-figures at all. For early modern audiences of biblical plays the narratives of the Bible's key figures were familiar. Their stories were the subject of sermons, cheap print, and household readings, and were reimagined in art, poetry, and ballads, as well as on stage. *Biblical Readings and Literary Writings* has investigated some of these rewritings of scripture and it has also considered more subtle invocations of the Bible in the period's literature. As the Bible's words, imagery, and topoi are woven into early modern plays and poems, audiences and readers are called to decipher the significance of brief biblical allusions and analogies.

But this book has not only demonstrated how literary writers used the Bible in a different ways to different ends. It has also demonstrated the extent to which early modern literary culture imbibes and scrutinizes dominant interpretative principles, practices, and readings. Writers shuffle between biblical texts in a manner that expects readers and audiences to understand their connectedness. Exegetical methodologies are defended at length but they are also stated, and debated, in brief through phrases such as 'no paine' and 'promised end'.[3] Readers and audiences of early modern literature today have, then, not only to discern references to biblical figures and texts that, for many, feel remote—they must also grapple with *how* the Bible is being read and used. To do so, as this book suggests, will open up new and enriched readings of the period's poetry and drama, and facilitate deeper engagement with early modern literary culture. *Biblical Readings and Literary Writings* works towards a fuller appreciation of the Bible's intricate relationship with early modern literary writings, and suggests some of the ways that this might be achieved.

My discussion of biblical culture and Protestant hermeneutics also aims to add to the growing body of scholarship on the Bible and cultures of biblical reading, as well as appeal to those scholars interested in early modern religion more generally. The constitutive tension that exists between the reformers' interpretative claims and their practices permeates literary as well as theological writings, as the preceding chapters have shown. This fact elucidates the extent to which Protestantism was reliant on a figural ontology, and the arguments I have made may interest those working on early modern conceptions of identity, history, and belief, as well as textual practices more generally. *Biblical Readings and Literary Writings* reminds that the relationship between biblical interpretation and literature transcends discrete genres—woodcuts, sermons, and plays,

[3] Lanyer, *Salve Deus*, 97–8: 1083; Shakespeare, *King Lear*, 5.3.263. See, respectively, the discussion in Chapter 5, pp. 158–9, and Chapter 3, p. 111.

as well as mothers' manuals and poetry, can advance sophisticated readings of scripture. Neither can interpretative innovation be associated with a particular profession or gender. The diversity of writers and breadth of genres considered by this book will, I hope, encourage scholars to explore further the impact of the Bible on a broad assortment of writings. Such investigations would improve our understanding of the typicality of biblical rewritings, and enhance our awareness of the multifarious contexts in which biblical readings take place.

Doubtless there is scope to press investigation of the complex encounter between the Bible and literature in other directions too. More work is needed on biblical plays in particular to dispel the assumption that such dramas have limited political and artistic value. Investigation of biblical allusions in the work of commercial playwrights, such as Thomas Middleton, John Webster, and Philip Massinger, has also not been exhausted. In various chapters I have gestured towards the rich body of biblical verse that was written in the sixteenth and early seventeenth centuries, most of which remains largely unexplored. Consideration of biblical poetry by writers including Thomas Jackson, Gervase Markham, and Alice Sutcliffe would deepen our awareness of reading habits and textual practices, particularly among lay writers. More broadly, there seems to be scope to situate what we already know about the biblical reading practices of English Protestants in relation to the interpretative practices of Catholicism, as well as those of reformed lay readers in other parts of Europe. Such a study would add to our increasing awareness of commonalities, rather than contrasts, in interpretative practices across confessional lines.

Biblical Readings and Literary Writings in Early Modern England, 1558–1625 emerges at a time when the Bible's influence on popular culture is being felt more expressly, and when the Bible, and confessional belief and practices, are of fervent interest and discussion in early modern studies. If we continue to explore the Bible's cultural impact in early modern society it will greatly enrich not only our understanding of the literature of this period, but the Bible's legacy in Western culture more generally.

Select Bibliography

PRIMARY SOURCES

A.G. *The widdoves mite cast into the treasure-house of the prerogatiues, and prayses of our B. Lady.* Saint-Omer: English College Press, 1619. STC (2nd ed.)/ 11490.

Abbot, George. *An exposition vpon the prophet Ionah Contained in certaine sermons, preached in S. Maries church in Oxford.* London: Richard Field, 1600. STC (2nd ed.)/34.

Abbot, George. *The reason vvhich Doctor Hill hath brought for the vpholding of Papistry, which is falselie termed the Catholike religion.* Oxford: Joseph Barnes, 1604. STC (2nd ed.)/37.

Abbot, George. *A sermon preached at Westminster May 26. 1608 at the funeral solemnities of the Right Honorable Thomas Earle.* London: Melchisedech Bradwood, 1608. STC (2nd ed.)/38.

Abbot, George. *The whole booke of Iob paraphrased or, made easie for any to understand.* London: Edward Griffin, 1639. STC (2nd ed.)/41.

Adams, Thomas. *The happines of the church, or, A description of those spirituall prerogatiues vvherewith Christ hath endowed her.* London: G.P., 1619. STC (2nd ed.)/121.

Adams, Thomas. *The white deuil, or The hypocrite vncased in a sermon preached at Pauls Crosse, March 7. 1612.* London: Melchisedech Bradvvood, 1613. STC (2nd ed.)/132.

Ainsworth, Henry. *Annotations upon the five books of Moses, the booke of Psalmes and the Song of Songs.* London: M. Flesher and J. Haviland, 1627. STC (2nd ed.)/219.

Ainsworth, Henry. *An arrovv against idolatrie Taken out of the quiver of the Lord of hosts.* Amsterdam: Giles Thorp, 1624. STC (2nd ed.)/222.

Ainsworth, Henry. *The orthodox foundation of religion.* London: R.C., 1641. Wing/A811.

Ainsworth, Henry. *Solomon's Song of Songs in English metre: with annotations and references to other Scriptures, for the easier understanding of it.* Amsterdam: Giles Thorp, 1623. STC (2nd ed.)/2775.

Andrewes, Bartimaeus. *Certaine verie worthie, godly and profitable sermons, vpon the fifth chapiter of the Songs of Solomon.* London: Robert Waldegraue, 1583. STC (2nd ed.)/585.

Andrewes, Lancelot. *Sermons by the Right Honorable and Reverend Father in God, Lancelot Andrevves, late Lord Bishop of Winchester. Published by His Majesties speciall command.* London: George Miller, 1629. STC (2nd ed.)/606.

Anon. *The Chronicle History of King Leir and his Three Daughters*. Ed. Sidney Lee. London: Chatto & Windus, 1909.

Anon. *The office of Christian parents, shewing how children are to be governed through all ages and times of their lives*. Cambridge: Cantrell Legge, 1616. STC 5180.

Aquinas, Thomas. *The 'Summa Theologica' of St Thomas Aquinas*. Trans. the Fathers of the Dominican Province, 27 vols. New York: Benzinger Brothers, 1947.

Articles, whereupon it was agreed by the archbishoppes and bishoppes of both prouinces, and the whole cleargie. London: Richarde Iugge and Iohn Cawood, 1571. STC (2nd ed.)/10038.11.

Augustine. *De Civitate Dei (The City of God)*. Ed. Thomas Merton and Marcus Dods. London: Random House, 2000.

Aylett, Robert. *The brides ornaments viz. fiue meditations, morall and diuine. 1. Knowledge, 2. zeale, 3. temperance, 4. bountie, 5. ioy*. London: William Stansby, 1625. STC (2nd ed.)/1000.5.

Aylett, Robert. *The Song of Songs, which was Salomons metaphrased in English heroiks by way of dialogue. With certayne of the brides ornaments*. London: William Stansby, 1621. STC (2nd ed.)/2771.

Babington, Gervase. *Certaine Plaine, briefe and comfortable notes upon everie Chapter of Genesis*. London: [A. Jeffes and P. Short], 1592. STC (2nd ed.)/1086.

Baldwin, William. *The canticles or balades of Salomon, phraselyke declared in Englysh metres*. London: William Baldwin, 1549. STC (2nd ed.)/2768.

Bale, John. *The Complete Plays of John Bale*. Ed. Peter Happé. Cambridge: D. S. Brewer, 1985–6.

Bale, John. *A Dialogue or communycacyon to be had at table between two children*. London: R. Foster, 1549. STC 1290.

Bale, John. *The image of both Churches after the most wonderfull and heauenly Reuelation of sainct Iohn the Euangelist, contayning a very fruitfull exposition or paraphrase vpon the same*. London: Thomas East, 1570. STC (2nd ed)/1301.

Bale, John. *The image of bothe churches after the moste wonderfull and heauenly Reuelacion of Sainct Iohn the Euangelist, contayning a very frutefull exposicion or paraphrase vpon the same*. London: Richard Iugge, 1548. STC (2nd ed.)/1297.

Bale, John. *The image of bothe churches after reulacion of saynt Iohan the euangelyst*. [Antwerp]: S. Mierdman, 1545. STC (2nd ed.)/1296.5.

Batman, Stephen. *A christall glasse of christian reformation wherein the godly maye beholde the coloured abuses vsed in this our present tyme*. London: Iohn Day, 1569. STC (2nd ed.)/1581.

Bayly, Lewis. *The practice of pietie directing a Christian how to walke that he may please God*. [London]: Robert Allott, 1616. STC (2nd ed.)/1606.5.

Becon, Thomas. *The iewel of ioye*. London: J. Daye and W. Seres, 1550. STC (2nd ed.)/1733.

Bentley, Thomas. *The fift lampe of virginitie conteining sundrie forms of christian praiers and meditations*. London: H. Denham, 1582. STC (2nd ed.)/1893.

Bentley, Thomas. *The monument of matrones conteining seuen seuerall lamps of virginitie, or distinct treatises; whereof the first fiue concerne praier and meditation:*

the other two last, precepts and examples, as the woorthie works partlie of men, partlie of women; compiled for the necessarie vse of both sexes out of the sacred Scriptures. London: H. Denham, 1582. STC (2nd ed.)/1892.

Bernard, Richard. *Dauids musick: or Psalmes of that royall prophet*. London: Felix Kyngston, 1616. STC (2nd ed.)/1935.

Bernard, Richard. *A key of knowledge for the opening of the secret mysteries of St. Johns mysticall revelation*. London: Felix Kyngston, 1617. STC (2nd ed.)/1943.

Beza, Théodore. *A briefe declaration of the chiefe points of Christian religion set forth in a table*. Trans. William Whittingham. London: Tho. Man, 1613. STC (2nd ed.)/2002.

Beza, Théodore. *Job expounded... partly in manner of a commentary, partly in manner of a paraphrase*. Cambridge: John Legatt, 1589. STC (2nd ed.)/2020.

Beza, Théodore. *A Learned Treatise of the Plague wherein the Two Questions, whether the plague be infectious or no, and, whether and how farr it may be shunned of Christians by going aside, are resolved*. London: Thomas Ratcliffe, 1665. Wing/B2196.

Beza, Théodore. *Master Bezaes sermons vpon the three chapters of the canticle of canticles wherein are handled the chiefest points of religion controversed and debated betweene vs and the aduersarie at this day, especially touching the true Iesus Christ and the true Church, and the certaine & infallible marks both of the one and of the other*. Oxford: Joseph Barnes, 1587. STC (2nd ed.)/2025.

The Bible that is, the Holy Scriptures contained in the Olde and Newe Testament. London: Christopher Barker, 1587.

Black, Sixt. *Sapientia Solomonis: Acted Before the Queen by the Boys of Westminster School January 17, 1565/6*. Ed. Elizabeth Rogers Payne. New Haven: Yale University Press, 1938.

Böhme, Jakob. *The fifth book of the authour, in three parts the first, Of the becoming man or incarnation of Jesus Christ*. London: J.M., 1659. Wing/B3405.

The Book of Common Prayer and Administration of the Sacraments and other Rites and Ceremonies of the Church of England in *Liturgy and Occasional Forms of Prayer Set Forth in the Reign of Queen Elizabeth*. Ed. William Keatinge Clay. Cambridge: Cambridge University Press, 1847.

The Book of Common Prayer: The Texts of 1549, 1559, and 1662. Ed. Brian Cummings. Oxford: Oxford University Press, 2011.

Brightman, Thomas. *A commentary on the Canticles or the Song of Salomon wherein the text is analised, the native signification of the words declared, the allegories explained, and the order of the times whereunto they relate observed*. London: John Field, 1644. Wing/B4681.

Brightman, Thomas. *A reuelation of the reuelation that is, the reuelation of St. Iohn opened clearely With a logicall resolution and exposition*. Amsterdam: [s.n.], 1615. STC (2nd ed.)/3755.

Brightman, Thomas. *The Reuelation of S. Iohn illustrated with an analysis & scholions Wherein the sence is opened by the Scripture, & the euent of things foretold, shewed by histories*. Leyden: John Classm, 1616. STC (2nd ed.)/3756.

Brightman, Thomas. *The Workes of that Famous, Reverend, and Learned Divine, Mr Thomas Brightman*. London: John Field, 1644. Wing/2305:09.

Brocardo, Iacopo. *The Reuelation of S. Ihon reueled or a paraphrase opening by conference of time and place such things as are both necessary, and profitable for the tyme present*. Trans. James Sandford. London: Thomas Marshe, 1582. STC (2nd ed.)/3810.

Broughton, Hugh. *A reuelation of the holy Apocalyps*. Middelburg: Richard Schilders, 1610. STC (2nd ed.)/3884.

Broughton, Richard. *A manual of praiers vsed by the fathers of the primatiue Church for the most part within the foure first hundred yeares of Christ, & al before the end of the sixt hundred yeare*. Lancashire: [Birchley Hall Press], 1618. STC (2nd ed.)/3899.

Bucer, Martin. *De Regno Christi. The Library of Christian Classics: Melanchthon and Bucer*. Trans. Wilhelm Pauck. Ed. Paul Larkin. Philadelphia: Westminster Press, 1969.

Bullinger, Heinreich. *A confutation of the Popes bull which was published more then two yeres agoe against Elizabeth the most gracious Queene of England, Fraunce, and Ireland, and against the noble realme of England together with a defence of the sayd true Christian Queene, and of the whole realme of England*. London: Iohn Day, 1572. STC (2nd ed.)/4044.

Bullinger, Heinreich. *A Hundred Sermons vpon the Apocalipis of Iesu Christe in dede by the angell of the Lorde: but seen or receyued and written by the apostle and Evangelist S. John*. London: John Day, 1561. STC (2nd ed.)/4061.

Bunny, Edmund. *Of the head-corner-stone: by builders still ouer-much omitted that is; a forme of teaching Iesus Christ, out of all the Holy Scriptures*. London: W. Iaggard, 1611. STC (2nd ed.)/4093.

Bünting, Heinrich. *Itinerarium totius Sacrae Scripturae. Or, the trauels of the holy patriarchs, prophets, iudges, kings, our sauiour Christ, and his Apostles*. London: Adam Islip, 1636. STC (2nd ed.)/4020.

Burton, Henry. *A tryall of priuate deuotions. Or, A diall for the houres of prayer*. London: Bernard Alsop, Thomas Fawcet, and Thomas Cotes, 1628. STC (2nd ed.)/4157.

Byfield, Nicholas. *Directions for the priuate reading of the Scriptures wherein besides the number of chapters assigned to euery day, the order and drift of the whole Scriptures is methodically set downe*. London: E. Griffin, 1618. STC (2nd ed.)/4214.

Calvin, John. *Calvin's Commentaries*. Trans. William Pringle. Grand Rapids, MI: Baker Books, 1989.

Calvin, John. *Commentary on... Matthew, Mark and Luke*. Trans. William Pringle. Edinburgh: Edinburgh Printing Company, 1845.

Calvin, John. *Commentaries on the New Testament*. Ed. D. W. Torrance and T. R. Torrance,12 vols. Edinburgh: Oliver & Boyd, 1959–65.

Calvin, John. *Calvin on the Epistle of Paul to the Galatians and Ephesians*. Trans. William Pringle. Edinburgh: Thomas Clark, 1841.

Calvin, John. *Corpus Reformatorum*. Ed. Guilelmus Baum. Brunsvigae: Wiegandt & Appelhans, 1863–1900.

Calvin, John. *A Defense of the Secret Providence of* God. Trans. Henry Cole. London: Sovereign Grace Union, 1927.

Calvin, John. *Institutes of the Christian Religion*. Ed. John T. McNeill. Trans. Ford Lewis Battles, 2 vols. Louisville: Westminster John Knox Press, 2006.

Calvin, John. *Sermons of Master Iohn Caluin, vpon the booke of Iob*. Trans. Arthur Golding. London: [Henry Bynneman], [1574]. STC (2nd ed.)/4445.

Cartwright, Thomas. *A Plaine explanation of the whole Revelation of Saint John. Very necessary and comfortable in these fayes of trouble and affliction in the Church. Penned by a faithful preacher, now with the God, for more private use, and now published for the further benefit of the people of God*. London: Nathaniel Newbery, 1622. STC (2nd ed.)/4710.5.

Certain Sermons or Homilies 1547–1571. Ed. Mary Ellen Rickey and Thomas B. Stroupe. Gainesville, FL: Scholars' Facsimiles and Reprints, 1968.

Charron, Pierre. *Of Wisdome three bookes written in French by Peter Charro[n] Doctr of Lawe in Paris*. Trans. Samson Lennard. London: [Eliot's Court Press], 1608. STC (2nd ed.)/5051.

Clapham, Henoch. *Three partes of Salomon his Song of Songs, expounded The first part printed before: but now re-printed and enlarged. The second and third partes neuer printed before. All which parts are here expounded and applied for the readers good*. London: Valentine Sims, 1603. STC (2nd ed.)/2772.

Clarke, Samuel. *A Collection of the lives of ten eminent divines famous in their generations for learning, prudence, piety and painfulness in the work of the ministry*. London: William Miller, 1662. Wing/C4506.

Collinges, John. *The intercourses of divine love betwixt Christ and the Church, or, The particular believing-soul as metaphorically expressed by Solomon in the second chapter of the Canticles*. London: A. Maxwel, 1676. Wing/C5323.

Cornelius, Heinrich. *A treatise of the nobilitie and excellencye of vvoman kynde*. Trans. Dauid Clapham. London: Thomae Bertheleti, 1542. STC (2nd ed.)/203.

Cowper, William. *Pathmos: or, A commentary on the Reuelation of Saint Iohn diuided into three seuerall prophecies* London: John Buge, 1619. STC (2nd ed.)/5931.

Crakanthorpe, Richard. *A sermon at the solemnizing of the happie inauguration of our most gracious and religious soueraigne King Iames wherein is manifestly proued, that the soueraignty of kings is immediately from God, and second to no authority on earth whatsoeuer*. London: VV. Iaggard, 1609. STC (2nd ed.)/5979.

Cranmer, Thomas. *The Byble in Englyshe that is to saye the conte[n]t of al the holy scrypture, both of ye olde, and newe testame[n]t*. London: Rychard Grafton, 1540. STC (2nd ed.)/2071.

Crashaw, William. *The Iesuites gospel*. London: E. A[llde], 1610. STC (2nd ed.)/6016.

Crowley, Robert. *The Psalter of Dauid newely translated into Englysh metre*. London: R. Grafton and S. Mierdman, 1549. STC (2nd ed.)/2725.

Deios, Laurence. *That the pope is that Antichrist*. London: George Bishop and Ralph Newberie, 1590. STC (2nd ed.)/6475.

Dekker, Thomas. *The Dramatic Works of Thomas Dekker*. Ed. Fredson Bowers, Vol. 2. Cambridge: Cambridge University Press, 1964.

Dekker, Thomas. *The Whore of Babylon*. Ed. Marianne Gateson Riely. New York: Garland, 1980.

Dent, Arthur. *The ruine of Rome: or An exposition vpon the whole Reuelation.* London: T. Creede, 1603. STC (2nd ed.)/6640.

Dixon, John. *The First Commentary on 'The Faerie Queene'*. Ed. Graham Hough. Stansted: privately published, 1964.

Dod, John. *A plaine and familiar [on] chapters of the Prouerbs of Salomon*. London: Humfrey Lownes, 1607. STC (2nd ed.)/6954.5.

Donne, John. *Essays in Divinity*. Ed. Evelyn Simpson. Oxford: Clarendon Press, 1952.

Donne, John. *The Sermons of John Donne*. Ed. George K. Potter and Evelyn Simpson, 10 vols. Berkeley: University of California Press, 1953–63.

Donne, John. *The Works of John Donne with a Memoir of his Life*. Ed. Henry Alford, 6 vols. London: John W. Parker, 1839.

Dove, John. *The conuersion of Salomon A direction to holinesse of life; handled by way of commentarie vpon the whole booke of Canticles*. London: W. Stansby, 1613. STC (2nd ed.)/7080.

Downame, George. *A Treatise concerning the Antichrist.* London: Cuthbert Burbie, 1603. STC (2nd ed.)/7120.

Downame, John. *Annotations upon all the books of the Old and Nevv Testament.* London: Evan Tyler, 1657. Wing (2nd ed., 1994)/D2064.

Downame, John. *A guide to godlynesse or a Treatise of a Christian life shewing the duties wherein it consisteth*. London: Felix Kingstone, 1622.

Drant, Thomas. *Two sermons preached the one at S. Maries Spittle on Tuesday in Easter weeke 1570 and the other at the court at Windsor the Sonday after twelfth day, being the viij of Ianuary, before in the yeare 1569*. London: John Daye, 1570. STC (2nd ed.)/7171.5.

Drayton, Michael. *The harmonie of the church Containing, the spirituall songes and holy hymnes, of godly men, patriarkes and prophetes: all, sweetly sounding, to the praise and glory of the highest. Now (newlie) reduced into sundrie kinds of English meeter: meete to be read or sung, for the solace and comfort of the godly*. London: T. Orwin, 1591. STC (2nd ed.)/7199.

Durham, James. *Clavis Cantici: Or, an Exposition of the Song of Solomon.* Edinburgh: George Swintoun and James Glen, 1668. Wing/D2802.

Fawkner, Antony. *Comfort to the Afflicted*. London: H. Lownes, 1626. STC (2nd ed.)/10718.

Fenner, Dudley. *The Song of Songs, that is, the most excellent song which was Solomons, translated out of the Hebrue into English meeter with as little libertie in departing from the wordes, as any plaine translation in prose can vse: and interpreted by a short commentarie*. Middelburgh: Richard Schilders, 1594. STC (2nd ed.)/2770.

Finch, Henry. *An exposition of the Song of Solomon: called Canticles Together with profitable obseruations, collected out of the same*. London: John Beale, 1615. STC (2nd ed.)/12113.

Finch, Richard. *The epiphanie of the church gathered out of the Holy Scriptures*. London: Roger Ward, 1590. STC (2nd ed.)/10877.5.

Forbes, Patrick. *An exquisite commentarie vpon the Reuelation of Saint Iohn VVherein, both the course of the whole booke, as also the more abstruse and hard places thereof not heretofore opened; are now at last most cleerely and euidently explane*. London: W. Hall, 1613. STC (2nd ed.)/11149.3.

Foxe, John. *Actes and monuments of matters most speciall and memorable, happenyng in the Church with an vniuersall history of the same*. Vol. 2 (first half). London: John Daye, 1583. STC (2nd ed.)/11225.

Foxe, John. *Actes and monuments of matters most speciall and memorable, happenyng in the Church with an vniuersall history of the same*. Vol. 2 (second half). London: John Daye, 1583. STC (2nd edn.)/11225.

Foxe, John. *Eicasmi seu meditations in Apocalypsin S. Joannis Apostoli et Evangelistae*. London: Thomas Dawson, 1587. STC (2nd ed.)/11237.

Franciscus, Junius. *The Apocalyps, or Reuelation of S.Iohn the apostle and euangelist of our Lord Iesus Christ With a brief and methodicall exposition vpon chapter by way of a little treatise, applying the words of S. Iohn to our last times*. Trans. Thomas Barber. Cambridge: Iohn Legat, 1596. STC (2nd ed.)/2990.

Fulke, William. *Praelections upon the sacred and holy Revaltion of S. John*. Trans. George Gifford. London: Thomas Purfoote, 1573. STC (2nd ed.)/11443.

Gataker, Thomas. *A good vvife Gods gift and, a vvife indeed. Tvvo mariage sermons*. London: John Hauiland, 1623. STC (2nd ed.)/11659.

Gataker, Thomas. *Of the nature and vse of lots a treatise historicall and theologicall*. London: Edward Griffin, 1619. STC (2nd ed.)/11670.

The Geneva Bible: 1560 Edition. Peabody: Hendrickson Publishers, 2007.

Gifford, George. *Fifteene sermons vpon the Song of Salomon*. London: Felix Kingston, 1598. STC (2nd ed.)/11854.

Gifford, George. *A godlie, zealous, and profitable sermon vpon the second chapter of Saint Iames*. London: Thomas East, 1582. STC (2nd ed.)/11860.

Gifford, George. *Sermons vpon the whole booke of Revelation*. London: Thomas Man, 1599. STC (2nd ed.)/11866.5.

Goodwin, John. *Anti-Cavalierisme, or, Truth Pleading As well the Necessity, as the Lawfulness of this present War, for the suppressing of that Butcherly brood of Cavalering Incendiaries, who are now hammering England, to make an Ireland out of it*. London: G.B and R.W, 1642. Wing/G1146.

Granger, Thomas. *Pauls crovvne of reioycing. Or The maner how to heare the word with profit*. London: T. S[nodham], 1616. STC (2nd ed.)/12182.

Greene, Robert. *Greenes vision vvritten at the instant of his death. Conteyning a penitent passion for the folly of his pen*. London: E. Allde, 1592. STC (2nd ed.)/12261.

Greenham, Richard. *A fruitful and Godly sermon containing necessary and profitable doctrine, for the reformation of our sinfull and wicked liues*. Edinburgh: Robert Walde-graue, 1595. STC (2nd ed.)/12319.

Greville, Fulke. *Certaine learned and elegant vvorkes of the Right Honorable Fulke Lord Brooke written in his youth*. London: E[lizabeth] P[urslowe], 1633. STC (2nd ed.)/12361.

Guild, William. *Loves entercours between the Lamb & his bride, Christ and his Church. Or, A clear explication and application of the Song of Solomon*. London: W. Wilson, 1658. Wing (2nd ed.)/G2206.

Guild, William. *Moses vnuailed: or Those figures which serued vnto the patterne and shaddow of heauenly things, pointing out the Messiah Christ Iesus*. London: John Budge, 1620. STC (2nd ed.)/12485.

Guild, William. *Popish glorying in antiquity turned to their shame*. London: Robert Allot, 1627. STC (2nd ed.)/12489.

Hakewill, George. *King Dauids vow for reformation of himselfe*. London: [Humphrey Lownes], 1621. STC (2nd ed.)/12616.

Hall, John. *Certayn chapters take[n] out of the Prouerbes of Salomo[n]*. London: Thomas Raynalde, 1550. STC (2nd ed.)/12631.

Hall, Joseph. *Salomons diuine arts, of 1. Ethickes, 2. Politickes, 3. Oeconomicks that is; the gouernment of 1. Behauiour, 2. Common-vvealth, 3. Familie. Drawne into method, out of his Prouerbs & Ecclesiastes. With an open and plaine paraphrase, vpon the Song of songs*. London: H[umphrey] L[ownes], 1609. STC (2nd ed.)/12712.

Hamilton, John. *A Facil traictise . . . Dedicate to his soverain Prince, the Kings Majestie of Scotland, King James the Saxt*. In *Catholic Tractates of the Sixteenth Century, 1573–1600*. Ed. Thomas Graves Law. Edinburgh: W. Blackwood & Sons, 1901.

Henslowe, Philip. *Henslowe's Diary*. Ed. R. A. Foakes. Cambridge: Cambridge University Press, 2006.

Herbert, George. *The Temple Sacred poems and private ejaculations*. Cambridge: Thom. Buck, and Roger Daniel, 1633. STC (2nd ed.)/13183.

Hoby, Margaret. *Diary of Lady Margaret Hoby, 1599–1605*. Ed. Dorothy M. Meads. Boston: Houghton Mifflin, 1930.

The Holie Bible faithfully translated into English, out of the Authentical Latin . . . By the College of Doway. Doway: Laurence Kellan, 1609–10. STC (2nd ed.)/2207.

Homes, Nathanael. *The Works of Dr. Nathanael Homes. A Commentary Literal or Historical and Mystical or Spiritual on the Whole Book of Canticles*. London: J. Legate, 1652. Wing/H2559.

Hooker, Richard. *The works of Mr. Richard Hooker (that learned and judicious divine), in eight books of ecclesiastical polity compleated out of his own manuscripts, never before published: with an account of his life and death*. London: Thomas Newcomb, 1666. Wing/H2631.

Hunnis, William. *Certayne Psalms drawen into English meter*. London: Ihon Harrington, 1550. STC (2nd ed.)/2727.

Hyperius, Andreas. *The course of Christianitie: or, As touching the dayly reading and meditation of the holy Scriptures*. London: Henry Bynneman, 1579. STC (2nd ed.)/11755.

I.B. *Virginalia. or Spirituall sonnets in prayse of the most glorious Virgin Marie*. Rouen: [s.n.], 1632. STC (2nd ed.)/3608.5.

James I. *The Works of the Most High and Mightie Prince, James, By grace of God*. London: Robert Barker, 1616. STC (2nd ed.)/14344.

Jerome, St. *Nicene and Post-Nicene Fathers (St Jerome: Letters and Select Works).* Ed. Philip Schaff and Henry Wace, Vol. 6. Grand Rapids, MI: Eerdmans, 1996.

Jewel, John. *A defence of the Apologie of the Churche of Englande conteininge an answeare to a certaine booke lately set foorthe by M. Hardinge.* London: Henry VVykes, 1567. STC (2nd ed.)/14600.5.

Journal of the House of Commons: 1547–1629. Vol. 1. London: HMSO, 1802.

Journal of the House of Lords: 1620–1628. Vol. 3. London: House of Lords, 1767–1830.

Joye, George. *A Present consolation for the suffers of persecution for rightwyseness.* Antwerp: S. Mierdman, 1544. STC (2nd ed.)/14828.

Junius, Franciscus. *Apocalypsis. A briefe and learned commentarie.* London: Richard Field, 1592. STC (2nd ed.)/2988.

Knell, Paul. *Israel and England paralleled.* London: [s.n.], 1648. Wing (2nd ed.)/K679.

Lanyer, Aemilia. *Salve Deus Rex Judaeorum. The Poems of Aemilia Lanyer.* Ed. Susanne Woods. Oxford: Oxford University Press, 1993.

Laud, William. *A sermon preached before his Maiesty, on Tuesday the nineteenth of Iune, at Wansted.* London: F. K[ingston], 1621. STC (2nd ed.)/15301.

Leigh, Dorothy. *The mothers blessing. Or the godly counsaile of a gentle-woman not long since deceased, left behind her for her children containing many good exhortations, and godly admonitions, profitable for all parents to leaue as a legacy to their children, but especially for those, who by reason of their young yeeres stand most in need of instruction.* London: Iohn Budge, 1616. STC (2nd edn.)/15402.

Leigh, William. *Queene Elizabeth paralleled in her Princely vertues with Dauid, Josua, and Hezekia.* London: T[homas] C[reede], 1612. STC (2nd ed.)/15426.

Lloyd, John. *A good help for weak memories, or, The contents of every chapter in the Bible in alphabetical dysticks.* London: Thomas Helder, 1671. Wing/L2655.

Loarte, Gasper. *Instructions and aduertisements, how to meditate the misteries of the rosarie of the most holy Virgin Mary.* London: W. Carter, 1597. STC (2nd ed.)/16646.

Loe, William. *Songs of Sion Set for the ioy of gods deere ones, vvho sitt here by the brookes of this vvorlds Babel, & vveepe vvhen they thinke on Hierusalem vvhich is on highe.* Hamburg: s.n., 1620. STC (2nd ed.)/16690.

Luther, Martin. *A Commentary on Saint Paul's Epistle to the Galatians.* London: J. Duncan, 1830.

Luther, Martin. *Das Newe Testament Deutzsch.* Wittenburg: M. Lotter, 1522.

Luther, Martin. *Luther's Works.* Ed. Jaroslav Pelikan and Helmut T. Lehmann. Philadelphia: Fortress Press, 1955–86.

Luther, Martin. *Selected Writings of Martin Luther, 1517–1520.* Ed. Theodore G. Tappert. Philadelphia: Fortress Press, 1965.

Luther, Martin. *Table Talk.* Trans. William Hazlitt. London: George Bell and Sons, 1902.

Luther, Martin. *Three Treatises.* Ed. Helmut T. Lehmann. Augsburg: Fortress Press, 1970.

Markham, Gervase. *The poem of poems. Or, Sions muse contayning the diuine song of King Salomon, deuided into eight eclogues*. London: Iames Roberts. 1596. STC (2nd ed.)/17386.

Marlorat, Augustine. *A Catholike exposition vpon the Reuelation of Sainct Iohn*. Trans. Arthur Golding. London: H. Binneman, 1574. STC (2nd ed.)/17408.

Mason, Thomas. *A revelation of the Revelation wherein is contayned, a most true, plaine, and briefe manifestation of the meaning and scope of all the Reuelation, and of euery mystery of the same: whereby the pope is most plainely declared and proued to bee Antichrist*. London: G. Eld, 1619. STC (2nd ed.)/17623.

Merbecke, John. *The holie historie of King Dauid*. London: Henrie Middleton, 1579. STC (2nd ed.)/17302.

Middleton, Thomas. *A Game at Chess*. Ed. T. H. Howard-Hill. Manchester: Manchester University Press, 2003.

Moffett, Peter. *A commentarie vpon the whole booke of the Prouerbs of Salomon*. London: Robert Robinson, 1596. STC (2nd ed.)/18246.

Morton, Thomas. *Salomon or A treatise declaring the state of the kingdome of Israel, as it was in the daies of Salomon Whereunto is annexed another treatise, of the Church: or more particularly, of the right constitution of a Church*. London: Robert Robinson, 1596. STC 1249:10.

Napier, John. *A Plaine Discovery of the whole Revelation*. Edinburgh: Robert Walde-graue, 1593. STC (2nd ed.)/18354.

Noot, Jan van der. *A theatre wherein be represented as wel the miseries & calamities that follow the voluptuous worldlings as also the greate ioyes and plesures which the faithfull do enioy*. London: Henry Bynneman, 1569. STC (2nd ed.)/18602.

Norden, John. *A progresse of pietie*. London: I. Windet, 1596. STC (2nd ed.)/18633.

Ockham, William of. *Summa totius logicae*. In *Philosophical Writings*. Ed. Philotheus Boehner, rev. ed. Stephen Brown. Indianapolis: Hackett Publishing Company, 1990.

Origen. *The Song of Songs*. Trans. R. P. Lawson. Westminster: Newman Press, 1957.

Pareus, David. *A commentary upon the divine Revelation of the apostle and evangelist, Iohn*. Trans. Elias Arnold. Amsterdam: C.P., 1644. Wing/P353.

Parr, Elnathan. *The grounds of diuinitie plainely discouering the mysteries of Christian religion, propounded familiarly in diuers questions and answeres*. London: N. O[kes], 1614. STC (2nd ed.)/19314.

Parrin, J. Paul. *Luther's Fore-Runners*. Trans. Samson Lennard. London: Nathanael Newbery, 1624. STC (2nd ed.)/19769.

Patrologia Latina. Ed. J. P. Migne, 217 vols. + 4 index vols. Paris: Garnier, 1841–61.

Peele, George. *The Love of King David and Fair Berthsabe*. In *The Dramatic Works of George Peele*. Ed. Charles Tyler Prouty, Vol. 3. New Haven: Yale University Press, 1970.

Perkins, William. *The arte of prophecying, or, A treatise concerning the sacred and onely true manner and methode of preaching*. Trans. Thomas Tuke. London: Felix Kyngston, 1607. STC (2nd ed.)/19735.4.

Perkins, William. *Christian oeconomie: or, A short survey of the right manner of erecting and ordering a familie according to the scriptures*. London: Felix Kyngston, 1609. STC (2nd ed.)/19677.

Perkins, William. *A Christian and plaine treatise of the manner and order of predestination and of the largenes of Gods grace*. Trans. Francis Cacot and Thomas Tuke. London: F. Kingston, 1606. STC (2nd ed.)/19683.

Perkins, William. *A Commentarie or Exposition upon the First Five Chapters of the Epistle to Galatians*. Cambridge: John Legat, 1604. STC (2nd ed.)/19680.

Perkins, William. *A godly and learned exposition or commentarie vpon the three first chapters of the Reuelation*. London: Adam Islip, 1606. STC (2nd ed.)/19732.

Perkins, William. *A golden chaine* or *The description of theologie containing the order of the causes of saluation and damnation, according to Gods word*. London: John Legat, 1600. STC (2nd ed.)/19646.

Perkins, William. *How to liue, and that well in all estates and times, specially when helps and comforts faile*. Cambridge: John Legat, 1601. STC (2nd ed.)/19728.

Perkins, William. *Lectures vpon the three first chapters of the Reuelation: preached in Cambridge anno Dom. 1595. by Master William Perkins, and now published for the benefite of this Church*. London: Richard Field, 1604. STC (2nd ed.)/19731.

Perkins, William. *A reformed Catholike: or, A declaration shewing how neere we may come to the present Church of Rome in sundrie points of religion*. Cambridge: Iohn Legat, 1598. STC (2nd ed.)/19736.

Perkins, William. *A warning against the idolatrie of the last times. And an instruction touching religious, or diuine worship*. Cambridge: Iohn Legat, 1601. STC (2nd ed.)/19763.5.

Perkins, William. *The Workes of that famous... Mr. William Perkins*. Cambridge: Iohn Legatt, 1612–13. STC (2nd ed.)/19650.

Pettus, John. *Volatiles from the history of Adam and Eve containing many unquestioned truths*. London: T. Bassett, 1674. Wing/P1912.

Plowden, Edmund. *Commentaries or Reports*. London: S. Brooke, 1816.

Prime, John. *A sermon briefly comparing the estate of King Salomon and his subiectes togither [sic] with the condition of Queene Elizabeth and her people*. Oxford: Ioseph Barnes, 1585. STC (2nd ed.)/20371.5.

Quarles, Francis. *Divine poems containing the history of Ionah. Ester. Iob. Sions sonets. Elegies*. London: Miles Flesher, 1630. STC (2nd ed.)/20533.

Quarles, Francis. *Emblemes*. London: G.M., 1635. STC (2nd ed.)/20540.5.

Quarles, Francis. *Militant Job with Meditations Divine and Moral*. London: Felix Kyngston, 1624. STC (2nd ed.)/20550.

Quarles, Francis. *Sions sonets. Sung by Solomon the King*. London: W. Stansby, 1625. STC (2nd ed.)/2776.

Rawlinson, John. *Vivat rex. A sermon preached at Paul Crosse on the day of his majesties happie inauguration, March 14 1614*. Oxford: John Lichfield and James Short, 1619. STC (2nd ed.)/20777.

Richard, Humfrey. *Job's Pietie*. London: George Norton, 1624. STC (2nd ed.)/13968.

Richard, Humfrey. *The Conflict of Job*. London: William Jaggard, 1607. STC (2nd ed.)/13967.

R[ogers], D[aniel]. *Matrimoniall Honour*. London: Th. Harper, 1642. Wing/R1797.

Rogers, Francis. *A sermon preached on September the 20. 1632 . . . at the funerall of William Proud*. London: Iohn Norton, 1633. STC (2nd ed.)/21175.

Rogers, Henry. *Blame for the bruised: Job 5:18–19*. London: Robert Allot, 1631. STC (2nd ed.)/21178.7.

Rogers, Thomas. *The faith, doctrine, and religion, professed, & protected in the realme of England, and dominions of the same expressed in 39 articles, concordablie agreed vpon by the reuerend bishops, and clergie of this kingdome*. Cambridge: Iohn Legatt, 1607. STC (2nd ed.)/21228.

Rogers, Thomas. *A golden chaine, taken out of the rich treasurehouse the Pslames of King Dauid: also, the pretious pearles of King Salomon published for the adorning of al true Christians which are the right nobilitie, against the triumphant returne of our blessed Sauiour, which is nigh at hande*. London: Henrie Denham, 1579. STC (2nd ed.)/21235.

Roper, Margaret More. *A Devout Treatise Upon the Pater Noster*. London: T. Berthelet, 1531. STC (2nd ed.)/10477.5.

Ross, Alexander Ross. *AN exposition on the Fourtene first chapters of Genesis*. London: B[ernard] A[lsop] and T[homas] F[awcet], 1626. STC (2nd ed.)/21324.

Sales, Francis de. *The Mystical Explanation of the Canticle of Canticles*. Trans. Henry B. Mackay. London: Burns & Oates, 1908.

Samuel, William. *An abridgeme[n]t of all the canonical books of the old Testament written in Sternholds meter*. London: William Seres, 1569. STC (2nd ed.)/21690.

Scott, Thomas. *The Belgick souldier dedicated to the Parliament. Or, vvarre was a blessing*. London: s.n., 1624. STC (2nd ed.)/22072.

Shakespeare, William. *King Lear. The Norton Shakespeare*. Ed. Stephen Greenblatt, Walter Cohen, Jean E. Howard, and Katharine Eisaman Maus. New York and London: W. W. Norton, 1997.

Sibbes, Richard. *Bovvels opened: or, A discovery of the near and dear love, union and communion betwixt Christ and the Church and consequently betwixt Him and every beleeving soul. Delivered in divers sermons on the fourth, fifth, and sixth chapters of the Canticles*. London: W. Godbid, 1658. Wing (2nd ed.)/S3731A.

Sibbes, Richard. *A heavenly conference between Christ and Mary after His resurrection. Wherein the intimate familiarity, and near relation between Christ and a believer is discovered*. London: John Rothwel, 1654. Wing (2nd ed.)/S3736A.

Sidney, Philip and Sidney, Mary. *The Psalms of Sir Philip Sidney and The Countess of Pembroke*. Ed. J. C. A. Rathmell. New York: New York University Press, 1963.

Smith, Jude. *A misticall deuise of the spirituall and godly loue betwene Christ the spouse, and the church or congregation Firste made by the wise Prince Salomon, and now newly set forth in verse by Iud Smith. Wherunto is annexed certeine other briefe stories. And also a treatise of prodigalitie, most fit and necessarie to be read [and] marked of all estates*. London: Henry Kirckham, 1575. STC (2nd ed.)/22805.

Smith, Thomas. *De Republica Anglorum*. Ed. Mary Dewar. Cambridge: Cambridge University Press, 1982.

Speght, Rachel. *A mouzell for Melastomus, the cynicall bayter of, and foule mouthed barker against Euahs sex*. London: Nicholas Okes, 1616. STC (2nd ed.)/23058.

Spenser, Edmund. *The Faerie Queene*. Ed. A. C. Hamilton. London and New York: Longman, 1998.

Spenser, Edmund. *The Faerie Queene*. Ed. Thomas P. Roche and Patrick C. O'Donnell. London: Penguin, 1987.

Stafford, Anthony. *The femall glory: or, The life, and death of our Blessed Lady, the holy Virgin Mary, Gods owne immaculate mother to whose sacred memory the authordedicates these his humble endeavours*. London: Thomas Harper, 1635. STC (2nd ed.)/23123.

Sternhold, Thomas. *The whole booke of Psalmes collected into Englysh metre*. London: John Day, 1562. STC (2nd ed.)/2430.

Stonely, Richard. *Richard Stonely's Diary*. Folger Shakespeare Library, MS V.a.459–61.

Stubbes, Philip. *A christal glasse for christian vvomen containing, a most excellent discourse, of the godly life and Christian death of Mistresse Katherine Stubs*. London: [T. Orwin], 1592. STC (2nd ed.)/23382.

Stubbes, Philip. *A motiue to good workes Or rather, to true Christianitie indeede*. London: Thomas Man 1593. STC (2nd ed.)/23397.

Sutcliffe, Alice. *Meditations of man's mortalitie. Or, A way to true blessednesse*. London: B[ernard] A[lsop] and T[homas] F[awcet], 1634. STC (2nd ed.)/23447.

Swetnam, Joseph. *The araignment of leuud, idle, froward, and vnconstant women or the vanitie of them, choose you whether: with a commendation of wise, vertuous and honest women*. London: George Purslowe, 1615. STC (2nd ed.)/23534.

Taverner, Richard. *The most sacred Bible, whiche is the Holy Scripture conteyning the Old and New Testament*. London: John Byddell, 1539. STC (2nd ed.)/2067.

Taylor, Thomas. *Christ revealed: or The Old Testament explained A treatise of the types and shadowes of our Saviour contained throughout the whole Scripture: all opened and made usefull for the benefit of Gods Church*. London: Miles Flesher, 1635. STC (2nd ed.)/23821.

Taylor, Thomas. *Christs victorie over the Dragon: or Satans downfall shewing the glorious conquests of our Saviour for his poore Church, against the greatest persecutors*. London: M[iles] F[lesher], 1633. STC (2nd ed.)/23823.

Taylor, Thomas. *Moses and Aaron, or, The types and shadovvs of our Saviour in the Old Testament opened and explained*. London: John Williams, 1653. Wing/T567.

Tuke, Thomas. *The practise of the faithfull containing many godly praiers both of morning and euening and other necessarie occasions*. London: Io. Beale, 1613. STC (2nd ed.)/24314.

Tyndale, William. *Doctrinal Treatises*. Ed. Henry Walter. Cambridge: Cambridge University Press, 1848.

Tyndale, William. *The Obedie[n]ce of a Christen man and how Christe[n] rulers ought to governe, where in also (if thou marke diligently) thou shalt fynde eyes to perceave the crafty conveyance of all iugglers*. Antwerp: J. Hoochstraten, 1528. STC (2nd ed.)/24446.

Tyndale, William. *The vvhole workes of W. Tyndall, Iohn Frith, and Doct. Barnes, three worthy martyrs, and principall teachers of this Churche of England collected and compiled in one tome together*. London: Iohn Daye, 1573. STC (2nd ed.)/24436.

Vaughan, Edward. *Ten introductions how to read, and in reading, how to vnderstand*. London: A. Islip, 1594. STC (2nd ed.)/24599.

Vives, Juan Luis. *A verie fruitfull and pleasant booke, called the instruction of a christian woman*. Trans. Richard Hyrde. London: Robert Walde-graue, 1585. STC (2nd ed.)/24862.

Wastell, Simon. *Microbiblion or The Bibles epitome: in verse Digested according to the alphabet, that the Scriptures we reade may more happily be remembered, and things forgotten more easily recalled*. London: Miles Flesher, 1629. STC (2nd ed.)/25102.

Weemes, John. *The Portraiture of the Image of God in Man*. London: [M. Flesher and G. Wood], 1627. STC (2nd ed.)/25217.

Whitaker, William. *A Disputation on Holy Scripture Against the Papists*. Trans. William Fitzgerald. Parker Society, No. 45. Cambridge: Cambridge University Press, 1849.

Willet, Andrew. *Hexapla in Genesin & Exodum: that is, a sixfold commentary upon the two first bookes of Moses, being Genesis and Exodus Wherein these translations are compared together*. London: John Haviland, 1633. STC (2nd ed.)/25685.

Williams, John. *Great Britains Salomon A sermon preached at the magnificent funerall, of the most high and mighty king, Iames, the late King of Great Britaine, France, and Ireland, defender of the faith*. London: Eliot's Court Press, 1625. STC (2nd ed.)/25723.

Williamson, Thomas. *THE SWORD of the spirit to smite in pieces that Antichristian GOLIAH, WHO DAILY DEFENDETH the Lords people the host of Israel*. London: Edward Griffin, 1613. STC (2nd ed.)/25740.

Wither, George. *The hymnes and songs of the Church diuided into two parts. The first part comprehends the canonicall hymnes, and such parcels of Holy Scripture as may properly be sung, with some other ancient songs and creeds. The second part consists of spirituall songs, appropriated to the seuerall times and occasions obserueable in the Church of England*. London: [John Bill], 1623. STC (2nd ed.)/25910a.

Wither, George. *The schollers purgatory discouered in the Stationers common-wealth, and discribed in a discourse apologeticall, asvvell for the publike aduantage of the Church, the state & vvhole common-vvealth of England, as for the remedy of priuate iniuryes*. London: G. Wood, 1624. STC (2nd ed.)/25919.

Woodward, Ezekias. *The Kings chronicle: In two sections; Wherein vve have the acts of the wicked and good kings of Iudah fully declared*. London: George Miller, 1643. Wing/W3494.

Wyclif, John. *Wyclif, Select English Writings*. Ed. Herbert E. Winn. London: Oxford University Press, 1929.

SECONDARY SOURCES

Alford, Stephen. *The Early Elizabethan Polity: William Cecil and the British Succession Crisis, 1558–1569.* Cambridge: Cambridge University Press, 2002.

Allen, Prudence. *The Concept of Women: The Aristotelian Revolution, 750 B.C.–A.D. 1250.* Grand Rapids, MI: Eerdmans, 1985.

Almond, Philip. *Adam and Eve in Seventeenth-Century Thought.* Cambridge: Cambridge University Press, 1999.

Altegoer, Diana B. *Reckoning Words: Baconian Science and the Construction of Truth in English Renaissance Culture.* London: Associated University Presses, 2000.

Alter, Robert. *The Art of Biblical Narrative.* New York: Basic Books, 1981.

Andersen, Jennifer L. and Sauer, Elizabeth. *Books and Readers in Early Modern England: Material Studies.* Philadelphia: University of Pennsylvania Press, 2002.

Appleby, David J. *Black Bartholomew's Day: Preaching, Polemic and Restoration Nonconformity.* Manchester: Manchester University Press, 2007.

Ardolino, Frank. *Apocalypse & Armada in Kyd's Spanish Tragedy.* Kirksville: Sixteenth Century Essays & Studies, 1995.

Astell, Ann W. *The Song of Songs in the Middle Ages.* Ithaca: Cornell University Press, 1990.

Auerbach, Erich. *Mimesis: The Representation of Reality in Western Literature.* Princeton: Princeton University Press, 1968.

Axton, Marie. *The Queen's Two Bodies: Drama and the Elizabethan Succession.* London: Royal Historical Society, 1977.

Backus, Irena Dorota. *Reformation Readings of the Apocalypse: Geneva, Zurich, and Wittenberg.* Oxford: Oxford University Press, 2000.

Ball, Bryan W. *A Great Expectation: Eschatological Thought in English Protestantism to 1660.* Leiden: E. J. Brill, 1975.

Barnes, Robin. *Prophesy and Gnosis: Apocalypticism in the Wake of the Lutheran Reformation.* Stanford: Stanford University Press, 1988.

Baroway, Israel. 'The Imagery of Spenser and the Song of Songs'. *Journal of English and Germanic Philology* 33.1 (January 1934): 23–45.

Bauckham, Richard. *The Theology of the Book of Revelation.* Cambridge: Cambridge University Press, 1993.

Bauckham, Richard. *Tudor Apocalypse: Sixteenth Century Apocalypticism, Millenarianism and the English Reformation from John Bale to John Foxe and Thomas Brightman.* Oxford: Sutton Courtenay Press, 1978.

Bawcutt, N. W. 'New Light on Middleton's Knowledge of Chess'. *Notes & Queries* 232 (1987): 301–2.

Beattie, Tina. *God's Mother, Eve's Advocate: A Marian Narrative of Women's Salvation.* London: Continuum Books, 2002.

Beilin, Elaine. *Redeeming Eve: Women Writers of the English Renaissance.* Princeton: Princeton University Press, 1987.

Bennet, Josephine Waters. *The Evolution of 'The Faerie Queene'.* Chicago: University of Chicago Press, 1942.

Besserman, Laurence L. *The Legend of Job in the Middle Ages*. Cambridge, MA: Harvard University Press, 1979.

Blackburn, Ruth. *Biblical Drama Under the Tudors*. The Hague: Mouton, 1975.

Bloch, Marc. *The Royal Touch: Sacred Monarchy and Scrofula in England and France*. Trans. J. E. Anderson. London: Routledge, 1973.

Bloom, Harold. *Ruin the Sacred Truths: Poetry and Belief from the Bible to the Present*. Cambridge, MA: Harvard University Press, 1989.

Borris, Kenneth. *Allegory and Epic in English Renaissance Literature: Heroic Form in Sidney, Spenser, and Milton*. Cambridge: Cambridge University Press, 2000.

Braunmuller, A. R. *George Peele: Criticism and Interpretation*. Boston: Twayne Publishers, 1983.

Brooks-Davies, Douglas. *Spenser's Faerie Queene: A Critical Commentary on Books I and II*. Manchester: Manchester University Press, 1977.

Brown, Sylvia, ed. *Women's Writing in Stuart England: The Mother's Legacies of Dorothy Leigh, Elizabeth Joscelin and Elizabeth Richardson*. Gloucestershire: Sutton Publishing, 1999.

Brownlee, Victoria. 'Literal and Spiritual Births: Mary as Mother in Seventeenth-Century Women's Writing'. *Renaissance Quarterly* 68.4 (Winter 2015): 1297–326.

Brownlee, Victoria and Gallagher, Laura, eds. *Biblical Women in Early Modern Literary Culture 1550–1700*. Manchester: Manchester University Press, 2015.

Buccola, Regina and Hopkins, Lisa, eds. *Marian Moments in Early Modern British Drama*. Aldershot: Ashgate, 2007.

Bullough, Geoffrey, ed. *Narrative and Dramatic Sources of Shakespeare*, 8 vols. London: Routledge & Kegan Paul; New York: Columbia University Press, 1957–75.

Burke, Mary E., Donawerth, Jane, Dove, Linda L., and Nelson, Karen, eds. *Women, Writing, and the Reproduction of Culture in Tudor and Stuart Britain*. Syracuse: Syracuse University Press, 1999.

Cambers, Andrew. *Godly Reading: Print, Manuscript and Puritanism in England, 1580–1720*. Cambridge: Cambridge University Press, 2011.

Cameron, Euan, ed. *The New Cambridge History of the Bible: Volume 3, From 1450 to 1750*. Cambridge: Cambridge University Press, 2016.

Campbell, Lily B. *Divine Poetry and Drama in Sixteenth-Century England*. Cambridge: Cambridge University Press, 1959.

Carr, David. 'Gender and the Shaping of Desire in the Song of Songs and its Interpretation'. *Journal of Biblical Literature* 119.2 (Summer 2000): 233–48.

Carter, Charles H. 'Gondomar: Ambassador to James I'. *The Historical Journal* 7.2 (1964): 189–208.

Cheney, Patrick, Hadfield, Andrew, and Sullivan, Garrett A., eds. *Early Modern English Poetry: A Critical Companion*. Oxford: Oxford University Press, 2007.

Cheney, Patrick and Silberman, Lauren, eds. *Worldmaking Spenser: Explorations in the Early Modern Age*. Lexington: University Press of Kentucky, 2000.

Christianson, Paul. *The Reformers and Babylon: English Apocalyptic Visions from the Reformation to the Eve of the Civil War.* Toronto: University of Toronto Press, 1978.

Clark, Stuart. *Thinking with Demons: The Idea of Witchcraft in Early Modern Europe.* Oxford: Oxford University Press, 1997.

Clark, Stuart. *Vanities of the Eye: Vision in Early Modern European Culture.* Oxford: Oxford University Press, 2013.

Clarke, Danielle. *The Politics of Early Modern Women's Writings.* Harlow: Longman, 2001.

Clarke, Danielle and Clarke, Elizabeth, eds. *'This Double Voice': Gendered Writing in Early Modern England.* Basingstoke: Macmillan, 2000.

Clarke, Elizabeth. *Politics, Religion and the Song of Songs in Seventeenth-Century England.* Basingstoke: Palgrave Macmillan, 2011.

Cogswell, Thomas. *The Blessed Revolution: English Politics and the Coming of War, 1621–1624.* Cambridge: Cambridge University Press, 1989.

Cohn, Norman. *The Pursuit of the Millennium: Revolutionary Millenarians and Mystical Anarchists of the Middle Ages.* London: Pimlico, 1957, rpt. 2004.

Colie, Rosalie L. and Flahiff, F. T., eds. *Some Facets of King Lear: Essays in Prismatic Criticism.* Toronto: University of Toronto Press, 1974.

Collins, John Joseph. *Apocalypse: The Morphology of a Genre.* Missoula: Scholars Press, 1979.

Collinson, Patrick. *The Reformation.* London: Weidenfeld & Nicolson, 2003.

Collinson, Patrick. *The Religion of Protestants: The Church in English Society 1559–1625.* Oxford: Clarendon Press, 1982.

Conway, M. D. *Solomon and Solomonic Literature.* London: Kegan Paul, 1899.

Cooper, Helen. *Shakespeare and the Medieval World.* London: A & C Black, 2010.

Copenhaver, Brian P. and Schmitt, Charles B. *A History of Western Philosophy: 3. Renaissance Philosophy.* Oxford: Oxford University Press, 1992.

Court, John M. *Approaching the Apocalypse: A Short History of Christian Millenarianism.* London: I. B. Tauris, 2008.

Crawford, Patricia. *Women and Religion in England, 1500–1720.* London: Routledge, 1993.

Cressy, David. *Literacy and the Social Order: Reading and Writing in Tudor and Stuart England.* Cambridge: Cambridge University Press, 1980.

Cummings, Brian. *The Literary Culture of the Reformation: Grammar and Grace.* Oxford: Oxford University Press, 2002.

Cunningham, Andrew and Grell, Ole Peter. *The Four Horsemen of the Apocalypse: Religion, War, Famine, and Death in Reformation Europe.* Cambridge: Cambridge University Press, 2001.

Dallett, Joseph B. 'Ideas of Sight in *The Faerie Queene*'. *English Literary History* 27 (1960): 87–121.

Daniell, David. *The Bible in English: Its History and Influence.* New Haven and London: Yale University Press, 2003.

Daniell, David. *William Tyndale: A Biography.* New Haven and London: Yale University Press, 1994.

Daniélou, Jean. *From Shadows to Reality: Studies in Biblical Typology of the Fathers.* Trans. Wulstan Hibberd. London: Burns & Oates, 1960.
DeNeef, A. Leigh. *Spenser and the Motives of Metaphor.* Durham, NC: Duke University Press, 1982.
Dickens, A. G. *The Counter Reformation.* London: Thames & Hudson, 1968.
DiPasquale, Theresa M. *Refiguring the Scared Feminine: The Poems of John Donne, Aemilia Lanyer and John Milton.* Pittsburgh: Duquesne University Press, 2008.
DiPasquale, Theresa M. 'Woman's Desire for Man in Lanyer's *Salve Deus Rex Judaeorum*'. *Journal of English and Germanic Philology* 99.3 (2000): 356–78.
Dolan, Francis. *Whores of Babylon: Catholicism, Gender, and Seventeenth-Century Print Culture.* Notre Dame, IN: University of Notre Dame Press, 2005.
Dollimore, Jonathan. *Radical Tragedy: Religion, Ideology, and Power in the Drama of Shakespeare and His Contemporaries.* Chicago: University of Chicago Press, 1984.
Donnelly, Philip J. *Milton's Scriptural Reasoning: Narrative and Protestant Toleration.* Cambridge: Cambridge University Press, 2009.
Doran, Susan and Freedman, Thomas S., eds. *The Myth of Elizabeth.* Basingstoke: Palgrave Macmillan, 2003.
Dove, Mary. *The First English Bible: The Text and Context of the Wycliffite Versions.* Cambridge: Cambridge University Press, 2007.
Dowling, Maria and Lake, Peter, eds. *Protestantism and the National Church in Sixteenth Century England.* London: Croom Helm, 1987.
DuBois, Page. *Torture and Truth.* London: Routledge, 1991.
Duffy, Eamon. *The Stripping of the Altars: Traditional Religion in England, 1400–1580.* New Haven: Yale University Press, 1992.
Ellington, Donna S. *From Sacred Body to Angelic Soul: Understanding Mary in Late Medieval and Early Modern Europe.* Washington, DC: Catholic University of America Press, 2001.
Elsky, Martin. *Authorizing Words: Speech, Writing, and Print in the English Renaissance.* Ithaca: Cornell University Press, 1989.
Elton, William. *King Lear and the Gods.* San Marino, CA: Huntington Library, 1966.
Emmerson, Richard. *Antichrist in the Middle Ages.* Manchester: Manchester University Press, 1981.
Ephraim, Michelle. *Reading the Jewish Woman on the Elizabethan Stage.* Aldershot: Ashgate, 2008.
Escobedo, Andrew. *Nationalism and Historical Loss in Renaissance England: Foxe, Dee, Spenser, Milton.* Ithaca: Cornell University Press, 2004.
Evans, Gillian R. *The Language of the Bible: The Earlier Middle Ages.* Cambridge: Cambridge University Press, 1984.
Evett, David. 'Types of King David in Shakespeare's Lancastrian Tetralogy'. *Shakespeare Studies* 18 (1981): 139–61.
Ewbank, Inga Stina. 'The House of David in Renaissance Drama: A Comparative Study'. *Renaissance Drama* 8 (1965): 3–40.
Fernie, Ewan. *Shame in Shakespeare.* London: Routledge, 2002.
Fine, Hillel A. 'The Tradition of a Patient Job'. *Journal of Biblical Literature* 74.1 (1955): 28–32.

Firth, Katherine R. *The Apocalyptic Tradition in Reformation Britain 1530–1645.* Oxford: Oxford University Press, 1976.

Fischlin, Daniel and Fortier, Mark, eds. *Royal Subjects: Essays on the Writings of James VI and I.* Detroit: Wayne State University Press, 2002.

Fissell, Mary E. *Vernacular Bodies: The Politics of Reproduction in Early Modern England.* Oxford: Oxford University Press, 2004.

Fleissner, Robert F. 'The "Nothing" Element in King Lear'. *Shakespeare Quarterly* 13 (1962): 67–70.

Flinker, Noam. *The Song of Songs in English Renaissance Literature: Kisses of Their Mouths.* Cambridge: D. S. Brewer, 2000.

Foucault, Michel. *Discipline and Punish: The Birth of the Prison.* New York: Vintage Books, 1979.

Foucault, Michel. *The Order of Things: An Archaeology of the Human Sciences.* Trans. A. Sheridan. London and New York: Routledge Classics, 2002.

Freeman, Thomas S. and Mayer, Thomas F., eds. *Martyrs and Martyrdom in England c.1400–1700.* Woodbridge: Boydell Press, 2007.

Freinkel, Lisa. *Reading Shakespeare's Will: The Theology of Figure from Augustine to the Sonnets.* New York: Columbia University Press, 2002.

Frontain, Raymond-Jean and Wojcik, Jan. *The David Myth in Western Literature.* West Lafayette: Purdue University Press, 1980.

Frye, Northrop. *The Great Code: The Bible and Literature.* London: Routledge & Kegan Paul, 1982.

Frye, Roland. *Shakespeare and Christian Doctrine.* London: Oxford University Press, 1963.

Galdon, Joseph A. *Typology and Seventeenth-Century Literature.* The Hague: Mouton, 1975.

Gardiner, Samuel R. *Prince Charles and the Spanish Marriage, 1617–1623.* London: Hurst and Blackett, 1869.

Gasper, Julia. *The Dragon and the Dove: The Plays of Thomas Dekker.* Oxford: Clarendon Press, 1990.

Gerrish, B. A. *The Old Protestantism and New Essays on the Reformation Heritage.* Edinburgh: T & T Clark, 1982.

Gilman, Ernest B. 'Word and Image in Quarles' "Emblemes"'. *Critical Inquiry* 6.3 (Spring 1980): 385–410.

Gless, Darryl J. *Interpretation and Theology in Spenser.* Cambridge: Cambridge University Press, 1994.

Goldberg, Jonathan. *Endlesse Worke: Spenser and the Structures of Discourse.* Baltimore: Johns Hopkins University Press, 1981.

Gordon, Bruce, ed. *Protestant History and Identity in Sixteenth-Century Europe, Volume 2: The Later Reformation.* Aldershot: Scholar Press, 1996.

Gray, Catherine. 'Feeding on the Seed of the Woman: Dorothy Leigh and the Figure of Maternal Dissent'. *English Literary History* 68 (2001): 563–92.

Gray, Madeleine. *The Protestant Reformation: Belief, Practice, and Tradition.* Brighton: Sussex Academic Press, 2003.

Green, Ian. *The Christian's ABC: Catechism and Catechizing in England c.1530–1740.* Oxford: Oxford University Press, 1996.

Green, Ian. *Print and Protestantism in Early Modern England.* Oxford: Oxford University Press, 2000.

Greenslade, S. L., ed. *The Cambridge History of the Bible: The West from the Reformation to the Present Day.* Cambridge: Cambridge University Press, 1963.

Gregerson, Linda. *The Reformation of the Subject: Spenser, Milton, and the English Protestant Epic.* Cambridge: Cambridge University Press, 1995.

Gregory, Brad S. *Salvation at Stake: Christian Martyrdom in Early Modern Europe.* Cambridge, MA: Harvard University Press, 1999.

Grell, Ole Peter and Scribner, Bob, eds. *Tolerance and Intolerance in the European Reformation.* Cambridge: Cambridge University Press, 1996.

Grogan, Jane. *Exemplary Spenser: Visual and Poetic Pedagogy in The Faerie Queene.* Farnham: Ashgate, 2009.

Grossman, Marshall, ed. *Aemilia Lanyer: Gender, Genre and the Canon.* Lexington: University Press of Kentucky, 1998.

Groves, Beatrice. *The Destruction of Jerusalem in Early Modern English Literature.* Cambridge: Cambridge University Press, 2015.

Groves, Beatrice. *Texts and Traditions: Religion in Shakespeare 1592–1604.* Oxford: Clarendon Press, 2007.

Guggisberg, Hans R. *Sebastian Castellio, 1515–1563.* Trans. Bruce Gordon. Aldershot: Ashgate, 2003.

Guibbory, Achsah. *Christian Identity: Jews & Israel in Seventeenth-Century England.* Oxford: Oxford University Press, 2010.

Hackett, Helen. *Virgin Mother, Maiden Queen: Elizabeth and the Cult of the Virgin Mary.* New York: St. Martin's Press, 1995.

Hackett, Helen. *Women and Romance Fiction in the English Renaissance.* Cambridge: Cambridge University Press, 2000.

Hadfield, Andrew, ed. *The Cambridge Companion to Spenser.* Cambridge: Cambridge University Press, 2001.

Haight, Gordon S. 'Francis Quarles in the Civil War'. *Review of English Studies* 12.46 (April 1936): 147–64.

Halio, Jay L., ed. *Critical Essays on Shakespeare's King Lear.* New York: G. K. Hall and Co., 1996.

Hamburgh, Harvey E. 'The Problem of Lo Spasimo of the Virgin in Cinquecento Paintings of the Descent from the Cross'. *Sixteenth Century Journal* 12.4 (1981): 45–75.

Hammond, Jeffrey A. 'The Bride in Redemptive Time: John Cotton and the Canticles Controversy'. *The New England Quarterly* 56.1 (March 1983): 78–102.

Hankins, John E. 'Spenser and the Revelation of St. John'. *Publications of the Modern Language Association* 60.2 (June 1945): 364–81.

Harbage, Albert, ed. *Annals of English Drama, 975–1700: An Analytical Record of All Plays, Extant or Lost, Chronologically Arranged and Indexed by Authors, Titles, Dramatic Companies.* London: Routledge, 1989.

Harris, Jonathan Gill. *Foreign Bodies and the Body Politic: Discourses of Social Pathology in Early Modern England.* Cambridge: Cambridge University Press, 1998.

Hart, Vaughan. *Art and Magic in the Court of the Stuarts.* London: Routledge, 1994.

Hattaway, Michael. 'Paradoxes of Solomon: Learning in the English Renaissance'. *Journal of the History of Ideas* 29.4 (October–December 1968): 449–530.

Hattaway, Michael. 'The Theology of Marlowe's *Doctor Faustus*'. *Renaissance Drama* 3 (1970): 51–78.

Heal, Bridget. *The Cult of the Virgin Mary in Early Modern Germany: Protestant and Catholic Piety 1500–1648.* Cambridge: Cambridge University Press, 2007.

Heller, Jennifer Louise. *The Mother's Legacy in Early Modern England.* Farnham: Ashgate, 2011.

Helm, Paul. *John Calvin's Ideas.* Oxford: Oxford University Press, 2004.

Hill, Christopher. *Antichrist in Seventeenth-Century England.* London: Verso, 1971.

Hill, Christopher. *The English Bible and the Seventeenth Century Revolution.* London and New York: Penguin Press, 1993.

Hill, Christopher. *Society and Puritanism in Pre-Revolutionary England.* Basingstoke: Palgrave Macmillan, 1997.

Hirsh, John C. *The Boundaries of Faith: The Development and Transmission of Medieval Spirituality.* Leiden: E. J. Brill, 1996.

Hodgson, Elizabeth. 'Prophesy and Gendered Mourning in Lanyer's *Salve Deus Rex Judaeorum*'. *Studies in English Literature* 43.1 (2003): 101–16.

Holloway, John. *The Story of the Night: Studies in Shakespeare's Major Tragedies.* London: Routledge, 1961, rpt. 2005.

Höltgen, Karl Josef. 'Quarles, Francis (1592–1644)'. *Oxford Dictionary of National Biography.* Oxford University Press, 2004. Online edition, January 2008. <http://www.oxforddnb.com/view/article/22945>, accessed 21 March 2011.

Hopkins, Lisa. *Shakespeare on the Edge: Border-Crossing in the Tragedies and the Henriad.* Aldershot: Ashgate, 2005.

Howard, Jean. *The Stage and Social Struggle in Early Modern England.* London: Routledge, 1994.

Hoy, Cyrus. *Introductions, Notes and Commentaries to Texts in 'The Dramatic Works of Thomas Dekker'.* Ed. Fredson Bowers. Cambridge: Cambridge University Press, 1980.

Hsia, R. Po-Chia. *Social Discipline in the Reformation: Central Europe 1550–1750.* London: Routledge, 1989.

Hume, Anthea. *Edmund Spenser: Protestant Poet.* Cambridge: Cambridge University Press, 1984.

Ishida, Tomoo, ed. *Studies in the Period of David and Solomon and Other Essays.* Winona Lake, IN: Eisenbrauns, 1982.

Johnson, Staley L. 'Elizabeth, Bride and Queen: A Study of Spenser's April Eclogue and the Metaphors of English Protestantism'. *Spenser Studies: A Renaissance Poetry Annual* 2 (1981): 75–89.

Johnston, Warren. *Revelation Restored: The Apocalypse in Later Seventeenth-Century England.* Woodbridge: Boydell Press, 2011.

Kallas, Endel. 'Martin Luther as Expositor of the Song of Songs'. *Lutheran Quarterly* 2 (1988): 323–42.

Kantorowicz, Ernst H. *The King's Two Bodies: A Study in Mediaeval Political Theology.* Princeton: Princeton University Press, 1957, rpt. 1997.

Kaske, Carol V. *Spenser and Biblical Poetics.* Ithaca and London: Cornell University Press, 1999.

Keenan, Hugh T., ed. *Typology and English Medieval Literature.* New York: AMS Press, 1992.

Keiper, Hugo, Bode, Christopher, and Utz, Richard J., eds. *Nominalism and Literary Discourse: New Perspectives.* Critical Studies 10. Amsterdam: Rodopi, 1997.

Kermode, Frank. *The Sense of an Ending: Studies in the Theory of Fiction with a New Epilogue.* Oxford: Oxford University Press, 1966, rpt. 2000.

Kermode, Frank. *Shakespeare: King Lear. A Casebook.* London: Macmillan, 1969, rpt. 1992.

Killeen, Kevin. *Biblical Scholarship, Science and Politics in Early Modern England: Thomas Browne and the Thorny Place of Knowledge.* Aldershot: Ashgate, 2009.

Killeen, Kevin. 'Chastising with Scorpions: Reading the Old Testament in Early Modern England'. *Huntington Library Quarterly* 73.3 (2010): 491–506.

Killeen, Kevin. 'Hanging up Kings: The Political Bible in Early Modern England'. *Journal of the History of Ideas* 72.4 (2011): 549–70.

Killeen, Kevin. *The Political Bible in Early Modern England.* Cambridge: Cambridge University Press, 2016.

Killeen, Kevin and Forshaw, Peter J., eds. *The Word and the World: Biblical Exegesis and Early Modern Science.* Basingstoke: Palgrave Macmillan, 2007.

Killeen, Kevin, Smith, Helen, and Willie, Rachel, eds. *The Oxford Handbook of the Bible in Early Modern England, c.1530–1700.* Oxford: Oxford University Press, 2015.

King, Christopher J. *Origen on the Song of Songs as the Spirit of Scripture: The Bridegroom's Perfect Marriage-Song.* Oxford: Oxford University Press, 2005.

King, John N. *English Reformation Literature: The Tudor Origins of the Protestant Tradition.* Princeton: Princeton University Press, 1982.

King, John N. *Spenser's Poetry and the Reformation Tradition.* Princeton: Princeton University Press, 1990.

King, John N. *Tudor Royal Iconography: Literature and Art in an Age of Religious Crisis.* Princeton: Princeton University Press, 1989.

Klassen, Walter. *Living at the End of the Ages: Apocalyptic Expectation in the Radical Reformation.* Lanham, MD: University Press of America, 1992.

Knight, G. W. *The Wheel of Fire: Interpretations of Shakespearean Tragedy.* London: Methuen, 1930, rpt. 1964.

Knott, John R. *Discourses of Martyrdom in English Literature, 1563–1694.* Cambridge: Cambridge University Press, 1993.

Knowles, Richard. 'How Shakespeare Knew *King Leir*'. *Shakespeare Survey* 55 (2002): 12–35.

Koester, Craig R. *Revelation and the End of All Things.* Grand Rapids, MI: Eerdmans, 2001.

Kolb, Robert. 'God's Gift of Martyrdom: The Early Reformation Understanding of Dying for the Faith'. *Church History* 64.3 (1995): 399–411.

Korshin, Paul J. *Typologies in England 1650–1820.* Princeton: Princeton University Press, 1982.

Kott, Jan. *Shakespeare Our Contemporary*. Trans. Boleslaw Taborski. Bristol: Methuen, 1965/1986.
Kramer, S. N. *The Sacred Marriage Rite*. Bloomington: Indiana University Press, 1969.
Krantz, Susan E. 'Thomas Dekker's Political Commentary in *The Whore of Babylon*'. *Studies in English Literature, 1500–1900* 35.2 (Spring 1995): 345–59.
Kreitzer, Beth. *Reforming Mary: Changing Images of the Virgin Mary in Lutheran Sermons of the Sixteenth Century*. Oxford: Oxford University Press, 2004.
Krier, Thresea M. *Gazing on Secret Sights: Spenser, Classical Imitation, and the Decorums of Vision*. Ithaca: Cornell University Press, 1990.
Kristeva, Julia. 'Stabat Mater'. In *The Female Body in Western Culture: Contemporary Perspectives*, ed. Susan R. Suleiman. Cambridge, MA: Harvard University Press, 1986.
Kuchar, Gary. 'Aemilia Lanyer and the Virgin's Swoon: Theology and Iconography in *Salve Deus Rex Judaeorum*'. *English Literary Renaissance* 37.1 (2007): 47–73.
Lake, Peter and Dowling, Maria, eds. *Protestantism and the National Church in Sixteenth Century England*. London: Croom Helm, 1987.
Langford, Michael J. *Providence*. London: SCM Press, 1981.
Lee, Maurice. *Great Britain's Solomon: James the VI and I in His Three Kingdoms*. Urbana: University of Illinois Press, 1990.
Leith, John H. *John Calvin's Doctrine of the Christian Life*. Louisville: Westminster/John Knox Press, 1989.
Levin, Carole. *The Reign of Elizabeth I*. Basingstoke: Palgrave Macmillan, 2002.
Levin, Carole, Carney, Jo Eldridge, and Barrett, Debra, eds. *Elizabeth I: Always Her Own Free Woman*. Aldershot: Ashgate, 2003.
Lewalski, Barbara K. *Protestant Poetics and the Seventeenth-Century Religious Lyric*. Princeton: Princeton University Press, 1979.
Loewenich, Walther von. *Luther's Theology of the Cross*. Trans. Herbert J. A. Bouman. Minneapolis: Augsburg Publishing House, 1976.
Longfellow, Erica. *Women and Religious Writing in Early Modern England*. Cambridge: Cambridge University Press, 2004.
Longman III, Temper. *Song of Songs*. Grand Rapids, MI: Eerdmans, 2001.
Lothian, John M. *King Lear: A Tragic Reading of Life*. Toronto: Clarke, Irwin & Co., 1949.
Loughlin, Marie H. '"Fast ti'd unto them in a golden Chaine": Typology, Apocalypse, and Women's Genealogy in Aemilia Lanyer's *Salve Deus Rex Judaeorum*'. *Renaissance Quarterly* 53 (2000): 133–79.
Luckyj, Christina. *'A moving Rhetoricke': Gender and Silence in Early Modern England*. Manchester: Manchester University Press, 2002.
Luxon, Thomas. *Literal Figures: Puritan Allegory and the Reformation Crisis in Representation*. Chicago: University of Chicago Press, 1995.
McBride, Kari Boyd and Ulreich, John C. 'Answerable Styles: Biblical Poetics and Biblical Politics in the Poems of Aemilia Lanyer and John Milton'. *Journal of English and Germanic Philology* 100 (2001): 333–54.

MacCaffrey, Isabel G. *Spenser's Allegory: The Anatomy of Imagination*. Princeton: Princeton University Press, 1976.

McCoy, Richard C. *Alterations of State: Sacred Kingship in the English Reformation*. New York: Columbia University Press, 2002.

MacCulloch, Diarmaid. *The Boy King Edward VI and the Protestant Reformation*. Berkeley: University of California Press, 2002.

MacCulloch, Diarmaid. *Reformation: Europe's House Divided*. London: Penguin, 2003.

McCullough, Peter E., Adlington, Hugh, and Rhatigan, Emma, eds. *The Oxford Handbook of the Early Modern Sermon*. Oxford: Oxford University Press, 2011.

McCullough, Peter E. and Ferrell, Lori Anne, eds. *The English Sermon Revised: New Studies in Early Modern Preaching*. Manchester: Manchester University Press, 2000.

McEachern, Clare and Shuger, Debora Kuller, eds. *Religion and Culture in Renaissance England*. Cambridge: Cambridge University Press, 1997.

McGrath, Alistair. *Intellectual Origins of the European Reformation*. Oxford: Blackwell, 1987.

McGrath, Alistair. *Luther's Theology of the Cross: Martin Luther's Theological Breakthrough*. Oxford: Blackwell, 1990.

Mallette, Richard. *Spenser and the Discourses of Reformation England*. Lincoln: University of Nebraska Press, 1997.

Maltby, Judith. *Prayer Book and People in Elizabethan and Early Stuart England*. Cambridge: Cambridge University Press, 2000.

Marshall, Peter. *Reformation England 1480–1642*. London: Arnold, 2003.

Martin, Randall, ed. *Women Writers in Renaissance England: An Annotated Anthology*. London and New York: Routledge, 2014.

Marx, Steven. *Shakespeare and the Bible*. Oxford: Oxford University Press, 2000.

Matter, Ann E. *The Voice of My Beloved: The Song of Songs in Western Medieval Christianity*. Philadelphia: University of Pennsylvania Press, 1990.

Mayer, Jean-Christophe, ed. *The Struggle for the Succession in Late Elizabethan England: Politics, Polemics and Cultural Representations*. Montpellier: University Press Paul-Valéry, 2004.

Miller, P. C. '"Pleasure of the Text, Text of Pleasure": Eros and Language in Origen's *Commentary on the Song of Songs*'. *Journal of the American Academy of Religion* 54.2 (Summer 1986): 241–53.

Milward, Peter. *Biblical Influences in Shakespeare's Great Tragedies*. Bloomington: Indiana University Press, 1987.

Miner, Earl, ed. *Illustrious Evidence: Approaches to English Literature of the Seventeenth Century*. Berkeley: University of California Press, 1975.

Miner, Earl, ed. *Literary Uses of Typology from the Late Middle Ages to the Present*. Princeton: Princeton University Press, 1977.

Molekamp, Femke. 'Reading Christ the Book in Aemilia Lanyer's *Salve Deus Rex Judaeroum* (1611): Iconography and the Cultures of Reading'. *Studies in Philology* 109.3 (2012): 311–32.

Molekamp, Femke. *Women and the Bible in Early Modern England: Religious Reading and Writing*. Oxford: Oxford University Press, 2013.

Monod, Paul Kléber. *The Power of Kings: Monarchy and Religion in Europe, 1589–1715*. New Haven: Yale University Press, 1999.

Morrissey, Mary. *Politics and the Paul's Cross Sermons, 1558–1642*. Oxford: Oxford University Press, 2011.

Muir, Kenneth. *King Lear: Critical Essays*. New York: Garland, 1984.

Mullan, David George. *Narratives of the Religious Self in Early-Modern Scotland*. Farnham: Ashgate, 2010.

Muller, Richard and Thompson, John L., eds. *Biblical Interpretation in the Era of the Reformation: Essays Presented to David C. Steinmetz in Honor of his Sixtieth Birthday*. Grand Rapids, MI: Eerdmans, 1996.

Mullet, Michael. *The Catholic Reformation*. London: Routledge, 1999.

Munns, Jessica and Richards, Penny, eds. *Gender, Power and Privilege in Early Modern Europe*. Harlow: Pearson, 2003.

Murphy, Roland E. and McBride, S. Dean, eds. *Origen in the Song of Songs: A Commentary on the Book of Canticles or the Song of Songs*. Minneapolis: Fortress Press, 1990.

Narveson, Kate. *Bible Readers and Lay Writers in Early Modern England: Gender and Self-Definition in an Emergent Writing Culture*. Aldershot: Ashgate, 2012.

Neff, Amy. 'The Pain of Compassio: Mary's Labour at the Foot of the Cross'. *The Art Bulletin* 80 (1998): 243–73.

Nethercot, Arthur H. 'The Literary Legend of Francis Quarles'. *Modern Philology* 20.3 (February 1923): 225–40.

Noble, Richard. *Shakespeare's Biblical Knowledge and the Use of the Book of Common Prayer as Exemplified in the Plays of the First Folio*. New York: Macmillan, 1935.

Norbrook, David. *Poetry and Politics in the English Renaissance*. Oxford: Oxford University Press, 2002.

Nuttall, A. D. *Why Does Tragedy Give Pleasure?* Oxford: Clarendon Press, 1996.

O'Callaghan, Michelle. *Thomas Middleton, Renaissance Dramatist*. Edinburgh: Edinburgh University Press, 2009.

O'Connell, Michael. *The Idolatrous Eye: Iconoclasm and Theater in Early-Modern England*. Oxford: Oxford University Press, 2000.

O'Hear, Natasha F. H. *Contrasting Images of the Book of Revelation in Late Medieval and Early Modern Art: A Case Study in Visual Exegesis*. Oxford: Oxford University Press, 2011.

O'Hear, Natasha and O'Hear, Anthony. *Picturing the Apocalypse: The Book of Revelation in the Arts over Two Millennia*. Oxford: Oxford University Press, 2015.

O'Leary, Stephen. *Arguing the Apocalypse: A Theory of Millennial Rhetoric*. Oxford: Oxford University Press, 1994.

O'Meara, Thomas. *Mary in Protestant and Catholic Theology*. New York: Sheed & Ward, 1966.

Ogden, Margaret S., ed. *A Bibliography of Middle English Texts.* Ann Arbor: University of Michigan Press, 1954.

Osherow, Michele. *Biblical Women's Voices in Early Modern England.* Aldershot: Ashgate, 2009.

Oxford Dictionary of National Biography. Oxford University Press, 2004. Online edition, January 2008.

Pack, Robert. *The Long View: Essays on the Discipline of Hope and Poetic Craft.* Amherst: University of Massachusetts Press, 1991.

Pack, Robert. *Willing to Choose: Volition and Storytelling in Shakespeare's Major Plays*. Sandpoint, ID: Lost Horse Press, 2007.

Palme, Per. *The Triumph of Peace: A Study of the Banqueting House.* London: Thames & Hudson, 1957.

Parish, Helen L. *Monks, Miracles and Magic: Reformation Representations of the Medieval Church.* New York: Routledge, 2005.

Parker, Barbara L. 'The Whore of Babylon and Shakespeare's *Julius Caesar*'. *Studies in English Literature, 1500–1900* 35.2 (1995): 251–69.

Parker, Patricia and Hartman, Geoffrey, eds. *Shakespeare and the Question of Theory*. London: Methuen, 1985, rpt. 2005.

Patrides, C. A. and Wittreich, Joseph, eds. *The Apocalypse in English Renaissance Thought and Literature.* Manchester: Manchester University Press, 1984.

Patterson, Annabel. *Censorship and Interpretation: The Conditions of Writing and Reading in Early Modern England.* Madison: University of Wisconsin Press, 1984.

Pattison, Bonnie L. *Poverty in the Theology of John Calvin.* Eugene, OR: Pickwick Publications, 2006.

Pelikan, Jaroslav. *Mary Through the Centuries: Her Place in the History of Culture.* New Haven: Yale University Press, 1996.

Pendergast, John S. *Religion, Allegory and Literacy in Early Modern England, 1560–1640: The Control of the Word.* Aldershot: Ashgate, 2006.

Perry, Curtis. *The Making of Jacobean Culture: James I and the Renegotiation of Elizabethan Literary Practice.* Cambridge: Cambridge University Press, 1997.

Phillippy, Patricia. 'Sisters of Magdalen: Women's Mourning in Aemilia Lanyer's *Salve Deus Rex Judaeorum*'. *English Literary Renaissance* 31.1 (2001): 78–106.

Pollard, William F. and Boenig, Robert, eds. *Mysticism and Spirituality in Medieval England.* Woodbridge: D. S. Brewer, 1997.

Poole, Kristen. '"The fittest closet for all goodness": Authorial Strategies of Jacobean Mothers' Manuals'. *Studies in English Literature, 1500–1900* 35.1 (Winter 1995): 69–88.

Pope, Marvin H. *Song of Songs.* New York: Doubleday, 1977.

Preus, James S. *From Shadow to Promise: Old Testament Interpretation from Augustine to the Young Luther*. Cambridge, MA: Harvard University Press, 1969.

Quilligan, Maureen. *The Language of Allegory: Defining the Genre.* Ithaca: Cornell University Press, 1979.

Quitslund, Beth. *The Reformation in Rhyme: Sternhold, Hopkins and the English Metrical Psalter, 1547–1603*. Aldershot: Ashgate, 2008.

Radzinowicz, Mary Ann. *Milton's Epics and the Book of Psalms.* Princeton: Princeton University Press, 1989.

Reddaway, W. F., ed. *Selected Documents of European History: Vol. II, 1492–1715.* New York: Henry Holt & Co., 1930.

Reeves, Marjorie. *The Influence of Prophecy in the Later Middle Ages: A Study in Joachimism.* Oxford: Clarendon Press, 1969.

Reibetanz, John. *The 'Lear' World: A Study of King Lear in Its Dramatic Context.* Toronto and Buffalo: University of Toronto Press, 1977.

Rhymer, Joseph. *The End of Time: Eschatology of the New Testament.* Slough: St Paul Publications, 1992.

Richey, Ester Gilman. *The Politics of Revelation in the English Renaissance.* Columbia: University of Missouri Press, 1998.

Richey, Ester Gilman. '"To Undoe the Booke": Cornelius Agrippa, Aemilia Lanyer and the Subversion of Pauline Authority'. *English Literary Renaissance* 27 (1997): 106–28.

Roberts, Wendy Miller. 'Gnosis in Aemilia Lanyer's *Salve Deus Rex Judaeorum*'. *Rocky Mountain Review of Language and Literature* 59.2 (2005): 11–28.

Robertson, D. 'The Experience of Reading: Bernard of Clairvaux's Sermons on the Song of Songs'. *Religion and Literature* 19 (1987): 1–20.

Rogers, John. 'The Passion of a Female Literary Tradition: Aemilia Lanyer's "Salve Deus Rex Judæorum"'. *Huntington Library Quarterly* 63.4 (2000): 435–46.

Ruether, Rosemary Radford. *Mary: The Feminine Face of the Church.* Philadelphia: Westminster Press, 1977.

Russell, D. S. *The Method and Message of Jewish Apocalyptic, 200 BC–AD 100.* Philadelphia: Westminster Press, 1964.

Ryrie, Alec. *Being Protestant in Reformation Britain.* Oxford: Oxford University Press, 2013.

Sæbø, Magne, ed. *Hebrew Bible/Old Testament: The History of Its Interpretation.* Vol. 2. Göttingen: Vandenhoeck & Ruprecht, 2008.

Scarisbrick, J. J. *Henry VIII.* Berkeley: University of California Press, 1968.

Scarry, Elaine. *The Body in Pain: The Making and the Unmaking of the World.* Oxford: Oxford University Press, 1985.

Scheper, George L. 'Reformation Attitudes toward Allegory and the Song of Songs'. *Publications of the Modern Language Association* 89.3 (May 1974): 551–62.

Schmitt, Charles B. and Skinner, Quentin, eds. *The Cambridge History of Renaissance Philosophy.* Cambridge and New York: Cambridge University Press, 1996.

Schreiner, Susan Elizabeth. *Where shall Wisdom Be Found? Calvin's Exegesis on Job from Medieval and Modern Perspectives.* Chicago: University of Chicago Press, 1994.

Scott, Sarah. 'The Empress of Babylon's "carbuncles and rich stones": The Metaphorizing of the Pox in Thomas Dekker's *Whore of Babylon*'. *Early Theatre* 7.1 (2004): 67–95.

Scribner, Robert. *For the Sake of Simple Folk: Popular Propaganda for the German Reformation.* Oxford: Clarendon Press, 1994.

Severs, J. Burke and Hartung, Albert E., eds. *A Manual of the Writings in Middle English 1050–1500*. New Haven: Connecticut Academy of Arts and Sciences, 1967–93.
Sewall, R. B. *The Vision of Tragedy*. New Haven: Yale University Press, 1965.
Shaheen, Naseeb. *Biblical References in Shakespeare's Comedies*. Newark: University of Delaware Press, 1993.
Shaheen, Naseeb. *Biblical References in Shakespeare's History Plays*. Newark: University of Delaware Press, 1989.
Shaheen, Naseeb. *Biblical References in Shakespeare's Plays*. Cranbury, NJ: Associated University Presses, 1999.
Shaheen, Naseeb. *Biblical References in Shakespeare's Tragedies*. Newark: University of Delaware Press, 1993.
Sharpe, Kevin and Zwicker, Steven N. *Reading, Society and Politics in Early Modern England*. Cambridge: Cambridge University Press, 2003.
Shell, Alison. *Catholicism, Controversy and the English Literary Imagination, 1558–1660*. Cambridge: Cambridge University Press, 1999.
Sherman, William H. *Used Books: Marking Readers in Renaissance England*. Philadelphia: University of Pennsylvania Press, 2008.
Shuger, Debora Kuller. *Habits of Thought in the English Renaissance: Religion, Politics and Dominant Culture*. Berkeley: University of California Press, 1990.
Shuger, Debora Kuller. *The Renaissance Bible: Scholarship, Sacrifice and Subjectivity*. Berkeley: University of California Press, 1994.
Shuger, Debora Kuller and McEachern, Claire, eds. *Religion and Culture in the English Renaissance*. Cambridge: Cambridge University Press, 1997.
Siegel, Paul N. *Shakespearean Tragedy and Elizabethan Compromise*. New York: New York University Press, 1957.
Sievers, Julie. 'Refiguring the Song of Songs: John Cotton's 1655 Sermon and the Antinomian Controversy'. *The New England Quarterly* 76.1 (March 2003): 73–107.
Simpson, James. *Burning to Read: English Fundamentalism and its Religious Opponents*. Cambridge, MA: Harvard University Press, 2007.
Sims, James H. *The Bible in Milton's Epics*. Gainesville, FL: University of Florida Press, 1962.
Sims, James H. *Dramatic Uses of Biblical Allusions in Marlowe and Shakespeare*. Gainesville, FL: University of Florida Press, 1966.
Skinner, Quentin. *The Foundations of Modern Political Thought, Vol. II*. Cambridge: Cambridge University Press, 1978.
Smalley, Beryl M. *The Study of the Bible in the Middle Ages*. Oxford: Blackwell, 1983.
Smith, John Hazel, ed. *Two Latin Comedies: Titus et Gesippus and Christus Triumphans*. Ithaca: Cornell University Press, 1973.
Smith, Susan L. 'The Bride Stripped Bare: A Rare Type of the Disrobing of Christ'. *Gesta* 34.2 (1995): 126–46.
Snook, Edith. *Women, Reading and the Cultural Politics of Early Modern England*. Aldershot: Ashgate, 2005.
Spinka, Matthew. *John Hus and the Czech Reform*. Hamden: Archon Books, 1966.

Steadman, John M. 'The Iconographical Background of Quarles' "Flesh" and "Spirit"'. *The Art Bulletin* 39.3 (September 1957): 231–2.

Steinmetz, David. 'Divided by a Common Past: The Reshaping of the Christian Exegetical Tradition in the Sixteenth Century'. *Journal of Medieval and Early Modern Studies* 27.2 (1997): 245–64.

Sternberg, Meir. 'The Politics of Biblical Poetic'. Lecture at Queen's University Belfast, 7 October 2010.

Stewart, Stanley. *The Enclosed Garden: The Tradition and the Image in Seventeenth-Century Poetry.* Madison: University of Wisconsin Press, 1966.

Streete, Adrian. '"An old quarrel between us that will never be at an end": Middleton's *Women Beware Women* and Late Jacobean Religious Politics'. *Review of English Studies* 60.244 (2009): 230–54.

Streete, Adrian. *Apocalypse and Anti-Catholicism in Seventeenth-Century English Drama.* Cambridge: Cambridge University Press, 2017.

Streete, Adrian, ed. *Early Modern Drama and the Bible: Contexts and Readings, 1570–1625.* Basingstoke: Palgrave Macmillan, 2011.

Streete, Adrian. 'Frances Quarles' Early Poetry and the Discourses of Jacobean Spenserianism'. *Journal of the Northern Renaissance* 1.1 (Spring 2009): 88–108.

Streete, Adrian. *Protestantism and Drama in Early Modern England.* Cambridge: Cambridge University Press, 2009.

Streete, Adrian. 'Reforming Signs: Semiotics, Calvinism and Clothing in Sixteenth-Century England'. *Literature and History* 12.1 (Spring 2003): 1–18.

Streete, Adrian. '"What bloody man is that?": Questioning Biblical Typology in *Macbeth*'. *Shakespeare* 5.1 (April 2009): 18–35.

Suleiman, Susan R., ed. *The Female Body in Western Culture: Contemporary Perspectives.* Cambridge, MA: Harvard University Press, 1986.

Sun, Emily. *Succeeding King Lear: Literature, Exposure, and the Possibility of Politics.* New York: Fordham University Press, 2010.

Tanner, J. P. 'The History of the Interpretation of the Song of Songs'. *Bibliotheca Sacra* 154.613 (1997): 23–46.

Tavard, George Henry. *The 1000 Faces of the Virgin Mary.* Collegeville, MN: Liturgical Press, 1996.

Teinmetz, D. C., Muller, R. A., and Thompson, J. L., eds. *Biblical Interpretation in the Era of the Reformation: Essays Presented to David C. Steinmetz in Honor of his Sixtieth Birthday.* Grand Rapids, MI: Eerdmans, 1996.

Tilley, Morris Palmer. *A Dictionary of the Proverbs in England in the Sixteenth and Seventeenth Centuries.* Ann Arbor: University of Michigan Press, 1950.

Thomas, Helen. 'Jacob and Esau—"Rigidly Calvinistic"?' *Studies in English Literature* 9.2 (1969): 199–213.

Trousdale, Marion. *Shakespeare and the Rhetoricians.* Chapel Hill: University of North Carolina Press, 1982.

Wallace, Ronald S. *Calvin's Doctrine of the Christian Life.* London: Oliver & Boyd, 1959.

Waller, Gary. *The Virgin Mary in Late Medieval and Early Modern English Literature and Popular Culture.* Cambridge: Cambridge University Press, 2011.

Walsham, Alexandra. *Providence in Early Modern England.* Oxford: Oxford University Press, 1999.

Warner, Marina. *Alone of all Her Sex: The Myth and Cult of the Virgin Mary.* New York: Routledge, 1988.

Waters, D. Douglas. *Duessa as Theological Satire.* Columbia: University of Missouri Press, 1970.

Watt, Tessa. *Cheap Print and Popular Piety 1550–1640.* Cambridge: Cambridge University Press, 1991.

Wayment, Hilary and Harrison, Kenneth. *The Windows of King's College Chapel, Cambridge: A Description and Commentary*. London: Oxford University Press, 1972.

Wells, Robin Headlam. *Spenser's Faerie Queene and the Cult of Elizabeth.* London and Canberra: Croom Helm, 1983.

Westbrook, Vivienne. *Long Travail and Great Paynes: A Politics of Reformation Revision*. London: Kluwer Academic, 2001.

White, Micheline. *English Women, Religion, and Textual Production, 1500–1625.* Burlington, VT: Ashgate, 2011.

White, Micheline. 'A Woman with Saint Peter's Keys?: Aemilia Lanyer's *Salve Deus Rex Judaeroum* (1611) and the Priestly Gifts of Women'. *Criticism* 45.3 (2003): 323–41.

White, Paul Whitfield. *Drama and Religion in English Provincial Society, 1485–1660.* Cambridge: Cambridge University Press, 2008.

White, Paul Whitfield. 'Predestination Theology in the Mid-Tudor Play *Jacob and Esau*'. *Renaissance and Reformation* 24.4 (1988): 291–301.

Wilcher, Robert. 'Francis Quarles and the Crisis of Royalism'. *Critical Survey* 5.3 (1993): 252–62.

Wilcox, Helen, ed. *Women and Literature in Britain, 1500–1700.* Cambridge: Cambridge University Press, 1996.

Williams, Daniel, ed. *Early Tudor England: Proceedings of the 1987 Harlaxton Symposium.* Woodbridge: Boydell Press, 1989.

Willis, Jonathan P. *Church Music and Protestantism in Post-Reformation England: Discourses, Sites and Identities.* Farnham: Ashgate, 2010.

Wittreich, Joseph A. *Visionary Poetics: Milton's Tradition and his Legacy.* San Marino, CA: Huntington Library, 1979.

Wood, Rufus. *Metaphor and Belief in The Faerie Queene.* Basingstoke: Macmillan Press, 1997.

Woodbridge, Linda. *Vagrancy, Homelessness, and English Renaissance Literature.* Urbana: University of Illinois Press, 2001.

Woodward, Jennifer. *The Theatre of Death: The Ritual Management of Royal Funerals in Renaissance England, 1570–1625.* Woodbridge: Boydell Press, 1997.

Yachnin, Paul. 'A Game at Chess and Chess Allegory'. *Studies in English Literature, 1500–1900* 22.2 (Spring 1982): 317–30.

Young, Alan R. 'The Written and Oral Sources of *King Leir* and the Problem of Justice in the Play'. *Studies in English Literature, 1500–1900* 15.2 (Spring 1975): 309–19.

Young, Francis. *English Catholics and the Supernatural, 1553–1829*. New York: Routledge: 2016.

Young, R. V. *Doctrine and Devotion in Seventeenth-Century Poetry: Studies in Donne, Herbert, Crashaw, and Vaughan*. Cambridge: D. S. Brewer, 2000.

Zaller, Robert. *The Discourse of Legitimacy in Early Modern England*. Stanford: Stanford University Press, 2007.

Zim, Rivkah. *English Metrical Psalms: Poetry as Praise and Prayer, 1535–1601*. Cambridge: Cambridge University Press, 1987.

Index Locorum

Index

'Figures are indicated by an italic *f* following the page number.'